Lecture Notes in Computer Scie

Commenced Publication in 1973
Founding and Former Series Editors:
Gerhard Goos, Juris Hartmanis, and Jan van Leeuwen

Jacques Julliand   Olga Kouchnarenko (Eds.)

B 2007:
Formal Specification
and Development in B

7th International Conference of B Users
Besançon, France, January 17-19, 2007
Proceedings

 Springer

Volume Editors

Jacques Julliand
Laboratoire d'Informatique de l'Université de Franche-Comté
CNRS, FRE 2661
16 route de Gray
25030 Besançon Cedex, France
E-mail: jacques.julliand@lifc.univ-fcomte.fr

Olga Kouchnarenko
Laboratoire d'Informatique de l'Université de Franche-Comté
CNRS, FRE 2661
16 route de Gray
25030 Besançon Cedex, France
E-mail: olga.kouchnarenko@lifc.univ-fcomte.fr

Library of Congress Control Number: 2006938539

CR Subject Classification (1998): D.2.1, D.2.2, D.2.4, F.3.1, F.4.2-3

LNCS Sublibrary: SL 2 – Programming and Software Engineering

ISSN   0302-9743
ISBN-10   3-540-68760-2 Springer Berlin Heidelberg New York
ISBN-13   978-3-540-68760-3 Springer Berlin Heidelberg New York

Springer is a part of Springer Science+Business Media

springer.com

© Springer-Verlag Berlin Heidelberg 2006
Printed in Germany

Typesetting: Camera-ready by author, data conversion by Scientific Publishing Services, Chennai, India
Printed on acid-free paper   SPIN: 11955757   06/3142   5 4 3 2 1 0

Preface

These proceedings record the papers presented at the Seventh International Conference of B Users (B 2007), held in the city of Besançon in the east of France. This conference was built on the success of the previous six conferences in this series, B 1996, held at the University of Nantes, France; B 1998, held at the University of Montpellier, France; ZB 2000, held at the University of York, UK; ZB 2002, held at the University of Grenoble, France; ZB 2003, held at the University of Turku, Finland; ZB 2005 held at the University of Surrey, Guildford, UK. B 2007 was held in January at the University of Franche-Comté, Besançon, France, hosted by the Computer Science Department (LIFC). LIFC has always placed particular emphasis on the applicability of its research and its relationship with industrial partners. In this context, it created in 2003 a company called LEIRIOS Technologies, which produces an automatic test generator tool (LTG) from models described in the B specification language. Other members of LIFC work on extensions of the B method for specifying and verifying dynamic properties.

All the submitted papers in these proceedings were peer reviewed by at least three reviewers drawn from the B committee, depending on the subject matter of the paper. The authors of the papers for B 2007 were from Australia, Canada, Finland, Germany, France, Switzerland, and the UK. The conference featured a range of contributions by distinguished invited speakers drawn from both industry and academia. The invited speakers addressed significant recent industrial applications of formal methods, as well as important academic advances serving to enhance their potency and widen their applicability.

The topics of interest to the conference included: industrial applications and case studies using B; integration of model-based specification methods in the software development lifecycle; derivation of hardware–software architecture from model-based specifications; expressing and validating requirements through formal models, in particular verifying security policies; theoretical issues in formal development (e.g., issues in refinement, proof process, or proof validation); model-based software testing versus proof-oriented development; tools supporting the B method; development by composition of specifications; validation of assembly of COTS by model-based specification methods; B extensions and/or standardization.

Our invited speakers for B 2007 were drawn from France, Ireland, Switzerland and the United States of America. Leslie Lamport is an American computer scientist. The papers by L. Lamport produced original and insightful concepts and algorithms to solve many fundamental problems in distributed systems. L. Lamport applies an elegant mathematical approach to very practical engineering problems. Joseph Morris, from Dublin City University, Ireland, is especially interested in developing mathematical methods of extracting guaranteed correct programs from formal specifications. David Chemouil works in the Flight

Software Department at the French Space Agency (CNES) in Toulouse. His activities include monitoring the development of flight software contracted by CNES and carrying out R&D on flight-software engineering. Paul Gibson from the Department of Computer Science at the National University of Ireland, Maynooth, is an expert in feature interaction. He is a consultant for the Irish government for the Irish e-voting system. He knows this system and its bugs very well and has presented the requirements for its formal – safe and secure – development. Laurent Voisin from the Swiss Federal Institute of Technology, Zurich, a member of the European IST project RODIN (Rigorous Open Development Environment for Complex Systems), presented Event-B modelling with the Rodin platform.

Besides its formal sessions, the conference included tool sessions, demonstrations, exhibitions, an industrial event and tutorials. In particular, the industrial event was constituted of an industrial invited talk and five communications of industry members. Eddie Jaffuel, senior consultant in LEIRIOS Technologies, talked about the specification process for model-based testing generation. Ian Oliver at Nokia Research Center in Finland presented experiences in using B and UML together in industrial developments. Mathieu Clabaut of Systerel Company presented a tool for firewall administration. Daniel Dollé and Didier Essaimé of Siemens Transportation Systems in Montrouge, France, used B in large-scale projects such as the Canarsie Line CBTC. Sarah Hoffman, Sophie Gabriele, Germain Haugou of STMicroelectronics and Lilian Burdy of ClearSy presented the use of the B method for the construction of microkernel-based systems. Neil Evans and Wilson Ifill of AWE (Atomic Weapons Establishment) in the UK presented a synthesis and some perspectives about the use of B at AWE for hardware verifications.

The B 2007 conference was initiated by the International B Conference Steering Committee (APCB). The University of Franche-Comté and the Computer Science Department LIFC provided local organization. Without the great support from local staff at the University of Franche-Comté, B 2007 would not have been possible. In particular, much of the local organization was undertaken by Bruno Tatibouët with the assistance of Brigitte Bataillard, Christine Bigey, Alain Giorgetti, Ahmed Hammad, Pierre-Alain Masson, Hassan Mountassir, François Piat and Laurent Steck. B 2007 was sponsored by Alstom, ClearSy System Engineering, INRETS (French National Institute for Transport and Safety Research), INRIA (National Institute of Research in Automatic and Computer Science), LEIRIOS Technologies, PARKEON (Parking Space Management Solution Industry), RATP, the local council of Doubs, the regional council of Franche-Comté and the town council of Besançon. We are grateful to all those who contributed to the success of the conference.

Online information concerning the conference is available under the following URL: `http://lifc.univ-fcomte.fr/b2007`

This web site and `http://www-lsr.imag.fr/B/` provide links to further online resources concerning the B method.

We hope that all participants and other interested readers benefit scientifically from these proceedings and also find them stimulating in the process.

October 2006   Jacques Julliand
                                                              Olga Kouchnarenko
                                                                Fabrice Bouquet
                                                             Marie-Laure Potet

Organization

Executive Committee

B 2007 was organized by the department of Computer Science, University of Franche-Comté.

Conference and Program Chair: Jacques Julliand
Co-chair and Invited Talks: Olga Kouchnarenko
Industrial Event: Marie-Laure Potet (University of Grenoble, France)
Tools Session: Fabrice Bouquet
Organizing Chair: Bruno Tatibouët
Proceedings: Alain Giorgetti
Web Site: François Piat
Demonstrations: Laurent Steck

Program Committee

Program Chair: Jacques Julliand, LIFC, University of Franche-Comté, France
Co-chair: Olga Kouchnarenko, LIFC, University of Franche-Comté, France

Richard Banach, University of Manchester, UK
Didier Bert, CNRS, University of Grenoble, France
Juan Bicarregui, CLRC, Oxfordshire, UK
Lilian Burdy, ClearSy, France
Michael Butler, University of Southampton, UK
Dominique Cansell, LORIA, University of Metz, France
Daniel Dollé, Siemens Transportation Systems, Paris, France
Steve Dunne, University of Teesside, UK
Mamoun Filali, CNRS, IRIT, Toulouse, France
Marc Frappier, University of Sherbrooke, Canada
Andy Galloway, University of York, UK
Henri Habrias, LINA, Université de Nantes, France
Regine Laleau, LACL, IUT Fontainebleau, France
Jean-Louis Lanet, Gemplus, France
Annabelle McIver, Macquarie University, Sydney, Australia
Luis-Fernando Mejia, Alstom Transport Signalisation, Paris, France
Marie-Laure Potet, University of Grenoble (Chair of industrial half-day)
Ken Robinson, University of New South Wales, Australia
Emil Sekerinski, McMaster University, Ontario, Canada
Helen Treharne, University of Surrey, UK
Mark Utting, University of Waikato, New Zealand
Véronique Viguié Donzeau-Gouge, CNAM, Paris, France
Marina Waldén, Åbo Akademi University, Turku, Finland

External Referees

Pascal André, University of Nantes, France
Christian Attiogbé, University of Nantes, France
Julien Brunel, Université Paul Sabatier, Toulouse, France
Xavier Crégut, ENSEEIHT, Toulouse, France
Andy Edmunds, University of Southampton, UK
Alain Giorgetti, University of Franche-Comté, Besançon, France
Pierre-Alain Masson, University of Franche-Comté, France
Hassan Mountassir, University of Franche-Comté, France
Mike Poppleton, University of Southampton, UK
Antoine Requet, Gemalto, Marseille, France
Jean-François Rolland, Université Paul Sabatier, Toulouse, France
Colin Snook, University of Southampton, UK
Bill Stoddart, University of Teesside, UK
David Streader, University of Waikato, New Zealand
Bruno Tatibouët, University of Franche-Comté, Besançon, France
Guy Vidal-Naquet, Ecole Supérieure d'Electricité, Gif-sur-Yvette, France

Support

B 2007 greatly benefited from the support of the following organizations:

CNRS
INRIA
LIFC
Ministère de l'Éducation Nationale
University of Franche-Comté

and sponsorship from:

Alstom
ClearSy System Engineering
INRETS
LEIRIOS Technologies
PARKEON
RATP
Local Council of Doubs
Regional Council of Franche-Comté
Town Council of Besançon

Table of Contents

Invited Talks

Regular Papers

Industrial Papers

Tool Papers

Invited Talk

E-Voting and the Need for Rigourous Software Engineering – The Past, Present and Future

J. Paul Gibson

Department of Computer Science,
National University of Ireland, Maynooth,
Ireland
pgibson@cs.nuim.ie

Abstract. In many jurisdictions around the world, the introduction of e-voting has been subject to wide-ranging debate amongst voters, politicians, political scientists, computer scientists and software engineers. A central issue is one of public trust and confidence: should voters be expected to put their faith in "closed" electronic systems where previously they trusted "open" manual systems?

As the media continues to report on the "failure" of e-voting machines, electoral administrators and e-voting machine manufacturers have been required to review their policies and systems in order to meet a set of ever changing requirements. Such an unstable problem domain stretches their understanding of the electoral process and their ability to apply a diverse range of technologies in providing acceptable electronic solutions. The breadth and depth of the issues suggest that no electoral administration can justifiably claim to have implemented a "trustworthy" electronic replacement for a paper system.

All e-voting systems rely substantially on the correct functioning of their software. It has been argued that such e-voting software is "critical" to its users, and so one would expect to see the highest standards being applied in the development of software in e-voting machines: this is certainly not the case for machines that have already been used. Furthermore, in jurisdictions where e-voting machines have just been procurred we shall see that the software in these machines is often of very poor "quality", even though it has been independently tested and accredited for use.

Throughout the presentation we will focus on the software engineering issues, and will consider the question of whether the formal methods community could have done more - and should do more - to help alleviate the costly problems that society is facing from badly developed software in a wide range of critical government information systems (and not just voting machines).

J. Julliand and O. Kouchnarenko (Eds.): B 2007, LNCS 4355, p. 1, 2006.

Using B Machines for Model-Based Testing
of Smartcard Software

Eddie Jaffuel

LEIRIOS Technologies
TEMIS Innovation - 18 Rue Alain Savary - 25000 Besançon, France
eddie.jaffuel@leirios.com
http://www.leirios.com

Abstract. Automated test generation from B abstract machines is commonly used in the smart card industry since 2003. Several domains are concerned such as mobile communication applications (e.g. SIM cards) [1], identity applications (e.g. health cards or identity cards) and banking applications. The model-based testing tool LTG (LEIRIOS Test Generator) [2] makes it possible to generate executable test scripts from a B formal model of the functional requirements. Therefore, the design of the test cases and the development of the test scripts are based on a modeling and automated test generation approach.

The model-based testing process is structured in 3 main steps:

Model. The first step consists in developing a behavior model using the B abstract machine notation. The model represents the expected behavior of the smart card application under test.

Configure test generation. The configuration of the test generation with LTG is based on model coverage criteria. Three families of criteria give a precise control over the test generation: decision coverage, operation effect coverage and data coverage.

Adapt. The generated test cases are then translated in executable test scripts using an adaptor customized for the test execution environment and the project.

This talk show how B abstract machines are developed in the context of model-based testing of smart card applications, how model coverage criteria makes it possible to generate accurate test cases and how those test cases are adapted into executable test scripts for a targeted test execution environment.

References

[1] E. Bernard, B. Legeard, X. Luck, and F. Peureux. Generation of test sequences from formal specifications: GSM 11-11 standard case study. *International Journal of Software Practice and Experience*, 34(10):915–948, 2004.

[2] M. Utting and B. Legeard. *Practical Model-Based Testing - A Tools Approach.* Morgan & Kauffman - Elsevier Science 2006. 528 pages, ISBN 0-12-372501-1.

J. Julliand and O. Kouchnarenko (Eds.): B 2007, LNCS 4355, p. 2, 2006.
© Springer-Verlag Berlin Heidelberg 2006

The Design of Spacecraft On-Board Software

David Chemouil

French Space Agency (CNES)

Abstract. This presentation deals with the way Space Systems and particularly Spacecraft On-Board Software are designed. I will try to show how the design of Space Systems is undergoing a shift from a seasoned-expert craft to a methodology based upon modelling. First, I will introduce Space Systems by presenting their applications and architecture. Then I will detail the design of such systems, insisting on systems and software aspects. Finally, I will describe some directions currently followed by CNES regarding modelling technologies. Among them, I will bring the notion of pre-proven business-specific refinement patterns to the forefront, as a possible (partial) solution to the reluctance to proof-based development methods in industry.

David Chemouil works in the On-Board Software Office at the French Space Agency (CNES) in Toulouse. His activities include monitoring the development of On-Board Software contracted by CNES and carrying out R&D on Embedded Software Engineering. David Chemouil holds a PhD in Computer Science from Université Paul Sabatier, Toulouse (2004).

J. Julliand and O. Kouchnarenko (Eds.): B 2007, LNCS 4355, p. 3, 2006.

Interpreting Invariant Composition in the B Method Using the Spec# Ownership Relation: A Way to Explain and Relax B Restrictions

Sylvain Boulmé and Marie-Laure Potet

LSR-IMAG, Grenoble, France
Sylvain.Boulme@imag.fr,
Marie-Laure.Potet@imag.fr

Abstract. In the B method, the invariant of a component cannot be violated outside its own operations. This approach has a great advantage: the users of a component can assume its invariant without having to prove it. But, B users must deal with important architecture restrictions that ensure the soundness of reasonings involving invariants. Moreover, understanding how these restrictions ensure soundness is not trivial. This paper studies a meta-model of invariant composition, inspired from the Spec# approach. Basically, in this model, invariant violations are monitored using ghost variables. The consistency of assumptions about invariants is controlled by very simple proof obligations. Hence, this model provides a simple framework to understand B composition rules and to study some conservative extensions of B authorizing more architectures and providing more control on components initialization.

1 Introduction

Approaches based on formal specifications or annotations become widespread. They are based on specifications by contract [18] and invariants [13]. When components like modules or objects, are involved, the notion of invariant requires a careful attention, both in specification and validation processes. In particular, several issues must be addressed [21]: which variables may an invariant depend on? when do invariants have to hold? It has been proved that a very lax approach, as initially adopted in JML [14,15], cannot be really implemented in static verifiers. Indeed, when components are involved, verification is also expected to be modular: invariants must be established without examining the entire program. Consequently, specifiers need a methodology to explicitly reason about invariants and their preservation in layered architectures.

In the B method [1], architectural restrictions ensure that when components are combined, their respective invariants are preserved without further proof obligations. Hence, in a well-formed architecture, invariant propagation and verification is a transparent process for developers. The simplicity of invariant composition and the control of proof obligations through composition are the main features in industrial uses of the B method. For example, the Météor project [2,9]

J. Julliand and O. Kouchnarenko (Eds.): B 2007, LNCS 4355, pp. 4–18, 2006.

involves about 1000 components, while keeping manageable the proof process. New projects as Roissy Val [3] and Line 1 of Paris involve even more components. For railway applications, constructors have developed methodological guides to build architectures which are adapted to the domain and fulfill architectural restrictions. The B method has also been used in the domain of smart card applications [17,24,5]. But, as detailed in section 5, reconciling B restrictions and natural architectures of applications is harder in this domain.

Alternatively, other approaches, like Spec# [16,6], are based on an explicit treatment of invariants validity. In the Spec# approach, invariants are properties that hold except when they are declared to be broken. The main difficulty of this approach is the specification overheads: developers must describe which invariants are expected to hold. Thus, the specification process becomes much more complex and error-prone. In this paper, we propose to relax architectural restrictions of B using Spec# ideas. But, we avoid Spec# specification overheads, by characterizing some patterns of architectures.

Section 2 introduces the principles of invariant composition in the B method and restrictions associated to this approach. Section 3 presents a meta-model of invariant composition, inspired from the Spec# approach. Section 4 shows how the invariant composition of the B method can be explained from our meta-model. Finally, section 5 proposes a new invariant composition principle, and illustrates the proposed approach through a case study.

2   A Brief Presentation of the B Method

At first, we recall some basic notions about the B method. The core language of B specifications is based on three formalisms: data are specified using a set theory, properties are first order predicates and the behavioral part is specified by *Generalized Substitutions*. Generalized Substitutions can be defined by the Weakest Precondition (*WP*) semantics, introduced by E.W. Dijkstra [10], and denoted here by $[S]R$. Here are two *WP* definition examples:

$[\,\text{PRE } P \text{ THEN } S \text{ END}]\,R \Leftrightarrow P \wedge [S]\,R$	pre-conditioned substitution
$[S_1 \,;\, S_2]\,R \qquad\qquad \Leftrightarrow [S_1]\,[S_2]\,R$	sequential substitution

Generalized substitutions can equivalently be characterized by two predicates, $\mathsf{trm}(S)$ and $\mathsf{prd}(S)$, that respectively express the required condition for substitution S to terminate, and the relation between before and after states (denoted respectively by v and v'). Weakest precondition calculus includes termination: we have $[S]R \Rightarrow \mathsf{trm}(S)$, for any R.

Definition 1 (trm and prd predicates)

$$\mathsf{trm}(S) \Leftrightarrow [S]true \qquad\qquad \mathsf{prd}_v(S) \Leftrightarrow \neg[S]\neg(v' = v)$$

2.1   Abstract Machine

As proposed by C. Morgan [19], B components correspond to the standard notion of state machines which define an initial state and a set of operations, acting on internal state variables. Moreover, an invariant is attached to an abstract machine: this is a property which must hold in observables states, i.e. states before and after operations calls. Roughly, an abstract machine has the following shape[1]:

```
MACHINE M
VARIABLES v
INVARIANT I
INITIALIZATION U
OPERATIONS
    o ← nom_op(i) ≙
        PRE P THEN S END ;
    ...
END
```

M is the component name, v a list of variable names, I a property on variables v, and U a generalized substitution. In the operation definition, i (resp. o) denotes the list of input (resp. output) parameters, P is the precondition on v and i, and S is a generalized substitution which describes how v and o are updated.

Proof obligations attached to machine M consist in showing that I is an inductive property of component M:

Definition 2 (Invariant proof obligations)

$$
\begin{array}{lll}
(1) & [U]I & \textit{initialization} \\
(2) & I \wedge P \Rightarrow [S]I & \textit{operations}
\end{array}
$$

2.2   Invariants Composition

Abstract machines can be combined, through the two primitives INCLUDES and SEES to build new specifications. We do not consider here the clause USES, which is not really used and supported by tools.

The first feature underlying invariant composition in the B method is invariant preservation by encapsulated substitutions. A substitution S is an encapsulated substitution relative to a given component M if and only if variables of M are not directly assigned in S, but only through calls to M operations. Thus, any encapsulated substitution relative to M preserves, by construction, invariant of M (see [23]). The second feature underlying invariant composition is a set of restrictions when components are combined together:

- M INCLUDES N means that operations of M can be defined using any N operations and M invariant can constrain N variables.
- M SEES N means that operations of M can only call read-only N operations and M invariant can not constrain N variables.

Moreover there is no cycle in INCLUDES and SEES dependencies and INCLUDES dependency relation is a tree (each machine can be included only once). These restrictions prevent from combining operations that constrain shared variables in inconsistent ways. Let us consider the following example:

---

[1] Some others rubrics are permitted such as constants, ... Because they have no particular effect on the composition process, we do not take them into account here.

MACHINE N	MACHINE M
VARIABLES x	INCLUDES N
INVARIANT $x \in NAT$	INVARIANT $even(x)$
INITIALIZATION $x := 0$	OPERATIONS
OPERATIONS	$incr2 \;\hat{=}\;$
$incr \;\hat{=}\; x := x + 1$;	BEGIN $incr$; $incr$ END
$r \leftarrow val \;\hat{=}\; r := x$	
END	END

(1)	$init$; $incr2$; $r \leftarrow val$; $incr2$;	admitted by B
(2)	$init$; $incr2$; $incr$; $incr2$;	rejected by B
(3)	$init$; $incr2$; $incr$; $incr$; $incr2$;	rejected by B

Sequence 1 is authorized because it combines a read-only operation of N with operations of M. Sequences 2 and 3 are rejected because they combine modifying operations of N and M. The reject of sequence 2 prevents the second call of operation $incr2$ to occur in a state where invariant of M is broken. But, sequence 3 is rejected although each operation-call happens in a state where all invariants visible from this operation are valid.

In practical experiments, these restrictions make the design of architectures difficult [4,12]. Actually, components can share variables only in a very limited way (at most one writer-several readers). Section 5 describes a smart card case study [5] illustrating problems raised by a real application.

3   A Meta-model for B Components Inspired from Spec#

The Spec# approach [6,16] proposes a flexible methodology for modular verification of objects invariants, which is based on a dynamic notion of ownership. An ownership relation describes which objects can constrain others objects, i.e. which object has an invariant depending on the value of another object. It is imposed that this relation is dynamically a forest. This allows to generate proof obligations ensuring that an object is not modified while it is constrained by the invariant of an other object. Dynamic ownership of an object can be transfered during execution, introducing some flexibility with respect to B restrictions. We directly present the Spec# approach in the framework of B components and generalized substitutions style.

Hence, this section proposes a new module language for B inspired from the Spec# approach. In section 4, this module language is considered as a kind of meta-model in which we interpret each composition mechanisms of B. This allows to check very simply the soundness of B proofs obligations with respect to components composition. And in section 5, we study how this meta-model can be used to relax B restrictions on composition. In the present state of our work, refinement of B is not considered, and let for future works.

3.1 Static Ownership and Admissible Invariants

In our module language, we first assume a relation *owns* between components: we write $(M, N) \in owns$ to express that "M owns N". This relation *owns* is called *static ownership* and is related to admissible invariants, i.e. the invariants which are not automatically rejected by the static analyzer. By definition 3 below, *admissible invariants* of M can only have free variables bound to components transitively owned by M. In the following, M.Inv denotes the invariant stated in component M, and M.Var denotes the set of variables declared in M, and $free(P)$ denotes the set of unbound variables appearing in formula P, and $owns^*$ is the reflexive and transitive closure of relation *owns*.

Definition 3 (Admissible invariant through the *owns* relation)

$$free(M.\text{Inv}) \subseteq \bigcup\nolimits_{N \in \ owns^*[M]} N.\text{Var}$$

Here, this notion of admissible invariant is the unique assumption about *owns*: correct instances of the meta-model must define *owns* such that their notion of admissible invariant matches exactly definition 3. In section 4, we show that if we consider that *owns* corresponds exactly to INCLUDES clauses between B components, then B is a quite simple instance of the meta-model. In section 5, in order to relax B restrictions related to INCLUDES clauses, we propose to consider *owns* only as a particular sub-relation of INCLUDES.

Actually, static ownership is related to validity of invariants: the invariant of a component M can not be *safely assumed*, when the state of a component transitively owned by M has been modified outside of M scope. Moreover, we will see that static ownership gives a hierarchical structure to validity of invariants: if the invariant of component M can be safely assumed, then all the invariants of components transitively owned by M can also be safely assumed.

3.2 Dynamic Ownership and Ghost Status Variable

Our module language controls the consistency of constraints on a component M by ensuring that in each state of the execution, M has at most one unique *dynamic owner*. Hence, validity of invariants is now precised: the invariant of a component X constraining an other component M can be safely assumed, only when X transitively *owns* a dynamic owner of M.

In order to express this control, each component M contains a ghost status variable, called M.st, and belonging to {invalid, valid, committed}. By definition, a component X is a *dynamic owner* of M if and only if $(X, M) \in owns$ and $X.\text{st} \neq$ invalid. And, for each component M, M.st is intended to satisfy:

– if M.st = invalid then M.Inv may be false. In particular, any modification on M variables is authorized. Moreover, M has no dynamic owner.
– if M.st = valid then M.Inv is established and M has no dynamic owner.
– if M.st = committed then M.Inv is established and M has a single dynamic owner.

More formally, for each component M, variable M.st has to verify the following meta-invariants:

$\mathcal{MI}_1$	M.st $\neq$ invalid $\Rightarrow$ M.Inv
$\mathcal{MI}_2$	M.st $\neq$ invalid $\wedge$ $(M, N) \in owns \Rightarrow N$.st $=$ committed
$\mathcal{MI}_3$	M.st $=$ committed $\wedge$ $(A, M) \in owns \wedge (B, M) \in owns$ $\wedge$ A.st $\neq$ invalid $\wedge$ B.st $\neq$ invalid $\Rightarrow A = B$

The first meta-invariant states that a component invariant can be safely assumed if its status is different from invalid. Meta-invariant $\mathcal{MI}_2$ imposes that when a component invariant is not invalid then components transitively owned by this component have to be declared as committed. Finally $\mathcal{MI}_3$ ensures that a component has at most one unique dynamic owner.

3.3 Preconditioned Assignment Substitution

In our module language, assignment substitution is preconditioned, but it can occur outside of the component where the assigned variable is bound (there is *a priori* no variable encapsulation). We have:

subst	trm	prd
N.Var $:= e$	$N.st =$ invalid	$N.st' = N.st \wedge N$.Var$' = e$

Meta-invariants $\mathcal{MI}_2$ and $\mathcal{MI}_3$ are obviously preserved by this substitution, because status variables remain unchanged. We want to prove that the assignment substitution preserves the meta-invariant $\mathcal{MI}_1$ for any component M, i.e.:

$$M.\text{st} \neq \text{invalid} \Rightarrow (N.\text{st} = \text{invalid} \Rightarrow [N.\text{Var} := e]M.\text{Inv})$$

There are three cases:

1. if $N = M$ then $\mathcal{MI}_1$ holds because hypotheses are contradictory.
2. if $(M, N) \in owns^+$ then the two hypotheses N.st $=$ invalid and M.st $\neq$ invalid are also contradictory due to $\mathcal{MI}_2$: N.st must be equal to committed.
3. if $(M, N) \notin owns^*$ then, due to definition 3, N.Var $\cap free(M.\text{Inv}) = \emptyset$. In this case M.Inv is obviously preserved by the assignment substitution N.Var $:= e$.

3.4 pack(M) and unpack(M) Substitutions

Substitutions are extended with two new commands pack(M) and unpack(M). The former requires the establishment of M invariant and the latter allows violation of M invariant. Status variables can only be modified via these commands. They can be invoked in M or outside of M. They are formally defined by:

subst	trm	prd
pack(M)	$\forall N.((M,N)\in owns \Rightarrow N.\text{st=valid})$ $\wedge\, M.\text{st} = \texttt{invalid}$ $\wedge\, M.\text{Inv}$	$\forall N.((M,N)\in owns \Rightarrow N.\text{st}'=\texttt{committed})$ $\forall N.(M{\neq}N \wedge\ (M,N)\notin owns \Rightarrow N.\text{st}'=N.\text{st})$ $\wedge\, M.\text{st}' = \texttt{valid}$ $\wedge\, M.\text{Var}' = M.\text{Var}$
unpack(M)	$M.\text{st} = \texttt{valid}$	$\forall N.((M,N)\in owns \Rightarrow N.\text{st}'=\texttt{valid})$ $\forall N.(M{\neq}N \wedge\ (M,N)\notin owns \Rightarrow N.\text{st}'=N.\text{st})$ $\wedge\, M.\text{st}' = \texttt{invalid}$ $\wedge\, M.\text{Var}' = M.\text{Var}$

Control of dynamic ownership appears in these commands. The precondition of pack(M) imposes that the components statically owned by M have no dynamic owners, then pack(M) makes M the dynamic owner of all the components that it statically owns. Of course, unpack(M) has the reverse effect. Here, let us note that the precondition of unpack(M) imposes that M has itself no dynamic owner. In other words, if we want to unpack a component N in order to modify it through a preconditioned assignment, we are first obliged to unpack its dynamic owner (and so on recursively). It is easy to prove that meta-invariants $\mathcal{MI}_1$, $\mathcal{MI}_2$ and $\mathcal{MI}_3$ are preserved by these pack and unpack.

Finally, each substitution S built from preconditioned assignment, pack and unpack constructors and other standard B substitutions satisfies proposition 1.

Proposition 1 (Meta-invariants preservation)

$$\mathcal{MI}_1 \wedge\ \mathcal{MI}_2 \wedge\ \mathcal{MI}_3 \wedge\ \text{trm}(S) \Rightarrow\ [S](\mathcal{MI}_1 \wedge\ \mathcal{MI}_2 \wedge\ \mathcal{MI}_3)$$

3.5   Revisiting Example of Section 2.2

substitution S_e	condition	status modification
$incr2$;	$M.\text{st} = valid$	
unpack(M) ;	$M.\text{st} = valid$	$M.\text{st} := \texttt{invalid} \| N.\text{st} := \texttt{valid}$
$incr$;	$N.\text{st} = valid$	
$incr$;	$N.\text{st} = valid$	
pack(M) ;	$N.\text{st} = valid$ $\wedge M.\text{Inv}$ $\wedge M.\text{st} = invalid$	$M.\text{st} := \texttt{valid} \| N.\text{st} := \texttt{committed}$
$incr2$;	$M.\text{st} = valid$	

In our meta-model, sequence 3 of example section 2.2 can be extended by pack and unpack substitutions such that if S_e denotes the resulting substitution, then we can prove trm(S_e). In the table above, we have represented the proof obligation generated for trm(S_e) by associating each basic step of the sequence to its precondition and its modification of the environment.

In order to express the B semantics of components M and N of the example into our meta-model, we impose that $(M,N) \in owns$ and that substitutions of modifying operations defined in a component X are implicitly bracketed by unpack(X) and pack(X). Hence, in calls to modifying operations of X, variable X.st is required to be valid before the call, and is ensured to be valid after the call. Moreover, we impose that this sequence starts in a state such that M.st = valid and N.st = committed. This interpretation of the B language is justified in section 4.

4   Encoding B Operations in This Meta-model

This section proposes to check the consistency of invariants in B architectures, by embedding B components into our meta-model, and verifying that proofs obligations of B allow to discharge the proof obligations from the meta-model.

First, we consider that $(M, N) \in owns$ if and only if M contains a clause "INCLUDES N". Indeed, clause SEES can not be included in the ownership relation defined section 3, because it does not authorize seen variables to be constrained by the invariant part. So, we consider a relation $sees$, such that $(M, N) \in sees$ if and only if M contains a clause SEES N. Moreover, if $(M, N) \in sees$, there is no meta-invariant like $\mathcal{MI}_2$ ensuring that validity of M invariant implies validity of N invariant. Indeed, modifying operations of N can be called while M is valid: this leads to an intermediary state where N is unpacked, but M not. Hence, below, the status of seen components is managed in preconditions of operations.

At last, we need to label B operations using status variables, according to implicit conditions of B with respect to component invariants. We distinguish three cases: the initialization process, operations belonging to component interfaces and local operations.

4.1   Initialization Process

In the B method, global initialization is an internal process which sequentializes local initializations in an order compatible with component dependencies. This step is analog to the Ada elaborate phase and is tool-dependent: depending on the architecture, several orders could be possible, resulting in different initial values. This global process can be described in the following way: let $<$ be a partial order defined by $N < M$ if and only if $(M, N) \in owns \cup sees$. From $<$ a total order is built giving in that an initialization procedure specified in the following way:

$$
\boxed{
\begin{array}{l}
\text{PRE } \forall N \ . \ (N \in COMP \Rightarrow N.\text{st} = \texttt{invalid}) \\
\text{THEN} \\
\quad U_1 \ ; \ \texttt{pack}(C_1) \ ; \\
\quad \cdots \\
\quad U_n \ ; \ \texttt{pack}(C_n) \ ; \\
\text{END}
\end{array}
}
$$

with C_i denoting the component labeled by i in the total order and U_i the initialization substitution of component C_i. $COMP$ represents the set of components concerned by the global initialization process. We proved that this initialization procedure terminates, and establishes meta-invariants $\mathcal{MI}_1$, $\mathcal{MI}_2$ and $\mathcal{MI}_3$ (thanks to proposition 1).

4.2   Interface Operations

In the same way, B operations of a component M can be labeled by status information. We consider two forms of operations: modifying operations and read-only operations. Let PRE P THEN S END be the definition of an operation belonging to interface of M. This operation can be labeled in the following way:

modifying case	PRE $P \wedge M.\mathrm{st} = \mathtt{valid}$ $\quad\quad \wedge \forall N .((M, N) \in (owns \cup sees)^+ \Rightarrow N.\mathrm{st} \neq \mathtt{invalid})$ THEN $\mathtt{unpack}(M)$; S ; $\mathtt{pack}(M)$ END
read-only case	PRE $P \wedge M.\mathrm{st} \neq \mathtt{invalid}$ $\quad\quad \wedge \forall N .((M, N) \in (owns \cup sees)^+ \Rightarrow N.\mathrm{st} \neq \mathtt{invalid})$ THEN S END

In the modifying case, direct assignments of M variables can occur because M is unpacked. For read-only operations, status precondition is weakest because a read-only operation does not contain assignment. Hence, read-only operations can be called, even if M is committed. Formula $\forall N .((M, N) \in (owns \cup sees)^+ \Rightarrow N.\mathrm{st} \neq \mathtt{invalid})$ preconditions, guarantees that invariants of transitively seen components are also valid, as said at the beginning of this section.

As before, proof obligations of termination contain proof obligations of B invariants, corresponding to termination of `pack` calls. Finally, if S does not contain explicit `pack` and `unpack` substitutions and respects B restrictions (M variables can be directly assigned, included variables are only assignable through operation calls and seen variables can not be modified in any way) then all status conditions are established by construction. In particular, any operation body S of component M fulfills the following property, for any component N:

Proposition 2 (Status preservation through B operations)

$$\mathcal{MI}_1 \wedge \mathcal{MI}_2 \wedge \mathcal{MI}_3 \wedge \mathsf{prd}(S) \Rightarrow N.\mathrm{st}' = N.\mathrm{st}$$

4.3   Local Operations

In B, local operations can be introduced at the level of implementation [8]. They authorize assignment of component variables as well as direct assignments of included variables[2]. Local operations can be seen as private operations allowing to factorize code. They do not have to preserve local invariant. Proof obligations given in [8] consists in proving the preservation of all invariants of included components. So, let M be a component which (transitively) includes components $N_1, \ldots, N_n$. A local operation in M, defined by the substitution PRE P THEN S END, can be labeled[3] in the following way:

---

[2] At the level of implementation, inclusion takes the form of an IMPORTS clause. Here we do not distinguish these two mechanisms, as it is done in B for the clause SEES.

[3] To simplify, we do not take into account seen components.

$$
\begin{aligned}
&\text{PRE } \ P \wedge \ M.\text{st} = \texttt{invalid} \ \wedge \ N_1.\text{st} = \texttt{valid} \ \wedge \ \ldots \ \wedge \ N_n.\text{st} = \texttt{valid} \\
&\text{THEN } \ \texttt{unpack}(N_1) \ ; \ \ldots \ ; \ \texttt{unpack}(N_n) \ ; \\
&\qquad S \ ; \\
&\qquad \texttt{pack}(N_1) \ ; \ \ldots \ ; \ \texttt{pack}(N_n) \ ; \\
&\text{END}
\end{aligned}
$$

Remark that several other forms of local operations would be possible. For instance, we should define friendly local operations that must be called in a state where the local invariant holds. Such operations would not require to repeat the invariant (or some part of it) in the precondition of a local operation, as it is often necessary. Similarly, developers could choose which variables are assigned and so which included components needs to be unpacked. This would avoid to reproved all imported invariants: this may be interesting even if such proofs are obvious. To introduce such flexibility we now define an extension of B language allowing to directly manipulate conditions on status variables and substitutions pack and unpack.

5   A More Flexible Composition Principle

Modifying the previous interpretation of B in our meta-model, this section proposes to extend B with a more flexible invariant composition principle, allowing to specify more sharing between components and more natural architectures. Specifications can now directly reference component status variables but only in precondition or assertion parts. Moreover, specifications can perform unpack and pack substitutions. By this way, developers can precisely state when invariants must hold. Now, invariant preservation proof obligation is no more an external process, but directly integrated into the language. Let PRE P THEN S END be an operation definition. Now, its proof obligation is:

$$
(\mathcal{MI}_1 \wedge \ \mathcal{MI}_2 \wedge \ \mathcal{MI}_3 \wedge P) \Rightarrow \mathsf{trm}(S)
$$

Such a proof obligation guarantees the consistent use of status variables. Moreover, if S contains some pack substitutions then the termination proof obligation contains proofs obligations relative to the validity of the expected invariants.

Finally, to obtain a powerful invariant composition principle, we propose a more flexible initialization process and a smaller notion of ownership than the B INCLUDES relation.

5.1   Initialization and Reinitialization Process

As stated section 4.1, in the B method initialization is a global process. Because more sharing is now admitted, we make explicit the initialization process in using operations which establish invariants (on the contrary to interface operations which preserve invariant). In this way, the developer can specify an initialization order in a precise way, avoiding uncontrollable non-determinism of B initialization process. At last, initializations can be invoked in any place, in order to reinitialize variables. Let U be the initialization substitution of component M. Several form of initialization operations are possible:

case 1	PRE M.st $=$ invalid THEN U ; pack(M) END
case 2	PRE M.st $=$ invalid $\wedge$ N.st $\neq$ invalid THEN U ; pack(M) END
case 3	PRE M.st $=$ invalid $\wedge$ N.st $=$ invalid THEN $N.Init$; U ; pack(M) END

Case 1 corresponds to initialization of a stand-alone machine. Case 2 corresponds to an initialization depending on another initialization, like when M sees N in B. Case 3 corresponds to an initialization performing another initialization: here, $N.Init$ denotes an initialization operation of component N. Case 3 implicitly happens in B when M includes N: in particular, the elaboration of M invariant involves initial values of N.

5.2   A Smaller *owns* Relation

Modular invariant composition is based on two orthogonal aspects: on one hand, it is necessary to control components that constrain shared variables and, on the other hand, it is also necessary to control assignment of shared variables. In the Spec# approach, the ownership relation allows to control in which way variables are constrained and the preconditioned assignment substitution allows to control when sets of variables can be updated. In B, these two aspects are syntactically grouped together through the two clauses clauses SEES and INCLUDES:

	read operation	modifying operation
variables can be constrained	INCLUDES	INCLUDES
variables cannot be constrained	SEES	–

The case uncovered by B corresponds to components that call any operations of a given component M but do not constrain its variables. In this case, there is no problem as soon as the shared component is not committed (all other components with an invariant depending on these variables are invalid). So, we narrow relation *owns* to only keep the subrelation corresponding to components whose variables are effectively strengthened by new invariants. Formally, we now define the *owns* relation as the smallest subrelation of INCLUDES$^+$ (the transitive closure of the relation induced by INCLUDES clauses) respecting the notion of admissible invariant (def. 3). Such a relation exists and is unique. All results of section 3 apply here.

With this smaller *owns* relation, we now have more meaningful architectures than before. Let us compare three approaches. Approach 1 is strict B, based on static restrictions about architectures. Approach 2 is the approach of section 4, in which the *owns* relation is assimilated to the clause INCLUDES. At last, approach 3 corresponds to the smaller definition of *owns* given above. We consider

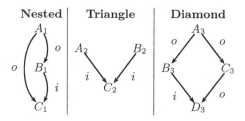

the three architectures given below. In the two first approaches, both kind of arrows represent an INCLUDES clause. In approach 3, o-arrows represent an *owns* pair, and i-arrows represent a INCLUDES pair that is not a *owns* pair.

In approach 1, all these architectures are rejected. In approach 2, architecture Nested1 is meaningless, because A_1 can be never packed. Indeed, B_1 must be packed before A_1, but when B_1 is packed, C_1 is committed, and A_1 can not be packed. On the contrary, in approach 3, A_1 can be packed because C_1 is not committed by B_1. Moreover, interface operations of B_1 can call interface operations of C_1. In approach 2, architecture Triangle can be used with restrictions: one of the two components A_2 or B_2 must be invalid because C_2 can be committed only once. In approach 3, C_2 is never committed, thus A_2 and B_2 can be packed and can freely call interface operations of C_2. Finally, architecture Diamond is also meaningless in approach 2 (A_3 can not be packed). On the contrary, in approach 3, interface operations of B_3 can call interface operations of D_3 when C_3 is invalid. In A_3, we may thus need to unpack C_3 before to call operation of B_3 and then repack C_3.

5.3   A Case Study

We present here an example extracted from the Java Card byte-code interpreter case study developed in the BOM project [FME'03]. A Java card virtual machine has a four components architecture:

- *PgMemory* contains the byte-code of the program to run. It performs an abstraction of the physical memory.
- *Installer* performs the loading of the byte-code into the memory of the card.
- *Interpreter* provides operations corresponding to each instruction of the virtual machine.
- *VM* is the main component, it provides an operation to install a program and run it step-by-step, using the operations of *Interpreter*.

In Java Card, the format of byte-code is required to satisfy well-formness properties that guarantee safety and security properties of the execution [20]: for instance, a valid instruction starts by an op-code directly followed by its well-typed parameters, a method entry point always refers an op-code, etc. These properties need to be expressed in the different components of our architecture:

- *PgMemory*: the byte-code stored in memory is well-formed (invariant I_{mem}).
- *Installer*: the byte-code already loaded is well-formed (invariant I_{inst}).

– *Interpreter*: the program counter always points to a valid instruction (invariant I_{interp}).

This architecture can not be directly implemented in B because invariants I_{inst} and I_{interp} constrain the state of $PgMemory$ (see the discussion in the conclusion). On the contrary, in the proposed approach, the diamond architecture on the right is adapted.

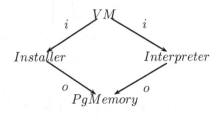

In VM, *Installer* and *Interpreter* do not need to be valid in the same time: when one is valid, it dynamically owns $PgMemory$ and the other is invalid. So the VM main operation performs the ownership transfer of $PgMemory$ in the following way:

> $PgMemory.Init$; $Installer.Init$; $Installer.load$;
> unpack($Installer$) ;
> $Interpreter.Init$; $Interpreter.exec$

6   Conclusion

The approach proposed here allows to express invariants which are only valid on some portions of programs. Such invariants can also be expressed in B by predicate of the form $co = i \Rightarrow I_i$ where co is a variable simulating an "ordinal counter" and I_i the expected invariant when $co = i$. Such forms of invariants are extensively used in B-event development. Nevertheless, this solution is not modular because variable co can not be updated by several components. For instance, a B solution for the case study of section 5.3 consists in building an architecture where *Installer* includes $PgMemory$, *Interpreter* sees $PgMemory$ and VM includes both *Installer* and *Interpreter*. The invariant I_{interp} is stated at the level of component VM, in the form $co = interp \Rightarrow I_{interp}$. This needs to add the precondition $co = interp$ to each operation of *Interpreter* (see [12] for a general solution). Variable co is assigned by VM, but, each *Interpreter* operation-call requires precondition $co = interp$ to be established. As stated in [4], this solution forces to specify some expected invariants in a top component, rather than in components where operations concerned by these invariants are defined. Moreover, invariants of the form $co = i \Rightarrow I_i$ may be confusing because such invariants should never be violated, but strongly depend on the control. The Spec# approach systematizes this solution, by introducing explicitly variables and statements relative to invariants validity. Hence, the notion of invariant validity is more explicit, while preserving soundness and modularity of invariant proofs.

The adaptation of the Spec# approach to B proposed in this paper leads to very simple proof obligations about status variables, most of them being obvious. Nevertheless, on the contrary to the B method in which invariant composition is a transparent process, the Spec# approach is very permissive making specification and proof an hard task. Hence, it is necessary to propose some patterns having good properties, like the different form of B operations described section 4. Moreover, it seems also possible to define a static analysis allowing to approximate whether status variables are used in a consistent way.

Other approaches have been studied in order to overcome B restrictions and in particular the single writer constraint. In [4], a rely-guarantee approach has been proposed in order to support architectures where two components A and B both need to constrain variables of C and to write into these variables. Basically, in this approach, the user must express in C what A and B are authorized to do on variables of C. Hence, both A and B know an abstraction of the other behavior on C, and can verify that this behavior is compatible with their own invariants. This approach is thus compatible with refinement (in particular, refinements of A and B refine their respective abstraction with respect to C). Our approach seems suitable for the multiple writers paradigm only when all ownership transfers between successive writers are performed via a reinitialization operation. But, in the other cases, when interface operations of writers are interleaved without reinitialization, then our approach is not modular with respect to the previous rely-guarantee approach: each ownership transfer requires a proof that the invariant of the new owner hold. On the contrary, the rely-guarantee approach of [4] does not authorize some combinations which are permitted by our approach. Indeed, our approach does not impose that invariants of all writers hold concurrently for all possible interleavings. Hence, it would be interesting to study the extension of our approach with rely-guarantee. Some proposals in this direction have already been studied for Spec# by Naumann and Barnett [7,22].

Finally, the main characteristics of the B method are its notion of component refinement and the monotonicity property allowing substitution of operation specifications by their implementations. Technically, refinement in B is based on invariants [11]: the relations between abstract and concrete data are expressed in a "gluing" invariant of the refining component. If we want to mix B refinement with our approach, we have the following problem: when we use some $\mathbf{pack}(M)$ outside of component M, we are obliged to prove that the invariant of M holds, but also that invariants of all refinements of M hold in order to ensure the substitutability principle. Let us remark that when $\mathbf{pack}(M)$ is used inside an operation of M, this problem does not occur: the proofs that gluing invariants hold are done in refining operations. Moreover, $\mathbf{unpack}(M)$ may occur outside of M without problem. Thus, in practice, it seems that refinement is compatible with our approach when it is restricted such that $\mathbf{pack}(M)$ calls occur only in component M. The case study of section 5 is an example where our approach accepts an architecture not admitted B, which is still compatible with refinement.

References

1. J.R. Abrial. *The B-Book*. Cambridge University Press, 1996.
2. P. Behm and all. Météor: A Successful Application of B in a Large Project. In *FM'99*, vol 1708 of *LNCS*, pages 348–387. Springer-Verlag, 1999.

3. F. Badeau and A. Amelot. Using B in a High Level Programming Language in an Industrial Project : Roissy VAL. In *ZB 2005*, vol 3455 of *LNCS*. Springer-Verlag, 2005.

4. M. Büchi and R. Back. Compositional Symmetric Sharing in B. In *FM'99*, vol 1708 of *LNCS*. Springer-Verlag, 1999.

5. D. Bert, S. Boulmé, M-L. Potet, A. Requet, and L. Voisin. Adaptable Translator of B Specifications to Embedded C programs. In *FME 2003: Formal Methods*, vol 2805 of *LNCS*. Springer, 2003.

6. M. Barnett, R. DeLine, M. Fähndrich, K.R.M. Leino, and W. Schulte. Verification of object-oriented programs with invariants. *Journal of Object Technology*, 3(6):27–56, 2004.

7. M. Barnett and D.A. Naumann. Friends need a bit more: Maintaining invariants over shared state. In *MPC*, vol 3125 of *LNCS*. Springer, 2004.

8. ClearSy. *Le Langage B. Manuel de reference, version 1.8.5*. ClearSy, 2002.

9. D.Dollé, D. Essamé, and J. Falampin. B à Siemens Transportation Systems- Une expérience industrielle. In *Développement rigoureux de logiciel avec la méthode B*, vol 22. Technique et Science Informatiques, 2003.

10. E.W. Dijkstra. *A discipline of Programming*. Prentice-Hall, 1976.

11. D. Gries and J. Prins. A New Notion of Encapsulation. In *Proc. of Symp. on Languages Issues in Programming Environments, SIGLPAN*, 1985.

12. H. Habrias. *Spécification formelle avec B*. Hermès Science, 2001.

13. C.A.R. Hoare. Proof of correctness of data representations. *Acta Informatica*, 1:271–281, 1972.

14. G. Leavens, A. Baker, and C. Ruby. JML: A notation for detailed design. In *Behavioral Specifications of Businesses and Systems*. Kluwer Academic Publishers, 1999.

15. G. Leavens, A.L. Baker, and C. Ruby. Preliminary design of JML: A behavioral interface specification language for Java. Technical report, TR 98-06i, Iowa State University, 2000.

16. K.R.M. Leino and P. Müller. Object invariants in dynamic contexts. In *ECOOP*, vol 3086 of *LNCS*, pages 491–516. Springer-Verlag, 2004.

17. J-L. Lanet and A. Requet. Formal Proof of Smart Card Applets Correctness. In *CARDIS'98*, vol 1820 of *LNCS*. Springer-Verlag, 1998.

18. B. Meyer. *Object-Oriented Construction*. Prentice-Hall, 1988.

19. C. Morgan and P.H.B. Gardiner. Data Refinement by Calculation. *Acta Informatica*, 27(6):481–503, 1990.

20. Sun Microsystems. Java Card^{TM} 2.2 Off-Card Verifier. Tech. report, Sun microsystems, 901 San Antonio Road, Palo Alto, CA 94303 USA, June 2002.

21. P. Müller, A. Poetzsch-Heffer, and G.T. Leavens. Modular Invariants for Layered Object Structures. *Science of Computer Programming*, 2006.

22. D.A. Naumann and M. Barnett. Towards imperative modules: Reasoning about invariants and sharing of mutable state. In *LICS 2004*. IEEE Computer Society, 2004.

23. M-L. Potet. *Spécifications et développements formels: Etude des aspects compositionnels dans la méthode B*. Habilitation à diriger des recherches, Institut National Polytechnique de Grenoble, 5 décembre 2002.

24. D. Sabatier and P. Lartigue. The Use of the B method for the Design and the Validation of the Transaction Mechanism for smart Card Applications. *Formal Methods in System Design*, 17(3):245–272, 2000.

Chorus Angelorum

Steve Dunne

School of Computing, University of Teesside
Middlesbrough, TS1 3BA, UK
s.e.dunne@tees.ac.uk

Abstract. We extend B's GSL by introducing new operators for angelic choice, thus widening its application from its original domain of
conjunctive computations to that of monotonic ones in general. We explore the impact of this on our theory of substitutions [6], discovering
two dual new normal forms for our new substitutions which we exploit
to formulate two new first-order tests of refinement between them.

1 Introduction

Angelic choice is much less familiar to most program developers as a programming concept than its demonic counterpart. Nevertheless, it has been directly
enlisted with successful effect in applications as diverse as constraint programming [12], the defining of proof tactics [14], the analysis of simple game plays
[2] and others in [18]. Moreover, angelic nondeterminism has long been recognised by refinement theorists as having an important role in refinement theory
[3,7,8]. A way of conceptualising angelic choice operationally is to recognise that
in general when a user runs a program he is doing so to achieve some purpose
or goal. When program execution encounters a demonic choice the user must
accept that this will be resolved capriciously and quite without regard to his
goal, whereas when an angelic choice is encountered he can intervene to resolve
the choice in whichever way best steers the execution towards the achievement
of his goal. Our aim in this paper is to explore the consequences of extending
the Generalised Substitution Language (GSL) with angelic choice.

After disposing of some preliminaries in Section 2, in Section 3 we initially
develop a theory of angelic substitutions, in which demonic choice is completely
replaced by angelic choice, and show that its properties are dual to those of [6].
Then in Section 4 we formulate our language of "extended" substitutions, in
which demonic choice and angelic choice co-exist. But a serious difficulty arises
here that, unlike in the case of ordinary and angelic substitutions, no obvious
before-after relational characterisation of our extended substitutions presents itself for us to utilise in a practicable test of refinement between such substitutions.
Fortunately, in Section 5 we are able to exploit recent work [4,15] on the relational characterisation of monotonic predicate transformers in terms of binary
multirelations [16] to formulate two alternative multirelational characterisations
of extended substitutions, yielding two interesting dual normal forms for them
and providing us with two alternative versions of our desired refinement test.

J. Julliand and O. Kouchnarenko (Eds.): B 2007, LNCS 4355, pp. 19–33, 2006.
© Springer-Verlag Berlin Heidelberg 2006

2   A Few Preliminaries

Variables and meta-variables. We will often use a single meta-variable to signify a list or *bunch* of basic variables. A bunch is essentially a flattened set, but –in contrast to set theory– bunch theory [9] makes no distinction between an element a and the singleton bunch comprised by a. In particular,

- bunch union is denoted by comma, thus u, v denotes the bunch comprising all the elements of u and of v;
- bunch difference is denoted by backslash, thus $u \setminus z$ denotes the bunch comprising all the elements of u which are not also in z;
- the empty bunch is denoted by null;
- we write $u : v$ to signify that u is a subbunch of v, which is to say that every element of u is an element of v.

Non-freeness. We write $x \setminus Q$ to mean that variable x does not appear free in predicate Q.

Syntactic substitution. When Q is a predicate, u a variable (or list of variables) and E an appropriately-typed expression, we write $Q\langle x/E\rangle$ to denote the predicate derived from Q by replacing all its free occurrences of (each component of) x by (the corresponding component of) E.

Applying substitutions to postconditions. We follow the usual B convention of denoting the weakest-precondition (wp) predicate-transformer effect of a substitution S on a postcondition Q by $[S]\,Q$. We adopt the syntactic convention that predicate-transformer application has a higher precedence than the ordinary logical connectives. Thus $[S]\,Q \wedge R$ means $([S]\,Q) \wedge R$ rather than $[S]\,(Q \wedge R)$.

Equality for Substitutions. In this paper we will meet angelic and "extended" (angelico-demonic) varieties of substitutions as well as conventional (demonic) ones. In all these cases we consider that two substitutions are the same if and only if they have the same frame of variables to which they assign values and the same wp predicate-transformer effect on every postcondition.

3   On the Side of the Angels

It took the genius of Jean-Raymond Abrial to invent generalised substitutions and thereby give us within the B Method [1] the convenience of expressing operations in an imperative fashion without forgoing any of the power of abstraction associated more commonly with the relational style of operation specification employed in other formal methods like Z [19] and VDM [13]. Associated with any generalised substitution are the characteristic predicates defined in Table 1, which in the context of their variable alphabets deriving from the substitution's frame can be interpreted as alphabetised relations [11]. Indeed, a generalised

Table 1. Characteristic predicates of a generalised substitution S with frame s

name	syntax	definition
termination	$\mathrm{trm}(S)$	$[S]\,\mathrm{true}$
feasibility	$\mathrm{fis}(S)$	$\neg\,[S]\,\mathrm{false}$
before-after predicate	$\mathrm{prd}(S)$	$\neg\,[S]\,s \neq s'$

substitution S with frame s is completely characterised by its characteristic predicates $\mathrm{trm}(S)$ and $\mathrm{prd}(S)$, as embodied in the "normal form" identity [6, Prop 4].

$$S \;\;=\;\; \mathrm{trm}(S) \mid @\; s' \,.\, \mathrm{prd}(S) \Longrightarrow s := s'$$

Anyone perplexed by meeting for the first time the double negation in the definition of $\mathrm{prd}(S)$ might reasonably ask why we can't instead just use $[S]\,s = s'$, which for the sake of discussion here we will call S's before-after "co-predicate" and denote by $\mathrm{crd}(S)$. The answer, of course, is that the nondeterminism expressible by generalised substitutions is demonic, and our co-predicate $\mathrm{crd}(S)$ doesn't accurately capture useful information about demonically nondeterministic behaviour whereas $\mathrm{prd}(S)$ does. Consider, for example, the substitution $x := 1 \;[]\; x := 2$. For $\mathrm{prd}(x := 1 \;[]\; x := 2)$ we obtain the useful predicate $x' = 1 \lor x' = 2$, whereas for $\mathrm{crd}(x := 1 \;[]\; x := 2)$ we obtain $x' = 1 \land x' = 2$ which merely collapses to false.

But now consider a variant of the GSL in which demonic choice has been replaced by angelic choice, which we will call the Angelic Substitution Language (ASL). We define its wp semantics in Table 2, in which A and B are typical angelic substitutions with respective frames a and b, Q a typical postcondition on the state, u a list of distinct variables and E is a corresponding list of appropriately typed values, w a bunch of variables not necessarily disjoint from a and z a bunch of variables which must be fresh with respect the state and hence non-free in Q.

Our ASL is a mirror-image of the GSL with properties which are dual to the latter's. Whereas in the GSL we can express all conjunctive computations, *i.e.* computations characterised by wp predicate transformers which distribute through all non-empty conjunctions of postconditions, in our ASL we can express all disjunctive computations, *i.e.* computations characterised by wp predicate transformers which distribute through all non-empty disjunctions of postconditions. We note that conjunctivity and disjunctivity are special cases of monotonicity, a predicate transformer being monotonic if it preserves the implication ordering between postconditions [5].

Table 2. The Angelic Substitution Language (ASL)

substitution name	syntax	frame	$[\text{subn}]\,Q$
skip	skip	null	Q
assignment	$u := E$	u	$Q\langle E/u\rangle$
precondition	$P \mid A$	a	$P \wedge [A]\,Q$
guard	$P \Longrightarrow A$	a	$P \Rightarrow [A]\,Q$
frame enlargement	A_w	a, w	$[A]\,Q$
bounded angelic choice	$A \sqcup B$	a, b	$[A]\,Q \vee [B]\,Q$
unbounded angelic choice	$\natural\, z\,.\,A$	$a \setminus z$	$\exists z\,.\,[A]\,Q$
sequential composition	$A\,;\,B$	a, b	$[A]\,[B]\,Q$

3.1   Characteristic Predicates of Angelic Substitutions

The characteristic predicates trm, fis and crd of an angelic substitution are formally defined in Table 3. We note that trm and fis are defined in the same way as for generalised substitutions, and we retain the same operational intuitions about them.

Table 3. Characteristic predicates of an angelic substitution A with frame a

name	syntax	definition
termination	$\text{trm}(A)$	$[A]\,\text{true}$
feasibility	$\text{fis}(A)$	$\neg\,[A]\,\text{false}$
before-after co-predicate	$\text{crd}(A)$	$[A]\,a = a'$

The following proposition highlights some tautologies relating the characteristic predicates in Table 3:

Proposition 3.1   (Properties of trm, fis and crd)
For any angelic substitution A and postcondition Q the following tautologies hold:

$$\text{fis}(A) \ \lor \ \text{crd}(A) \qquad\qquad\qquad\qquad 3.1.1$$

$$\text{crd}(A) \ \Rightarrow \ \text{trm}(A) \qquad\qquad\qquad\qquad 3.1.2$$

$$\text{fis}(A) \ \lor \ [A]Q \qquad\qquad\qquad\qquad 3.1.3$$

$$[A]Q \ \Rightarrow \ \text{trm}(A) \qquad\qquad\qquad\qquad 3.1.4$$

Proof: Each follows trivially from the monotonicity of A. □

3.2 Normal Form of an Angelic Substitution

In order to establish a normal form for angelic substitutions analagous to that given in [6, Prop 4] for generalised substitutions, we first need the following dual of [6, Prop 3]:

Proposition 3.2 (Conjunctivity with a frame-independent conjunct)
Let A be an angelic substitution with frame a and Q and R be predicates on the state such that $a \setminus R$. Then

$$[A](Q \land R) \ = \ [A]Q \ \land \ (\text{fis}(A) \Rightarrow R)$$

Proof: By structural induction over the constructs of the ASL in Table 2. □

Because the nondeterminism featuring in the ASL is angelic rather than demonic the boot is now on the other foot with respect to prd and crd. The ordinary before-after predicate $\text{prd}(A)$ of an angelically nondeterministic substitution A doesn't capture any useful information about A's behaviour whereas the co-predicate $\text{crd}(A)$ does. Consider the angelic substitution $x := 1 \sqcup x := 2$. For $\text{prd}(x := 1 \sqcup x := 2)$ we obtain $x' = 1 \land x' = 2$ which merely collapses to false, whereas for $\text{crd}(x := 1 \sqcup x := 2)$ we obtain the useful predicate $x' = 1 \lor x' = 2$. It turns out that an angelic substitution is completely characterised by its fis and crd. In fact we have the following interesting dual of [6, Prop 4]:

Proposition 3.3 (Normal form of an angelic substitution)
For any angelic substitution A with frame a

$$A \ = \ \text{fis}(A) \ \Longrightarrow \ \natural\, a'.\, \text{crd}(A) \mid a := a'$$

Proof: Trivially, the right-hand substitution's frame is also a. We must also show that the left-hand and right-hand substitutions have the same wp effect on an arbitrary postcondition Q. This follows from Props 3.2 and 3.1.3, the definition of $\text{crd}(A)$ and the ASL wp definitions in Table 2. □

3.3 Refinement of Angelic Substitutions

Our fundamental notion of refinement for angelic substitutions is the same as for ordinary generalised substitutions:

Definition 1 (Angelic refinement)

For any pair of angelic substitutions A and B with respective frames a and b we say A is refined by B, written $A \sqsubseteq B$, if and only if B's frame encompasses that of A, and B is always guaranteed to establish any postcondition Q that A is:

$$A \sqsubseteq B \qquad =_{df} \qquad a : b \quad \text{and for every } Q, \quad [A]\,Q \; \Rightarrow \; [B]\,Q$$

Intuitively, we refine an angelic substitution by *increasing* its angelic nondeterminism and *reducing* its vestigial drastic demonic nondeterminism by weakening its termination precondition. Thus, for example, we have that

$$y < 7 \mid x := 7 \quad \sqsubseteq \quad y < 11 \mid (x := 7 \sqcup \text{skip})$$

Clearly Definition 1 is impractical if we actually want to check whether one given angelic substitution refines another, since it entails testing against every postcondition Q. Fortunately, we have the following proposition which provides the basis for a more practicable check:

Proposition 3.4 (Angelic refinement in terms of fis and crd)

For any pair of angelic substitutions A and B with respective frames a and b

$$A \sqsubseteq B \qquad \Leftrightarrow \qquad a : b \; \wedge \; (\text{fis}(B) \Rightarrow \text{fis}(A)) \; \wedge \; (\text{crd}(A_b) \Rightarrow \text{crd}(B))$$

Proof: ($\Rightarrow$) follows from Definition 1 and the definitions of fis and crd, while ($\Leftarrow$) follows from Prop 3.3 and the ASL wp definitions in Table 2. $\qquad\qquad \square$

3.4   Conjugacy and Determinism

Every generalised substitution has a corresponding angelic substitution known as its *conjugate*, and conversely. If T is a generalised or angelic substitution with frame t we denote its conjugate by T^o and define it by

$$\text{frame}(T^o) \; = \; t \quad \text{and} \quad [T^o]\,Q \; = \; \neg\,[T]\neg\,Q$$

It has the property that $T^{oo} = T$. For a generalised substitution S with frame s we have

$$S^o \quad = \quad \text{trm}(S) \implies \natural\, s' \,.\, \text{prd}(S) \mid s := s'$$

Conversely, for an angelic substitution A with frame a we have

$$A^o \quad = \quad \text{fis}(A) \mid @\, a' \,.\, \text{crd}(A) \implies a := a'$$

The GSL and ASL overlap, since a substitution may be both conjunctive and disjunctive, which will be the case as long as it involves no non-trivial choices. We call a substitution which is both conjunctive and disjunctive *quasi-deterministic* because it behaves deterministically from states within its termination precondition (trm) and feasibility guard (fis). Moreover, such a substitution may be its own conjugate, in which case it is properly *deterministic*. Equivalently, a substitution T is deterministic exactly if $\text{prd}(T) = \text{crd}(T)$.

4   The Cosmic Struggle

We have seen that our angelic substitutions enjoy a range of interesting properties dual to those enjoyed by ordinary generalised substitutions [1,6]. Of course, in our ASL we have had to sacrifice the ability to express demonically nondeterministic behaviour with any real finesse, since all we have there to express demonic behaviour is the blunt instrument of preconditioning. Yet it is often important to be able to express both demonic and angelic nondeterminism with similar degrees of finesse in the same computation [2]. This motivates us to reinstate the GSL's original demonic choice operators alongside the angelic ones of our ASL, and so to obtain a new language which subsumes both the GSL and the ASL within it. We call this the Extended Substitution Language (ESL). Its syntax and wp semantics are given in Table 4, where M and N represent typical extended substitutions with respective frames m and n. Notice that in our ESL we have replaced the GSL's original symbol $[]$ for bounded demonic choice by the symbol $\sqcap$ commonly used in other formalisms such as CSP [10,17], in order to emphasize its duality with bounded angelic choice $\sqcup$.[1]

Extended substitutions express monotonic computations, *i.e.* computations characterised by monotonic wp predicate transformers. The interrelationship between our three substitution languages is illustrated in Figure 1.

4.1   Riding for a Fall?

The characteristic predicates trm and fis are defined for extended substitutions in the same way as for generalised substitutions and angelic substitutions, and we retain the same operational intuitions about them. Unfortunately, though, neither the before-after predicate prd nor co-predicate crd which we have already encountered adequately captures the behaviour of a monotonic computation. For example, let M be $(x := 1 \sqcap x := 2) \sqcup x := 3$ We find that $\mathrm{prd}(M)$ is false while $\mathrm{crd}(M)$ is $x' = 3$, which even together fail to capture fully the actual behaviour of M. So we have as yet no obvious relational characterisation of extended substitutions like the trm-prd one for generalised substitutions or the fis-crd one for angelic substitutions.

This is a potentially devastating deficiency in our theory of extended substitutions, since without an adequate relational characterisation of extended substitutions we are unable to formulate an effective first-order test of refinement which generalises those with which [6, Prop 7] and Proposition 3.4 provide us respectively for generalised and angelic substitutions. Fortunately, a binary-multirelational representation of monotonic computations has recently emerged which we can utilise to redeem our theory, as we explain in the next section.

---

[1] The symbols $\sqcap$ and $\sqcup$ are of course borrowed from Lattice Theory [2]. Our use of them here in our ESL is justified since it transpires our bounded demonic and angelic choices are respectively the binary meet and join operators of the refinement lattice of ESL programs.

Table 4. The Extended Substitution Language (ESL)

substitution name	syntax	frame	$[\text{subn}]\,Q$
skip	skip	null	Q
assignment	$u := E$	u	$Q\langle E/u\rangle$
precondition	$P \mid M$	m	$P \wedge [M]\,Q$
guard	$P \Longrightarrow M$	m	$P \Rightarrow [M]\,Q$
frame enlargement	M_w	m, w	$[M]\,Q$
bounded demonic choice	$M \sqcap N$	m, n	$[M]\,Q \wedge [N]\,Q$
unbounded demonic choice	$\textcircled{c}\,z\,.\,M$	$m \setminus z$	$\forall z\,.\,[M]\,Q$
bounded angelic choice	$M \sqcup N$	m, n	$[M]\,Q \vee [N]\,Q$
unbounded angelic choice	$\natural\,z\,.\,M$	$m \setminus z$	$\exists z\,.\,[M]\,Q$
sequential composition	$M \,;\, N$	m, n	$[M]\,[N]\,Q$

5 Paradise Regained

Rewitsky [16] formulates a relational representation, further explored in [15], of monotonic computations based on what are called *binary multirelations*. Rewitsky's representation has also subsequently been adapted by Cavalcanti *et al* [4] into an alphabetised predicative form favoured for incorporation into the Unifying Theories of Programming (UTP) [11].

5.1 Up-Closed Binary Multirelations

A *binary multirelation* R from a set X to a set Y is a relation of the form $X \leftrightarrow \mathbb{P}(Y)$. It is said to be *up-closed* if it has the property that for all elements x of X and subsets U, V of Y

$$x \mapsto U \in R \ \wedge \ U \subseteq V \ \Rightarrow \ x \mapsto V \in R$$

In Rewitzky's interpretation such an up-closed R represents a heterogeneous monotonic computation starting in X and finishing (if at all) in Y, in the following way. First, from the starting state x the angel chooses any set U from among all those sets of final states related to x under R. The demon then concludes the computation by choosing an actual final state y from the set U which the angel has chosen. Two special cases arise which deserve comment. First, the

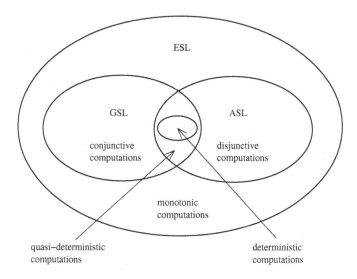

Fig. 1. The hierarchy of substitution languages

starting state x may be outside the domain of R so that there is no available set U whatsoever for the angel to choose. Such a frustration of the angel represents a win for the demon, the computation being taken in this case as having aborted (diverged). Second, if $x \mapsto \emptyset \in R$ the empty subset is available for the angel to choose, which will utterly frustrate the demon since he then has no potential states from which to choose an actual final state. This represents a win for the angel, the computation being taken in this case as having succeeded miraculously.

It is shown in [16] that this binary multirelation representation of monotonic computations is complete in the sense that there is an isomorphism between monotonic predicate transformers and up-closed binary multirelations, so every computation characterised by a monotonic wp predicate transformer is represented by an up-closed binary multirelation of appropriate type, while every up-closed binary multirelation represents a monotonic computation. In particular, the interpretation of the following two extreme binary multirelations is interesting:

- the empty relation represents the everywhere-aborting computation abort, since the angel is everywhere frustrated;
- the maximal relation $X \times \mathbb{P}(Y)$ represents the everywhere-miraculous computation magic, since from every starting state the angel can choose the empty set of final states to frustrate the demon.

5.2   An Alternative Interpretation

Rewitzky's interpretation of the up-closed binary multirelation $R : X \leftrightarrow \mathbb{P}(Y)$ as a monotonic computation from X to Y is not the only one possible. We can alternatively interpret R by reversing the order of choices of the angel and the demon, so that now from the starting state x the demon first chooses any set U from among all those sets of final states related to x under R, the angel then concluding the computation by choosing an actual final state y from the set U which the demon has chosen. Once again, the interpretation of the following two extreme binary multirelations is interesting:

- the empty relation now represents the everywhere-miraculous computation magic, since the demon is everywhere frustrated;
- the maximal relation $X \times \mathbb{P}(Y)$ now represents the everywhere-aborting computation abort, since from every starting state the demon can choose the empty set of final states to frustrate the angel.

This second interpretation is adopted in [4] since it fits more readily into the existing UTP framework where refinement is customarily modelled by reverse implication, so we will therefore call it the Cavalcanti interpretation. In lattice-theoretic terms it is the dual or conjugate of the Rewitzky interpretation.

5.3 Alphabetising a Binary Multirelation

Let x be a variable which ranges over values in X, and let u be a variable which ranges over $\mathbb{P}(Y)$, which is to say u denotes sets of values in Y, and let P be a predicate over alphabet x, u. Then P characterises a binary multirelation R such that $R \in X \leftrightarrow \mathbb{P}(Y)$ where $R \ =_{df} \ \{x, u \mid x \in X \ \wedge \ u \subseteq Y \ \wedge \ P\}$.

5.4 Characteristic Predicates of an Extended Substitution

Let M be an extended substitution with frame m, and let u be fresh with respect to the alphabet of M. Then we define the (before-after) *power predicate* of M, denoted $\mathrm{pod}(M)$, as $\neg \ [M] \, m \notin u$. It is in fact the predicate of the alphabetised form of the binary multirelation whose Cavalcanti interpretation is the monotonic computation which M expresses. Intuitively, therefore, $\mathrm{pod}(M)$ relates individual starting states to various sets of final states, one of which the angel must choose to offer the demon, from which he in turn chooses the actual final state.

Similarly, we define the (before-after) *power co-predicate* of M, denoted $\mathrm{cod}(M)$, as $[M] \, m \in u$. This is the predicate of the alphabetised form of the binary multirelation whose Rewitzky interpretation is the monotonic computation which M expresses. Note that the monotonicity of M ensures that both $\mathrm{pod}(M)$ and $\mathrm{cod}(M)$ are up-closed. We also note the duality implicit in the fact that $\mathrm{cod}(M) \ = \ \mathrm{pod}(M^o)$. Intuitively, therefore, $\mathrm{cod}(M)$ relates individual starting states to various sets of final states, one of which the demon must choose to offer the angel, from which she in turn chooses the actual final state.

In contemplating the predicates $\mathrm{pod}(M)$ and $\mathrm{cod}(M)$ we must be careful to appreciate the type of the variable u which appears in them. This denotes sets of final states of M. This state space may itself be characterised by several variables, so in general u will denote a set of bindings of these variables, corresponding, for example, to a set of bindings of the appropriate schema type in Z [19]. Alternatively, by assuming an implicit universal lexical ordering on our variable names, we can represent these sets of values simply as sets of tuples.

We summarise all the characteristic predicates of an extended substitution in Table 5. Note that $\text{fis}(M)$ and $\text{trm}(M)$ can be derived from $\text{pod}(M)$, since

$$\text{fis}(M) \;=\; \exists\,u\;.\;\text{pod}(M) \qquad \text{and} \qquad \text{trm}(M) \;=\; \neg\,\text{pod}(M)\langle\emptyset/u\rangle$$

Dually, they can also be derived from $\text{cod}(M)$, since

$$\text{trm}(M) \;=\; \exists\,u\;.\;\text{cod}(M) \qquad \text{and} \qquad \text{fis}(M) \;=\; \neg\,\text{cod}(M)\langle\emptyset/u\rangle$$

Table 5. Characteristic predicates of an extended substitution M with frame m

name	syntax	definition
termination	$\text{trm}(M)$	$[M]\,\text{true}$
feasibility	$\text{fis}(M)$	$\neg\,[M]\,\text{false}$
before-after power predicate	$\text{pod}(M)$	$\neg\,[M]\,m \notin u$
before-after power co-predicate	$\text{cod}(M)$	$[M]\,m \in u$

5.5   Two Normal Forms of an Extended Substitution

The following two propositions give us alternative normal forms for an extended substitution:

Proposition 5.3   (Demonic normal form of an extended substitution)
For any extended substitution M with frame m

$$M \;=\; @\,u\;.\;\text{pod}(M) \;\Longrightarrow\; \natural\,m'\;.\;m' \in u \mid m := m'$$

Proof: Trivially, the right-hand substitution has the same frame m as the left-hand one M. We also have to prove that the application of the right-hand substitution to an arbitrary postcondition Q gives $[M]\,Q$, *i.e.*

$$[\,@\,u\;.\;\text{pod}(M) \;\Longrightarrow\; \natural\,m'\;.\;m' \in u \mid m := m'\,]\,Q \;\;\Leftrightarrow\;\; [M]\,Q$$

Proof $(\Rightarrow)$

$$[\,@\,u\;.\;\text{pod}(M) \;\Longrightarrow\; \natural\,m'\;.\;m' \in u \mid m := m'\,]\,Q$$
$$\equiv \qquad \{\text{ ESL semantics from Table 4 }\}$$
$$\forall\,u\;.\;\text{pod}(M) \;\Rightarrow\; \exists\,m'\;.\;m' \in u \wedge Q\langle m'/m\rangle$$

$\equiv$ { defn of pod(M) }
$\quad \forall u \; . \; \neg \, [M]\, m \notin u \;\; \Rightarrow \;\; \exists\, m' \; . \; m' \in u \wedge Q\langle m'/m\rangle$
$\equiv$ { logic }
$\quad \forall u \; . \; [M]\, m \notin u \; \vee \; \exists\, m' \; . \; m' \in u \wedge Q\langle m'/m\rangle$
$\Rightarrow$ { specialise u as $\{m \mid \neg\, Q\}$ }
$\quad [M]\, m \notin \{m \mid \neg\, Q\} \; \vee \; \exists\, m' \; . \; m' \in \{m \mid \neg\, Q\} \wedge Q\langle m'/m\rangle$
$\equiv$ { set theory }
$\quad [M]\, Q \; \vee \; \exists\, m' \; . \; m' \in \{m \mid \neg\, Q\} \wedge Q\langle m'/m\rangle$
$\equiv$ { change name of bound variable }
$\quad [M]\, Q \; \vee \; \exists\, m \; . \; m \in \{m \mid \neg\, Q\} \wedge Q$
$\equiv$ { set theory }
$\quad [M]\, Q \; \vee \; \exists\, m \; . \; \neg\, Q \wedge Q$
$\equiv$ { logic }
$\quad [M]\, Q \; \vee \; \exists\, m \; . \; \text{false}$
$\equiv$ { logic }
$\quad [M]\, Q$

Proof ($\Leftarrow$):

$\quad \text{true}$
$\equiv$ { monotonicity of M }
$\quad (\forall m \; . \; Q \Rightarrow m \notin u) \;\; \Rightarrow \;\; [M]\, Q \;\; \Rightarrow \;\; [M]\, m \notin u$
$\equiv$ { logic }
$\quad [M]\, Q \;\; \Rightarrow \;\; (\forall m \; . \; Q \Rightarrow m \notin u) \;\; \Rightarrow \;\; [M]\, m \notin u$
$\equiv$ { logic }
$\quad [M]\, Q \;\; \Rightarrow \;\; \neg\, [M]\, m \notin u \;\; \Rightarrow \;\; \neg\,(\forall m \; . \; Q \Rightarrow m \notin u)$
$\equiv$ { logic }
$\quad [M]\, Q \;\; \Rightarrow \;\; \neg\, [M]\, m \notin u \;\; \Rightarrow \;\; (\exists m \; . \; m \in u \wedge Q)$
$\equiv$ { make quantification over u explicit }
$\quad \forall u \; . \; [M]\, Q \;\; \Rightarrow \;\; \neg\, [M]\, m \notin u \;\; \Rightarrow \;\; (\exists m \; . \; m \in u \wedge Q)$
$\equiv$ { $u \setminus [M]\, Q$ }
$\quad [M]\, Q \;\; \Rightarrow \;\; \forall u \; . \; \neg\, [M]\, m \notin u \;\; \Rightarrow \;\; (\exists m \; . \; m \in u \wedge Q)$
$\equiv$ { change name of bound variable }
$\quad [M]\, Q \;\; \Rightarrow \;\; \forall u \; . \; \neg\, [M]\, m \notin u \;\; \Rightarrow \;\; (\exists m' \; . \; m' \in u \wedge Q\langle m'/m\rangle)$
$\equiv$ { defn of pod(M) }
$\quad [M]\, Q \;\; \Rightarrow \;\; \forall u \; . \; \text{pod}(M) \;\; \Rightarrow \;\; (\exists m' \; . \; m' \in u \wedge Q\langle m'/m\rangle)$
$\equiv$ { ESL semantics from Table 4 }
$\quad [M]\, Q \;\; \Rightarrow \;\; [\; @\, u \; . \; \text{pod}(M) \;\; \Longrightarrow \;\; \natural\, m' \; . \; m' \in u \mid m := m' \;]\, Q$

$\square$

Proposition 5.4 (Angelic normal form of an extended substitution)
For any extended substitution M with frame m

$$M \;=\; \natural\, u \,.\, \mathrm{cod}(M) \;\mid\; @\, m' \,.\, m' \in u \implies m := m'$$

Proof: Dual of Prop 5.3.   □

5.6   Refinement of Extended Substitutions

Our fundamental notion of refinement for extended substitutions is the same as
for ordinary generalised substitutions and angelic substitutions:

Definition 2 (Refinement for extended substitutions)
For any pair of extended substitutions M and N with respective frames m and n
we say M is refined by N, written $M \sqsubseteq N$, if and only if N's frame encompasses
that of M, and N is always guaranteed to establish any postcondition Q that
M is:

$$M \sqsubseteq N \qquad =_{df} \qquad m : n \quad \text{and for every } Q, \;\; [M]\,Q \;\Rightarrow\; [N]\,Q$$

Like Definition 1 for angelic substitutions, Definition 2 is impractical if we actually want to check whether one given extended substitution refines another, since
it entails testing against every postcondition Q. Fortunately, we can use either
of our new characteristic predicates pod or cod as the basis of a more practicable
first-order test of refinement, as revealed in the following two propositions:

Proposition 5.5 (Refinement by pod)
For extended substitutions M and N with respective frames m and n:

$$M \sqsubseteq N \qquad \Leftrightarrow \qquad m : n \;\wedge\; (\mathrm{pod}(N) \Rightarrow \mathrm{pod}(M_n))$$

Proof: Follows from the demonic normal forms of M_n and N, and up-closedness
of pod.   □

Proposition 5.6 (Refinement by cod)
For extended substitutions M and N with respective frames m and n:

$$M \sqsubseteq N \qquad \Leftrightarrow \qquad m : n \;\wedge\; (\mathrm{cod}(M_n) \Rightarrow \mathrm{cod}(N))$$

Proof: Follows from the angelic normal forms of M_n and N, and up-closedness
of cod.   □

5.7   An Example Refinement

We will illustrate the use of Prop 5.6 with a small example. Let

$$M \;=\; (\,x := 0 \sqcap x := 1 \sqcap \mathrm{skip}\,) \;\sqcup\; (\,x := 1 \sqcap x := 2\,)$$

$$N \;=\; (\,x := 2 \sqcup \mathrm{skip}\,) \sqcap\; x := 1$$

In this case M and N have the same frame x so $M_n = M$. We will demonstrate
that $M \sqsubseteq N$ by proving that $\mathrm{cod}(M) \Rightarrow \mathrm{cod}(N)$. We therefore calculate

$$
\begin{aligned}
cod(M) \quad &= \quad [M]\, x \in u \\
&= \quad [(x := 0 \sqcap x := 1 \sqcap skip) \sqcup (x := 1 \sqcap x := 2]\, x \in u \\
&= \quad [x := 0 \sqcap x := 1 \sqcap skip]\, x \in u \ \lor\ [\, x := 1 \sqcap x := 2]\, x \in u \\
&= \quad (0 \in u \land 1 \in u \land x \in u\,) \ \lor\ (1 \in u \land 2 \in u) \\
&= \quad 1 \in u \ \land\ ((0 \in u \land x \in u) \ \lor\ 2 \in u) \\
&= \quad 1 \in u \ \land\ (0 \in u \lor 2 \in u) \ \land\ (x \in u \lor 2 \in u)
\end{aligned}
\tag{1}
$$

$$
\begin{aligned}
cod(N) \quad &= \quad [N]\, x \in u \\
&= \quad [(x := 2 \sqcup skip) \sqcap x := 1]\, x \in u \\
&= \quad [\, x := 2 \sqcup skip\,]\, x \in u \ \land\ [x := 1]\, x \in u \\
&= \quad (2 \in u \lor x \in u) \ \land\ 1 \in u
\end{aligned}
\tag{2}
$$

whence it is clear that $(1) \Rightarrow (2)$.   □

6   Conclusion

We have developed a theory of extended (angelico-demonic) substitutions, the main fruits of which are our two dual normal forms with their corresponding simple refinement test for pairs of such substitutions, based respectively on our new dual notions of power predicate, pod, and power co-predicate, cod. We have seen how Abrial's original conception of generalised substitutions, intended for expressing only conjunctive computations, has proved surprisingly well adaptable to the wider realm of monotonic computations.

References

1. J.-R. Abrial. *The B-Book: Assigning Programs to Meanings*. Cambridge University Press, 1996.
2. R.-J. Back and J. von Wright. *Refinement Calculus: A Systematic Introduction*. Springer-Verlag New York, 1998.
3. R.J.R. Back and J. von Wright. Combining angels, demons and miracles in program specifications. *Theoretical Computer Science*, 100:365–383, 1992.
4. A. Cavalcanti, J.C.P. Woodcock, and S.E. Dunne. Angelic nondeterminism in the unifying theories of programming. *Formal Aspects of Computing*, 18(3):288–307, 2006.
5. E.W. Dijkstra and C.S. Scholten. *Predicate Calculus and Program Semantics*. Springer Berlin, 1990.
6. S.E. Dunne. A theory of generalised substitutions. In D. Bert, J.P. Bowen, M.C. Henson, and K. Robinson, editors, *ZB2002: Formal Specification and Development in Z and B*, number 2272 in Lecture Notes in Computer Science, pages 270–290. Springer, 2002.
7. P.H.B. Gardiner and C.C. Morgan. Data refinement of predicate transformers. *Theoretical Computer Science*, 87:143–162, 1991.
8. P.H.B. Gardiner and C.C. Morgan. A single complete rule for data refinement. *Formal Aspects of Computing*, 5:367–382, 1993.
9. E.C.R. Hehner. Bunch theory: a simple set theory for computer science. *Information Processing Letters*, 12(1):26–30, 1981.

10. C.A.R. Hoare. *Communicating Sequential Processes*. Prentice-Hall, 1985.

11. C.A.R. Hoare and He Jifeng. *Unifying Theories of Programming*. Prentice Hall, 1998.

12. R. Jagaeesan, V. Shanbhogue, and V. Saraswat. Angelic nondeterminism in concurrent constraint programming, 1991. Xerox technical report.

13. C.B. Jones. *Systematic Software Development Using VDM (2nd edn)*. Prentice-Hall, 1990.

14. A.P. Martin, P.H.B. Gardiner, and J.C.P. Woodcock. A tactical calculus. *Formal Aspects of Computing*, 8(4):479–489, 1996.

15. C.E. Martin, S.A Curtis, and I. Rewitzky. Modelling nondeterminism. In D. Kozen, editor, *Mathematics of Program Construction*, number 3125 in Lecture Notes in Computer Science, pages 228–251. Springer, 2004.

16. I. Rewitzky. Binary multirelations. In H. de Swart, E. Orlowska, G. Schmit, and M. Roubens, editors, *Theory and Application of Relational Structures as Knowledge Instruments*, number 2929 in Lecture Notes in Computer Science, pages 259–274. Springer, 2003.

17. A.W. Roscoe. *The Theory and Practice of Concurrency*. Prentice-Hall, 1998.

18. N. Ward and I.J. Hayes. Applications of angelic nondeterminism. In P.A. Bailes, editor, *Proc. of the 6th Australian Software Engineering Conference (ASWEC91)*, pages 391–404. Australian Computer Society, 1991.

19. J. Woodcock and J. Davies. *Using Z: Specification, Refinement and Proof*. Prentice Hall, 1996.

Augmenting B with Control Annotations

Wilson Ifill[1,2], Steve Schneider[1], and Helen Treharne[1]

[1] Department of Computing, University of Surrey
[2] Atomic Weapons Establishment, Aldermaston, Reading, UK

Abstract. CSP‖B is an integration of the process algebra Communicating Sequential Processes (CSP), and the B-Method, which enables
consistent controllers to be written for B machines in a verifiable way.
Controllers are consistent if they call operations only when they are
enabled. Previous work has established a way of verifying consistency
between controllers and machines by translating control flow to AMN
and showing that a *control loop invariant* is preserved. This paper offers an alternative approach, which allows fragments of control flow expressed as *annotations* to be associated with machine operations. This
enables designers' understanding about local relationships between successive operations to be captured at the point the operations are written,
and used later when the controller is developed. Annotations provide a
bridge between controllers and machines, expressing the relevant aspects
of control flow so that controllers can be verified simply by reference to
the annotations without the need to consider the details of the machine
operations. This paper presents the approach through two instances of
annotations with their associated control languages, covering recursion,
prefixing, choice, and interrupt.

1 Introduction

The design and implementation of critical systems benefits from development in
a formal method such as the B-Method, which models systems in terms of state
and operations. However, this approach does not support specifications of execution patterns directly, and so approaches such as Event-B [6] and CSP‖B [8]
have been proposed to incorporate action specification with B. This paper develops the CSP‖B approach, which offers a clean separation of control from data
manipulation. The developments presented here fall within the scope of AWE's
System-B project, which involves collaborative research into the use of CSP‖B
to specify co-designs [5] and to formally investigate systems designs of large scale
developments.

One motivation for the work is a desire to enable Engineers to describe many
aspects of design within a single notation. We introduce control annotations
into the B-Method to enable the formal capture of control flow fragments in
B during the development of the B machines. We generate proof obligations to
demonstrate that the set of executions allowable by the annotations do not cause
operations to diverge. The benefit of this approach is that only the semantics
of the machine operations is required in checking the annotations, and these

J. Julliand and O. Kouchnarenko (Eds.): B 2007, LNCS 4355, pp. 34–48, 2006.
© Springer-Verlag Berlin Heidelberg 2006

checks are similar in size and difficulty to standard B machine consistency checks. Annotations can be checked against controllers written in CSP, which describe the flow of control explicitly. There is no need to check the CSP directly against the full B description, in contrast to previous CSP‖B work where it was necessary to translate the entire CSP controller into AMN in order to check it. Once the annotations are shown to be correct with respect to the B machine we can evaluate controllers against the annotations without further reference to the machine. Machines can be refined and implemented in the normal way while remaining consistent with the controller.

This paper describes the extendable framework for introducing annotations and controllers and presents two exemplars. This paper is not concerned with I/O operations. In Section 2, we briefly introduce the approach. In Section 3 we demonstrate the framework by using a simple language for controllers, the NEXT annotation for B operations, and define the notion of consistency between them. Section 4 presents a worked example of a simple traffic control system. In Section 5 we introduce an interrupting annotation FROM-ANY, add the CSP interrupt operator to the controller language, and extend the notion of consistency. We develop the worked example in Section 6 to illustrate the new annotation and its use. Finally in Section 7 we discuss further directions and related work.

We assume the reader is familiar with the Abstract Machine Notation of the B-Method [1]. We restrict our attention in this paper to correct B machines: those for which all proof obligations have already been discharged. We use I to refer to the invariant of the machine, T to refer to the machine's initialisation, P_i to refer to the precondition of operation Op_i, and B_i to refer to the body of operation Op_i.

Controllers will be written in a simple subset of the CSP process algebraic language [4,7]. The language will be explained as it is introduced. Controllers are considered as *processes* performing *events*, which correspond to operations in the controlled B machine. Thus operation names will appear in the controller descriptions as well as the B machine definitions.

2   The General Framework

The approach proposed in this paper introduces *annotations* on B operations as a mechanism for bridging the gap between B machines and CSP controllers, whilst maintaining the separation of concerns. The approach consists of the following components:

- **Machine definition:** The controlled component must first be defined.
- **Annotations:** The initialisation and the operations in the machine definition are annotated with fragments of control flow.
- **Annotation proof obligations:** Verification conditions that establish consistency of the annotations with the controlled machine. This means that the fragments of control flow captured by the annotations really are appropriate for the machine.

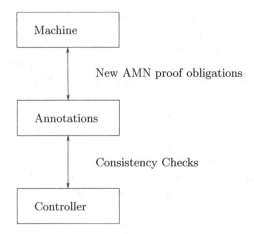

Fig. 1. Relationship between the different parts of the approach

- **Controller:** This is a process that describes the overall flow of control for the B machine.
- **Consistency checking:** Establishing that the controller is consistent with the annotations—that every part of the control flow is supported by some annotation.

Checking a CSP controller against a machine is thus reduced to checking it against the annotations and verifying that the annotations are appropriate for the machine. The relationship between the different parts of the approach is illustrated in Figure 1.

The framework presented here is quite general, in that it may be applied to a variety of annotations and control languages. The first step to be taken is therefore to fix on the control language and the associated annotations to be incorporated into the AMN machine descriptions. The key result that these build up to is expressed in Theorem 1, though the underlying theory will not be expanded in this paper for reasons of space.

3   A First Approach

We will demonstrate the approach firstly with a simple model to illustrate how the aspects of the approach interrelate. The first kind of annotation we consider is the NEXT annotation, and we use an extremely simple controller language consisting only of prefixing, choice, and recursion. These go naturally together because the NEXT annotation is concerned with successive operations, and the controller language allows simple loops of sequences of operations.

3.1   The NEXT Annotation

We annotate an operation of a B machine with a NEXT annotation. Currently, we introduce this as a comment included with the description of the operation, so that it is invisible to current tools. However, in principle tools could be modified to recognise an additional ANNOTATION clause to introduce the additional information into operation descriptions.

A NEXT annotation on an operation Op_i introduces another operation Op_j, or set of operations $Op_j, \ldots, Op_k$, which should be enabled after Op_i is executed. The NEXT annotation is written as follows:

$$Op_i \mathrel{\widehat{=}} \textbf{PRE} \ \ P_i \ \ \textbf{THEN} \ \ B_i \ \ \textbf{END} \ \ /* \ \{ \ Op_j, \ldots, Op_k \ \} \ \text{NEXT} \ */$$

3.2   Annotation Proof Obligations

The annotation corresponds to the assertion that, following the execution of Op_i, operations Op_j through to Op_k are available for execution. This gives rise to the following proof obligation, which requires that the precondition of each of the listed operations is enabled:

Definition 1 (NEXT **Proof Obligation for Operations**). *The proof obligation associated with a* NEXT *annotated operation* Op_i *is given as:*

$$(I \wedge P_i \Rightarrow [B_i](P_j))$$
$$\wedge \ \ldots$$
$$\wedge \ (I \wedge P_i \Rightarrow [B_i](P_k))$$

If the conjunction of proof obligations for all the annotations are discharged then we say that the annotations are consistent with the machine. This ensures that any controller which only calls operations that are listed, following execution of Op_i, can be sure that those operations will be enabled.

Definition 2 (NEXT **Proof Obligation for Initialisation**). *The proof obligation associated with the annotation*

$$T / * \{ Op_j, \ldots, Op_k \} NEXT * /$$

on initialisation T *is given by*

$$[T](P_j)$$
$$\wedge \ \ldots$$
$$\wedge \ [T](P_k)$$

This establishes that all of the listed operations are enabled following initialisation. Thus, any controller which only begins with such operations will be consistent with the annotations.

We will use $next(Op_i)$ to identify the set of operations given in the NEXT annotation. Thus from the annotation above we have that $next(Op_i) = \{ Op_j, \ldots, Op_k \}$. We also use $next(INITIALISATION)$ to identify the set of operations in the annotation of the INITIALISATION clause. To ensure that there is no deadlock in the system, it is sufficient that every operation, and the INITIALISATION, has a NEXT annotation.

3.3 A Simple Controller Language

We will begin with the following simple controller language, which allows only event prefix, choice, and recursion:

Definition 3 (Controller Syntax)

$$R ::= a \rightarrow R \mid R \;\square\; R \mid S$$

Here, the event a is an operation name, and S is a process variable. Recursive definitions are then given as $S \mathbin{\widehat{=}} R$. In a controller definition, all process variables used are bound by some recursive definition. The results presented in this paper require that all recursive definitions are *guarded*, which means that at least one event must occur before a recursive call.

3.4 Consistency

We can now give a definition of consistency between a controller and the annotations on a B machine. The key underlying idea is that whenever one event Op_j follows another Op_i in the controller's execution, then there must be an annotation that underpins this, ensuring that the associated operation Op_j is guaranteed to be enabled after Op_i has occurred.

To do this, we first capture the initial events $init(R)$ for a controller R:

Definition 4 (initial elements of CSP controller process)

$$init(a \rightarrow R1) = \{a\}$$
$$init(R1 \;\square\; R2) = init(R1) \cup init(R2)$$
$$init(S) = init(R) \qquad where\ S \mathbin{\widehat{=}} R$$

Note that in a controller definition the process variable S must be bound by some recursive definition $S \mathbin{\widehat{=}} R$, and this defines $init(S)$.

For example, if $LOOP \mathbin{\widehat{=}} a \rightarrow b \rightarrow LOOP$, then $init(LOOP) = a$.

A controller will be *step-consistent* with a collection of annotations if all consecutive events are allowed by the occurrence of some annotation. In the case where the only kind of annotation is NEXT, it is straightforward to define step-consistency, and we do this over the structure of the syntax.

Definition 5 (Step-consistency of NEXT Annotated Machines and Controllers). *The* step-consistency *of a controller R with the annotations of machine M is defined structurally over the syntax of R as follows:*

1. *$a \rightarrow R$ is step-consistent with M's annotations if $init(R) \subseteq next(a)$ and R is step-consistent with M's annotations.*
2. *$R1 \;\square\; R2$ is step-consistent with M's annotations if $R1$ is step-consistent with M's annotations and $R2$ is step-consistent with M's annotations.*
3. *S is step-consistent with M's annotations.*

A family of recursive definitions $S \mathbin{\widehat{=}} R$ is step-consistent with M's annotations if each R is step-consistent with M's annotations.

There is one additional aspect of consistency required: that the initial state of the machine is consistent with the starting point of the controller. This is captured as *initial-consistency*:

Definition 6 (Initial-Consistency of NEXT Annotated Machines and Controllers). *A controller R is* initially-consistent *with the annotations of machine M if init(R) ⊆ next(INITIALISATION).*

Definition 7 (Consistency). *A controller R is* consistent *with the annotations of machine M if it is step-consistent with M's annotations and initially-consistent with M's annotations.*

The main result of this section is the following theorem:

Theorem 1. *If R is consistent with the annotations of a machine M, and the annotations of M are consistent with machine M, then operations of M called in accordance with the control flow of R will never be called outside their preconditions.*

The key feature of the proof of this theorem is an argument that no trace of R leads to an operation of M called outside its precondition. This is established by building up the traces of R and showing that at each step an operation called outside its precondition cannot be introduced, by appealing to the relevant annotation and applying its proof obligation.

The benefit of this theorem is that the details of the operations of M are required only for checking the consistency of the annotations, and are not considered directly in conjunction with the controller. The annotations are then checked against the controller using the definition of consistency above. This enables a separation of concerns, treating the annotations as an abstraction of the B machine.

4   Example: Carcassonne Traffic Control System

We use the example of a traffic light system to illustrate the ideas introduced in the previous section.

A traffic control system for the main street of the walled Cité of Carcassonne is specified. The main street is narrow and is heavily used by tourists and some motor vehicles brave enough to edge through the alley. The system must allow traffic up into the cité market square from the moat or down from the square to the moat gate along the same single width road. The system must allow time for motor vehicles to clear the road before changing direction. A B machine that offers a choice between the traffic flows is given in Figure 2. A controller consistent with the annotations is given in Figure 3. We note that the controller given here is more restrictive than necessary; it is not the weakest controller consistent with the annotations.

In order to show that *Lights_CTRL* is an appropriate controller for *Lights*, we make use of the annotations. We must show that the annotations are consistent with the machine, and we must also show that the controller is consistent with the annotations. We consider each of these in turn.

MACHINE *Lights*
SETS *COMMAND* = { *Stop* , *Go* }
VARIABLES *Moat* , *Square*
INVARIANT *(Moat = Stop* ∨ *Square = Stop)*
$\qquad\qquad$ ∧ *Moat* ∈ *COMMAND* ∧ *Square* ∈ *COMMAND*
INITIALISATION *Moat* , *Square* := *Stop* , *Stop* /* { Stop_All } NEXT */

OPERATIONS
$\quad$ **Stop_All** ≙ **PRE** *true* **THEN** *Moat, Square* := *Stop, Stop* **END**
$\qquad$ /* { Go_Moat, Go_Square } NEXT */ ;
$\quad$ **Go_Moat** ≙ **PRE** *Moat = Stop* ∧ *Square = Stop* **THEN** *Moat* := *Go* **END**
$\qquad$ /* { Stop_All, Stop_Moat } NEXT */ ;
$\quad$ **Stop_Moat** ≙ **PRE** *Moat = Go* **THEN** *Moat* := *Stop* **END**
$\qquad$ /* { Go_Moat, Go_Square } NEXT */ ;
$\quad$ **Go_Square** ≙ **PRE** *Moat = Stop* ∧ *Square = Stop* **THEN** *Square* := *Go* **END**
$\qquad$ /* { Stop_All, Stop_Square } NEXT */ ;
$\quad$ **Stop_Square** ≙ **PRE** *Square = Go* **THEN** *Square* := *Stop* **END**
$\qquad$ /* { Go_Moat, Go_Square } NEXT */
END

Fig. 2. Lights machine

$$Lights\_CTRL \;\hat{=}\; Stop\_All \rightarrow S\_CTRL$$

$$S\_CTRL \;\hat{=}\; (Go\_Moat \rightarrow Stop\_Moat \rightarrow S\_CTRL)$$
$$\Box \,(Go\_Square \rightarrow Stop\_Square \rightarrow S\_CTRL)$$

Fig. 3. Lights Controller

4.1 Consistency of Annotations with the Machine

The proof obligations associated with the annotations (eliding the invariant) are
as follows:

– **Initialisation:** The initialisation clause must establish the precondition of
all the operations identified in its annotation; in this case this is *Stop_All*,
with precondition *true*. From Definition 2, we must prove

$$[Moat, Square := Stop, Stop](true).$$

– **Stop_All:** There are two next operations, *Go_Moat* and *Go_Square*, and so
there will be a proof obligation associated with each of them. In fact each
of them have the same precondition: *Moat = Stop* ∧ *Square = Stop*. Hence
the two proof obligations are identical, and correspond to

$$I \wedge P_{Stop\_All} \Rightarrow [Moat, Square := Stop, Stop](Moat = Stop \wedge Square = Stop).$$

– **Go_Moat:** There are two next operations, *Stop_All* and *Stop_Moat*, identified in the annotation. For *Stop_All*, the precondition is *true*, so the proof

obligation is $I \wedge P_{Go\_Moat} \Rightarrow [Moat := Go](true)$. Considering $Stop\_Moat$, its precondition is $Moat = Go$, so the corresponding proof obligation is

$$I \wedge P_{Go\_Moat} \Rightarrow [Moat := Go](Moat = Go).$$

- **Go_Square:** The annotation and hence the proof obligations for this operation are entirely similar to those for Go_Moat, but assigning to $Square$ this time.
- **Stop_Moat:** There are two next operations, Go_Moat and Go_Square, so there will be a proof obligation associated with each. The proof obligation associated with Go_Moat is given by $I \wedge P_{Stop\_Moat} \Rightarrow [B_{Stop\_Moat}](P_{Go\_Moat})$, which expands to

$$(Moat = Stop \vee Square = Stop) \wedge (Moat = Go)$$
$$\Rightarrow [Moat := Stop](Moat = Stop \wedge Square = Stop)$$

The proof obligation associated with Go_Square is entirely similar, since the precondition for Go_Square is the same as that of Go_Moat.
- **Stop_Square:** The annotation and hence the proof obligations for this operation are entirely similar to that for $Stop\_Moat$.

In all cases the proof obligations are discharged. Note that in the case of $Stop\_Moat$ the invariant and its precondition are necessary for establishing that the operation body establishes the precondition of the next operations.

Discharging the proof obligations means that the annotations are a correct description of allowable sequences of operations. Thus they can be used to verify the appropriateness of the controller.

4.2   Consistency of the Controller with the Annotations

To show that the controller $Lights\_CTRL$ is consistent with $Lights$ we apply the definitions of step-consistent and initially-consistent. Let R_CTRL be the body of the definition of S_CTRL. Then it is necessary to show that R_CTRL is step-consistent with the annotations of the $Lights$ machine.

Step-consistency is established by considering the parts of the definition of R_CTRL:

- The process variable S_CTRL is step-consistent, by the definition of step-consistency for process variables.

- $Stop\_All \rightarrow S\_CTRL$: the prefix rule for step-consistency from Definition 5 requires that $init(S\_CTRL) \subseteq next(Stop\_All)$. This is true in this case, since the process variable S_CTRL is step-consistent and
  $init(S\_CTRL) = \{Go\_Moat, Go\_Square\} = next(Stop\_All)$.

- $Stop\_Moat \rightarrow S\_CTRL$: this is step-consistent, since the process variable S_CTRL is step-consistent and
  $init(S\_CTRL) = \{Go\_Moat, Go\_Square\} = next(Stop\_Moat)$.

- $Go\_Moat \rightarrow Stop\_Moat \rightarrow S\_CTRL$: step-consistency follows from the fact that $Stop\_Moat \rightarrow S\_CTRL$ is step-consistent, and

$$
\begin{aligned}
init(Stop\_Moat \rightarrow S\_CTRL) &= \{Stop\_Moat\} \\
&\subseteq \{Stop\_Moat, Stop\_All\} \\
&= next(Go\_Moat).
\end{aligned}
$$

- $Stop\_Square \rightarrow S\_CTRL$: this is step-consistent, since the process variable S_CTRL is step-consistent, and
  $init(S\_CTRL) = \{Go\_Moat, Go\_Square\} = next(Go\_Square)$.

- $Go\_Square \rightarrow Stop\_Square \rightarrow S\_CTRL$: step-consistency follows from the fact that the process $Stop\_Square \rightarrow S\_CTRL$ is step-consistent, and

$$
\begin{aligned}
init(Stop\_Square \rightarrow S\_CTRL) &= \{Stop\_Square\} \\
&\subseteq \{Stop\_Square, Stop\_All\} \\
&= next(Go\_Square).
\end{aligned}
$$

- $Go\_Moat \rightarrow Stop\_Moat \rightarrow S\_CTRL \,\square\, Go\_Square \rightarrow Stop\_Square \rightarrow S\_CTRL$: this is step-consistent, due to the step-consistency of both sides of the choice.

Initial-consistency follows from the fact that

$$next(INITIALISATION) = init(Lights\_CTRL).$$

Thus, S_CTRL is consistent with the annotations of the machine *Lights*, and so the controller is appropriate for the machine.

5   Introducing FROM-ANY Annotations and Interrupts

Section 2 introduced the key components of the annotation approach that provide a framework for developing controlled systems. In general there will be a variety of annotations that we will want to make use of, and a richer language for controllers. These will have an impact on the consistency relationship, and on the underlying proofs which will need to be adapted to accommodate the changes.

In this section we will extend the controller language to include interrupts, which are commonly used to introduce interruptions in the control flow between one operation and the next. A further annotation will be introduced to accompany this extension to the controller language, and we will see the impact on the notion of consistency.

5.1   The FROM-ANY Annotation

The introduction of interrupts in the control language gives rise to another annotation, the FROM-ANY annotation.

The FROM-ANY annotation is written /* FROM-ANY */. This annotation is added to an operation which can follow *any* previous operation (including itself), and can also follow initialisation. It will naturally be used on an operation which follows an interrupt, since such an operation might follow any previous operation, allowing for the fact that the operation might happen anywhere.

Its use in an arbitrary operation Op_i is given as follows:

$$Op_i \mathrel{\widehat{=}} \textbf{PRE} \ \ P_i \ \ \textbf{THEN} \ \ B_i \ \textbf{END} \ \ /* \ \text{FROM-ANY} \ */ \ ;$$

5.2   Annotation Proof Obligation

The annotation corresponds to the claim that after the execution of any operation, Op_i will always be available to execute. The annotation gives rise to the following proof obligation: that the precondition P_i of Op_i is enabled after any precondition, and also that it is enabled after initialisation:

Definition 8 (FROM-ANY **Proof Obligations**). *The proof obligation associated with a* FROM-ANY *annotated operation* Op_i *is given as:*

$$\forall \, op \in OPERATIONS \bullet P_{op} \ \wedge I \Rightarrow [B_{op}]P_i \ \wedge$$
$$[T]P_i$$

where T is the initialisation of the machine.

A condition sufficient to establish the proof obligation of Definition 8 is the assertion $I \Rightarrow P_i$. Its use is captured as a lemma:

Lemma 1. *If $I \Rightarrow P_i$ for an operation Op_i with a* FROM-ANY *annotation, then the proof obligations on Op_i associated with this annotation are all true.*

When it holds, this is a simpler condition to establish. It may not always hold, since it is stronger than the FROM-ANY proof obligations. However, note that if those proof obligations hold then the invariant of the machine could be strengthened to include P_i, in which case the lemma will then hold.

Operations can be annotated with both a FROM-ANY annotation and a NEXT annotation. The former indicates what the operation can follow, and the latter indicates what can come next.

For a machine M, we define *from-any(M)* to be the set of operations of M that are annotated with a FROM-ANY clause.

5.3   Controller Language

We introduce an interrupt operator to the control language as follows:

Definition 9 (Controller Syntax)

$$R ::= a \rightarrow R \mid R \mathbin{\square} R \mid R \mathbin{\triangle} R \mid S$$

The global interrupt operator, $\triangle$, permits the second controller fragment to interrupt the former at any point, even before the first action of the former has been performed. However, we do not rely on an interrupt establishing initial-consistency. There should always be a *next* annotation in the INITIALISATION.

The $init(R)$ function was defined on controllers by means of a structural induction over the controller syntax. Thus the introduction of an interrupt clause into the controller syntax necessitates a revision to the definition of $init(R)$, as follows:

Definition 10 (init on CSP controller process)

$$init(a \rightarrow R1) = \{a\}$$
$$init(R1 \ \square \ R2) = init(R1) \cup init(R2)$$
$$init(R1 \ \triangle \ R2) = init(R1) \cup init(R2)$$
$$init(S) = init(R) \qquad where \ S \cong R$$

The first event that can be performed by $R1 \ \triangle \ R2$ is either a first event from $R1$, or else a first event from $R2$ following the occurrence of the interrupt.

5.4   Consistency

We again provide a definition for consistency between a controller and the annotations. This is again separated into a notion of step-consistency, which is concerned with successive events; and initial-consistency, regarding the initial state of the system.

The notion of step-consistency now needs to take account of a further clause in the controller language, and the fact that the machine M has more than one kind of annotation. Thus the definition has one additional clause. We introduce $from\text{-}any(M)$ to denote the set of operations of M with a FROM-ANY annotation.

Definition 11 (Step-consistency of NEXT and FROM-ANY Annotated Machines and Controllers). *The* step-consistency *of a controller R with the annotations of machine M is defined structurally over the syntax of R as follows:*

1. *$a \rightarrow R$ is step-consistent with M's annotations if $init(R) \subseteq (next(a) \cup from\text{-}any(M))$ and R is step-consistent with M's annotations.*
2. *$R1 \ \square \ R2$ is step-consistent with M's annotations if $R1$ is step-consistent with M's annotations and $R2$ is step-consistent with M's annotations.*
3. *$R1 \ \triangle \ R2$ is step-consistent with M's annotations if $R1$ is step-consistent with M's annotations, $R2$ is step-consistent with M, and $init(R2) \subseteq from\text{-}any(M)$.*
4. *S is step-consistent with M's annotations.*

A family of recursive definitions $S \cong R$ is step-consistent with M's annotations if each R is step-consistent with M's annotations.

In the case for $a \rightarrow R$, we require that every operation b that R can perform first, which are those operations in $init(R)$, must be able to follow a, either because b is in $next(a)$ and hence identified explicitly as an operation that can follow a, or because b is in $from\text{-}any(M)$, and hence can follow anything.

In the case for interrupt, we have that $R1$ must be step-consistent with M because all executions of $R1$ are possible executions of $R1 \triangle R2$; $R2$ must also be step-consistent since control can pass to $R2$; and every operation that $R2$ can initially perform must be able to follow anything, since the interrupt can occur at any point.

The cases for choice and for recursion are similar to the previous version of step-consistency.

Definition 12 (Initial-Consistency of NEXT and FROM-ANY Annotated Machines and Controllers). *A controller R is* initially-consistent *with the annotations of machine M if $init(R) \subseteq next(INITIALISATION) \cup from\text{-}any(M))$.*

As stated previously, a controller R is consistent with the annotations of a B machine M if it is step-consistent and initially-consistent with the annotations of M.

Once again we have everything in place to establish the main theorem of this section:

Theorem 2. *If R is consistent with the annotations of a machine M, and the annotations of M are consistent with machine M, then operations of M called in accordance with the control flow of R will never be called outside their preconditions.*

6   Example Continued

We develop the example of the Carcassonne traffic control system. We wish to extend the controller so that normal operation can be interrupted at any point with all lights being set to *Stop*. The resulting controller is given in Figure 4.

The NEXT annotations of the machine *Lights* are not sufficient to establish consistency with *Lights_CTRL2*, and in particular the interrupt requires consideration. The only event immediately following the interrupt is *Stop_All*, so we require a FROM-ANY annotation on that operation in addition to the NEXT annotation it already has. The resulting operation is as follows:

Stop_All $\widehat{=}$ **PRE** *true* **THEN** *Moat, Square := Stop, Stop* **END**
    /* { Go_Moat, Go_Square } NEXT */
    /* FROM-ANY */

This annotation introduces an additional proof obligation. Since the precondition P_{Stop_All} of *Stop_All* is *true*, it follows that $I \Rightarrow P_{Stop\_All}$, and hence by Lemma 1 that the annotation is consistent with the machine.

It remains to show that the new controller *Lights_CTRL2* is consistent with the annotated machine. Initial-consistency, and most of the step-consistency cases are similar to those seen in the consistency check for *Lights_CTRL* and

$$Lights\_CTRL2 \cong Stop\_All \rightarrow S\_CTRL2$$

$$S\_CTRL2 \cong S\_INNER \triangle Stop\_All \rightarrow S\_CTRL2$$

$$S\_INNER \cong (Go\_Moat \rightarrow Stop\_Moat \rightarrow S\_INNER)$$
$$\square \, (Go\_Square \rightarrow Stop\_Square \rightarrow S\_INNER)$$

Fig. 4. A Second Lights Controller

we do not repeat them here. However, the new conditions are required to consider the interrupt construction $S\_INNER \triangle Stop\_All \rightarrow S\_CTRL2$. Step-consistency requires us to check three conditions:

1. S_INNER is step-consistent: this follows from the definition of step-consistency on process variables.
2. $Stop\_All \rightarrow S\_CTRL2$ is step-consistent: this follows since S_CTRL2 is step-consistent and

$$
\begin{aligned}
init(S\_CTRL2) &= \{\, Go\_Moat, Go\_Square, Stop\_All \,\} \\
&= \{\, Go\_Moat, Go\_Square \,\} \cup \{\, Stop\_All \,\} \\
&= next(Stop\_All) \cup \textit{from-any}(Lights)
\end{aligned}
$$

3. $init(Stop\_All \rightarrow S\_CTRL2) \subseteq \textit{from-any}(Lights)$. This follows from the fact that $init(Stop\_All \rightarrow S\_CTRL2) = \{Stop\_All\}$ and that $Stop\_All$ has a FROM-ANY annotation.

Thus we conclude that $Lights\_CTRL2$ is an appropriate controller for the machine $Lights$.

7   Discussion

We are currently investigating further extensions to the framework. Operations with input and output arise naturally in B machines, and can have the annotations described previously. However, the situation is more complex, since controllers can also pass information from one operation call to another. This can lead to complications in the definitions of step-consistency, and it is necessary to carry around information obtained from previous operation calls when reasoning about step-consistency. This also gives rise to parameterised recursive definitions. Query operations are of particular interest, since it appears that different considerations apply: they do not change the state of the machine, but require output which can affect control flow.

The current approach requires separate construction of annotations and of controllers. One longer term aim of this line of research is the ability to synthesise controllers from the machine annotations. Such a controller would be the weakest controller consistent with a machine, and other consistent controllers would then be refinements. This is a topic of future research.

We now consider related work. The notion of incorporating temporal properties in B is not new. Abrial and Mussat [2] introduced the temporal operators of *next*, *eventually* and *leadsto*. In the case of *leadsto* (written $\rightsquigarrow$) they focus on identifying predicates P and Q such that if P holds at any point then Q eventually must hold, together with a list of events that make progress towards satisfying the final predicate Q. Their approach does not explicitly define the order in which these events must occur nor whether they occur more than once, the clause simply identifies which events can be performed in order to satisfy the $P \rightsquigarrow Q$ predicate. They use these predicates to express properties of the system which must hold when the temporal ordering of events is considered. We are using annotations to give us a handle on what operations are allowed to be performed when considering the temporal ordering of operations. We do not use them as a basis for expressing properties of a system and therefore use distinct clauses to define a possible ordering on operations in a novel way. Our approach does resonate with [2] in that we do not change the proof obligations that already exist but also identify additional proof obligations in order to ensure that the temporal orderings suggested by the annotations are sensible ones.

More recent work on Event-B and B$^\#$ [6] introduces proof obligations both for feasibility (that events and initialisation do not block), and for deadlock-freedom of a system (that the disjunction of the event guards in the system is true). The control is left implicit, but the properties are sufficient to ensure that at any stage the execution can continue.

The approach presented in this paper makes the control flow explicit, and thus deadlock-freedom would follow directly from the deadlock-freedom of a consistent controller, provided the operations are non-blocking. Feasibility and deadlock-freedom obligations cannot be expressed directly in terms of the operation annotations presented here, but this is to be expected: The information in an annotation is more directive, whereas deadlock-freedom is a general property which does not contain specific control information within it.

We could represent our running example in Event-B as follows:

stopall = **when** true **then** c := 1 **end**
gosquare = **when** c=1 **then** c:= 2 **end**
stopquare = **when** c=2 **then** c:= 1 **end**
gomoat = **when** c=1 **then** c := 3 **end**
stopmoat = **when** c=3 **then** c:= 1 **end**

The predicates in the guards determine whether an event is enabled or not and governs when an event can be performed. In this approach the control flow is implicit and not always straightforward to understand or extract. As we saw in our example it is possible to allow either **gosquare** or **gomoat** to be performed when both variables are in the state *Stop* because the next annotation of the stop all operation refers to both these operations. In our approach this was translated to an external choice in CSP. In Event-B if more than one guard is true then the decision as to which event is performed is internal. Because we are only dealing with temporal ordering at the level of traces this distinction is not significant. However, contrary to normal B consistency one important difference is that we do not need to examine the preconditions of all the operations to identify the next set of possible operations. By using annotations we can clearly see which operations should be available to be performed following an operation because we can look at each operation in isolation. Note that there may be other operations that are enabled but not mentioned in an annotation—this could possibly be because the designer providing the annotations does not want them to happen at that point.

The approach in [9] combines CSP and B so that CSP captures, primarily, the event aspect of the design, whereas the B captures the state evolution. Each CSP controller directs a single B machine via communication channels. Controllers may also interact with other controllers. In [9], consistency between the pre-conditioned B machine and the CSP controllers is established in two ways. Firstly, by showing that operations are always called within their preconditions, which establishes divergence freedom. Guarded controllers present the possibility of controller deadlock. A second, consistency condition establishes that controllers are deadlock free. Consistency is investigated using the weakest preconditions of guarded commands [3], by translating the controller into AMN and demonstrating that it preserves a control loop invariant (CLI). In contrast, in this paper we establish divergence freedom by showing that the controller is consistent with the machine annotations. If every operation has a next annotation then the machine is also deadlock-free.

Acknowledgements. We are grateful to Neil Evans for his comments and suggestions on this paper, and to the anonymous reviewers for their thorough reviewing and insightful comments.

References

1. J-R. Abrial. *The B-Book: Assigning Programs to Meaning.* Cambridge University Press, 1996.
2. J-R. Abrial and L. Mussat. Introducing dynamic constraints in B. In *B'98*, number 1393 in LNCS. Springer, 1998.
3. E. W. Dijkstra. *A Discipline of Programming.* Prentice Hall PTR, 1997.
4. C.A.R. Hoare. *Communicating Sequential Processes.* Prentice-Hall, 1985.
5. A. McEwan and S. Schneider. A verified hardware development using CSP‖B. In *Fourth ACM-IEEE International Conference on Formal Methods and Models for Codesign*, 2006.
6. C. Métayer, J-R. Abrial, and L. Voisin. Event-B language, 2005. RODIN deliverable 3.2, Project IST-5111599.
7. S. Schneider. *Concurrent and Real-time Systems: The CSP Approach.* John Wiley and Sons, 1999.
8. S.A. Schneider and H.E. Treharne. CSP theorems for communicating B machines. *Formal Aspects of Computing*, 17(4):390–422, 2005.
9. H. Treharne. *Combining Control Executives and Software Specifications.* PhD thesis, Royal Holloway, University of London, 2000.

Justifications for the Event-B Modelling Notation*

Stefan Hallerstede

ETH Zurich
Switzerland
halstefa@inf.ethz.ch

Abstract. Event-B is a notation and method for discrete systems modelling by refinement. The notation has been carefully designed to be simple and easily teachable. The simplicity of the notation takes also into account the support by a modelling tool. This is important because Event-B is intended to be used to create complex models. Without appropriate tool support this would not be possible. This article presents justifications and explanations for the choices that have been made when designing the Event-B notation.

1 Introduction

In this article we present an overview of the Event-B notation and provide justifications for the choices made when developing the notation. The Event-B notation is targeted at an incremental modelling style where models are found by trial and error. As such it is best explained by referring to concrete modelling problems resulting from this approach. For this reason we present the justifications as a list of problem statements. The guiding principles when designing the notation were its intended simplicity and the aim to make learning it easy. Usually notations get more complicated and less consistent as they evolve. As Event-B has evolved from classical B [1] and Action Systems [10] we were aware of this danger and took a considerable amount of time to discuss the notation.

Event-B [6] is a modelling notation and method for formal development of discrete systems based on refinement; see e.g. [1,10]. An Event-B model is associated with proof obligations that permit us to reason about it. This is essential for a modelling method: we must be able to reason about models written in it. In order to explain specific traits of modelling, we compare requirements for a programming notation to those for a modelling notation. There are some similarities between programming and modelling, and between the proof obligations to establish properties of programs and models. However, there are differences that have an impact on the notations used. The most notable difference is that for modelling we use refinement, introducing more detail in a step-wise fashion;

---

* This research was carried out as part of the EU research project IST 511599 RODIN (Rigorous Open Development Environment for Complex Systems) http://rodin.cs.ncl.ac.uk.

J. Julliand and O. Kouchnarenko (Eds.): B 2007, LNCS 4355, pp. 49–63, 2006.

whereas for programming we use verification [11] where all detail is introduced in a single step, i.e. when writing the program.

Event-B has been designed with tool support in mind and we have drawn on our experience with the tool Click'n'Prove [4] during the discussions. The user of an Event-B tool should be presented with proof obligations that (1) are not trivial and (2) can be easily related to the model.

The first point should allow the user to focus on the interesting part of a problem. Usually, the proportion of more challenging proof obligations makes only a small percentage of all proof obligations. We are aware that automated theorem provers can discharge most of the trivial proof obligations that appear when modelling systems. However, even as theorem provers improve further and get more powerful, modelling will remain difficult. The reason for this is that modelling is an exploratory activity that requires ingenuity in order to arrive at a meaningful model.

The second point is important because we consider proving properties about a model one of the major facilities to gain understanding of the model. When a proof obligation cannot be proved, it should be almost obvious what needs to be changed in the model. When modelling, we usually do not simply represent some system in a formal notation; but we learn about the system and eliminate misunderstandings, inconsistencies, and specification gaps. In particular, in order to eliminate misunderstandings, we first must develop an understanding of the system.

This article is organised as follows. Section 2 gives a brief overview of the Event-B notation. In Section 3 we discuss important points about the notation by stating a list of problems and the solutions we have chosen.

2   The Event-B Modelling Notation

Event-B [6], unlike classical B [1], does not have a fixed syntax. Instead it is a collection of modelling elements that are stored in a repository. This decision has been taken so that Event-B can be more easily extended with new constructs, say, to incorporate probability [17] or CSP [13,19]. Still, we present the basic notation for Event-B using some syntax. We proceed like this to improve legibility and help the reader remembering the different constructs of Event-B. The syntax should be understood as a convention for presenting Event-B models in textual form rather than defining a language. More reasons for this approach are discussed in Section 3.

Event-B models are described in terms of the two basic constructs *contexts* and *machines*. Contexts contain the static part of a model whereas machines contain the dynamic part. This is presented in Section 2.1. Contexts can be *extended* by other contexts and *referenced* by machines. Machines can be *refined* by machines. This is presented in Section 2.2.

The semantics of an Event-B model is characterised by *proof obligations*. In fact, proof obligations have a two-fold purpose. On the one hand, they show that a model is sound with respect to some behavioural semantics. On the other hand, they serve to verify properties of the model. This goes so far that we only focus on the proof obligations and do not present a behavioural semantics at all. This approach permits us to use the same proof obligations for very different modelling domains, e.g., reactive, distributed and concurrent systems [5], sequential programs [2], electronic circuits [15], or mixed designs [8], not being constrained to semantics tailored to a particular domain. Event-B is a calculus for modelling that is independent of the various models of computation. We believe that this uniformity is a key to teaching the various aspects of systems modelling.

As a prerequisite to Section 3 which provides the justifications, Sections 2.1 and 2.2 give a brief overview of Event-B.

2.1 Contexts and Machines

Contexts provide axiomatic properties of Event-B models. They play also an important rôle in model parameterisation (see Section 3.10) and model instantiation [6] which is not discussed in detail in this article. Contexts may contain *carrier sets*, *constants*, *axioms*, and *theorems*. Carrier sets are similar to types but both, carrier sets and constants, can be instantiated as is customary in algebraic specification, e.g., [9]. Axioms describe properties of carrier sets and constants. Theorems are derived properties that can be proved from the axioms. Proof obligations associated with contexts are straightforward: the stated theorems must be proved. In this article we focus on (the more interesting) proof obligations associated with machines.

Machines provide behavioural properties of Event-B models. Machines M may contain *variables*, *invariants*, *theorems*, *events*, and *variants*. Variables v define the state of a machine. They are constrained by invariants $I(v)$. Possible state changes are described by means of events. Each event is composed of a *guard* $G(t, v)$ and an *action* $S(t, v)$, where t are *local variables* the event may contain. The guard states the necessary condition under which an event may occur, and the action describes how the state variables evolve when the event occurs. An event can be represented by the term

$$\text{any } t \text{ where } G(t, v) \text{ then } S(t, v) \text{ end} \quad . \tag{1}$$

The short form

$$\text{when } G(v) \text{ then } S(v) \text{ end} \tag{2}$$

is used if event e does not have local variables, and the form

$$\text{begin } S(v) \text{ end} \tag{3}$$

if in addition the guard equals true. A dedicated event of the form (3) is used for *initialisation*. The action of an event is composed of several *assignments* of the form

$$x := E(t, v) \tag{4}$$

$$x :\in E(t, v) \tag{5}$$

$$x :| Q(t, v, x'), \tag{6}$$

where x are some variables, $E(t, v)$ expressions, and $Q(t, v, x')$ a predicate. Assignment form (4) is *deterministic*, the other two forms are *nondeterministic*. Form (5) assigns x to an element of a set, and form (6) assigns to x a value satisfying a predicate. The effect of each assignments can also be described by a before-after predicate:

$$BA(x := E(t,v)) \quad \hat{=} \quad x' = E(t,v) \tag{7}$$

$$BA(x :\in E(t,v)) \quad \hat{=} \quad x' \in E(t,v) \tag{8}$$

$$BA(x :\mid Q(t,v,x')) \quad \hat{=} \quad Q(t,v,x') \quad . \tag{9}$$

A before-after predicate describes the state just before an assignment has occurred (represented by unprimed variable names x) and the state just after the assignment has occurred (represented by primed variable names x'). All assignments of an action $S(t, v)$ occur simultaneously which is expressed by conjoining their before-after predicates, yielding a predicate $A(t, v, x')$. Variables y that do not appear on the left-hand side of an assignment of an action are not changed by the action. Formally, this is achieved by conjoining $A(t, v, x')$ with $y' = y$, yielding the before-after predicate of the action:

$$BA(S(t,v)) \quad \hat{=} \quad A(t,v,x') \wedge y' = y \quad . \tag{10}$$

In proof obligations we represent the before-after predicate $BA(S(t, v))$ of an action $S(t, v)$ by directly by the predicate

$$S(t,v,v') \quad .$$

Proof obligations serve to verify certain properties of a machine. All proof obligations in this article are presented in the form of sequents: "antecedent" $\vdash$ "succedent".

For each event of a machine, *feasibility* must be proved:

$$\vdash \quad \frac{I(v) \wedge G(t,v)}{(\exists v' \cdot S(t,v,v'))} \quad . \tag{11}$$

By proving feasibility we achieve that $S(t, v, v')$ provides an after state whenever $G(t, v)$ holds. This means that the guard indeed represents the enabling condition of the event.

Invariants are supposed to hold whenever variable values change. Obviously, this does not hold a priori for any combination of events and invariants and, thus, needs to be proved. The corresponding proof obligation is called *invariant preservation*:

$$\vdash \quad \frac{I(v) \wedge G(t,v) \wedge S(t,v,v')}{I(v')} \quad . \tag{12}$$

Similar proof obligations are associated with the initialisation event of a machine. The only difference is that the invariant does not appear in the antecedent of the proof obligations (11) and (12). For brevity we do not treat initialisation differently from ordinary events of a machine. The required modifications of the concerned proof obligations are obvious. We also do not discuss deadlock freeness, see [6].

2.2 Context and Machine Relationships

Context extensions is a mechanism to introduce more detail into the axiomatic properties of a model by adding carrier sets, constants, and axioms, or simply to add derived properties in the form of theorems. There are no specific proof obligations dealing with context extension. In order to structure axiomatic properties, contexts may extend several other contexts, see [6].

Context references provide the means to access axiomatic properties from machines. A machine may reference several contexts. In that case we say the machine *sees* these contexts. Seeing more than one context is particularly useful in conjunction with decomposition [6].

Machine refinement provides a means to introduce more detail about the dynamic properties of a model [6]. For more on the well-known theory of refinement we refer to the Action System formalism that has inspired the development of Event-B [10]. We present some important proof obligations for machine refinement. As mentioned before, the user of Event-B is not presented with a behavioural model but only with proof obligations. The proof obligations describe the semantics of Event-B models.

A machine CM can refine at most one other machine AM. We call AM the *abstract* machine and CM a *concrete* machine. The state of the abstract machine is related to the state of the concrete machine by a *glueing invariant* $J(v, w)$, where v are the variables of the abstract machine and w the variables of the concrete machine.

Each event ea of the abstract machine is *refined* by one or more concrete events ec. Let abstract event ea and concrete event ec be:

$$ea \quad \widehat{=} \quad \text{any } t \text{ where } G(t, v) \text{ then } S(t, v) \text{ end} \tag{13}$$

$$ec \quad \widehat{=} \quad \text{any } u \text{ where } H(u, w) \text{ then } T(u, w) \text{ end} \quad . \tag{14}$$

Somewhat simplified, we can say that ec refines ea if the guard of ec is stronger than the guard of ea, and the glueing invariant $J(v, w)$ establishes a simulation[1] of ec by ea:

$$\vdash \begin{array}{l} I(v) \land J(v, w) \land H(u, w) \land \boldsymbol{T}(u, w, w') \\ (\exists t \cdot G(t, v) \land (\exists v' \cdot \boldsymbol{S}(t, v, v') \land J(v', w'))) \end{array} \quad . \tag{15}$$

In the course of refinement usually *new events* ec are introduced into a model. New events must be proved to refine the implicit abstract event *skip* that does nothing. Moreover, it may be proved that new events do not collectively diverge by proving that a *variant* $V(w)$ is decreased by each new event:

$$\vdash \begin{array}{l} I(v) \land J(v, w)) \land H(u, w)) \land \boldsymbol{T}(u, w, w') \\ V(w) \in \mathbb{N} \land V(w') < V(w) \end{array} \quad , \tag{16}$$

where we assume that the variant expression is a natural number. It can be more elaborate [6] but this is not relevant here.

---

[1] More specifically, it establishes a *forward* simulation [22].

3   Modelling Problems and Solutions

In this section we present justifications for the Event-B notation, most in the form of pairs of problem statement and our solution. It resumes many discussions about the notation and method. Two major objectives during these discussions were to make the notation as simple as possible and to make learning it easy by avoiding exceptions and inconsistencies. This section is the heart of the article. The problems are not sorted according to importance. They are all important in the sense that they contribute to the overall simplicity of the Event-B notation and method.

3.1   Terminology

When writing about Event-B we found that by careless choice of terminology certain concepts are difficult to convey. For instance, instead of the word "machine", we could use "model" or "system". As a consequence, in an introductory text about B we would have phrases like: "*A model consists of models and contexts.*", or "*A system is a model of a system.*". Such phrases are a hurdle that is difficult to overcome by beginners learning Event-B. We analysed texts on Event-B, and have chosen a terminology that, we believe, is neutral with respect to modelling domains, and does not conflict with habitual modelling terminology. This is the reason why, in the end, we have chosen the word "machine" over its alternatives.

3.2   Labels

Problem. Usually the invariant of a machine $I(v)$ is a conjunction of predicates

$$I_0(v) \ \wedge \ I_1(v) \ \wedge \ \ldots \ \wedge \ I_k(n) \ \wedge \ \ldots \ \wedge \ I_n(v) \quad . \tag{17}$$

When treating proof obligation (12) that serves to verify invariant preservation,

$$\vdash \begin{array}{l} I(v) \ \wedge \ G(t,v) \ \wedge \ \boldsymbol{S}(t,v,v') \\ I(v') \quad , \end{array} \tag{12}$$

we use basic sequent calculus to split the conjunction in the succedent. The aim of this is to achieve more manageable proof obligations. Instead of (12) we generate n proof obligations

$$\vdash \begin{array}{l} I(v) \ \wedge \ G(t,v) \ \wedge \ \boldsymbol{S}(t,v,v') \\ I_k(v') \quad . \end{array} \tag{18}$$

The advantage of this is that proof obligations are much smaller. The problem introduced by this technique is the following. When a model is changed it can be costly and sometimes even not possible to relate proofs belonging to previously generated proof obligations. In our concrete case of (18), if we modify the model, e.g., by inserting a predicate $I_j(v)$ into the list (17) and changing $S(t,v)$, then all indices after the insertion point change and, at the same time, many of the predicates $I_k(v')$ of (17) change. This makes it very difficult to relate existing proofs to their associated proof obligation, stopping us from reusing them efficiently. This problem exists generally if a model contains many theorems, invariants, or events.

Solution. Individual axioms, theorems, invariants, events, guards, and actions are labelled. For instance, the invariant of a model is a list of labelled predicates:

inv_0: $I_0(v)$
inv_1: $I_1(v)$
$\vdots$
inv_k: $I_k(v)$
$\vdots$
inv_n: $I_n(v)$.

Let e be an event with label **evt**, then instead of proof obligation (12) we generate several proof obligations (18) with names

"**evt/inv_k/***inv*"   ,

where the last segment of the name "/*inv*" depends on the proof obligation. It gives an indication about what is being proved. Now it is very easy to locate old proofs for this proof obligation by name, independently of the complexity of changes made to a model. The same approach is followed for all proof obligations associated with Event-B models. The predicates $I_k(v)$ are treated like atomic predicates during proof obligation generation so that there is an immediate correspondence between models and their proof obligations.

An additional benefit of the labels is that they can be used in the documentation of a model. They can also be useful to make the informal requirements better traceable into the model, because all Event-B modelling elements can be easily referenced by their label.

3.3   Feasibility

Problem. The intention of specifying a guard of an event is that the event may always occur when the guard is true. There is, however, some interaction between guards and nondeterministic assignments (5) and (6), namely $x :\in E(t,v)$ and $x :| Q(t,v,x')$.

We say an assignment is *feasible* if there is an after-state satisfying the corresponding before-after predicate. The first form (5) is not feasible for some t and v if $E(t,v)$ denotes the empty set, and the second form (6) is not feasible if $Q(t,v,x')$ is false. This means that the guard of an event could effectively be stronger than specified if the guard was true in some state but the assignment not feasible. Such implicit specification quickly leads to models that are difficult to comprehend.

Solution. For each event its feasibility (11) must be proved. Note, that for deterministic assignments the proof of feasibility is trivial (one-point rule). Also note, that feasibility of the initialisation of a machine yields the existence of an initial state of the machine. It is not necessary to require an extra initialisation theorem as used, e.g., in Z [20].

3.4 Nondeterministic Assignments

Problem. When generating proof obligations such as (12) or (15) we use for each variable two names, an unprimed name to refer to the before-state and a primed name for the after-state of the action. In classical B nondeterministic assignments were denoted by

$$x :\mid Q(t, y, x_0, x) \quad , \tag{19}$$

where x_0 denotes the value of x in the before-state and y refers to the before-state for all other variables. This notation requires renaming x_0 into x and x into x' in the proof obligations. We want to avoid renaming of variables as much as possible in order to improve readability of the proof obligations. Furthermore, note the notational inconsistency of subscripting some before-state names (x_0, for variables that may be changed by the assignment) but not others (y, for variables that are not changed by the assignment). This notation is traditionally used with predicate transformers, e.g., [16].

Solution. The problem is solved easily by writing on the right-hand side of (19) a before-after predicate. Then the problem of renaming disappears, as well as the notational inconsistency. This explains the notation (6) used in Event-B. With this notation the predicate $Q(t, v, x')$ is copied without change into proof obligations, see (9). This notation follows the style of operation specifications in Z [20].

3.5 Witnesses

Problem. In Section 3.2 we say that separate proof obligations are generated corresponding to the labelled elements (provided by the user), e.g., events or invariants. However, this is not directly possible for proof obligation (15):

$$\vdash \begin{array}{l} I(v) \ \wedge\ J(v, w) \ \wedge\ H(u, w) \ \wedge\ \boldsymbol{T}(u, w, w') \\ (\exists t \cdot G(t, v) \ \wedge\ (\exists v' \cdot \boldsymbol{S}(t, v, v') \ \wedge\ J(v', w'))) \end{array} \quad . \tag{15}$$

The two existential quantifiers in the succedent stop us from decomposing it into more manageable pieces.

Solution. As mentioned in Section 2.2 proof obligation (15) describes a *simulation* of the concrete event by the abstract event. This is an intuitive concept, i.e. we have an idea of how the simulation "works". In other words, the required instantiations of the existentially quantified variables are well-understood. These can be specified as *witnesses* in an Event-B model rather than being elaborated during proof. Let $t = E(u, v, w, w')$ be the witnesses for the local variables t, and $v' = F(u, v, w, w')$ be the witnesses for the global variables v' corresponding to the after-state.

By a witness we usually understand an expression to replace one of the existentially quantified variables. But the technique can easily be generalised to predicative witnesses, i.e., by providing a predicate $P(x, u, v, w, w')$ for a variable x, where x stands for t or v'. In this generalisation the witness is not defined by an equation as previously. It just has to satisfy the less restrictive predicate $P(x, u, v, w, w')$. Of course, a predicative witness must not be void and, as a consequence, gives rise to a new proof obligation

$$\vdash \begin{array}{l} I(v) \,\wedge\, J(v,w) \,\wedge\, H(u,w) \,\wedge\, \boldsymbol{T}(u,w,w') \\ (\exists x \cdot P(x,u,v,w,w')) \end{array} \;,$$

resembling feasibility described in Section 3.3 above.

Whatever the means by which witnesses have been specified, simple or predicative: once the two existential quantifiers have been eliminated by instantiation, we can split the proof obligation into three larger blocks for the guard $G(\ldots)$, the abstract before-after predicate $\boldsymbol{S}(\ldots)$, and the glueing invariant $J(\ldots)$. From there we can continue as described in Section 3.2, further decomposing the proof obligation. For instance, we obtain several (named) proof obligations for invariant preservation by splitting $J(\ldots)$:

$$\vdash \begin{array}{l} I(v) \,\wedge\, J(v,w) \,\wedge\, H(u,w) \,\wedge\, \boldsymbol{T}(u,w,w') \\ J_k(F(u,v,w,w'),w') \end{array} \;. \tag{20}$$

By using witnesses in models, a part of the proof has been moved into modelling itself. The price to pay is that one has to think about proving while modelling. We do not see this as a problem because we think that modelling and proving should not be considered different activities. Note, that providing witnesses is a constructive proof technique. In modelling we prefer this over non-constructive techniques where the exact nature of the refinement relationship of the two events is left undetermined. The aim of modelling is always to increase our understanding of a model.

Using simple techniques and conventions, most of the witnesses used in (20) can be determined automatically. This frees us in practice from having to search for many witnesses.

For the *global variables* x, of an abstract machine, that are linked to the global variables y of a concrete machine by an equality invariant $x = y$, the instantiation is trivial using the one-point rule. In practice, equality invariants are assumed to hold whenever variable names are reused during refinement. Then such a variable z of the abstract machine is renamed into, say, $z1$ and variable z of the concrete machine is linked to $z1$ by the invariant $z = z1$.

For *local variables* of events we do not have invariants that we could use to find witnesses. However, most instantiations appear in practice for local variables. So we need an efficient and simple way to find witnesses for local variables. To this end, we introduce the following *convention*: when a local variable name ℓ is used in a concrete and a corresponding abstract event, then the abstract ℓ is instantiated with the concrete ℓ. Conceptually, we treat instantiation of local variables similarly to that of global variables.

3.6   Programming Versus Modelling

In this short section we discuss some general points about modelling that predetermine some of the choices we have made in Event-B (those presented in Sections 3.7 to 3.10). Our discussion contrasts *modelling* and *programming* because in computing science modelling is often understood to be a form of programming. We propose to see them as activities of different nature with different aims.

The most important characteristic of a program is that it can be executed to perform some computation. When we conceive a model, we do not think about execution. We do not even require that it could be executed. How would we execute "pressing a button" when this is supposed to be done by a person in a model we have developed. It is impossible to do this and it was never our intention. In Event-B a model usually contains elements with such characteristics because we usually *include the environment* of a computing artefact, if we are developing one. In fact, nothing in Event-B requires that a model has anything to do with computation at all.

Modelling is much more concerned with observation of a model as transitions between its states occur and with reasoning about properties of the model. Models often are already useful when they are still very abstract by helping us to understand the system being modelled. The major concern in programming is execution. Properties of programs are usually directly linked to the implementation. They do not capture the system as a whole. Accordingly, programming offers a lot of support for expressing how something is computed.

Modelling is difficult without refinement. The amount of detail in a complete model of a complex system is too high to be written in a single model. In fact, we can write such models but, in practice, we cannot reason about them anymore. Refinement solves this problem by allowing us to introduce gradually more and more detail, reasoning at each refinement step about the so-enriched model. Programming usually begins with a large amount of detail necessary for the implementation of a program. Hence, it is too late to reason about it if the program is of high complexity.

Programming is associated with programming notations that have many construct convenient for programming. They are based on the assumption that the program is to be executed and that the development begins with the implementation of the program. None of this holds for modelling. We certainly do not want to begin by implementing something and we do not want our models to be restricted to those that can be executed. Concluding, we are not interested in supporting programming notation. In addition to this general discussion Sections 3.7 to 3.10 present some more technical points about constructs otherwise customary in programming.

3.7   Sequential Composition

In addition to the general problem discussed in Section 3.6 there are some technical problems we encounter with sequential composition. While modelling we usually learn about the system we are modelling. For this reason we frequently have to switch back and forth between a model and its associated proof obligations. This switching should be as effortless as possible in order to focus on learning and on improving the model instead of analysing proof obligations with respect to their significance for the model. We cannot achieve this when we use sequential composition.

Problem. Sequential composition can make proof obligations difficult to understand. We give two little examples to motivate the problem.

Assume we have an invariant $I(x, y)$ and we want to verify that the program

$$x := E(x, y) \; ; \; y := F(x, y) \tag{21}$$

preserves the invariant. Using a standard definition of sequential composition (e.g., [1,16]), we derive the following proof obligation

$$\vdash \begin{array}{l} I(x, y) \\ I(E(x, y), F(E(x, y), y)) \end{array} \quad .$$

The succedent is the invariant $I(x, y)$ rewritten according to (21). To understand the proof obligation we have to trace backwards through (21). This quickly increases the difficulty of proof obligations. In the case of (21) this is simple. Using many assignments in sequence, the problem gets more and more difficult. The following example demonstrates this on a more concrete example. In addition, it makes use of a non-deterministic assignment which aggravates the problem.

Let $x \in \mathbb{Z}$ and $y \in \mathbb{Z}$ be two integer variables; let program P be defined by:

$$
\begin{array}{ll}
P \; \widehat{=} & \textsf{begin} \\
& \quad x := y - 1 \; ; \\
& \quad y :\in \{x + 1, x - 1\} \; ; \\
& \quad x := y * x \; ; \\
& \quad y := y * y - x \\
& \textsf{end}
\end{array}
$$

Suppose we have specified invariant (22) that relates x and y:

$$x + y = x * y \tag{22}$$

The proof obligation to verify that (22) is an invariant of P would be a sequent as shown below[2]:

$$\vdash \begin{array}{l} x \in \mathbb{Z} \quad \wedge \quad y \in \mathbb{Z} \quad \wedge \quad y_1 \in \{y, y - 2\} \quad \wedge \quad x + y = x * y \\ y_1 * (y-1) + (y_1 * y_1 - y_1 * (y-1)) = y_1 * (y-1) * (y_1 * y_1 - y_1 * (y-1)) \end{array}$$

Note, that we had to rename y as a consequence of the appearance of the non-deterministic assignment. Now we have to judge whether this sequent is true or false. We can use a theorem prover to help us. If we think it does not hold we have to change the program. But even in this simple case it is not obvious what change in the program would cause the desired change of the proof obligation.

One could suggest that an automated theorem prover should discharge this proof obligation, should it be true. Unfortunately, there is no decision procedure for general arithmetic expressions. So this will not work.

When modelling we usually encounter sequents that are not provable because we rarely get a model correct the first time. As a consequence, we expect that we

---

[2] The proof of the claim is much easier once the following three consequences of (22) are used: $x \in \{0, 2\}$, $y \in \{0, 2\}$, and $x = y$.

get sufficient support for improving the model. The best way to achieve this is an immediate correspondence between the model we write and the proof obligations that result from it.

Solution. Event-B does not contain sequential composition. This does not mean, however, that we cannot model sequential programs in Event-B [2].

3.8   Conditional Statements

We present a problem of technical nature caused by conditional statements besides the problems discussed in Section 3.6.

Problem. The greatest problem with conditional statements in refinement is that we cannot avoid generating superfluous proof obligations. Worse, these proof obligations are often difficult to understand. Let $x \in \mathbb{Z}$ be an integer variable, $a \in \text{BOOL}$ and $b \in \text{BOOL}$ boolean variables, and $m \in \mathbb{Z} \to \mathbb{Z}$ a total function. Furthermore, let program P be defined by:

$$
\begin{aligned}
P \quad \widehat{=} \quad &\text{if } a = \text{FALSE} \wedge b = \text{FALSE then} \\
&\quad x := m(x + 1) \\
&\text{else} \\
&\quad x := m(x - 1) \\
&\text{end}
\end{aligned}
$$

We carry out a simple data-refinement of P by program Q defined below:

$$
\begin{aligned}
Q \quad \widehat{=} \quad &\text{if } (1 - A) * (1 - B) = 0 \text{ then} \\
&\quad x := m(x - 1) \\
&\text{else} \\
&\quad x := m(x + 1) \\
&\text{end}
\end{aligned}
$$

where $A \in \{0, 1\}$ and $B \in \{0, 1\}$ are two integer variables refining a and b, respectively, using the glueing invariant[3]

$$
a = \text{bool}(A = 1) \wedge b = \text{bool}(B = 1) \quad .
$$

Even in this simple example it can not immediately be seen that the refinement proof obligation below has a contradictory hypothesis. The situation is much worse when more realistic programs are considered.

$$
\begin{aligned}
& a = \text{bool}(A = 1) \\
& b = \text{bool}(B = 1) \\
& \neg((1 - A) * (1 - B) = 0) \\
& \neg(a = \text{FALSE} \wedge b = \text{FALSE}) \\
\vdash \quad & m(x + 1) = m(x - 1)
\end{aligned}
$$

In particular, note that we have to discharge a proof obligation that is completely insignificant with respect to the refinement relationship of P and Q. Had we used

---

[3] The notation $\text{bool}(P)$ is used to denote the boolean value corresponding to truth or falsehood of predicate P.

a case-statement with 10 branches, 90 out of 100 proof obligations would have been of this kind. We cannot solve this problem because it is in general not decidable which branches are supposed to refine which.

Solution. Event-B does not contain conditional statements. One could suggest to name the different branches of the conditional statement and specify the refinement relationship. But this would effectively remove the conditional statement. In fact, it corresponds to the approach chosen in Event-B where each branch would correspond to a separate event. The conditional statement is not essential for the development of sequential programs in Event-B [2].

3.9   Undefinedness

Problem. Any model may contain expressions that are *conditionally defined*, e.g., $1 \div x$ which is not defined for $x = 0$. A detailed discussion of this problem can be found in [7,12].

Solution. In our quest for simplicity we prefer not to deviate from classical logic which has the additional advantage of being in wide-spread use. In Event-B well-definedness of expressions is treated on the level of type-checking. Type-checking works in two passes. The first pass checks whether expressions are correctly typed independently of whether they are defined everywhere. The second pass creates well-definedness proof obligations that must be discharged by proof. This technique is similar to predicate sub-typing described in [18].

3.10   Parameterisation

Problem. Often a model depends on a number of parameters, e.g., the number of components in a distributed system or the size of some buffer. We do not want to write a new model each time we need different parameter values. In programming notations, e.g. Ada [21], parameterisation (also called "gener-icity") is used to choose specific implementation types and constants left open for customisation. This permits the development of libraries that can be reused by instantiating the parameters appropriately. For a modelling method this approach is not appropriate because the reuse is catered for execution whereas we need reuse catered for reasoning. In algebra a different form of instantiation is used. For instance, we first develop group theory and then instantiate groups with geometric transformations. Once we have proved that the transformations form a group, we can reuse everything we have proved about groups for transformations. This technique has been adopted in algebraic specification notations, e.g. CASL [9].

Solution. In Event-B parameterisation is algebraic. Event-B provides carrier sets and constants that are contained in contexts. Carrier sets and constants can be instantiated. After the axioms of the context have been proven to hold for the instantiated carrier sets and constants all theorems that have been derived from them can be reused. Machines that reference a context are parameterised by that context [6].

3.11 Openness

Problem. Devising a formal method requires a lot of foresight. We would like the method to be used for years to come, estimating where it could be useful and making reasonable restrictions on the development processes in which it would be used.

Solution. Being pessimistic about our capacity to predict the future and the ability to dictate changes, radical or not, to industries that could profit from the method, we choose not to finalise Event-B. We expect it to evolve according to the different needs and application domains. We propose an approach where the method from which we depart is open with respect to extensions and even changes. Still, when extending the method great care should be taken not to complicate the existing theory. In order to be able to serve a larger community duplication of concepts should be avoided and each single concept should have a simple and unambiguous interpretation.

4 Conclusion

It took a considerable amount of time to make many of the decisions presented in Section 3. We believe this effort will pay off in terms of the ease with which Event-B can be used and taught. We have not presented all decisions we have made, in particular, with respect to the notation used for predicates and expressions. In comparison to classical B their syntax has been simplified considerably. The improvements of the notation used for predicates and expressions has much less to do with constraints imposed by the need of tool support than with legibility. For a discussion of notational conventions for predicates and expressions see also [14].

We believe it is important to make the reasoning underlying the notation publicly available. This is particularly true in the light of Section 3.11. We hope that all extensions to Event-B will be made cautiously so that the notation keeps its simplicity and a lot of notation and associated methodology can be shared between different communities.

At ETH Zurich the RODIN modelling platform for Event-B is being developed that implements the techniques presented in this article. A description of the RODIN platform is published separately [3].

Acknowledgement. This article reports on results from discussions about Event-B that took place over several months with at least one meeting per week. The other two participants were Jean-Raymond Abrial and Laurent Voisin, both also at ETH Zurich.

References

1. J.-R. Abrial. *The B-Book: Assigning Programs to Meanings.* CUP, 1996.
2. J.-R. Abrial. Event based sequential program development: Application to constructing a pointer program. In K. Araki, S. Gnesi, and D. Mandrioli, editors, *FME*, volume 2805 of *LNCS*, pages 51–74. Springer, 2003.

3. J.-R. Abrial, M. Butler, S. Hallerstede, and L. Voisin. An open extensible tool environment for Event-B. In Z. Liu and J. He, editors, *ICFEM*, volume 4260 of *LNCS*, pages 588–605. Springer, 2006.
4. J.-R. Abrial and D. Cansell. Click'n'Prove: Interactive Proofs within Set Theory. In *TPHOL*, volume 2758 of *LNCS*, pages 1–24, 2003.
5. J.-R. Abrial, D. Cansell, and D. Méry. A mechanically proved and incremental development of IEEE 1394 tree identify protocol. *FAC*, 14(3):215–227, 2003.
6. J.-R. Abrial and S. Hallerstede. Refinement, Decomposition and Instantiation of Discrete Models: Application to Event-B. *Fundamentae Informatica*, 2006.
7. J.-R. Abrial and L. Mussat. On using conditional definitions in formal theories. In D. Bert et al., editor, *ZB*, volume 2272 of *LNCS*, pages 242–269, 2002.
8. Jean-Raymond Abrial. Event driven system construction, 1999.
9. E. Astesiano, M. Bidoit, B. Krieg-Brückner, H. Kirchner, P. D. Mosses, D. Sannella, and A. Tarlecki. CASL - the common algebraic specification language. *TCS*, 286:153–196, 2002. Special issue on Abstract Data Types.
10. R.-J. Back. Refinement Calculus II: Parallel and Reactive Programs. In J. W. deBakker, W. P. deRoever, and G. Rozenberg, editors, *Stepwise Refinement of Distributed Systems*, volume 430 of *LNCS*, pages 67–93. Springer, 1989.
11. M. Barnett, B.-Y. E. Chang, R. DeLine, B. Jacobs, and K. R. M. Leino. Boogie: A modular reusable verifier for object-oriented programs. In F. S. de Boer et al., editor, *FMCO 2005*, volume 4111 of *LNCS*, 2006.
12. P. Behm, L. Burdy, and J.-M. Meynadier. Well defined B. In D. Bert, editor, *B'98: 2nd Int. B Conference*, volume 1393 of *LNCS*, pages 29–45. Springer, 1998.
13. M. Butler. csp2B: A practical approach to combining CSP and B. *FAC*, 12(3):182–198, 2000.
14. E. W. Dijkstra. The notational conventions I adopted, and why. Technical Report EWD1300, University of Texas, 2000.
15. Stefan Hallerstede. Parallel hardware design in B. In D. Bert et al., editor, *ZB*, volume 2651 of *LNCS*, pages 101–102. Springer, 2003.
16. Carroll Morgan. *Programming from Specifications: Second Edition*. PHI, 1994.
17. C.Morgan, T.Hoang, and J.Abrial. The Challenge of Probabilistic Event B. In H. Treharne at al., editor, *ZB*, volume 3455 of *LNCS*, pages 162–171. Springer, 2005.
18. J. Rushby, S. Owre, and N. Shankar. Subtypes for specifications: Predicate sub-typing in PVS. *IEEE Trans. Soft. Eng.*, 24(9):709–720, 1998.
19. S. Schneider and H. Treharne. CSP theorems for communicating B machines. *FAC*, 17(4):390–422, 2005.
20. J. M. Spivey. *The Z Notation: A Reference Manual*. PHI, 2nd edition, 1992.
21. S. T. Taft and R. A. Duff, editors. *Ada 95 Reference Manual*. Springer, 1997.
22. J.Woodcock and J.Davies. *Using Z. Specification, Refinement, and Proof*. PH, 1996.

Automatic Translation from Combined *B* and CSP Specification to Java Programs

Letu Yang and Michael R. Poppleton

Dependable Systems and Software Engineering
University of Southampton
Southampton, SO17 1BJ, UK
{ly03r,mrp}@ecs.soton.ac.uk

Abstract. A recent contribution to the formal specification and verification of concurrent systems is the integration of the state- and event-based approaches B and CSP, specifically in the ProB model checking tool. At the implementation end of the development, concurrent programming in Java remains a demanding and error-prone activity, because of the need to verify critical properties of safety and liveness as well as functional correctness. This work contributes to the automated development of concurrent Java programs from such integrated specifications.

The JCSP package was originally designed as a proven clean Java concurrency vehicle for the implementation of certain CSP specifications. In the context of best current Java concurrent programming practice, we extend the original JCSP package to support the integrated B and CSP specification by implementing new channel classes. We propose rules for the automated translation of the integrated specification to multi-threaded Java using the extended JCSP channel classes. We briefly present a prototype translation tool which extends ProB, with a worked example, and conclude with a strategy for formally verifying the translation.

1 Introduction

Concurrency in multithreaded Java programming has always been seen as a problematic area [Pu00], to the extent that expert practitioner advice has been to avoid it where possible [MW]. The difficulty arises from the low level of the methods provided, the responsibility of the programmer for guaranteeing various awkward concurrency properties - including safety, liveness, and fairness - and the complexities of scale. The recent JDK 5.0 issue [Go04] has improved matters somewhat by raising the level of abstraction in the concurrency model, introducing constructs such as *semaphore* and *mutex*. Abstraction has also been raised, principally in package *util.concurrency* by deprecating low-level *Thread* methods such as *stop, resume* and *suspend* and replacing them with high-level thread-safe facilities. Safety properties have been made more tractable by the provision of a common cross-platform Java Memory Model [MPA05]. However, as the concurrency model of Java programs is described in natural language, it is still difficult to detect and avoid liveness and fairness problems in such programs.

J. Julliand and O. Kouchnarenko (Eds.): B 2007, LNCS 4355, pp. 64–78, 2006.
© Springer-Verlag Berlin Heidelberg 2006

The difficulty of concurrency motivated the development of formal languages for modelling concurrent processes such as CSP [SS00] and CCS [RM89]. The capability of formal and automated [MK99, FS03] verification of safety and liveness properties in such concurrency models, before transformation into code, has added real value to industrial systems, including hardware systems[JP04], software systems[JL04], and communication protocols [SD04]. Formal analysis techniques have been applied to concurrent Java programs: [LP05] and [BM02] provide languages to add assertions to Java programs, and employ runtime verification techniques to verify the assertions. Such approaches are concerned with the satisfaction of assertions, not explicit verification against a formal concurrency model. An explicit formal concurrency model, which can be verifiably transformed into a concurrent Java program, represents a useful contribution.

One recent trend in formal approaches to system design is to integrate the state- and event-based approaches. State-based specification is appropriate when data structure and its atomic transition is relatively complex; event-based specification is preferred when design complexity lies in behaviour, i.e. event and action sequencing between system elements. In general of course, significant systems will present design complexity, and consequently require rich modelling capabilities, in both aspects. [Bu99, TS99] have proposed the integration of the state-based B method [Ab96] and CSP, an event-based process algebra. The ProB [BL05] tool supports model checking of combined B and CSP specifications[1]. A composite specification in ProB uses B for data definition and operations. A CSP specification is employed as a filter on the invocations of atomic B operations, thus guiding their execution sequence.

Peter Welch's JCSP package [PM00a] provides a high-level concurrency model for Java, implementing the *Occam* language [ST95], a concurrent programming language that directly implements a subset of CSP. JCSP is based on the point-to-point communication model of *Occam*. The correctness of the JCSP translation of the *Occam* channel to a JCSP channel class has been formally proved [PM00b]: the CSP model of the JCSP channel communication is shown to refine the CSP/*Occam* concurrency model. Raju [RR03] has developed a tool to translate subset CSP models directly to JCSP. The tool does not extend beyond the *Occam* subset of CSP, and does not scale, in our experience, beyond small textbook examples. Furthermore, through our experience with JCSP and Raju's tool, we find that the point-to-point *Occam* communication model limits the capability of JCSP for developing concurrent systems based on other concurrency models.

Being event-based, CSP is insufficiently expressive of the data aspect of systems; JCSP is similarly limited. In [RR03], data declaration and assignment are manually added to the Java programs generated by the tool; this can easily break the correctness of the system model which is proved by FDR tool.

Motivated by both the Java concurrency issues and the integrated formal method approaches, we present a translation strategy, which converts combined B and CSP specifications in ProB into Java programs using an extended JCSP

---

[1] We will call this notation B+CSP for shorthand.

package. The design of the translation rules has taken some inspiration from [OC04], which defines a translation from *Circus* to JCSP.

In Section 2, we briefly introduce the existing JCSP package. We then discuss the reasons for extending the original package, and the new features of the extended JCSP package. In Section 3, we demonstrate the translation strategy from the combined B and CSP specification to Java programs, and discuss the translation tool which implements these rules in Prolog. In Section 4, we illustrate the translation with a Chef-and-Dining-Philosophers example. In Section 5, we outline the verification required of this translation process as future work. Section 6 discuss future work and conclusions.

2   The Extended JCSP Package

2.1   JCSP

JCSP [PM00a] is a Java package for developing concurrent Java Programs. It implements the *Occam* subset of the CSP language [SS00], as well as some other features of CSP, in a series of process and channel classes. The *Occam* language definition is based on that of CSP, but is aimed at modelling channel communication. *Occam* channels are based on CSP events. However, *Occam* channels are only applied for modelling point to point communication, while CSP events are used in more general concurrency models. In Figure 1, the concurrency model of JCSP and *Occam* is briefly illustrated in CSP syntax. CSP processes *ProcA* and *ProcB* synchronize with each other on channel A, while B and C are unsynchronized channels. The synchronization happens when *ProcB* is ready to output data y at $A!y$, and *ProcA* is ready to input data x at $A?x$.

$$ProcA = A?x \rightarrow B \rightarrow ProcA$$
$$ProcB = C \rightarrow A!y \rightarrow ProcB$$

Fig. 1. A CSP specification for Occam/JCSP concurrency

A Java application using the *JCSP* package consists of a number of objects of *JCSP* process classes running in parallel. The process objects communicate with each other via objects of JCSP channel classes. All the process classes used here implement an abstract JCSP process class `CSProcess`. The channel classes all inherit the `inputchannel` and `outputchannel` interfaces of the JCSP package. JCSP supports two process objects synchronizing and communicating data through a JCSP channel object. A JCSP process blocks when it requires a data communication with the other process on a specific channel. Only when both the output and input side processes of the channel are ready for the data communication, is the data is transmitted through the channel.

Since the JCSP channel classes implement only the *Occam* channels (as opposed to more general CSP events) the communication between two processes is the only synchronization supported by JCSP channel classes. Although

Any2OneChannel and *Any2AnyChannel* classes handle more than two processes, the synchronization still only involves two processes. For *Any2OneChannel*, many writer processes and one reader process are associated on the channel. All the requests from writer processes are grouped into a queue. At a given time, only the reader and one writer actually synchronize with each other and pass data through the channel. Thus the synchronization model still is the point-to-point communication of *Occam*.

JCSP does support synchronization between more than two channels with a *Barrier* class. However, *Barrier* is not implemented as a JCSP channel class, and uses a simple counter to resolve the synchronization. Therefore it can not help to do multi-way synchronization in a manner faithful to the CSP concurrency model.

2.2   Why We Extend JCSP

As the JCSP package was designed to implement the *Occam* subset of CSP in Java, it cannot be directly used for translating the combined B and CSP specification in ProB. The reasons for this are twofold.

For the CSP part, the combined specification uses a bigger CSP subset than that of JCSP package. Important CSP language features, especially some concurrency facilities such as Alphabetized Parallel, are not supported by JCSP. In developing a concurrent Java system, the synchronization between more than two threads on a certain data transition is a typical concurrency problem, which can be easily specified using CSP. This problem is also identified by JDK5.0, and in *java.util.concurrency* package, a *CyclicBarrier* class is build to implement this synchronization in a high-level facility. However, modelling this kind of concurrency in *Occam* gives the programmer extra work implementing the synchronization on the shared thread. Implementing them in JCSP also requires extra facility classes to resolve the synchronization.

Figure 2 shows the CSP specification of a parallel hardware interface. The interface reads eight bits from eight different channels, and when all the bits are ready, it generates a byte from the bits. In the specification, each bit process *B(i)* gets a bit using event *get(i)?bit*, and then waits for the *makebyte* event. The bit processes interleave with each other. The parallel interface process *PI* repeatedly makes bytes with the *makebyte* event, when all the bits are ready. The *Main* process requires all the processes to synchronize on the *makebyte* event. As the CSP model of this example has nine processes synchronizing on the same event, it can not be directly translated into Java using the original JCSP package.

The channel used in JCSP and *Occam* is obliged to communicate data between two processes, while the combined channel we propose uses a more general definition of CSP event. The CSP event can optionally have data parameters, with decorations denoting input, output or dot data, which can be either input or output. Parameters are similarly specified in the B+CSP specification. In the extended JCSP, we implement these kind of CSP events in Java with the new channel class.

$B(i) = get(i)?bit \rightarrow makebyte.byte \rightarrow B(i)$
$PI = makebyte.byte \rightarrow PI$
$Bsys = ||| \ i{:}1..8@ \ B(i)$
$Main = PI \ /\!|\{makebyte\}|/ \ Bsys$

---

* $|||$ *declares a set of interleaving processes*
* $A/\!|c|/B$ *is the syntax for Alphabetized Parallel, which means that processes A and B synchronize on a set of events c*

Fig. 2. CSP specification of Parallel Interface

Since the JCSP package is designed for implementing CSP specifications in Java, it has no facility to implement the B part of the combined specification in Java. Therefore we need a strategy for translating the B specifications into Java. Fortunately, the B specification used for the automatic translation is mainly from the B0 subset of the B language, which represents a simple programming language designed to be automatically translatable to target languages of choice. The B+CSP channel combines a B operation wih a CSP event; the operational semantics of this is given in [BL05].

2.3 The Extended JCSP Package

The JCSP package is extended with new channel and facility classes. The new "parallel/choice" channel class *PaChoChannel* implements the features of combined B and CSP specifications which are not included in the original JCSP package. The facility classes implement external choice for the extended channel class.

The extended channel and facility classes are designed as an add-on package for the original JCSP. JCSP process classes can declare and use the new channel classes in a similar manner to using the original JCSP channel classes. As all the changes have been preserved inside the channel and facility classes, there are no significant changes in using them in process classes.

Class *PaChoChannel* supports synchronization between more than two processes. It keeps track of all the processes associated with this channel. When all the associated processes are ready, the data operations in the channel are triggered. After the data operations complete, all the associated processes are notified.

PaChoChannel also supports the *dot* event $c.v$, where c is a CSP event and v is a data item on it. The synchronization of *dot* data channels is not only decided by the name of the channels, but also by the *dot* data values. Two processes, using the same channel c but with different values of v (e.g. $c.x$, $c.y$), will not synchronize with each other. This implementation is based on the B+CSP semantics. The input $c?x$ and output $c!x$ events are also supported by the new channel class.

With the implementation of the above two CSP language features, the new JCSP package can support *Alphabetized Parallel* of CSP, an important facility for specifying concurrent systems. Furthermore, some new facility classes implement *external choice* for the extended channel classes.

The main issue for implementing the B part of the combined specification is how to implement the data transitions of a B operation into a combined channel class. The *PaChoChannel* class implements the *Serializable* interface of Java, and has an abstract method *run*. The subclasses of *PaChoChannel* overwrite the *run* method by putting in the target Java code of the B data transitions. The *run* method is executed when all the associated processes are ready for the execution of the channel class.

Thus, the extended JCSP package supports a bigger subset of CSP than the original JCSP, as well as providing facilities to implement the B part of the combined specifications in Java. This makes it possible to translate the combined B and CSP specifications into Java programs. An example with the extended channel class is discussed in Chapter 4.

The synchronization supported by the extended channel class is implemented with concurrency primitives from Java monitors, which exclude the facilities deprecated by Java 5.0. The correctness of this implementation needs to be verified; a formal proof strategy is proposed later in Section 5.

3   Translation Strategy and Tool

A series of translation rules are developed to structure the automatic translation. The rules are used recursively to generate a set of Java classes from a combined B and CSP specification. We discuss some of the key translation rules in this section. The translation tool implements the translation rules in Prolog.

3.1   Translation Strategy and Rules

In the translation, each combined B+CSP channel is translated into an object of a channel class. Each process in the CSP part of the combined specification is translated into an object of a JCSP process class. Indexed processes are translated into different objects of the same JCSP process class. Their indices are treated as parameters of the JCSP class constructor.

Translation of the MAIN Process. The translation strategy is mainly based on the execution behaviour of the system which is specified in the MAIN process, which is the core process of the CSP part. The translation rules set generates the executable Java class for the target application. It starts with the MAIN process with rule *Main Proc Decl*, and recursively generates process classes for all the associated CSP processes.

Through this procedure, the translation gathers information of all the CSP channels v, B sets S, and variables and constants s. Rule *Set Def* generates Java classes to represent B set S. All the variables are declared and initialized by rule *Par Def*. The rule generates the declaration and initialization of the variables with the information from the B part. v is expanded with rule *Ch Def*, which will declare the channel objects for all the channels, and generate channel classes.

Finally, it generates the code for declaring the MAIN process object, including the code of the *run* call.

Table 1. Rule 0: Rule for Declaring Main Process

Name	*Main Proc Decl*
CSP	**MAIN**
B	**MACHINE** M
Java	$\langle MAIN \rangle^{ProcDecl}$
	public class M_machine {
	public static void main(){
	$\langle S \rangle^{SetDef}$
	$\langle s \rangle^{ParDef}$
	$\langle v \rangle^{ChDef}$
	new $\langle M \rangle^{ProcCName}(\langle s \rangle^{ParList}, \langle v \rangle^{ChList})$**.run();**
	}
	}

Support of Multi-way Synchronization. One important feature of the extended JCSP channel is the support of multi-way synchronization. The parallel structure is handled by rules from the rule set *ProcE*. For example, the combination of the indexed parallel processes is translated by rule *ProcE (Re-Parallel)*.

Table 2. Rule 9: Rule for Replicated Alphabetized Parallel

Name	*ProcE (Re-Parallel)*
CSP	$[\| \ v \ \|]$n:a@ P(n)
Java	**CSProcess[] procs = {**
	new $\langle P \rangle^{ProcCName}(\langle s \rangle^{ParList}, \langle v \rangle^{ChList}, \langle v_1 \rangle^{ChList}, a_1),$
	.....
	new $\langle P \rangle^{ProcCName}(\langle s \rangle^{ParList}, \langle v \rangle^{ChList}, \langle v_n \rangle^{ChList}, a_n)$
	}
	new Parallel(procs).run();

In rule *ProcE (Re-Parallel)* (Table 2), $\langle P \rangle^{ProcCName}$ refers to the name of the indexed process class, while each process object from $P(a_1)$ to $P(a_n)$ is an instance of that process class. These process objects synchronize on a set of channels v. Each process object may include a set of channels v_n, which do not synchronize with other indexed processes here. *PaChoChannel* class provides *ready* methods to support multi-way synchronization. When a JCSP process is ready for the execution of a channel, it calls the *ready* method of the channel, and waits for other processes which also synchronize on this channel. As there may or may not be data on the channel, different implementations of the *ready* methods are provided. Table 3 shows the different rules for translating the *ready* call.

Ready call rules for input/no input on channel are given in Table 3. The ready calls including output parameters are discussed in the following section. For rule *Par Vec*, the set *is* of input parameters are grouped into **Vector**, and performs as a single parameter for **ready** method.

Table 3. Rule 6: Rule for Channel Call, ready

Name	*Ch Call (ready I)*
CSP	*cc.is*
B	*cc(is) Instruction*
Java	$\langle cc \rangle^{ChName}$.**ready**($\langle is \rangle^{ParVec}$);
Name	*Ch Call (ready II)*
CSP	*cc*
B	*cc Instruction*
Java	$\langle cc \rangle^{ChName}$.**ready**();

Translation of Combined Channels. The main issue in translating the combined B+CSP channels is how to resolve the parameters from both B and CSP sides. In the original JCSP, as there is no data transition inside the channel, a data x on a channel Ch is simply passed through the channel. Here a process with channel $Ch!x$ synchronizes with a process with $Ch?x$ event.

Table 4. Rule 29: Rule for Extended Channel Classes

Name	ChC
B	$os \leftarrow cc(is)$ *Instruction*

Java	**public class** $\langle cc \rangle^{ChCName}$ **extends PaChoChannel {**
	 $\quad \langle is \rangle^{ParDef}$
	 $\quad \langle os \rangle^{ParDef}$
	 $\quad$ **public** $\langle cc \rangle^{ChCName}(\langle is \rangle^{ParDef})${
	 $\quad\quad \langle is \rangle^{ParRel}$
	 $\quad$ }
	 $\quad$ **public void run(){**
	 $\quad\quad \langle Instruction \rangle^{BInstruction}$
	 $\quad$ }
	 }

Therefore, in the target Java program, two process classes use the **read** and *write* methods of JCSP channel classes to communicate the data:

Process 1:
```
...
run(){
    ...; Ch.write(x); ...
}
...
```

Process 2:
```
...
run(){
    ...; x = Ch.read(); ...
}
...
```

To resolve the parameter issue for the combined B+CSP channel, we need to examine the operational semantics of B+CSP in [BL05]. The operational semantics of the combined B+CSP channel are: $(\sigma,P) \rightarrow_A (\sigma',P')$. σ and σ' are the before and after B states for executing operation o, while P and P' are the before and after processes for processing channel ch. The combined channel A is a unification of the CSP channel $ch.a_1, ..., a_j$ and the B operation $o = o_1,...,o_m \leftarrow op(i_1,...,i_n)$, where $j = m + n$. Therefore, the combined B+CSP channel A can be expressed as: $A.s_1.....s_m.s_{m+1}.....s_{m+n}$.

In the translation, both $o_1 ... o_m$ and $i_1 ... i_n$ are treated as parameter lists for the channel classes. In rule _ChC_ (Table 4), $o_1,..,o_m$ are translated into Java objects os, which are the output parameters, and $i_1,...,i_n$ are translated into is, which are the input parameters. Rule _Par Def_ obtains information from the B specification as before. In the channel class, is are static parameters whose values won't be changed. os are private parameters of the channel class and are made externally visible by being returned by the **ready** method. os are returned as a Java **Vector**, as defined in rule _Par Vec_.

The two translation rules in Table 5 show how the process gets the output parameters from the **ready** call.

Table 5. Rule 6 (continue): Rule for Channel Call, ready

Name	Ch Call (ready III)
CSP	$cc.is.os$
B	$os \leftarrow cc(is)$ Instruction
Java	$\langle os \rangle^{ParVec} = \langle cc \rangle^{ChName}.\mathbf{ready}(\langle is \rangle^{ParVec});$
Name	Ch Call (ready IV)
CSP	$cc.os$
B	$os \leftarrow cc$ Instruction
Java	$\langle os \rangle^{ParVec} = \langle cc \rangle^{ChName}.\mathbf{ready}();$

Translation of B. B0 is a concrete low-level deterministic imperative programming language. It is the target language for generating concrete programs from verified abstract B machines, and it is translatable to high-level programming languages [BB1, VT02].

The B0 language only includes concrete B substitutions and only handles concrete data. It is easy to correctly find corresponding data instructions in high-level programming languages for the concrete substitutions. There are two correctness issues in translating B0 into a high-level programming language. The first is how to translate parameter passing of B operations to the high-level programming language. The above discussion on translating the combined B+CSP channel answered this issue for our translation. The other issue concerning the correctness of the translation is how to represent some B0 data structures in a high-level language. Usually, high-level languages provide better support for the arithmetic data, such as integer and boolean. The only concern here is some complex data structures, such as sets and arrays. Java fully supports array structures which easily represent the B0 array. Currently B0 sets are translated into *enum* static classes.

3.2 Translation Tool

The automatic translation tool is constructed as part of the ProB tool. Our translation tool is also developed in *SICStus* Prolog, which is the implementation language for ProB.

In ProB, the B+CSP specification is parsed and interpreted into Prolog terms, which express the operational semantics of the combined specification. The translation tool works in the same environment as ProB, acquires information on the combined specification from the Prolog terms, and translates the information into the Java program.

4 Examples

In this section we illustrate how the translation tool works. The example we used here is a simplified version of the *Wot, no Chicken* example from [We00]. The example was originally constructed for emphasizing fairness issues in the wait/notify strategy of Java concurrent programming. We use the example to demonstrate the automatic production of a concurrent Java program from a B+CSP specification. Our version of the example is simplified in omitting the lazy philosopher who raises the fairness issues.

This example includes a chef who cooks chicken, a canteen which is used to store the chicken, and several philosophers who consume the chicken. The chef spends some time to cook a number of chickens and then put them in the canteen. The philosophers take time to think, then take chicken from the canteen and eat. The CSP specification in Figure 3 shows the behaviour of the system. The *Main* process is the core process. It consists of a *Chef* process, and several *Chicken(i)* processes and Philosopher processes *Phil(i)*. The *Phil(i)* processes do not synchronize with each other, while all the *Chicken(i)* processes synchronize on the *put* event. The *Phil(i)* processes and *Chicken(i)* processes synchronize on the *getchicken(i)* event. The *Chef* process synchronizes with other processes on the *put* event.

$Main = SYSTEM[\{put\}|]Chef$
$Phil(i) = gotocanteen.i \rightarrow getchicken.i \rightarrow backtoseat.i \rightarrow eat.i \rightarrow thinking.i \rightarrow Phil(i)$
$Chef = cook \rightarrow put \rightarrow Chef$
$Chicken(i) = put \rightarrow getchicken.i \rightarrow Chicken(i)$
$PHILS = ||| \ i{:}N@ \ Phil(i)$
$CHICKENS = [|put|] \ i{:}N@ \ CHICKEN(i).$

$SYSTEM = PHILS[\{getchicken\}|]CHICKENS$

Fig. 3. Chef-Philosophers example: CSP part

```
MACHINE chicken                              canteen := canteen - 1
......                                     END;
SETS                                        eat(pp) =
    PhilStates = {thinking, hungry, full} ;     SELECT pp:Phils THEN
......                                            chicken(pp) := 0 ||
OPERATIONS                                       state(pp) := full
    ......                                    END;
    gotocanteen(pp) =                        backtoseat(pp) =
        SELECT pp:Phils THEN                     SELECT pp:Phils THEN
        state(pp) := hungry                      state(pp) := eating
    END;                                     END;
    getchicken(pp) =                         ......
        SELECT pp:Phils THEN            END
        chicken(pp) := 1 ||
```

Fig. 4. Chef-Philosophers example: B part

The B specification in Figure 4 gives a part of the B specification of the combined specification. It shows the canteen and philosopher part of the chef-philosopher example. All the B operations use SELECT statements instead of PRE statements. PRE aborts when the condition is not satisfied, which means it is not guaranteed to terminate.

The execution of the B operations are guarded by the CSP specification. Therefore, the translation tool generates a JCSP process object for each process in the CSP specification.

In Figure 5, the *Phils* process groups all the interleaving *Phil* processes into a process array. Using the translation rule for indexed interleaving, which is similar to the rule for indexed parallel in Table 2, the target *Phils.java* class builds an array **procs** for all the *Phil* process objects, and runs all of them in parallel. All the associated channel objects are passed to the process object through its constructor as parameters. The index numbers of all the *Phil* processes are also passed to them as parameters. A target JCSP process class, which is translated

```
public class Phils implements CSProcess{          backtoseat, eat, thinking, 2),
    PaChoChannel gotocanteen;                 new Phil(gotocanteen, getchicken,
    PaChoChannel getchicken;                       backtoseat, eat, thinking, 3),
    PaChoChannel backtoseat;                  new Phil(gotocanteen, getchicken,
    PaChoChannel eat;                              backtoseat, eat, thinking, 4),
    PaChoChannel thinking;                    new Phil(gotocanteen, getchicken,
    /* Constructor of the class */                backtoseat, eat, thinking, 5)
    public void run(){                           };
        CSProcess[] procs = {                   new Parallel(procs).run();
            new Phil(gotocanteen, getchicken,  }
                backtoseat, eat, thinking, 1),  }
            new Phil(gotocanteen, getchicken,
```

Fig. 5. Target Java Class: *Phils.java*

from the *Phil(i)* process, is shown in Figure 6. All the channel objects in the *Phil.java* are created by the superior process *Phils*. So a process *Phil(i)* needs to synchronize on some shared channel objects with other processes. The *Phil*

```
public class Phil implements CSProcess{          while(true){
    PaChoChannel gotocanteen;                        gotocanteen.dotready(this,num);
    PaChoChannel getchicken;                         getchicken.dotready(this,num);
    PaChoChannel backtoseat;                          backtoseat.dotready(this,num);
    PaChoChannel eat;                                eat.dotready(this,num);
    PaChoChannel thinking;                           thinking.dotready(this,num);
    Integer num;                                 }
    /* Constructor of the class */               }
    public void run(){                       }
```

Fig. 6. Target Java Class: *Phil.java*

process objects synchronize with **Chicken** process objects on *getchicken.n* channel objects. The execution sequence of all channel objects in the **run** method implements the trace semantics of the CSP process *Phil(i)*. When the process is ready for the execution of a channel object, it calls the **ready** method, blocks itself, and waits for other processes, which also synchronize on this channel, to be ready for execution.

In the process class, channel objects are declared as instances of *PaChoChannel* classes. Actually, they have their own channel classes which extend *PaChoChannel* class. Therefore, when a undefined channel class is referred, it needs to be generated from the combined specification of the channel. The *Eat.java* class in Figure 7 is the target channel class of *eat* channel. This channel class is generated using translation rule *ChC*, which is discussed in the previous section.

```
public class eat extends PaChoChannel{            public synchronized void run(){
    Integer[] chicken;                                 Integer dotvalueint =
    PhilStates state;                                    (Integer)curdotvalue;
    public getchicken(Integer[] chicken,              chicken[dotvalueint.intValue()] = 0;
        PhilStates[] state){                          state[dotvalueint.intValue()] =
        super();                                          PhilStates.FULL;
        this.state = state;                        }
        this.chicken = chicken;                }
    }
}
```

Fig. 7. Target Java Class: *Eat.java*

In the **run** method of the **eat** class, **chicken** is a global array which records the number of chickens that each philosopher has. Changing the **chicken** record of the current philosopher to 0 implements the data transition *chicken(pp) := 0* in the B operations. *PhilStates* is a enumeration class which indicates the status of a philosopher. It can be THINKING, HUNGRY and FULL. After a philosopher eats a chicken, his status changes to FULL. The global array *state* is used to store the status of all the philosophers. Changing the status of the current philosopher to FULL implements the data transition *state(pp) := full* in B operation *eat*.

5   Correctness Proof Strategy

A correctness verification is required for the translation. In [RR03, OC04], the translations are discussed without considering the correctness of the translations. Formal verification which proves the correctness of the translation in terms of semantic models of the specification and Java programs respectively would be the best solution. We propose a more modest approach based on [WM00] for future work. The new *PaChoChannel* class is designed to represent the behaviour of the combined B+CSP channel in the target Java application. To use the new channel class more confidently, we still need to formally prove that it is a correct implementation of the combined B+CSP channel.

In [WM00], the correctness of Welch's original JCSP channel classes is proved. Each JCSP channel class (i.e. Java implementation) is formally specified by a CSP model. The desired channel behaviour (which the JCSP class implements) is also specified in CSP. The refinement checking tool FDR is used to prove the two CSP models equivalent: that is, JCSP refines CSP and CSP refines JCSP. A number of such proofs are required: there are a number of JCSP channel classes, implementing the various capabilities of CSP channels. The proof strategy starts with the simple *One2OneChannel* class without alternation, and gradually builds formal models for more complex JCSP channel classes.

To prove the correctness of the *PaChoChannel* class, a similar strategy is proposed: to prove that the implementation refines the specification. First, a B+CSP model for the *PaChoChannel* class is built. Then, the required behaviour of the combined B+CSP channel is specified with B+CSP specifications. As the ProB tool supports refinement checking between B+CSP models, we can prove the *PaChoChannel* class correctly implements (i.e. refines) the B+CSP channel.

The construction of a concrete model for the *PaChoChannel* class with full functionality will be a significant task, as will its verification. Hence we would start with an abstract model of *PaChoChannel* with simple functionality, gradually building concrete models with incremental data and concurrency capabilities.

6   Related Work and Conclusion

Our work aims at automatically generating concurrent Java programs from proven formal specifications. To achieve this, we extend the original JCSP package to implement the combined B and CSP specification in Java. A set of translation rules are developed to formalize the translation, and the automatic translation tool is built upon the translation rule set. We also propose a formal verification strategy for proving the correctness of the translation.

There is a similar tool [RR03] to translate a pure CSP specification into a Java program using the original JCSP package. As it is not very convenient to use CSP specification to model data aspect of systems, the target Java code of this tool always needs further manual revision to add data elements. However, manual revision has the danger that the concurrency model of JCSP may be broken by such revision. From our experience, the tool only works on some specific examples, and seems unstable.

In [OC04], a set of translation rules are proposed for translating a subset of the *Circus* specification language to Java using JCSP. The translation is restricted because the JCSP package lacks the ability to implement data transitions of the *Circus* language. Therefore, [OC04] proposes future work to extend JCSP to support the full *Circus* semantics. They also plan to develop an automatic translation tool using their rules.

[MK99] presents a strategy of using a process algebra language, FSP (Finite State Processes) to build a formal concurrency model of Java concurrent programming. The $LTSA$ (*Labelled Transition System Analyser*) tool is adopted to translate the FSP descriptions to a graphical representation. It also checks desirable and undesirable properties of the FSP model. However, it doesn't provide exhaustive rules or tool support to link the FSP syntax with the Java language. The development of the concurrent Java code relies on users' experience of this approach. Correctness of the target Java program cannot be proved formally.

JML [LP05] and Jassda [BM02] are runtime verification approaches for using formal methods to help develop concurrent Java programs. They both have assertion languages to specify pre- and post-conditions, and temporal properties of Java programs. The assertions can be checked at runtime to see whether they are preserved during the execution of the Java programs. The Java programs still need to be constructed manually.

An ambitious project [VH00] developed a tool *Java Path Finder* (JPF), which integrates model checking, program analysis and testing for Java programs. The JPF tool can generate a state model of the Java program via the support of its own Java Virtual Machine(JVM^{JPF}). Accordingly, formally defined properties and assertions can be verified in the state model. To avoid state explosion, the Java language features that can be used in *JPF* are restricted.

Future plans include a substantial case study using the translation tool. The stability and scalability of the translation strategy and the tool will be the focus of this exercise. The development of a GUI (Graphical User Interface) is also planned. It will provide facilities for configuring the translation, and interfacing with the target Java application.

Acknowledgements. We would like to thank Denis A. Nicole for his very helpful comments.

References

[BB1]   Didier Bert, Sylvain Boulmé, Marie-Laure Potet, Antoine Requet, Laurent Voisin.: Adaptable Translator of B Specifications to Embedded C Programs In FME 2003: Formal Methods, LNCS 2805, pp. 94-113, Pise, Sept. 2003.

[BL05]   M. J. Butler and M. Leuschel.: Combining CSP and B for Specification and Property Verification. FM 2005: 221-236

[BM02]   M. Brörken and M. Möller.: Jassda Trance Assertions: Runtime Checking the Dynamic of Java Programs. In International Conference on Testing of Communicating Systems, 2002.

[Bu99]   M. J. Butler.: csp2B: A Practical Approach to Combining CSP and B. In World Congress on Formal Methods, pages 490-508, 1999.

[FS03]   Formal Systems(Europoe) Ltd.: Failures-Divergence Refinement: FDR2 User Manual, 2003

[Go04]   B. Goetz.: Concurrency in JDK 5.0. Technical report, IBM, 2004.

[JL04]   J. Lawrence.: Practical Application of CSP and FDR to Software Design. In 25 Years Communicating Sequential Processes, 151-174, 2004.

[JP04]   J. Peleska.: Applied Formal Methods - From CSP to Executable Hybrid Specifications. In 25 Years Communicating Sequential Processes, 293-320, 2004.

[Ab96]   J.-R. Abrial.: The B-Book: Assigning Programs toMeanings. Cambridge University Press, 1996.

[LP05]   G. T. Leavens, E. Poll, C. Clifton, Y. Cheon, C. Ruby, D. Cok, P. Muller, and J. Kiniry.: JML Reference Manual. 2005.

[MK99]   J.Magee and J. Kramer.: Concurrency: State Models & Java Programs. John Wiley and Sons, 1999.

[MPA05] J. Manson, W. Pugh, and S. V. Adve.: The Java Memory Model. In POPL 05: Proceedings of the 32nd ACM SIGPLAN-SIGACT , 378-391, New York, NY, USA, 2005. ACM Press

[MW]   H. Muller and K. Walrath.: Threads and Swing. http://java.sun.com/products/jfc/tsc/articles/threads/threads1.html

[OC04]   M. Oliveira and A. Cavalcanti.: From Circus to JCSP. In Sixth International Conference on Formal Engineering Methods, November 2004.

[Pu00]   W. Pugh.: The Java Memory Model is Fatally Flawed. Concurrency: Practice and Experience, **12(6)**(2000) 445-455

[PM00a] P. H. Welch and J. M. Martin.: A CSP Model for Java Multithreading. In ICSE 2000, pages 114-122, June 2000.

[PM00b] P. H. Welch and J. M. Martin.: Formal Analysis of Concurrent Java System. In Communicating Process Architectures 2000.

[RM89]   R.Milner.: Communication and Concurrency. Prentice-Hall, Inc., 1989.

[RR03]   V. Raju, L. Rong, and G. S. Stiles.: Automatic Conversion of CSP to CTJ, JCSP, and CCSP. In Communicating Process Architectures 2003, pages 63-81, 2003.

[SD04]   S. Schneider and R. Delicata.: Verifying Security Protocols: An Application of CSP. In 25 Years Communicating Sequential Processes, 243-263, 2004.

[SS00]   S. Schneider.: Concurrent and Real-Time System: The CSP Approach. John Wiley and Sons LTD, 2000.

[ST95]   S.-T. M. Limited.: Occam 2.1 Reference Manual, 1995.

[TS99]   H. Treharne and S. Schneider.: Using a Process Algebra to Control B Operations. In IFM, pages 437-456, 1999.

[VH00]   W. Visser, K. Havelund, G. Brat, and S. Park.: Model checking programs. In Int. Conf. on Automated Software Engineering, 2000

[VT02]   J. C. Voisinet, B. Tatibouet and A. Hammand.: JBTools: An experimental platform for the formal B method. In PPPJ' 2002 , 137-140, 2002.

[We00]   P. Welch. Wow, no chicken? http://wotug.ukc.ac.uk/parallel/groups/wotug/java/discussion/3.html.

[WM00]   P. H. Welch and J. M. Martin.: Formal Analysis of Concurrent Java System. In Communicating Process Architectures, 2000

Symmetry Reduction for B by Permutation Flooding

Michael Leuschel[1], Michael Butler[2], Corinna Spermann[1], and Edd Turner[2]

[1] Institut für Informatik, Universität Düsseldorf
Universitätsstr. 1, D-40225 Düsseldorf
{leuschel,spermann}@cs.uni-duesseldorf.de
[2] School of Electronics and Computer Science, University of Southampton
Highfield, Southampton, SO17 1BJ, UK
{mjb,ent03r}@ecs.soton.ac.uk

Abstract. Symmetry reduction is an established method for limiting the amount of states that have to be checked during exhaustive model checking. The idea is to only verify a single representative of every class of symmetric states. However, computing this representative can be non-trivial, especially for a language such as B with its involved data structures and operations. In this paper, we propose an alternate approach, called permutation flooding. It works by computing permutations of newly encountered states, and adding them to the state space. This turns out to be relatively unproblematic for B's data structures and we have implemented the algorithm inside the PROB model checker. Empirical results confirm that this approach is effective in practice; speedups exceed an order of magnitude in some cases. The paper also contains correctness results of permutation flooding, which should also be applicable for classical symmetry reduction in B.

Keywords: B-Method, Tool Support, Model Checking, Symmetry Reduction.[1]

1 Introduction

The B-method [1] is a theory and methodology for formal development of computer systems. It is used in industry in a range of critical domains. In addition to the proof activities it is increasingly being realised that validation of the initial specification is important, as otherwise a correct implementation of an incorrect specification is being developed. This validation can come in the form of *animation*, e.g., to check that certain functionality is present in the specification. Another useful tool is *model checking*, whereby the specification can be systematically checked for certain temporal properties. In previous work [14], we have presented the PROB animator and model checker to support those activities. Implemented in Prolog, the PROB tool supports automated consistency checking and deadlock checking of B machines and has been recently extended for

---

[1] This research is partially supported by the EU funded project: IST 511599 RODIN (Rigorous Open Development Environment for Complex Systems).

J. Julliand and O. Kouchnarenko (Eds.): B 2007, LNCS 4355, pp. 79–93, 2006.

automated refinement checking [15], also allowing properties to be expressed in CSP [4].

However, it is well known that model checking suffers from the exponential state explosion problem; one way to combat this is via *symmetry reduction* [6]. Indeed, often a system to be checked has a large number of states with symmetric behaviour, meaning that there are groups of states where each member of the group behaves like every other member of the group. In the case of B machines this arises, e.g., when using deferred sets, where one set element can be replaced by another without affecting the behaviour of the machine. The classical approach to symmetry reduction requires the determination of a so-called *representative* for every symmetry group; the idea being that it is sufficient to check just the representative. Computing such a representative, at least for a formalism such as B with its sophisticated data structures and operations, is a non-trivial task. In this paper we present an alternate way to add symmetry reduction to B, which we have incorporated into ProB's model checking algorithm. Indeed, while it is not trivial to pick a (unique) representative for every symmetry group, it is relatively straightforward in B to generate from a given state a set of symmetric states, essentially by permuting the elements of deferred sets. Our new algorithm uses that fact to achieve symmetry reduction; the basic idea being that when a new state is added to the state space all symmetric states are also added. While this can result in a considerable number of symmetric states being added, we show that—in the absence of counterexamples—all of them would have been explored using the classical model checking algorithm anyway. We have implemented this algorithm, and have evaluated it on a series of examples. Our experiments show that big savings can be achieved (exceeding an order of magnitude).

2   Motivation and Overview

Let us examine the following simple B machine, modelling a system where a user can login and logout with session identifiers being attributed upon login.

```
MACHINE LoginVerySimple
SETS Session
VARIABLES active
INVARIANT  active<:Session
INITIALISATION active := {}
OPERATIONS
  res <-- Login = ANY s WHERE s:Session & s/: active THEN
                    res := s || active := active \/ {s} END;
  Logout(s) = PRE s: active THEN active := active - {s} END
END
```

This machine contains the deferred set Session. For animation, the user has to select some finite size for this set [14]. Figure 1 contains the full state space generated by ProB for this machine, where the cardinality of Session was set to 3 (and PROB has automatically generated three elements *Session*1, *Session*2 and *Session*3 of that set). One can see that the states 2,3,4 are symmetric, in the sense that:

- the states can be transformed into each other by permuting the elements of the set `Session`;
- if one of the states satisfies (respectively violates) the invariant, then any of the other states must also satisfy (respectively violate) the invariant;
- if one of the states can perform a sequence of operations, then any other state can perform a similar sequence of transitions; possibly substituting operation arguments (in the same way that the state values were permuted). E.g., state 2 can perform *Logout*(*Session*1), state 3 can be obtained from state 2 by replacing Session1 with Session2, and, indeed, state 3 can perform *Logout*(*Session*2).

The same holds for the states 5,6 and 7.

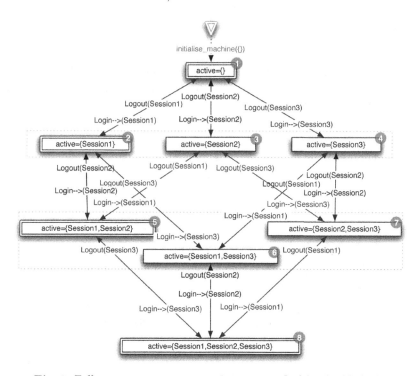

Fig. 1. Full state space; representatives are marked by double boxes

Classical Approach to Symmetry Reduction. In classical symmetry reduction, one would compute a representative for every set of symmetric states. A possible choice for such representatives for the above example would be the states 1,2,5,8; shown as boxes with double borders in Figure 1. When a model checker with symmetry reduction encounters state 3, it would compute its representative (i.e., state 2) which is already in the state space. Thus state 3 would not need to be checked. The same holds for state 4.

Deciding whether two states can be considered symmetric (also called the "orbit problem") is tightly linked to detecting graph isomorphisms (see, e.g., [6][Chapter 14.4.1]). Indeed, one can directly employ algorithms for detecting graph isomorphisms, by converting the system states into graphs and then checking whether these graphs are isomorphic. One efficient approach is by computing the canonical form of the graphs (called certificates in [12]). Such an approach also looks promising for B, but requires careful extension due to the data structures and operations of B.

New Approach. The new algorithm we present in this paper works the other way around to classical symmetry reduction: when a new state is added to the state space, we at the same time (proactively so to speak) add all states which can be obtained by permuting the deferred set values of the state. This is based on the three insights below:

- **Insight 1:** Whereas it is difficult to find out if two states are symmetric and compute a representative, it is actually quite straightforward to generate symmetric permutation of a given state; at least in B. Indeed, symmetry in B occurs usually due to the use of deferred sets; this was the case in the example above. One thus simply has to permute the deferred set elements that occur in the given state.

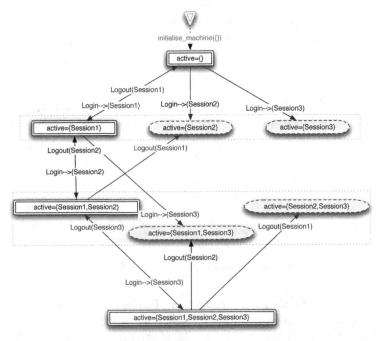

Fig. 2. Full state space after permutation flooding

- **Insight 2:** In order to prevent symmetric states from being checked, we can simply add the permutations to the state space and mark them as "already processed."
- **Insight 3:** The obvious drawback of generating all permutations is that there can be many such permutations, "flooding" the state space. However, they would all have been encountered during an exhaustive model check anyway! Thus—at least when compared to classical model checking in the absence of counterexamples—we have nothing to lose by using the new algorithm. We gain that for the permuted states we do not have to compute the invariant, nor compute the enabled operations and their effect. Furthermore we apply the permutation generation only to one representative of each symmetry group; all the other representatives will be detected by straightforward state hashing and identity checking using normalisation [14].

An illustration of the approach on the above example can be found in Figure 2. When adding the state $active = \{Session1\}$ the two symmetric states $active = \{Session2\}$ and $active = \{Session3\}$ are also added to the state space. Similarly, when adding $active = \{Session1, Session2\}$ its two symmetric states are also added. As can be seen, a reduction in the checking effort has been achieved: only 4 of the 8 states have to be checked (i.e., the invariant evaluated and the enabled operations computed).

3   The Algorithm

Informal Explanation Recall, that in B there are two ways to introduce sets into a B machine: either as a parameter of the machine (by convention parameters consisting only of upper case letters are sets; the other parameters are integers) or via the SETS clause. Sets introduced in the SETS clause are called *given sets*. Given sets which are explicitly enumerated in the SETS clause are called *enumerated sets*, the other given sets are called *deferred sets*.

Informally, two states are symmetric when the invariant has the same truth value in both states and when they can both execute the same sequences of operations (possibly up to some renaming of data values). While in the general case it is undecidable whether two states are symmetric or not, we can generate for a given state s a set of states which are guaranteed to be symmetric. The simplest approach is to permute the deferred set elements within s. This is what we have done in the example in the previous section. One may wonder why we only permute the deferred set elements, and not the elements of enumerated sets. Indeed, in the example above, if we replace Session by an enumerated set Session = {Session1, Session2, Session3} then the state space would remain unchanged (Figure 1 would remain exactly the same) as would the symmetry groups. However, without further knowledge about the machine, we have no guarantee that this would always be the case. Indeed, as the elements Session1, Session2, Session3 can now be referenced by name, they could be used in the invariant or in the precondition of a machine. For example, Session1:active => not(Session2:active) could be used as a precondition of an operation. This would break the symmetry, meaning that we would generate permutation states which are *not* symmetric to the original state. In other words, by not checking the permutation states we may fail to detect an invariant violation or deadlock. Similarly, if the above condition appears inside the invariant, the state $active = \{Session1, Session3\}$ would satisfy the invariant, while the permutation $active = \{Session1, Session2\}$ would not. Later, in Section 6, we will explain how this restriction can be somewhat relaxed; but for the time being we will only permute deferred set elements. Integers, booleans and enumerated sets will not be permuted.

Formalisation. The state space of a machine is defined as the cartesian product of the types of each of the machine variables and constants. We represent the machine constants and variables by a vector of variables $v1, \ldots, vn$ (denoted V). The normal form for a B operation operating on the variables V with inputs x and outputs y is characterised by a predicate $P(x, V, V', y)$. Characterising a B operation of the form $X \longleftarrow op(Y)$ as a predicate in this way gives rise to a labelled transition relation on states: state s is related to state s' by event $op.a.b$, denoted by $s \rightarrow^M_{op.a.b} s'$, when $P(a, s, s', b)$ holds. Further details may be found in [15]. We also add a special state *root*, where we define $root \rightarrow^M_{initialise} s$ if s satisfies the initialisation and the properties clause. We now describe how to generate permutation states.

Definition 1. *Let DS be a set of disjoint sets. A permutation f over DS is a total bijection from $\cup_{S \in DS} S$ to $\cup_{S \in DS} S$ such that $\forall S \in DS$ we have $\{f(s) \mid s \in S\} = S$.*

We can now define permutations for B machines, which permute deferred set elements, respecting the typing (i.e., we only permute within each deferred set).

Definition 2. *Let M be a B Machine with deferred sets $DS_1, \ldots, DS_k$ and enumerated sets $ES_1, \ldots, ES_m$. A function f is called a permutation for M iff it is a permutation over $DS_1, \ldots, DS_k$. We extend f to B's other basic datatypes, requiring that f must not permute integer, boolean or enumerated values:*
  – $f(x) = x$ if $x : \mathbb{Z}$ or $x : BOOL$ or $x : ES_j$ (for some j)
Values in B are either elements of given sets (including boolean values and integers), pairs of values, or sets of values. We recursively lift such an f to pairs and sets as follows:
  – $f(x \mapsto y) = f(x) \mapsto f(y)$
  – $f(\{x_1, \ldots, x_n\}) = \{f(x_1), \ldots, f(x_n)\}$
We also extend the domain of this function f to state vectors by defining
  – $f(\langle v_1, \ldots, v_k \rangle) = \langle f(v_1), \ldots, f(v_k) \rangle$

Take for example a B machine with deferred sets $DS_1 = \{s_1, s_2\}$ and $DS_2 = \{r_1, r_2\}$. Then $f = \{s_1 \mapsto s_2, s_2 \mapsto s_1, r_1 \mapsto r_1, r_2 \mapsto r_2\}$ is a permutation over $\{DS_1, DS_2\}$. Applying f to states we have for example $f(\langle s_1 \rangle) = \langle s_2 \rangle$, $f(\langle r_1, 5 \rangle) = \langle r_1, 5 \rangle$, $f(\langle \{s_1, s_2\} \rangle) = \langle \{s_1, s_2\} \rangle$, $f(\langle \{s_2\}, s_1 \rangle) = \langle \{s_1\}, s_2 \rangle$, $f(\langle \{s_1\}, \{1 \mapsto s_1\}, \{\{\}, \{s_2\}\} \rangle) = \langle \{s_2\}, \{1 \mapsto s_2\}, \{\{\}, \{s_1\}\} \rangle$. Observe that constants are part of the state and are thus also permuted by f.[2] We can now define when two states are a permutation of each other:

Definition 3. *Let s, s' be two states of a B Machine with deferred sets $DS_1, \ldots,$ DS_k. The state s is a permutation the state of s' iff there exists a permutation f over $\{DS_1, \ldots, DS_i\}$ such that $s' = f(s)$.*

In order to generate all permutation states of a given state s we thus simply need to enumerate all possible permutations over $\{DS_1, \ldots, DS_i\}$. In our implementation we have added one improvement: if the state s only contains the deferred set values $V \subset \cup_{i=1..k} DS_i$ then we only need to generate "partial" permutations (i.e., we do not have to map elements which do not occur in s).

   We can now formalise our model checking algorithm. Below, *error* is a function which returns true if the argument is an error state: usually, this means an invariant violation or a deadlock.

Algorithm 3.1 *[Consistency Checking with Permutation Flooding]*

>   **Input:** An abstract machine M
> $Queue := \{root\}$; $Visited := \{\}$; $Graph := \{\}$
>   **while** $Queue$ is not empty **do**
>   state := pop($Queue$); $Visited := Visited \cup \{state\}$
>   **if** $error(state)$ **then**
>   **return** counter-example trace in $Graph$ from $root$ to $state$
>   **else**
>   **for all** $succ, Op$ such that $state \rightarrow^M_{Op} succ$ **do**
> $Graph := Graph \cup \{state \rightarrow_{Op} succ\}$
>   **if** $succ \notin Visited$ **then**
>   **if** random(1) $< \alpha$ **then** add $succ$ to front of $Queue$
>   **else** add $succ$ to end of $Queue$ **end if**
> $Visited := Visited \cup \{s | \exists f.f$ is a permutation function $\wedge s = f(succ)\}$
>   **end if**
>   **end for**
>   **end if**   **od**
>   **return** ok

Note that all elements of $Queue$ and $Visited$ have associated hash values. It is therefore usually quite efficient to decide whether $succ \notin Visited$. We have implemented this algorithm within PROB, and we provide empirical results later in Section 5. In the following section we will justify the soundness of the approach.

4   Soundness Results

The permutation flooding algorithm optimises the standard exhaustive checking algorithm of PROB by assuming that if a state satisfies the invariant, then all

---

[2] If that is not desired then one could simply impose on the allowed permutations, that for all deferred set elements c occurring in the constants we have $f(c) = c$.

permutations of that state also satisfy the invariant. It also assumes that if a state can reach another state violating the invariant (or exhibiting a deadlock), then all permutations of that state can also reach a state violating the invariant (or with a deadlock). This section outlines the correctness of these assumptions. A key theorem in showing this is that given a state s and a permuted state $f(s)$, the truth value of predicate P in state s is equivalent to the truth value of P in state $f(s)$.

The values of free variables in B expressions and predicates are either elements of given sets (including Boolean values and integers), pairs of values, or sets of values. We find it convenient to represent the state as a substitution of the form $[v1, \ldots, vn := c1, \ldots, cn]$, where $v1, \ldots, vn$ (denoted V) are the variables in any B expression/predicate and $c1, \ldots, cn$ (denoted C) are the values. Such variables include state variables, machine constants, quantified variables and local operations variables.

For expression E, we write $E[V := C]$ to denote the value of E in state $[V := C]$. This value will be an element of some type constructed from the given sets of a machine. Similarly for predicate P, we write $P[V := C]$ to denote the boolean truth value of P in state $[V := C]$. Most B set operators are defined in terms of other more basic operators and/or set comprehension[3]. This means we can focus on the core predicate and expression syntax as defined in [1]. This core syntax is shown in figures 3 and 4[4].

$$
\begin{aligned}
E ::= \; &Var \\
| \; &Enum \\
| \; &(E, E) \\
| \; &E \times E \\
| \; &\mathbb{P}(E) \\
| \; &\{x \,|\, x \in S \wedge P\} \\
| \; &E(E)
\end{aligned}
\qquad\qquad
\begin{aligned}
P ::= \; &P \wedge P \\
| \; &\neg P \\
| \; &E = E \\
| \; &\forall x.(x \in S \implies P) \\
| \; &E \in E
\end{aligned}
$$

Fig. 3. Core syntax for expressions   **Fig. 4.** Core syntax for predicates

The goal is now to prove that the permutation function f used in permutation flooding will preserve the evaluation of *any expression or predicate*. This is expressed by the following theorem.

Theorem 1. *For any expression E, predicate P, state $[V := C]$ and permutation function f:*

---

[3] For example, $S \subseteq T \; \Leftrightarrow \; \forall x.(x \in S \implies x \in T)$.

[4] To simplify the presentation we have ignored integer and boolean expressions. These are never permuted by the algorithm. However an integer expression may contain a subexpression of the form $max(S)$ or $card(S)$, where S is a set. The set S in $max(S)$ must be a set of integers and therefore will never be permuted. The set S in $card(S)$ can be any finite set and therefore may be permuted. Such permutation is sound since the injectivity of f means that for any set S, $card(S) = card(f(S))$.

$$f(E[V := C]) = E[V := f(C)]$$
$$P[V := C] \Leftrightarrow P[V := f(C)]$$

The theorem can be proved by structural induction over expression and predicate terms. The induction is mutual since expressions may contain predicates and vice versa. We don't present the full proof here, but it is instructive to consider two case of the structural induction. Firstly, consider the base case where E is an enumerated value ev:

$f(ev[V := C])$
$= f(ev)$ ev has no free variables
$= ev$ $f(ev)=ev$
$= ev[V := f(C)]$ ev has no free variables

The case of an equality predicate makes use of the injectivity of f:

$(E1 = E2)[V := f(C)]$
$\Leftrightarrow E1[V := f(C)] = E2[V := f(C)]$ substitution distributes
$\Leftrightarrow f(E1[V := C]) = f(E2[V := C])$ induction hypothesis
$\Leftrightarrow E1[V := C] = E2[V := C]$ f is injective
$\Leftrightarrow (E1 = E2)[V := C]$

Corollary 1. *From Theorem 1 we can conclude that every state permutation f for a B machine M satisfies*

- $\forall s \in S : s \models I$ *iff* $f(s) \models I$
- $\forall s_1 \in S, \forall s_2 \in S:$ $s_1 \rightarrow^M_{op.a.b} s_2$ $\Leftrightarrow$ $f(s_1) \rightarrow^M_{op.f(a).f(b)} f(s_2)$.

In terms of the terminology of [6][Chapter 14], we have thus shown that our permutations are *automorphisms* wrt B's transition relation between states and that the truth value of the invariant is preserved by our permutations. Note that by induction, it follows from Corollory 1 that, if we can execute a trace t from a state s_1 to another state s_2, then we can execute a corresponding trace t' from $f(s_1)$ to $f(s_2)$. This ensures that we do not miss out deadlocks or reachable classes of symmetric states by checking just a single representative of a class. It also ensures that we do not miss out on traces (up to renaming); which is important for B's refinement notion and will enable us (in future) to use permutation flooding for symmetry reduction during refinement checking [15].

Proof. (Sketch) for Corollary 1.
The first point about invariant preservation is obvious. It is also trivial to show that enabling of op is preserved by f by applying Theorem 1 to the guard and pre-condition of op. The fact that the parameters and return values of an operation are linked can be easily proven by adding new variables to the machine for the arguments and return values and applying Theorem 1 with P being the characteristic predicate of the operation op.

From the above results we can also derive an efficiency result for permutation flooding, namely that all permutation states of some reachable state are also part of the reachable state space (this is nicely illustrated in Figures 1 and 2). In practical terms, this means, in case we exhaustively explore the entire state space, we have nothing to lose by applying permutation reduction.

5   Empirical Results

In a first phase we have performed classical consistency and deadlock checking with and without permutation flooding, on a series of examples using PROB's model checker. The results can be found in Table 1. The column "Nodes" contains the number of nodes for which the invariant was checked and the outgoing transitions computed. The experiments were all run on a multiprocessor system with 4 AMD Opteron 870 Dual Core 2 GHz processors, running SUSE Linux 10.1, SICStus Prolog 3.12.5 (x86_64-linux-glibc2.3) and PROB version 1.2.0.[5] scheduler0.mch and scheduler1.ref are the machines presented in [15]. The scheduler machine is a variation of scheduler0.mch, and is taken from [13]. In all the schedulers the deferred sets are the process identifiers. USB is a specification of a USB protocol, developed by ClearSy. The deferred set are the data transfers. RussianPostalPuzzle is a B model of a cryptographic puzzle (see, e.g., [10]). In this case, the deferred set is the number of available keys and locks.

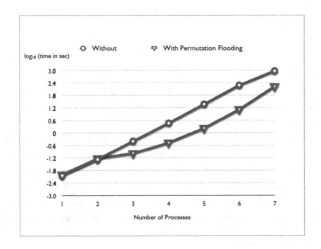

Fig. 5. Model Checking time and evaluated nodes and transitions for scheduler1.ref

Analysis of the results: The results are very encouraging. As can be seen, the permutation flooding algorithm pays off, sometimes achieving an order of magnitude reduction. However, we do not get a fundamental change of the runtime complexity, as Fig. 5 clearly shows. Still, Table 1 shows that a considerable

---

[5] Note that neither SICStus Prolog nor PROB take advantage of multiple processors.

Table 1. Model checking with and without (wo) permutation flooding

Machine	Card	Time wo (s)	Time with	Speedup	Nodes wo	Nodes with	Transitions wo	Transitions with
scheduler	1	0.01	0.01	1.0	4	4	5	5
(from [13])	2	0.04	0.03	1.6	11	7	25	16
	3	0.09	0.04	2.1	36	11	121	38
	4	0.43	0.07	6.0	125	16	561	75
	5	1.97	0.23	8.6	438	22	2481	131
	6	8.63	1.22	7.1	1523	29	10489	210
	7	36.63	9.87	3.7	5232	37	42617	316
Russian	1	0.05	0.05	1.0	15	15	24	24
PostalPuzzle	2	0.32	0.21	1.6	81	48	177	105
	3	1.32	0.46	2.9	441	119	1227	331
	4	8.73	1.90	4.6	2325	248	7869	838
	5	54.06	12.18	4.4	11985	459	47795	1826
scheduler0	1	0.01	0.01	1.0	5	5	6	6
(from [15])	2	0.07	0.05	1.5	16	10	37	23
	3	0.28	0.07	4.1	55	17	190	59
	4	0.98	0.20	5.0	190	26	865	121
	5	4.52	0.75	6.0	649	37	3646	216
	6	20.35	4.74	4.3	2188	50	14581	351
scheduler1	1	0.01	0.01	1.0	5	5	6	6
(refines	2	0.05	0.06	0.9	27	14	62	32
scheduler0)	3	0.41	0.11	3.8	145	29	447	94
	4	2.96	0.34	8.6	825	51	2948	211
	5	23.93	1.70	14.1	5201	81	19925	405
	6	192.97	13.37	14.4	37009	120	145926	701
	7	941.46	167.95	5.61	297473	169	506084	1127
USB.mch	1	0.21	0.26	0.8	23	23	652	652
	2	7.70	3.03	2.5	415	214	13120	6736
	3	283.05	47.92	5.9	7663	1398	248540	45302

amount of nodes do not need to be evaluated for invariant violations or computing the possible outgoing transitions. Hence, our method will pay off especially for machines with more complicated invariants or complicated operations. In the machines above the invariants were actually very simple. For example, scheduler1's invariant only contains typing information. We have thus produced an elaboration of scheduler 1 with a more complicated invariant. The results can be found in Figure 2, and they confirm our expectation that for more complicated machines the permutation flooding algorithm can be even more beneficial (e.g., being 68.5 times faster than classical model checking for 5 processes). However, for simple machines such as the scheduler or scheduler0, the bottleneck is the generation of the permutations. This explains why the relative performance improvements drop off for these simple machines for higher cardinalities of the deferred sets.

Table 2. Further Experiments

Machine	Card	Time wo (s)	Time with	Speedup	Nodes wo	Nodes with	Transitions wo	Transitions with
scheduler1[+]	2	0.23	0.14	1.7	27	14	62	32
(with more	3	1.81	0.37	4.9	145	29	447	94
complicated	4	32.48	1.97	16.4	825	51	2948	211
invariant)	5	766.19	11.18	68.5	5201	81	19925	405

6   Extending the Algorithm for Enumerated Sets

In this section we discuss how to extend our algorithm for enumerated given sets. It is clear that if an enumerated set element is referenced in the invariant or in the precondition or guard of an operation, that this can cause unsoundness of permutation flooding. We have seen that in Section 3. But what if the set element is only referenced in the body of an operation? Let us look at the following example.

```
MACHINE SymCounterEx
SETS   S={s1,s2,s3}
VARIABLES x
INVARIANT  x:POW(S) & card(x)=1
INITIALISATION  x : (x:POW(S) & card(x)=1)
OPERATIONS   add = BEGIN x := x \/ {s1} END
END
```

Here we have three initial states: $x = \{s1\}$, $x = \{s2\}$, $x = \{s3\}$. They are all symmetric wrt the INVARIANT as well as wrt all Preconditions and Guards of all operations. Still, it is unsound to just examine one representative. Suppose we check $x = \{s1\}$. This state does not violate the invariant and we detect that executing add in the state loops back itself and we would incorrectly report that the invariant is not violated by the machine, while it is when executing the add operation from either $x = \{s2\}$ or $x = \{s3\}$.

It is instructive to examine exactly where the proof of Section 4 fails if we permute enumerated sets. It is in Theorem 1, when we have an element of a given set as the expression. In this case we no longer have $f(ev) = ev$. As a result, we no longer have that evaluating the expression and then applying the permutation gives the same result as applying the permutation first and then evaluating the expression; breaking the symmetry results. However, if we do not use an enumerated set element inside *any* expression, the proof still goes through. This thus provides a way to extend our correctness results and methodology for enumerated sets.

This idea has also been implemented inside PROB. The basic idea is that, for every enumerated given set ES_i, we compute the values $D_{ES_i} \subseteq ES_i$ which are *not* referenced syntactically inside the invariant, properties, initialisation or the operations of a B machine. If $card(D_{ES_i}) > 1$ then we will permute the values in

D_{ES_i} in the same way as deferred set values were substituted for each other. We thus extend Definition 2 by allowing f to be a permutation over $\{DS_1, \ldots, DS_k\}$ $\cup \{D_{ES_i} \mid 1 \leq i \leq m \land card(D_{ES_i}) > 1\}$.

Let us examine this extended algorithm on the example above. Figure 6 shows the correct state space computed by PROB, where $s2$ and $s3$ are considered symmetric wrt each other but not wrt $s1$. As can be seen, the invariant violation is detected. (It can also be seen that PROB inserts artificial permute operations. This is to provide the user with a better feedback when using the animator.)

One may wonder how often in practice a given set would be defined and only part of its elements referenced inside the machine. One typical example is when the set is actually a deferred set, but was enumerated for animation purposes (to give meaningful names to the set elements). This case is actually quite common.

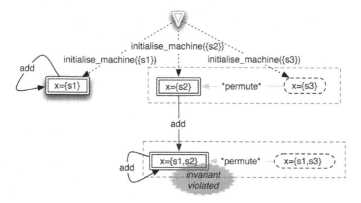

Fig. 6. Full state space after permutation flooding for SymCounterEx

7 Discussion, Related and Future Work

Future Work. One interesting avenue for further research is to use the permutation flooding idea also for refinement checking. This could be achieved by suitably taking the "permute" transitions inserted by PROB (see, e.g., Fig. 6) into account. Another idea is to use symmetry reduction when evaluating predicates with existential or universal quantification, to cut down on the number of values that need to be tested for the quantified variables. For example, to evaluate the formula $\forall x.x \subseteq DS \Rightarrow P$ one would only have to evaluate P for one representative per symmetry group. Finally, PROB has recently been extended to be able to treat set comprehensions and lambda abstractions symbolically. These are converted into a closure and are only evaluated on demand. For this extension, we would need to adapt the permutation so that it permutes the values stored inside the closures.

Related Work. The line of research developing symmetry reduction for temporal logic model checking is the inspiration for the present article. Symmetry reduction in model checking dates back to [11] and [5], more recent works being [17,18].

One difference with those works is that in our case we do not consider temporal logic formulas, but B's criteria of invariant violations, deadlocks and refinement. Another important difference is the complexity of B's data structures and operators, making the orbit problem [6] particularly tricky. Still, it should be possible to extend this line of research for B, by using algorithms from graph theory [12] and systems such as NAUTY [16].

As our experiments have indicated, classical symmetry reduction by computing a normal form (i.e., a representative of the set of symmetric states) may in principle be able to achieve even better results than our approach. The drawback of our method is that all permutations are added all of the time (for one representative per class). Depending on the B machine being checked, this may be unnecessary work as by pruning symmetric states initially, many of the later symmetric states may not be reachable anymore. E.g., in Fig 1, this is not the case, but one could imagine that by pruning 3 and 4, states 6 and 7 became unreachable. A classical symmetry reduction algorithm would thus not have to compute a normal form for 6 and 7, whereas we will still add the states 6 and 7 as permutations of 5 to the state space. Furthermore, when invariant violations are present, adding permutations could result in the model checker taking longer to find the first counterexample. However, there will also be cases where permutation flooding is better than a classical symmetry reduction algorithm, namely when the data values inside the individual states get complicated, thus making the computation of the normal form of the state graphs expensive. In our case, the complexity of computing the permutations does not depend on the complexity of the data values being used (they just need to be traversed once); only on the number of deferred set elements occurring inside the state. In summary, a main advantage of our approach lies in its simplicity, along with the fact that it can naturally deal with complicated data structures (such as the closures discussed above).

Another class of related work is the one using symmetry for efficient testing of satisfiability of boolean formulas. These works (e.g., [7], [2,3] or [8]) use symmetry breaking predicates, which are determined using algorithms from graph theory and which ensure that a subset of the state space will be ignored. Other related work in the formal methods area is the BZ testing tool (BZTT) [13]. This is a test-case generation tool, that also contains an animator. In contrast to PROB, this animator keeps constraints about the variables of a machine, rather than explicitly enumerating possible values. As a side benefit, this gives a simple form of symmetry reduction for the deferred set elements (e.g., the states 2,3,4 in Fig. 1 could be represented by a single state of the form $active = \{s\}$ with the constraint $s \in Session$), but in general not for enumerated sets. Also, the symbolic approach seems difficult to scale up to more complicated B operators (such as set comprehensions, lambda abstractions, existential quantifications, etc., which are not supported by BZTT).

Conclusion. In conclusion, we have presented a new way to achieve symmetry reduction for model checking B specifications. The algorithm proceeds by computing permutations of the states encountered during the model checking, and adding those permutations to the state space, marking them as already processed. We have presented a formalisation of this approach, along with correctness results. We have also compared our approach to classical symmetry reduction, arguing that either approach has its advantages and drawbacks. We have implemented the algorithm inside the PROB toolset and have evaluated the approach on a series of examples. The empirical results were very encouraging, the speedups exceeding an order of magnitude in some cases.

References

1. J.-R. Abrial. *The B-Book*. Cambridge University Press, 1996.
2. F. A. Aloul, A. Ramani, I. L. Markov, and K. A. Sakallah. Solving difficult SAT instances in the presence of symmetry. In *DAC*, pages 731–736. ACM, 2002.
3. F. A. Aloul, K. A. Sakallah, and I. L. Markov. Efficient symmetry breaking for boolean satisfiability. *IEEE Trans. Computers*, 55(5):549–558, 2006.
4. M. Butler and M. Leuschel. Combining CSP and B for specification and property verification. In *Proceedings of Formal Methods 2005*, LNCS 3582, pages 221–236, Newcastle upon Tyne, 2005. Springer-Verlag.
5. E. M. Clarke, T. Filkorn, and S. Jha. Exploiting symmetry in temporal logic model checking. In C. Courcoubetis, editor, *CAV'93*, LNCS 697, pages 450–462. Springer-Verlag, 1993.
6. E. M. Clarke, O. Grumberg, and D. Peled. *Model Checking*. MIT Press, 1999.
7. J. M. Crawford, M. L. Ginsberg, E. M. Luks, and A. Roy. Symmetry-breaking predicates for search problems. In *KR 1996*, pages 148–159, 1996.
8. P. T. Darga, M. H. Liffiton, K. A. Sakallah, and I. L. Markov. Exploiting structure in symmetry detection for CNF. In S. Malik, L. Fix, and A. B. Kahng, editors, *DAC*, pages 530–534. ACM, 2004.
9. E. A. Emerson and A. P. Sistla. Symmetry and model checking. *Formal Methods in System Design*, 9(1/2):105–131, 1996.
10. S. Flannery. *In Code: A Mathematical Adventure*. Profile Books Ltd, 2001.
11. C. N. Ip and D. L. Dill. Better verification through symmetry. In *Computer Hardware Description Languages and their Applications*, pages 97–111, 1993.
12. D. L. Kreher and D. R. Stinson. *Combinatorial Algorithms: Generation, Enumeration, Search*. CRC Press, 1999.
13. B. Legeard, F. Peureux, and M. Utting. Automated boundary testing from Z and B. In *Proceedings FME'02*, LNCS 2391, pages 21–40. Springer-Verlag, 2002.
14. M. Leuschel and M. Butler. ProB: A model checker for B. In K. Araki, S. Gnesi, and D. Mandrioli, editors, *FME 2003: Formal Methods*, LNCS 2805, pages 855–874. Springer-Verlag, 2003.
15. M. Leuschel and M. Butler. Automatic refinement checking for B. In K.-K. Lau and R. Banach, editors, *Proceedings ICFEM'05*, LNCS 3785, pages 345–359. Springer-Verlag, 2005.
16. B. McKay. Nauty users guide. Available at http://cs.anu.edu.au/people/bdm/nauty/.
17. A. P. Sistla. Employing symmetry reductions in model checking. *Computer Languages, Systems & Structures*, 30(3-4):99–137, 2004.
18. A. P. Sistla and P. Godefroid. Symmetry and reduced symmetry in model checking. *ACM Trans. Program. Lang. Syst.*, 26(4):702–734, 2004.

Instantiation of Parameterized Data Structures for Model-Based Testing

Fabrice Bouquet, Jean-François Couchot, Frédéric Dadeau, and Alain Giorgetti

LIFC – INRIA Cassis project
FRE CNRS 2661, University of Franche-Comté
16 route de Gray, 25030 Besançon cedex, France
{bouquet,couchot,dadeau,giorgetti}@lifc.univ-fcomte.fr

Abstract. Model-based testing is bound, by essence, to use the enumerated data structures of the system under test (SUT). On the other hand, formal modeling often involves the use of parameterized data structures in order to be more general (such a model should be sufficient to test many implementation variants) and to abstract irrelevant details. Consequently, the validation engineer is sooner or later required to instantiate these parameters. At the current time, this instantiation activity is a matter of experience and knowledge of the SUT. This work investigates how to rationalize the instantiation of the model parameters.

It is obvious that a poor instantiation may badly influence the quality of the resulting tests. However, recent results in instantiation-based theorem proving and their application to software verification show that it is often possible to guess the smallest most general data enumeration. We first provide a formal characterization of what a most general instantiation is, in the framework of functional testing. Then, we propose an approach to automate the instantiation of the model parameters, which leaves the specifier and the validation engineer free to use the desired level of abstraction, during the model design process, without having to satisfy any finiteness requirement.

We investigate cases where delaying the instantiation is not a problem. This work is illustrated by a realistic running example. It is presented in the framework of the BZ-Testing-Tools methodology, which uses a B abstract machine for model-based testing and targets many implementation languages.

1 Introduction

Model-based testing (MBT) [7] is the process of using a formal model to derive tests cases that are to be run on an implementation, named the *system under test* (SUT). The model is designed by a validation engineer from an informal specification, without looking at the implementation, except for the signatures of control and observable methods. Nevertheless, several factors influence the design of this model, among which the fact that the test methodology only supports finite data structures.

When writing a formal model from an informal specification, the validation engineer develops a complementary skill of formal specifier. Thus, he/she can

J. Julliand and O. Kouchnarenko (Eds.): B 2007, LNCS 4355, pp. 94–108, 2006.

take benefit of some specific features of formal modeling. One of them is the possibility to abstract details of the informal specification by designing an initial model with parameters. In the B method, this first model is called an abstract machine, and the parameters can be either machine parameters or abstract (i.e. not enumerated) sets. Then, coming back to his/her validation activity, the engineer has to make all the model data finite, by instantiating them cleverly. Up to now, this instantiation is performed by hand from the specifier's knowledge of the SUT and the informal specification.

However, since the engineer does not (have to) know all the implementation and informal specification details, his/her instantiation work is somewhat artificial and not optimal, neither in time nor in quality. Indeed, a poor instantiation may not exploit all the possibilities of the model: it may leave "dead code" in it, and no test case will be produced for this dead part of the model, leaving a –possibly important– part of the SUT not validated.

The first contribution of this work is the formalization (as a proof obligation) of the "most general instantiation" of a formal model with respect to a coverage criterion, corresponding to the idea of leaving no execution case without an associated test. Checking this proof obligation corresponds to dead code detection. The second contribution is to show how to discharge this proof obligation in a theorem prover or a constraint solver. The third contribution is a method based on sorted logic to find an approximation of the most general instantiation. This work is presented in the framework of the BZ-Testing-Tools [1], an approach performing model-based testing from B machines.

The paper is organized as follows. Section 2 presents a running example, a GSM11-11 specification that will be used to illustrate our approach. Section 3 introduces the principles of model-based testing, as performed within the BZ-Testing-Tools. The proof obligation defining the most general instantiation is given in Sect. 4. The techniques for solving this proof obligation are detailed in Sect. 5. The novel instantiation method proposed to guide them is presented in Sect. 6. Finally, Section 7 concludes and presents future work.

2   Running Example

Our running example is a simplified B model of the interface between the Subscriber Identity Module (SIM) and the Mobile Equipment (ME) within the GSM 11.11 (Global System for Mobile communication) digital cellular telecommunications system. It is based on an informal specification [8] produced by the Special Mobile Group (SMG). Section 2.1 briefly presents the aims of the GSM 11.11 standard and describes a parameterized B model of a fragment of it, written for test purposes. Then, Section 2.2 analyzes a former experience on this example where the instantiation was at the charge of the specifier.

2.1   Informal and Formal Specifications

The GSM 11.11 is a standard for the second generation of mobile phones. In this system, the mobile phone embeds a writable card (the SIM: Subscriber Identity

Module) containing security and application data. The SIM stores data in files hierarchically organized in a tree structure. The tree root and the other tree internal nodes are respectively called the *master file* (*MF*) and the *dedicated files* (*DF*). They are the *directories* of the file structure. The tree leaves are called the *elementary files* (*EF*).

```
MACHINE
  gsm1(FILES)
CONSTANTS
  MF, DF,
  EM, /* Elementary Files under the MF */
  ED, /* Elementary Files under a DF */
  FA,
  mf, dg, dt
PROPERTIES
  MF ⊆ FILES ∧ DF ⊆ FILES ∧
  EM ⊆ FILES ∧ ED ⊆ FILES ∧
  MF ∩ DF = ∅ ∧ MF ∩ EM = ∅ ∧
  MF ∩ ED = ∅ ∧ DF ∩ EM = ∅ ∧
  DF ∩ ED = ∅ ∧ EM ∩ ED = ∅ ∧
  FILES = MF ∪ DF ∪ EM ∪ ED ∧
  FA ∈ ED ⟶ DF ∧
  mf ∈ FILES ∧ dg ∈ FILES ∧ dt ∈ FILES ∧
  MF = { mf } ∧ DF = { dg, dt } ∧
  ei ∈ EM
VARIABLES
  cd, cf
INVARIANT
  cd ∈ (MF ∪ DF) ∧ cf ⊆ (EM ∪ ED) ∧
  card (cf) ≤ 1 ∧
  ( cf = ∅ ∨
    (cf ≠ ∅ ∧ cf ⊆ ED ∧ cd ∈ DF) ∨
    (cf ≠ ∅ ∧ cf ⊆ EM ∧ cd = mf) )
INITIALISATION
  cd := mf || cf := ∅
OPERATIONS
  sw ⟵ SELECT_FILE(ff) =

PRE
  ff ∈ FILES
THEN
  IF (ff ∈ (DF ∪ MF))
  THEN
    /* The last selected file is cd */
    IF (
      ( cd = mf ∧ ff ∈ DF ) ∨
      ( cd = dg ∧ ff = dt ) ∨
      ( cd = dt ∧ ff = dg ) ∨
      ( cd ∈ DF ∧ ff = mf ) ∨
      ( ff = cd ) ∨ ff = mf ))
    THEN
      cd := ff || cf := ∅ || sw := 9000
    ELSE
      sw := 9404 /* Not activable. */
    END
  ELSE /* ff is an EF */
    IF (
      ( ff ∈ EM ∧ cd = mf ) ∨
      ( ff ∈ ED ∧ cd ∈ DF
        ∧ FA(ff) = cd ) ∨ ff ∈ cf )
    THEN
      cf := {ff} || sw := 9000
    ELSE
      sw := 9404
    END
  END
END
```

Fig. 1. A small B model for the GSM 11-11 SIM - ME interface

During a communication between the SIM and the ME (Mobile Equipment), the SIM is passive: it only answers to requests sent by the ME, which reads and modifies the SIM files through functions defined in the communication interface. Our model focuses on the SELECT function of this communication interface, because it is the only one which interacts in a complex manner with the file structure. This B machine, shown in Fig. 1, is simplified and its identifiers are shortened in order to fit in the format of this paper. We now describe it in details.

The gsm1.mch machine is parameterized with the non empty finite set *FILES* of all the files present on the SIM card. Since the master file is unique, it is modeled in B by the *mf* constant. The SIM card can store files for many applications but our model focuses on the main one, namely the GSM application, whose dedicated files are all directly under the *MF*. Consequently, the model distinguishes four types of files: master file, dedicated file, elementary file under the master file and elementary file under a dedicated file. These four types are respectively modeled in B by the four pairwise disjoint sets *MF*, *DF*, *EM* and *ED* whose union is the set *FILES* of all the SIM files[1]. The property $MF = \{mf\}$ states that there is a unique master file and the property $DF = \{dg, dt\}$ fixes the set of dedicated files used by the GSM application. These two identifiers respectively represent the directories DF_GSM and DF_TELECOM containing the application data and some telecommunication service features. The file structure is completely defined by the total function *FA* which maps each elementary file in *ED* to its *FA*ther, the dedicated file containing it. The data are completed with the *ei* constant, representing the *EF_ICCID*, an *EF* at the *MF* level storing a unique identification number for the SIM.

The SELECT function is the sole function which can select a SIM file. More precisely, it aims at selecting a directory to become the new *current directory* and an *EF* to become the new *current elementary file*, in conformance with some access rules. It is modeled by the *SELECT_FILE* operation, which assigns a value to the two state variables *cd* (current directory) and *cf* (current *EF*).

The initialization chooses the master file as current directory. One can infer from the informal specification that there is always a single selected directory. Consequently, the variable *cd* takes its values in $MF \cup DF$. The informal specification also expects that there is always zero or one selected *EF*. Consequently, the variable *cf* is defined as a set of elementary files (i.e. is included in $EM \cup ED$) and its value is the empty set when no *EF* is selected. The property that its cardinality should be zero or one is added to the machine invariant. The last part of the invariant checks that the current *EF*, when selected, is always a child of the current directory.

The SELECT function works as follows. If the candidate for selection *ff* is a directory, it is selected iff it is the master file, the current directory, an immediate child, a sibling or the father of the current directory. Now, if *ff* is an *EF*, it is selected iff it is a child of the current directory or was already selected.

2.2 A Previous Experience

In a former work [2], members of our team have published a B model for the GSM 11.11 (named `gsm_revue.mch`), where all the sets were enumerated and where the file structure was modeled by a binary relation, itself enumerated as a set of pairs. After generating tests sequences, the authors have noticed that a branch of the model was never activated (this phenomenon is reproduced by the first ELSE branch of our running example, marked with `/* Not activable. */`).

The explanation for this phenomenon can be threefold. Firstly, the informal specification may be contradictory. Secondly, there may be a discrepancy between the informal specification, assumed contradiction-free, and branches of the B model, making these branches inconsistent. Thirdly, the enumeration of sets in `gsm_revue.mch` may be too restrictive to activate each branch.

After a closer look, the main explanation appeared to be a discrepancy between specifications: The informal specifier has indeed written that "Selecting a *DF* or the *MF* [always] sets the current directory", whereas the formal specifier

---

[1] Note that, for this use of the B machine for generating tests, it is equivalent to consider the *FILES* machine parameter as an abstract set.

has added a case of failure for this selection. The test campaign revealed that this case was not activable, for the enumerated file structure of `gsm_revue.mch`, but the question remained open, whether this property was general or due to a too restrictive enumeration. Our contribution is a methodology, described in Sect. 4, 5 and 6, to answer such a question. In the present case, it gives two answers. Firstly, the branch remains dead for any tree structure of height 1, meaning that the specifier choice of one *DF* and four *EF* was general enough for such a detection. Secondly, this branch becomes activable when one considers at least one dedicated file of depth 2.

From this example, it is clear that detecting "dead code" in a B model is a cumbersome and error-prone activity. We want to investigate ways to assist it with tools. Since the first two explanations for dead branches involve an informal side, they cannot be fully automatized. We therefore focus on the third explanation, i.e. an instantiation of data which is not general enough to activate each branch, by setting a framework where this instantiation is automatically performed.

This instantiation guessing method is based on tools supporting hereditary finite data structures. This excludes inductive structures and binary relations in all their generality. Thus, the model `gsm_revue.mch` has been revised by replacing the binary relation defining the file structure with a total function associating its father to each elementary file. When limited to *DF* of depth 1, this leads to `gsm1.mch`, used in the following sections to illustrate how the guessing method proceeds to find a good instantiation of the sets of files in this tree structure. The method will prove that no instantiation of these sets can activate the branch marked `/* Not activable. */` in Fig. 1, i.e. that the specifier choice in `gsm_revue.mch` was not that restrictive.

Now, in order to prove that a *DF* of depth 2 is sufficient to activate this dead branch, we have also written a larger model, named `gsm2.mch`[2]. Finally, note that the idea of considering such DFs, excluded in version 5.0.0 of the standard, is not artificial, since version 6.2.0. of the GSM 11.11 standard allows their existence.

3   Principles of Model-Based Testing from B Machines

This section describes model-based testing (MBT) from B machines, as performed in the BZ-Testing-Tools [1]. This process takes as an input a B abstract machine, representing the system under test (e.g. wiper controller, smart card, speed control device, etc.) from a functional point of view. Test targets are derived from this model according to different coverage criteria, chosen by the validation engineer. Once the test target is defined, the model is animated (using a boundary model-checking approach) in order to build a complete test case. This test generation process relies on a set-theoretic solver, named CLPS-BZ [3], interfaced with constraint logic programming.

---

[2] Available at `http://lifc.univ-fcomte.fr/~couchot/specs/gsm2.mch`.

We present in this section the principles of test target definition, and the associated coverage criteria. Then we introduce the CLPS-BZ solver. Finally, we present the test target conditions of consistency.

3.1   Definition of the Test Targets

The BZ-Testing-Tools approach considers a test case as the activation of a system behavior within a pertinent system state. This represents the *behavioral coverage*. In addition, a *decision coverage* is considered to cover the different possibilities of a disjunctive decision predicate, providing a specific coverage criterion. Finally, the *data coverage* is obtained by a boundary analysis of the data –input parameters and state variables– involved in the behavior. These three items give the outline of the subsection.

Behavioral Coverage. A behavior can be seen as an operation in which no branching exists. It is computed as a path in the control flow graph of a B machine operation, in which each branching structure (IF, ASSERT or CHOICE substitutions) creates a choicepoint. The behavioral coverage of the B machine consists in producing one test target for the activation of each behavior, by considering an *activation condition* for each behavior, as the conjunction of all the predicates along the considered path.

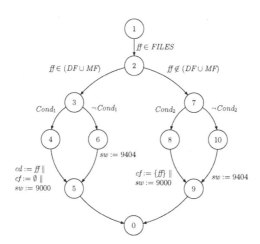

Fig. 2. Control-flow graph of the *SELECT_FILE* operation

The Fig. 2 presents the control flow graph of the SELECT_FILE operation, from the running example, where $Cond_1$ is the first IF condition that is

$$(cd = mf \wedge ff \in DF) \vee (cd = dg \wedge ff = dt) \vee$$
$$(cd = dt \wedge ff = dg) \vee (cd \in DF \wedge ff = mf) \vee$$
$$(ff = cd) \vee (ff = mf)$$

and $Cond_2$ is the second IF condition that is

$$(f\!f \in EM \wedge cd = m\!f) \vee (f\!f \in ED \wedge cd \in DF \wedge FA(f\!f) = cd) \vee f\!f \in cf.$$

Definition 1 (Set of Activation Conditions). *The set of activation conditions of a substitution is the set of activation conditions for each behavior extracted from an operation. We denote by act(Op) the set of activation conditions for an operation Op.*

Decision Coverage. The decision coverage is achieved by performing different rewritings on the disjunctive predicates labeling the control-flow graph.

We consider four rewritings, each one deserving a particular decision coverage criterion. Table 1 distinguishes these rewritings. It consists in creating a bounded choice ([]) between the different elements of the rewriting, expanding the control flow graph in as many subgraphs.

Table 1. Definition of the rewritings of the disjunctive predicates

Id	Rewriting of $P_1 \vee P_2$	Decision Coverage
1	$P_1 \vee P_2$	DC and SC
2	$P_1 \; [] \; P_2$	D/CC
3	$(P_1 \wedge \neg P_2) \; [] \; (\neg P_1 \wedge P_2)$	FPC
4	$(P_1 \wedge P_2) \; [] \; (P_1 \wedge \neg P_2) \; [] \; (\neg P_1 \wedge P_2)$	MCC

Rewriting 1 (RW1, for short) consists in leaving all the disjunctions unchanged. This rewriting satisfies the Decision Coverage (DC, for short), and Statement Coverage (SC) criterion. Rewriting 2 (RW2, for short) consists in creating a choice between the two predicates. Thus, the first branch and the second branch independently have to succeed when being evaluated. This rewriting satisfies the Decision/Condition Coverage criterion (D/CC) since it satisfies the DC and the Condition Coverage (CC) criteria. Rewriting 3 (RW3, for short) consists in creating an exclusive choice between the two predicates. Only one of the sub-predicates of the disjunction is checked at one time. This rewriting satisfies the Full Predicate Coverage (FPC) [11] criterion. Rewriting 4 (RW4, for short) consists in testing all the possible values for the two sub-predicates to satisfy the disjunction. This rewriting satisfies the Multiple Condition Coverage (MCC) criterion.

The decomposition of operation *SELECT_FILE* from the example into RW1-behaviors is given by Table 2.

Data Coverage. The data coverage consists in performing a boundary analysis of the data that are involved in the behaviors, depending on their types. A boundary analysis consists in selecting a data value at its extremum (either minimum or maximum) of its domain within the context of the behavior activation. The extremum is chosen depending on the data types; basically, atoms are enumerated, integers are selected at their bounds, sets are selected as their

Table 2. RW1-Behaviors extracted from the example

Behavior	Activation Condition
b_1	$ff \in \mathit{FILES} \wedge ff \in \mathit{MF} \cup \mathit{DF} \wedge ((cd = mf \wedge ff \in \mathit{DF}) \vee$ $(cd = dg \wedge ff = dt) \vee (cd = dt \wedge ff = dg) \vee$ $(cd \in \mathit{DF} \wedge ff = mf) \vee (ff = cd) \vee (ff = mf))$
b_2	$ff \in \mathit{FILES} \wedge ff \in \mathit{MF} \cup \mathit{DF} \wedge (cd \neq mf \vee ff \notin \mathit{DF}) \wedge$ $(cd \neq dg \vee ff \neq dt) \wedge (cd \neq dt \vee ff \neq dg)$ $(cd \notin \mathit{DF} \vee ff \neq mf) \wedge (ff \neq cd) \wedge (ff \neq mf)$
b_3	$ff \in \mathit{FILES} \wedge ff \notin \mathit{MF} \cup \mathit{DF} \wedge ((ff \in \mathit{EM} \wedge cd = mf) \vee$ $(ff \in \mathit{ED} \wedge cd \in \mathit{DF} \wedge \mathit{FA}(ff) = cd) \vee ff \in cf)$
b_4	$ff \in \mathit{FILES} \wedge ff \notin \mathit{MF} \cup \mathit{DF} \wedge (ff \notin \mathit{EM} \vee cd \neq mf) \wedge$ $(ff \notin \mathit{ED} \vee cd \notin \mathit{DF} \vee \mathit{FA}(ff) \neq cd) \wedge ff \notin cf$

minimal and maximal cardinality. This data selection is recursively performed on the elements of pairs.

It is important to notice that this step requires finite data structures so that a bound for data can be selected.

3.2   The CLPS-BZ Constraint Solver

Originally designed to animate B machines, the CLPS-BZ constraint solver [3] is a set-theoretic solver combined with a finite domain solver on integers. It allows the acquisition and the evaluation of constraints written using B-like basic operators.

CLPS-BZ uses an arc-consistency algorithm, whose worst-case complexity is $\mathcal{O}(ek^3)$ where e is the number of constraints and k is the cardinality of the largest data domain, for checking the satisfiability of the constraint system. Such an algorithm checks only the consistency between the adjacent edges within the constraint graph. As a consequence, the consistency of the whole constraint system can only be ensured by the enumeration of the solutions, performed using a forward-checking labeling algorithm, whose complexity is $\mathcal{O}(ek^2)$.

3.3   Behavior Consistency Condition

Each test case targets one behavior, extracted from the machine operations. Thus, a test case is relevant only if the target behavior is activable, i.e. its activation condition is consistent. The following definition formalizes this notion of behavior consistency, in the context of the machine properties and invariant.

Definition 2 (Behavior Consistency). *A behavior b_i is consistent iff the formula*

$$P \wedge B \wedge (\exists X . I \wedge a_i) \tag{1}$$

is satisfiable, where P (resp. I) is the predicate of the PROPERTIES (resp. INVARIANT) clause, X is the tuple of the machine state variables, a_i is the activation condition corresponding to the behavior b_i and B is the formula

$$\bigwedge_E \bigwedge_{e_j, e_k \in E}^{1 \leqslant j < k \leqslant l} e_j \neq e_k$$

precising that the elements of the set E are pairwise distinct, for each set $E = \{e_1, \ldots, e_l\}$ enumerated in the SETS clause.

/* Part coming from the PROPERTIES clause P */
$MF \subseteq FILES \wedge DF \subseteq FILES \wedge EM \subseteq FILES \wedge ED \subseteq FILES \wedge$
$MF \cap DF = \emptyset \wedge MF \cap EM = \emptyset \wedge MF \cap ED = \emptyset \wedge DF \cap EM = \emptyset \wedge$
$DF \cap ED = \emptyset \wedge EM \cap ED = \emptyset \wedge FILES = MF \cup DF \cup EM \cup ED \wedge$
$FA \in ED \longrightarrow DF \wedge mf \in FILES \wedge dg \in FILES \wedge dt \in FILES \wedge$
$MF = \{mf\} \wedge DF = \{dg, dt\} \wedge e_i \in EM \wedge$
$\exists\, cd, cf\,.$ /* Part coming from the INVARIANT clause I */   (2)
   $cd \in (MF \cup DF) \wedge cf \subseteq (EM \cup ED) \wedge \mathbf{card}(cf) \leq 1 \wedge$
   $\big(cf = \emptyset \vee (cf \neq \emptyset \wedge cf \subseteq ED \wedge cd \in DF) \vee$
     $(cf \neq \emptyset \wedge cf \subseteq EM \wedge cd = mf)\big) \wedge$
$\exists\, ff\,.$ /* Activation condition of behavior b_4 */
   $ff \in FILES \wedge ff \notin MF \cup DF \wedge (ff \notin EM \vee cd \neq mf) \wedge$
   $(ff \notin ED \vee cd \notin DF \vee FA(ff) \neq cd) \wedge ff \notin cf$

Fig. 3. b_4 consistency proof obligation

For instance, Fig. 3 shows the consistency condition of the fourth RW1-behavior extracted from our example, provided the *FILES* set is enumerated.

Up to now, all the sets were enumerated and the existential quantifications in (1) were expanded in disjunctions. This consistency was checked by the CLPS-BZ solver and the inconsistent behaviors were used to eliminate test cases.

However, the detection of many inconsistent behaviors could be a sign of weakness of the formal model with respect to the testing methodology, namely a too narrow instantiation of its data structures. Our purpose is to improve the testing methodology by adding a tool that guesses a "good" instantiation. We therefore formalize in the next section a notion of most general instantiation for a B model, that makes all its behaviors activable.

4   Most General Instantiation

Intuitively, we are looking for an instantiation of a B machine that makes each of its behaviors activable from at least one of the reachable machine states.

Under the assumption that the reachable states are characterized by the IN-VARIANT clause, this condition can be formalized by the following definition, where $F(X_i)$ denotes the formula obtained from formula F by replacing the tuple of state variables X with X_i.

Definition 3 (Activation Condition). *All the behaviors of a B machine are activable if*

$$P \wedge B \wedge \bigwedge_{\{i | b_i \text{ is a machine behavior}\}} \exists X_i \,.\, I(X_i) \wedge a_i(X_i) \qquad (3)$$

is satisfiable for each behavior b_i, where P, B and a_i have the same meaning as in Sect. 3.3 and X_i is a distinct tuple of state variables for each behavior b_i.

The tuple of state variables in (3) is distinct for each behavior, because each behavior may be activable from a different reachable state.

Now, a model of (3) is an instantiation with enumerated sets of all the B machine parameters and abstract sets. We suggest to call it the **most general instantiation**, since it makes the instantiated machine as general as the parameterized one, for a given testing coverage criterion. Another feature of this instantiation is that it minimizes the sum of the cardinalities of the instantiating sets.

In practice, the method to compute this most general instantiation is twofold. First of all, the behaviors that are not activable for any instantiation are detected by checking the satisfiability of (1) without enumerating the parametric sets. The specifier is informed that his/her specification contains some dead code whatever the parameter values are. Then, the inconsistent behaviors are ignored and a constraint solver is combined with an instantiation procedure to find an instantiation that make all the remaining consistent behaviors activable in a reachable state.

The next sections detail the techniques involved in this method.

5   Checking the Consistency

Finding a model for (3) may take benefit of any satisfiability decision procedure: a negative answer suggests that the specifier should modify the model whereas a positive one ensures the existence of a general instantiation and is therefore an intermediate step before computing it. This satisfiability can be checked either with a suitable prover or with a constraint solver, provided the data structures are first made finite.

In the proof-based approach, we exploit the existing bam2rv[3] tool that translates set-theoretic formulas into first order equational formulas ready to be discharged in the haRVey prover [6]. The choice of this tool is motivated by its compliance with set-theoretic formulas and its scalability [5].

Before applying the constraint-based approach, each machine parameter is constrained to be equal to (or included in) an arbitrary enumerated superset. For instance, the set $S = \{a01, a02, a03, \ldots, a30\}$ can be used as a superset of *FILES*, since the informal specification [8] allows a maximum of 30 files to exist on the card. The resulting constraints are then discharged into the CLPS-BZ solver, already used in the model-based testing methodology presented in Sect. 3.

In practice, for efficiency reasons, we first check whether each behavior is consistent, and then check the satisfiability of (3) restricted to the consistent behaviors. Table 3 summarizes the experimental results[4] obtained with each tool

---

[3] http://lifc.univ-fcomte.fr/~giorgett/Rech/Software/bam2rv/index.html
[4] Run on a P4 2.4 GHz with 640Mb RAM.

applied to the RW1-behaviors from Table 2. The third (resp. fourth) column gives the time consumed to check the satisfiability with the constraint $FILES \subseteq S$ (resp. $FILES = S$). The fifth column gives the first instantiation found by CLPS-BZ. The last column gives the time consumed by the proof-based approach with haRVey.

Table 3. Consistency results for the RW1-behaviors

Behavior	Satisfiable?	CLPS$_\subseteq$	CLPS$_=$	Instance	haRVey
b_1	yes	0.4 s	0.3 s	$FILES = \{dg, dt, mf\}, ff = dg,$ $DF = \{dg, dt\}, MF = \{mf\},$ $ED = \emptyset, EM = \{e_i\}, FA = \emptyset$	0.4 s
b_2	no	0.3 s	0.3 s		0.4 s
b_3	yes	0.4 s	0.3 s	$FILES = \{dg, dt, mf, e_i\}, ff = e_i,$ $DF = \{dg, dt\}, MF = \{mf\},$ $ED = \emptyset, EM = \{e_i\}, FA = \emptyset$	0.5 s
b_4	yes	> 1 h	0.5 s		0.3 s

Globally, an interesting result is that proving a consistency **for any value** of *FILES* with the haRVey prover is not much more time consuming than checking it with CLPS-BZ **for a unique enumeration** of *FILES*, with 30 elements.

A second result is that all the methods answer that the behavior b_2 is not activable. As announced in Sect. 2, the corresponding behavior extracted from the larger model `gsm2.mch` is proved to be activable by haRVey (or by CLPS-BZ after enumerating *FILES* with 30 elements) in less than one second.

Finally, the main result concerns b_4. For that behavior the enumeration strategy of CLPS-BZ takes too much time (more than one hour) when *FILES* is constrained to be included in S. It is so because the detection by arc-consistency is not sufficient and CLPS-BZ continues by instantiating from the initial *FILES* enumeration, which is too large. The next section will address this problem. For the moment, since haRVey gives a result, the combination of both tools is satisfactory.

The next step of the method, checking the satisfiability of (3), presents the same difficulty as the former one, since (3) is just a generalization of (1) to many behaviors. Hence, in (3), a coarse choice of the superset size would again make the solver diverge. The next section presents a method that aims at avoiding such a combinatorial explosion by restricting the size of the superset S.

6   Sort-Based Instantiation

The previous section ends with the idea that coarsely bounding the size of the machine parameter may make the instantiation process diverge. In order to reduce this problem, this section puts a bridge between the investigated challenge of guessing a "good" instantiation and classical methods from automated reasoning in first order many-sorted logics.

The underlying idea is that the sets we want to instantiate often come from a partitioning of more global sets, hence are pairwise disjoint. Consequently, they can be seen as sorts and the consistency and activation conditions can be seen as formulas to satisfy in a first order many-sorted logic. In such a logic, the choice of an Herbrand universe for each sort corresponds to the instantiation of the associated set. Another use of a many-sorted version of the Herbrand interpretation to verify software can be found for instance in [9].

Let us now detail the instantiation method derived from this simple idea and illustrate it on the consistency condition of behavior b_4.

A static analysis of the CONSTANTS and PROPERTIES clauses can detect that some abstract sets partition larger abstract sets. This analysis starts with the abstract sets declared as machine parameters (or in the SETS clause). They are considered as primary sorts. Then, the analysis iterates the following two steps: firstly, it considers that any set inclusion whose right member is a sort defines its left member as a sort too; secondly, it checks whether the sorts introduced so are pairwise disjoint. In our example, it is obvious that the primary sort is *FILES* and that the other sorts are *MF, DF, EM* and *ED*. The predicates defining the sorts are then removed from the formula. In (2), the first three lines of predicates are removed so.

It is now possible to assign one sort or more to each variable. We consider the non obvious case where a variable may have many sorts i.e. when it belongs to (or is included into) a union of sets. For instance the predicate $cd \in MF \cup DF$ is interpreted by *cd* is either of sort *MF* or of sort *DF*. Similarly, the elements of *cf* are either of sort *EM* or of sort *ED*.

Each set-theoretic predicate (cardinality, inclusion, equality) is firstly translated into a formula where the sole predicates are equality and membership. The set equality is decomposed into two inclusions. Each union (resp. intersection) is subsequently translated into a disjunction (resp. conjunction). For instance

$$cf \subseteq (EM \cup ED) \wedge \mathtt{card}(cf) \leqslant 1 \qquad (4)$$

is translated into

$$\forall x . (x \in cf \Rightarrow (x \in EM \vee x \in ED)) \wedge \forall x, y . (x \in cf \wedge y \in cf) \Rightarrow x = y \qquad (5)$$

where x and y are fresh variables whose sort comes from *cf*, i.e. is either *EM* or *ED*.

We are left with deciding the satisfiability of the formula in a many-sorted first order logic with equality and membership. We classically begin with considering a Skolem form of the formula. For instance, the quantifications on *cd*, *cf* and $f\!f$ in (2) are removed and these variables are replaced with the fresh constants $\overline{cd}$, $\overline{cf}$ and $\overline{f\!f}$.

A formula of a first order many-sorted logic is satisfiable if and only if it has a many-sorted Herbrand model [9]. We compute then the *graph of sort dependency* whose nodes are labelled with the sorts and whose oriented edges encode the dependency between sorts: a sort s depends of the sorts $s_1, \ldots, s_n$ if there is a functional symbol whose signature is $s_1, \ldots, s_n \rightarrow s$. These functional symbols are either already present in the quantified formula or are introduced by the skolemization step. For instance, Figure 4 shows the graph resulting from the skolemization of (2). It contains only one edge, which goes from the sort ED to the sort DF since the sole non constant functional symbol in the skolemization of (2) is FA.

Fig. 4. Graph of sort dependency of (2)

We compute then the Herbrand universe by firstly considering the constants of each sort and secondly building new terms with the functional symbols in the formula in accordance with the sorts. The computation (and thus the resulting Herbrand universe) is finite if and only if the graph of sort dependency is acyclic, which is the case for our example.

An interesting point in this procedure is the treatment of terms that may have many sorts, like $\overline{cd}$ with the sorts MF and DF in our example. This corresponds to a disjunction that a thinner notion of behavior could decompose. We suggest in this case to add a distinct fresh constant for each sort. For instance, for the behavior b_4, cd_{4a} and cd_{4b} are respectively added in the sorts MF and DF.

This choice has the advantage that it is meaningful for the specifier: each new constant corresponds to a distinct execution case in a behavior. Moreover, the constant name can encode this case (like a and b in our example), thus offering a complete traceability of the origin of each constant. The result is obviously an upper approximation of the desired instantiation, but it reflects the degree of precision of the coverage criterion that has produced these behaviors.

One may think that this procedure could be refined by interpreting each enumerated set on its set of constants (for instance MF interpreted on $\{mf\}$ and DF on $\{dg, dt\}$). However, such an optimization would require equating two constants and propagating this information through terms and sorts. Since this propagation is already developed in the CLPS-BZ solver, we suggest not to implement this optimization, but let the solver do the remaining work.

For the behavior b_4 of the running example, the sort-based instantiation is $MF \subseteq \{mf, \overline{cd_{4a}}, \overline{ff_{4a}}\}$, $DF \subseteq \{dg, dt, \overline{cd_{4b}}, \overline{ff_{4b}}, FA(\overline{ff_{4d}})\}$, $EM \subseteq \{e_i, \overline{ff_{4c}}\}$ and $ED \subseteq \{\overline{ff_{4d}}\}$. Then, starting from this result, CLPS-BZ finds the following most general instantiation, $MF = \{mf\}$, $DF = \{dg, dt\}$, $EM = \{e_i\}$, $ED = \{\overline{ff_{4d}}\}$, later called mgi_1, in less than one second.

Finally, the sort-based instantiation found for the conjunction of the three consistent behaviors b_1, b_3 and b_4 is $MF \subseteq \{mf, \overline{cd_{1a}}, \overline{ff_{1a}}, \overline{cd_{3a}}, \overline{ff_{3a}}, \overline{cd_{4a}}, \overline{ff_{4a}}\}$, $DF \subseteq \{dg, dt, \overline{cd_{1b}}, \overline{ff_{1b}}, FA(\overline{ff_{1d}}), \overline{cd_{3b}}, \overline{ff_{3b}}, FA(\overline{ff_{3d}}), \overline{cd_{4b}}, \overline{ff_{4b}}, FA(\overline{ff_{4d}})\}$, $EM \subseteq \{e_i, \overline{ff_{1c}}, \overline{ff_{3c}}, \overline{ff_{4c}}\}$ and $ED \subseteq \{\overline{ff_{1d}}, \overline{ff_{3d}}, \overline{ff_{4d}}\}$. Again in less than one second, CLPS-BZ finds a most general instantiation that appears to be mgi_1 again.

7   Conclusion and Future Work

The global aim of the present work was to unburden the specifier from instantiating the parameters of his/her formal model, when this model is designed to guide the automated generation of tests. When this formal model is a B machine, it proposed a way to assist the instantiation phase, by guessing an enumeration that is sufficient to be employed within the test generation process. The resulting enumeration is general enough for activating all the consistent behaviors extracted from the B machine operations. If it exists, then this enumeration serves to initialize the SUT. Otherwise, it means that no data is suitable for testing the wholeness of the SUT. The specifier is then invited to cut his/her model in separate parts, in a way that remains to be defined.

This approach is related to test data generation with tools such as Korat [4]. Korat aims at producing complex Java structures (such as balanced trees, etc.) from a boolean method describing the properties of the structure and a bound on the size of the structure. This approach aims at providing test data as inputs for Java unit tests. Basically, one may think that our approach is similar, since we both rely on constraint solving for instantiating the data structures. Nevertheless, the bound used by Korat is user-defined, whereas our approach proposes to automatically compute it.

For conciseness, this work has been restricted to the RW1 decision coverage, but it is directly extensible to the RW2, RW3 and RW4 ones. Furthermore, the sort-based instantiation is presented for one level of sorts, but holds for many levels too. Since the key is an acyclic graph of sorts, the method is suitable for many data structures like arrays, trees of bounded depth (as seen in the gsm2.mch) ...

It is important to notice that although our approach has been presented in the context of model-based testing, it can be employed for other purposes such as model-checking using ProB [10]. Indeed, the ProB model-checker also requires finite data domains. Such an instantiation phase could be performed as a preprocess, that would allow all the operations to be activable, improving the results of a model verification.

References

1. F. Ambert, F. Bouquet, S. Chemin, S. Guenaud, B. Legeard, F. Peureux, N. Vacelet, and M. Utting. BZ-TT: A Tool-Set for Test Generation from Z and B using Contraint Logic Programming. In *Formal Approaches to Testing of Software, FATES 2002 workshop of CONCUR'02*, pages 105–120, 2002.
2. E. Bernard, B. Legeard, X. Luck, and F. Peureux. Generation of test sequences from formal specifications: GSM 11-11 standard case study. *International Journal of Software Practice and Experience*, 34(10):915–948, 2004.
3. F. Bouquet, B. Legeard, and F. Peureux. CLPS-B: A constraint solver to animate a B specification. *International Journal on Software Tools for Technology Transfer, STTT*, 6(2):143–157, 2004.
4. C. Boyapati, S. Khurshid, and D. Marinov. Korat: automated testing based on java predicates. In *ISSTA'02: Proceedings of the ACM SIGSOFT international symposium on Software testing and analysis*, pages 123–133. ACM Press, 2002.

5. J.-F. Couchot, D. Déharbe, A. Giorgetti, and S. Ranise. Scalable automated proving and debugging of set-based specifications. *Journal of the Brazilian Computer Society (JBCS)*, 9(2):17–36, 2003. ISSN 0104-6500.

6. D. Déharbe and S. Ranise. Applying light-weight theorem proving to debugging and verifying pointer programs. In *ENTCS*, volume 86. Elsevier, 2003.

7. I.K. El-Far and J.A. Whittaker. Model-based software testing. *Encyclopedia of Software Engineering*, 1:825–837, 2002.

8. European Telecommunications Standards Institute. *GSM Technical Specification*, 1995. http://www.ttfn.net/techno/smartcards/gsm11-11.pdf.

9. Pascal Fontaine and E. Pascal Gribomont. Decidability of invariant validation for parameterized systems. In *Tools and Algorithms for Construction and Analysis of Systems (TACAS)*, volume 2619 of *LNCS*, pages 97–112. Springer, 2003.

10. M. Leuschel and M. Butler. ProB: A model checker for B. In *FME 2003: Formal Methods*, volume 2805 of *LNCS*, pages 855–874. Springer, 2003.

11. A. Jefferson Offutt, Yiwei Xiong, and Shaoying Liu. Criteria for generating specification-based tests. In *5th International Conference on Engineering of Complex Computer Systems (ICECCS '99)*, pages 119–. IEEE Computer Society, 1999.

Verification of LTL on B Event Systems⋆

Julien Groslambert

Université de Franche-Comté - LIFC - CNRS
16 route de Gray - 25030 Besançon cedex France
groslambert@lifc.univ-fcomte.fr

Abstract. This paper proposes a way to verify temporal properties expressed in LTL (Linear Temporal Logic) on B Event Systems. The method consists in generating a B representation of the Büchi automaton associated with the LTL property to verify. We establish the consistency of the generated event system implies the satisfaction of the LTL property on the executions of the original event system. We also characterize the subset of LTL preserved by the B refinement and we propose another refinement relation, with necessary and sufficient condition for preserving any given LTL property.

Keywords: LTL, Büchi Automaton, Verification, Refinement.

1 Introduction

Formal modelling is a widely spread practice in the software developpment. Modelization languages are used to formally describe the systems to study, leading to safer implementations.

The B method [1] is an incremental software engineering process, starting from the building of an abstract system which is later on refined to reach an implementation. For each step, properties have to be checked to ensure the correctness of the specification. In the case of a B abstract event systems, the specifier has to ensure that the invariant is established by the initialization and preserved by the execution of an event. This is the *verification process* which aims at checking the correctness of the specification.

Our aim is to check that the model has an expected behavior, i.e., satisfies the requirements of an informal specification. For that, one can express the requirement as formal properties that are checked on the model. A fundamental framework for such a verification is provided by temporal logics, describing the behavior of the specification over (discrete) time. In [4], Abrial and Mussat addresses the verification of temporal requirements in the B framework, by introducing a dynamic modality $P \rightsquigarrow Q$ intuitively meaning that, after a state where P holds, a state where Q holds must inevitably be reached in the future.

In this paper, we extend the work of Abrial and Mussat by addressing the verification of properties expressed in Linear Temporal Logic (LTL) and we study

---

⋆ Research partially founded by the french ACI *Geccoo*.

J. Julliand and O. Kouchnarenko (Eds.): B 2007, LNCS 4355, pp. 109–124, 2006.

their preservation by the B refinement of event systems. The three contributions of the paper are: (1) A method, close to the one of Alpern and Schneider [7], allowing the verification of LTL properties within the B framework without extending it. The approach is the following: from an event system M and a LTL property ϕ, we build an event system M_ϕ such that the consistency of M_ϕ implies that all the execution paths of M satisfies ϕ. The method is shown to be sound; (2) A characterization of the LTL fragment that is preserved by the B refinement; (3) A new refinement relation, called the ϕ-refinement, that is both necessary and sufficient to preserve a given property ϕ.

This paper is composed as follows. Section 2 recalls notions about B event systems, defines LTL syntax and semantics and recalls well-known results about these notions. Section 3 explains how a LTL formula can be verified within the B framework. The verification is done through the expression in a B machine of the automaton associated with the LTL formula. We establish the soundness of the methodology. Section 4 recalls the notion of B refinement and define the notion of preservation of LTL properties during the refinement. Section 5 characterizes the subset of LTL preserved by the B refinement, whereas Section 6 proposes a new refinement relation, the ϕ-refinement. Section 7 concludes and presents the perspectives for future work.

Nota bene. Proofs of theorems and propositions are not included in this paper but can be found in [13].

2   Preliminaries

This section introduces the theoretical background of the paper. First, we recall in Sect 2.1 general notions about B event systems. Section 2.2 defines the notions of traces and execution paths associated to event systems. Section 2.3 presents the Linear Temporal Logic (LTL) and gives its syntax and semantics over a path of an event system. Section 2.4 presents the structure of Büchi automata, used for the verification of LTL.

2.1   B Event System

First introduced by J.-R Abrial [1,2], Event B is both a formal development method and a specification language. B event systems are particular B machines where all operations are *events*. Intuitively, an *event* has no precondition and can only modify the internal state of the system. For formally defining a B event system, we need to recall the notion of *Generalized Substitution* and *Weakest Precondition Calculus*.

B predicates on a set of variables x are denoted $P(x), Q(x), \ldots$. When there is no ambiguity on x, we simply denote $P, Q, \ldots$. We consider in this paper the following primitive generalized substitutions, (denoted $S, T, \ldots$): Simple or multiple variable substitution $(x, y \ldots := E, F \ldots)$; guarded substitution $(P \implies T)$; sequence $(S; T)$; bounded choice $(S[]T)$ and unbounded choice $(@z.S)$. Given a substitution S and a post-condition Q we are able to compute the weakest precondition P such that, if P is satisfied, Q is satisfied after the execution of S.

The weakest precondition, defined in [1] is denoted $[S]Q$. We denote by $\langle S \rangle$ the expression $\neg[S]\neg Q$, intuitively meaning that if $\langle S \rangle$ is satisfied, there exists a computation of S terminating in a state satisfying Q. Given a B generalized substitution S, there exists three particular predicates: a *termination* predicate $\mathsf{trm}(S)$ denoting the termination of S, a *pre-post predicate*, denoted $\mathsf{prd}_x(S)$ relying the values x before the execution of S with the value x' after the execution of S; and a *feasibility* predicate $\mathsf{fis}(S)$.

Definition 1 $(\mathsf{prd}_x, \mathsf{fis}(S), \mathsf{trm}(S)$ [1]$)$. *Let S be a substitution. The predicates* prd_x, $\mathsf{fis}(S)$, $\mathsf{trm}(S)$ *are defined as follows*

$$\mathsf{prd}_x(S) = \langle S \rangle (x = x') \qquad \mathsf{fis}(S) = \langle S \rangle (true) \qquad \mathsf{trm}(S) = [S](true)$$

In the rest of the paper, *events* are characterized as follows:

Definition 2 (Events). *An* event e *is defined by a predicate G, called the* guard *of e and a generalized substitution T called the* action *of e such that $G \Rightarrow \mathsf{fis}(T)$ and $\mathsf{trm}(T) \Leftrightarrow true$.*

From now on, given an event e, we denote $\mathsf{guard}(e)$ its guard and $\mathsf{action}(e)$ its action. A B event system is defined as follows.

Definition 3 (B event system).
An event system M *is a tuple $< x_M, I_M, \mathsf{Init}_M, \mathsf{Interface}_M >$ where*

- x_M *is a set of variables;*
- I_M *is a predicate over x_M called* invariant;
- Init_M *is a substitution called* initialization;
- $\mathsf{Interface}_M$ *is a set of events.*

Figure 1 displays an example of B event system, describing a system composed of two platforms: an *input* platform and an *output* (respectively modeled by two booleans De and Dt). A platform is empty (resp. busy, i.e., a piece is on the platform) is modeled by a value set to FALSE (resp. TRUE. An event load permits to load a piece on the input platform. An event unload puts the piece on the output platform and an event discard leaves out the piece from the output platform. In this paper, we are interested in the verification of *event systems without deadlock* since we aim at reasonning over infinite executions. An event system is without deadlock if in each state, at least one event can be executed.

Definition 4 (B system without deadlock). *An event system M is* without deadlock *if:*

$$I_M \Rightarrow \bigvee_{e \in \mathsf{Interface}_M} \mathsf{guard}(e)$$

We only consider, from now on, B event systems without deadlock, since we reason about infinite executions of event. It is straightforward to notice that the B event system displayed in Fig. 1 is without deadlock.

A fundamental notion for B event systems is the notion of *consistency*. We say that a B event system is consistent if the initialisation establishes the invariant and if each event of the system preserves it.

```
MACHINE
    Robot                                    Unload = SELECT Dt = TRUE
VARIABLES                                                 ∧ De = FALSE
    De,Dt                                           THEN Dt := FALSE
INVARIANT                                               || De := TRUE
    Dt ∈ BOOL ∧ De ∈ BOOL                        END;
INITIALISATION
    Dt := FALSE || De := FALSE            Discard = SELECT De = TRUE
OPERATIONS                                           THEN De := FALSE
    Load = SELECT Dt = FALSE                         END
           THEN Dt := TRUE        END
           END;
```

Fig. 1. Example of a B event system

Definition 5 (Consistency of an Event System [1]). *An event system M is* consistent, *denoted* $M \models true$ *if* $[\mathsf{INIT}_M]I$ *and* $\forall e \in \mathsf{Interface}_M.(I_M \Rightarrow [e]I_M)$.

In [4], Abrial and Mussat have introduced a dynamic modality *leadsto*, denoted $P \rightsquigarrow Q$.

It intuitively means that when a state satisfying P is reached, there is inevitably in the future a state satisfying Q. Figure 2 displays the declaration of the modality $P \rightsquigarrow Q$. Notice that the user must provide a variant V that must decrease for each event, for proving that P leads inevitably to Q (as in a termination proof). Although the *leadsto* modality permits to express some temporal require-

Fig. 2.

ment on B event systems, it is not expressive enough to directly specify all the requirement we are interested in.

Temporal requirements on the example. Our aim is to verify that a B event system satisfies a temporal property. We illustrate our approach by addressing the verification of the following three properties on the example given in Fig 1:

$$An\ unload\ can\ only\ occurs\ when\ the\ output\ platform\ is\ free \qquad (\phi_S)$$

$$When\ the\ output\ platform\ is\ not\ free,\ it\ is\ inevitably\ free \qquad (\phi_{L1})$$

$$If\ after\ a\ certain\ time,\ there\ is\ always\ at\ least\ one\ piece\ on\ the\ system,$$
$$then\ both\ platforms\ are\ infinitely\ often\ busy \qquad (\phi_{L2})$$

These properties have a semantics over the *execution paths* of the event system. The next subsection defines the notion of *trace* and execution *path*, on which these properties will be formally expressed.

2.2   Traces and Execution

LTL formulae are defined on infinite executions [17]. Then, we first define the notion of *trace* of a B event system. Intuitively, a trace of a system M is an infinite sequence of events starting with the initialisation. Notice that our approach could be extended to B event systems with deadlock, since a finite execution can be extended into an infinite execution by infinitely repeating the last state [6].

Definition 6 (Trace). *An infinite sequence of events $e_0, e_1, e_2, \ldots, e_i, \ldots$ is a trace of the B event system M if and only if*

- e_0 *is the initialization of M and,*
- $\forall i > 0.(e_i \in \mathsf{Interface}_M)$ *and*
- $\forall i \geq 0.[e_0; \ldots; e_i]\mathsf{guard}(e_{i+1})$.

We denote by $\mathsf{Traces}(M)$ the set of all the infinite traces of M. Our trace definition differs from the one in [9] since we use a *complete* trace semantics. Given a trace, a *path* is a sequence of states reached during its execution.

Definition 7 (Path). *Let x_M be the state variables of a B event system M. Let $t = e_0, e_1, e_2, \ldots, e_i, \ldots \in \mathsf{Traces}(M)$ and let σ be an infinite sequence of variables value $s_0, s_1, s_2, \ldots$. Then, σ is a path associated to t, denoted $\sigma \in \mathsf{path}(t)$ if:*

- $[x'_M := s_0]\mathsf{prd}_{x_M}(\mathsf{action}(e_0))$
- $\forall i > 0.([x_M := s_{i-1}]\mathsf{guard}(e_i) \wedge [x_M, x'_M := s_{i-1}, s_i]\mathsf{prd}_{x_M}(\mathsf{action}(e_i)))$

Notice that several paths can be associated with a trace in $\mathsf{Traces}(M)$ because of the potential indeterminism of the events. In the rest of the paper, given a B event system M, we denote Σ_M the set of paths obtained from $\mathsf{Traces}(M)$ ($\Sigma_M = \{\sigma | \sigma \in \mathsf{path}(t) \wedge t \in \mathsf{Traces}(M)\}$). Given $\sigma \in \Sigma_M$, we denote by s_i the ith state of the path σ. Given an execution path σ the *path suffix* σ_i denotes the infinite path $s_i, s_{i+1}, s_{i+2} \ldots$. Given a state s_i and a predicate $P(x_M)$, s_i satisfies $P(x_M)$, denoted $s_i \models P(x_M)$ iff $[x_M := s_i]P(x_M)$.

The *leadsto* modality has a semantics over a path.

Definition 8 (*leadsto* Semantics). *The modality $P \rightsquigarrow Q$ is satisfied on a B event system M if $\forall i \geq 0.\forall \sigma \in \Sigma_M.(\sigma_i \models P \Rightarrow \exists j > i.(\sigma_j \models Q))$*

The LTL logic, expressing properties over paths, is now presented.

2.3   LTL

The basic LTL operators [17] are $\mathsf{F}\ P$ ("eventually P"), meaning that there is eventually a state in the future where P holds; $\mathsf{G}\ P$ ("always P"), meaning that all the states in the future satisfy P; $\mathsf{X}\ P$ ("next P") meaning the next state of the execution satisfies P; and finally $P\ \mathsf{U}\ Q$, meaning that all the future states satisfy P until a state where Q holds is reached.

Syntax of LTL. The syntax of LTL is built from atomic propositions, here B predicates, the logical connectives ($\wedge, \vee, \neg, \ldots$) and the above temporal operators.

Definition 9 (Syntax of LTL). *Let P be a B predicate, syntax of LTL is:*

$$\phi, \psi ::= \phi \wedge \psi \mid \neg\phi \mid \phi\mathsf{U}\psi \mid \mathsf{X}\phi \mid P$$

This is the minimal definition. We also add the following shortcuts.

$\phi \vee \psi$	$\equiv_{def}$	$\neg(\neg\phi \wedge \neg\psi)$	$\mathsf{F}\phi$	$\equiv_{def}$	$true\mathsf{U}\phi$
$\mathsf{G}\phi$	$\equiv_{def}$	$\neg\mathsf{F}\neg\phi$	$\psi\mathsf{R}\phi$	$\equiv_{def}$	$\neg(\neg\psi\mathsf{U}\neg\phi)$
$\phi \Rightarrow \psi$	$\equiv_{def}$	$\neg\phi \vee \psi$			

Semantics of LTL. We define the semantics of an LTL property ϕ with respect to an execution σ, denoted $\sigma \models \phi$, as follows.

Definition 10 (Semantics of LTL). *Let σ be an execution, let P be a B predicate, let $i \in \mathbb{N}$, let ϕ and ψ two LTL formulae. We inductively define $\sigma_i \models \phi$ as follows:*

$$
\begin{array}{|lll|lll|}
\hline
\sigma_i \models P & iff & s_i \models P & \sigma_i \models \phi \wedge \psi & iff & \sigma_i \models \phi \text{ and } \sigma_i \models \psi \\
\sigma_i \models \neg\phi & iff & \neg(\sigma_i \models \phi) & \sigma_i \models \psi\mathsf{U}\phi & iff & \exists j.(j \geq i \wedge \sigma_j \models \phi \wedge \\
\sigma_i \models \mathsf{X}\phi & iff & \sigma_{i+1} \models \phi & & & \forall k.(i \leq k < j \Rightarrow \sigma_k \models \psi)) \\
\hline
\end{array}
$$

Given a B event system M, we write $M \models \phi$, meaning that the event system M satisfies the LTL property ϕ if $\forall \sigma \in \Sigma_M.(\sigma \models \phi)$.

Notice that the modality $P \leadsto Q$ is equivalent to the property $\mathsf{G}(P \Rightarrow \mathsf{F}Q)$.

Examples of LTL formulae. In LTL, the temporal properties ϕ_S, ϕ_{L1} and ϕ_{L2} can be respectively expressed by

$$\mathsf{G}((\mathtt{Dt = true} \wedge \mathsf{X}\,(\mathtt{Dt = false})) \Rightarrow \mathtt{De = false}) \qquad (\phi_S)$$

$$\mathsf{G}(\mathtt{Dt = true} \Rightarrow (\mathsf{F}\ \mathtt{Dt = false})) \qquad (\phi_{L1})$$

$$(\mathsf{FG}(\mathtt{Dt = true} \vee \mathtt{De = true})) \Rightarrow (\mathsf{GF}\ (\mathtt{Dt = true} \wedge \mathtt{De = true}))) \qquad (\phi_{L2})$$

The LTL expressions of Property ϕ_S, ϕ_{L1} and ϕ_{L2} are explained as follows:

ϕ_S In all the states of the execution (G), if the input platform is not free ($\mathtt{Dt = true}$) and it is free in the next state ($\mathsf{X}\,(\mathtt{Dt = false})$), i.e., an unload occurs, then the output platform must be free ($\mathtt{De = false}$) in the current state.

ϕ_{L1} In all the states of the execution (G), if the input mechanism in not free ($\mathtt{Dt = true}$) then it must eventually (F) be free ($\mathtt{Dt = false}$) in the future.

ϕ_{L2} If, after a finite number a states, the system is never empty ($\mathsf{FG}(\mathtt{Dt = true} \vee \mathtt{De = true})$) then both platforms are busy infinitely often (GF).

Safety and Liveness Properties. A fundamental notion in LTL is the notion of safety and liveness property. Informally, a safety property means that "something bad must never happen", whereas liveness properties means "something good must eventually happen" [15]. Property ϕ_S is a safety property, since it expresses that a particular configuration – when a dischargement occurs and the evacuation platform is not free – must never happen. Property ϕ_{L1} is a liveness property, since when a particular configuration of the system occurs – the input mechanism is not free – the system must inevitably reach a state satisfying a property – here a state where the input mechanism is free. Property ϕ_{L2} is also a liveness property. Notice that Property ϕ_{L2} is a special kind of *liveness* called *fairness* in the Litterature [18].

Similarly to the verification of the *leadsto* primitive in [4], the verification of liveness properties needs that the specifier gives a wellfounded variant for proving the termination, whereas verification of safety properties does not. Therefore, we need to characterize safety and liveness formulae.

Characterization of safety and liveness. The characterization of safety and liveness properties is given by the following theorem, due to Alpern and Schneider.

Theorem 1 (Characterization of Safety and Liveness [6]). *The charac-terization of safety and liveness in the* LTL *is decidable.*

So, if the LTL property ϕ is a liveness property, the user must also provide a variant V. Our aim is, given a LTL property ϕ and an event system M, to prove that $M \models \phi$. For this verification, we first express LTL formulae in an intermediate formalism: Büchi automaton.

2.4 Büchi Automata

In this subsection, we give the definition of Büchi automata, further used for the verification of LTL properties and we give well known results about this class of automata.

Definition 11 (Büchi Automata). *A Büchi automaton $\mathcal{A}$ on an alphabet $\mathcal{P}red$ (here $\mathcal{P}red$ is a set of B predicates) is a tuple $< Q, q_0, Q_f, R >$ where Q is a finite set of states, $q_0 \in Q$ is the initial state, $Q_f \subseteq Q$ is the set of the all accepting states and $R \subseteq Q \times \mathcal{P}red \times Q$ is a finite set of transition rules.*

Then we define the *acceptance* a a Büchi automata.

Definition 12 (Synchronisation function and Acceptance). *Let $\mathcal{A} =< Q, q_0, Q_f, R >$ be a Büchi Automata. Let σ be a path. The synchronisation func-tion f from $\mathbb{N}$ to 2^Q is defined inductively as follows:*

- *$f(0) = \{q_0\}$*
- *$\forall i > 0.$ if $\sigma_{i-1} \models p$ and $q \in f(i-1)$ and $(q, p, q') \in R$, then $q' \in f(i)$.*

An execution σ is accepted by the automaton $\mathcal{A}$, denoted $\sigma \models \mathcal{A}$, if

$$\forall i \in \mathbb{N}. f(i) \neq \{\} \qquad (C_{Sync})$$

$$\text{There is an infinite set of indexes } i \text{ such that } f(i) \cap Q_f \neq \{\}. \qquad (C_{Buchi})$$

The condition C_{Buchi}, intuitively meaning that the path contains an infinite num-ber a states synchronized with an accepting state of the automamta, is called the acceptance condition of the Büchi Automaton.

Given a set Σ of executions, the set Σ is accepted by the automaton $\mathcal{A}$, denoted $\Sigma \models \mathcal{A}$, if $\forall \sigma \in \Sigma.(\sigma \models \mathcal{A})$. The link between LTL and Büchi automata is given by the following well-known theorem.

Theorem 2 (LTL and Büchi Automata). *For all LTL properties, there exists a Büchi Automaton $\mathcal{A}_\phi$ such that $\sigma \models \phi \Leftrightarrow \sigma \models \mathcal{A}_\phi$.*

Figure 3 displays the Büchi automata $\mathcal{A}_{\phi_S}$ and $\mathcal{A}_{\phi_{L_1}}$ associated respectively with the LTL properties ϕ_S and ϕ_{L1} [1]. The next section explains how to translate these automata into B.

---

[1] These Büchi automata have been obtained with the tool an on-line version of the tool LTL2BA [11] that can be found at http://www.ti.informatik.uni-kiel.de/~fritz/ABA-Simulation/ltl.cgi. The automaton obtained from ϕ_{L2} is not dis-played here for place reason. It is composed of 5 states and 12 transitions.

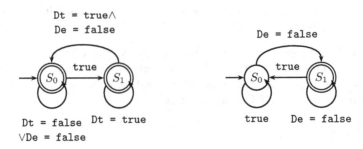

Fig. 3. Examples of Büchi automata for ϕ_S and ϕ_{L_1}

3 Expression of Büchi Automata in B

In this section, we show how to express a Büchi automaton as a B machine. Starting from a B event system $M =< x_M, I_M, \mathsf{Init}_M, \mathsf{Interface}_M >$ and a LTL property ϕ we first generate the Büchi automaton $\mathcal{A}_\phi$. Second from M and $\mathcal{A}_\phi =< Q, q_0, Q_f, R >$ (where $Q = \{q_0, \dots, q_n\}$), we create a new event system M_ϕ that includes a B model BA_ϕ of $\mathcal{A}_\phi$. In M_ϕ, events of M are synchronized with BA_ϕ. The correctness of M_ϕ implies that all the executions of M satisfies ϕ.

The generation of M_ϕ is done as follows(see Fig. 4): (i) we encode the states and transitions of the automaton in a B machine BA_ϕ; (ii) we synchronize the B event system M with BA_ϕ; (iii) we express the condition C_{Sync} of the Büchi automaton by an invariant; (iv) we express the condition C_{Buchi} of the Büchi automaton, by a *leadsto* modality.

(i) Encoding in B a Büchi automata consists in (a) encoding its states and (b) encoding its transitions.

    (a) In general, Büchi automata are indeterminist: a state of the event system M can be synchronized with several states q_i of the automata $\mathcal{A}_\phi$. Therefore, in the Machine BA_ϕ we declare a boolean variable $[\![q_i]\!]_B$ for each states q_i of $\mathcal{A}_\phi$. The value boolean variable $[\![q_i]\!]_B$ is $TRUE$ means that the current state of the event system is synchronized with $[\![q_i]\!]_B$. The first state of an execution must always be synchronized with the initial state q_0 of the automata. Therefore, we initialize the variable $[\![q_0]\!]_B$ to $TRUE$ and the others to $FALSE$.

    (b) The transitions of the automata are expressed by an operation *automata* that updates the boolean variables $[\![q_i]\!]_B$ representing the states w.r.t. the set of transition rules R of the Büchi automata. The operation *automata* takes as parameters the state variables x_M. The precondition of *automata* only contains the typing predicate of x_M (denoted by $\mathsf{Type}(x_m)$). The action of *automata* represents the transitions relations of R. For each $q' \in Q$ and for each rule $(q, p, q') \in R$, the variable $[\![q']\!]_B$ is set to $TRUE$ if $[\![q]\!]_B$ is $TRUE$ and if x_M satisfies the predicate p. Notice that a disjunction over the rules is needed because of the indeterminism of the automata: q' can be the right hand side of several rules.

```
MACHINE                                    SYSTEM
BA_φ                                        M_φ
VARIABLES                                   INCLUDES
    ⟦q₀⟧_B, ..., ⟦qₙ⟧_B                      BA_φ
INVARIANT                                   VARIABLES
⟦q₀⟧_B ∈ BOOL ∧...∧ ⟦qₙ⟧_B ∈ BOOL          x_M
INITIALIZATION                              INVARIANT
    ⟦q₀⟧_B := TRUE ‖                            I_M ∧ │(⟦q₀⟧_B = TRUE ∨...∨ ⟦qₙ⟧_B = TRUE)│_{I_φ}
    ⟦q₁⟧_B := FALSE ‖ ... ‖                  EVENTS
    ⟦qₙ⟧_B := FALSE                              e_i = SELECT guard(e_i)
OPERATION                                            THEN action(e_i) │‖ automata(x_M)│
automata(x_M) = PRE Type(x_m)                        END
    THEN                                    MODALITIES
    ⟦q₀⟧_B := ⋁_{q_j∈Q∧(q_j,p,q₀)∈R}             SELECT ⋀_{q∈S_f}(⟦q⟧_B = FALSE)
        (p(x_M) ∧ ⟦q_j⟧_B = TRUE)                   LEADSTO ¬(⋀_{q∈S_f}(⟦q⟧_B = FALSE))│_{D_φ}
    ‖...‖                                           VARIANT V_φ
    ⟦qₙ⟧_B := ⋁_{q_j∈Q∧(q_j,p,qₙ)∈R}             END
        (p(x_M) ∧ ⟦q_j⟧_B = TRUE)          END
    END
END
```

Fig. 4. The event system $M_φ$ and machine $BA_φ$

(ii) We *synchronize* the B machine $BA_φ$ with the event system M by including $BA_φ$ in $M_φ$ and by adding to each event of $M_φ$ an invocation of the operation *automata* in parallel of its action.

(iii) We check the condition C_{Sync}, i.e., each state of the execution must be synchronized with at least one state of $\mathcal{A}_φ$. For that, $M_φ$ contains an invariant $I_φ$ expressing the disjunction of the boolean variables $⟦q⟧_B$ representing the states of the automata. If a state s_i of the execution is not synchronized with any state of $\mathcal{A}_φ(f(i) = \{\})$, then all variables $⟦q⟧_B$ have the value false: the invariant $I_φ$ is not satisfied.

(iv) Finally, we check the Büchi acceptance condition (C_{Buchi}), i.e., that the path contains an infinite number of states synchronized with an accepting state of the automata, $M_φ$ contains a *leadsto* modality $D_φ$ ensuring that, if the current state is not synchronized with any accepting state ($⋀_{q∈S_f}(⟦q⟧_B = FALSE)$), it will in the future be synchronized with an accepting state. This is verified thanks to the decrease of the variant $V_φ$ given by the user.

The *consistency* of the event system $M_φ$ (see Def. 5,Sect. 2.1) implies that all the executions of M satisfy $φ$. The soundness of the method is established by the following Theorem.

Theorem 3 (Soundness). *Given a B event system M and a LTL property $φ$.*

$$\text{if} \quad M_φ \models TRUE \quad \text{then} \quad M \models φ$$

The proof uses the fact that executions of $M_φ$ are exactly the same as executions of M modulo the introduction of the new variables. The invariant $I_φ$ and the *leadsto* modality $D_φ$ ensure that conditions C_{Sync} and C_{Buchi} are satisfied. The example of the event system $M_φ$ and the machine $BA_φ$ for the event system in

Fig 1 and for the Properties ϕ_S can be found in [13]. This work is implemented as an extension of the JAG tool (see [12,14] Table 1 displays the results of the proof obligation generation of LTL properties on two B models, a communication protocol (T=1) and a Javacard application (Demoney).

4   LTL and Refinement

This section recalls notions about the refinement of B event systems (Sect. 4.1, characterizes the relation between abstract and refined traces (Sect. 4.2) and defines the preservation of LTL properties during the refinement (Sect. 4.3).

4.1   Event B Refinement

Refining an event system consists in refining both its state and its events. Variables of the refined system M_r and the abstract one M_a are related through an abstraction relation, expressed in terms of a *gluing* invariant $I_{M_r}(x_{M_a}, x_{M_r})$ connecting variables of the abstract event system to the variables of the refined one. Syntactically, the refined system M_r must at least contain all the events of its abstraction (Interface(M_a) $\subseteq$ Interface(M_r)). Given an event e in Interface(M_a), we denote e_a its abstract definition and e_r its refined definition. The refined event system may also contains a set E_{new} of *new* events (E_{new} = Interface(M_r) − Interface(M_a)). We now recall the proof obligations of the B event refinement.

Definition 13 (Refinement [2]). *Let M_a and M_r be two event systems, M_r is a refinement of M_a, denoted $M_a \sqsubseteq M_r$ if the following conditions are satisfied:*

C_{init}	Initialization refinement	$[Init_{M_r}] < Init_{M_a} > I_{M_r}$
C_{old}	Old events refinement	$\forall e \in$ Interface(M_a)$.(I_{M_a} \wedge I_{M_R} \Rightarrow [e_r] < e_a > I_{M_R})$
C_{new}	New events refinement	$\forall e \in E_{new}.(I_{M_a} \wedge I_{M_R} \Rightarrow [e_r] <$ skip $> I_{M_R})$
C_{dead}	No dead-lock introduction	$I_{M_a} \wedge I_{M_R} \Rightarrow (\bigvee_{e_a \in \text{Interface}(M_a)}$ guard(e_a) $\Rightarrow \bigvee_{e_r \in \text{Interface}(M_r)}$ guard(e_r)
C_{live}	No Live-lock introduction	$\exists V \in \mathbb{N}.\forall e_r \in$ Enew(M_r). $I_{M_a} \wedge I_{M_R} \Rightarrow (n := V)[e_r](V < n)$

Table 1. Results of the proof obligation generation

Example	Property	# of PO	Example	Property	# of PO
Robot	Property ϕ_S	3	Protocol T = 1	$(P \wedge XQ) \Rightarrow (X\neg R)$	4
Robot	Property ϕ_{L1}	9	Protocol T = 1	FG$P \Rightarrow$ FGQ	12
Robot	Property ϕ_{L2}	9	Demoney	G($P \Rightarrow$ GP)	7
			Demoney	G($P \Rightarrow$ X($Q \vee R$))	7

We denote by $\mathsf{Traces}(M_r)$ the traces of the event system M_R and Σ_{M_R} its paths. They are defined as for an abstract system (see Def. 6 and Def. 7, Sect.2.2).

4.2   Relation Between Abstract and Refined Path

This subsection characterizes the relation between traces of an abstract event system and its refinement. First, the relation between abstract and refined traces is done through an abstraction operator that "forgets" the new events.

Definition 14 (Abstraction of Traces). *Let M_a and M_r be two event systems, let $t_r \in \mathsf{Traces}(M_r)$. The abstraction of $t_r = e_{r_0}, e_{r_1}, ...,$ denoted $\mathsf{a}(t_r)$ is the sequence of events inductively defined as*

- $\mathsf{a}(e_{r_0}, e_{r_1}, ...) = e_{a_0}, \mathsf{a}(e_{r_1}, ...)$ *if $e_{r_0} \notin E_{new}$ or $e_{r_0} = \mathsf{Init}_M$.*
- $\mathsf{a}(e_{r_0}, e_{r_1}, ...) = \mathsf{a}(e_{r_1}, ...)$ *if $e_{r_0} \in E_{new}$.*

All the abstractions of the refined traces are included into the set of abstract traces.

Proposition 1 (Traces Inclusion). *Given $\mathsf{Traces}(M_a)$ and $\mathsf{Traces}(M_r)$,*

$$\forall t_r \in \mathsf{Traces}(M_r).(\exists t_a \in \mathsf{Traces}(M_a).(t_a = \mathsf{a}(t_r))).$$

4.3   Preservation of LTL Properties

The variable state may change during the refinement, therefore we need to define the satisfaction of a LTL property modulo a *gluing* invariant. For that, we first define the satisfaction of a predicate over the abstract variables on a state of the refined system, i.e., a satisfaction modulo a *gluing* invariant.

Definition 15 (Satisfaction of a Predicate Modulo a Gluing Invariant). *Let M_a and M_r be two event systems such that $M_a \sqsubseteq M_r$. A predicate $P(x_{M_a})$ is satisfied on the state s of M_r, denoted $s \models_{I_{M_r}} P(x_{M_a})$ if*

$$[x_{M_r} := s]I_{M_r}(x_{M_a}, x_{M_r}) \Rightarrow P(x_{M_a})$$

Then, the definition of the satisfaction of a LTL property modulo a *gluing* invariant is as follows.

Definition 16 (Semantics of a LTL Modulo a Refinement). *Let M_a and M_r be two event systems such that $M_a \sqsubseteq M_r$. Let σ be an execution of M_r, let $P(x_{M_a})$ be a predicate, let $i \in \mathbb{N}$, let ϕ and ψ two LTL formulae, we inductively define $\sigma_i \models_{I_{M_r}} \phi$ as follows:*

$\sigma_i \models_{I_{M_r}} P$ $\quad$ if $s_i \models_{I_{M_r}} P$	$\sigma_i \models_{I_{M_r}} \phi \wedge \psi$ $\quad$ if $\sigma_i \models_{I_{M_r}} \phi$ and $\sigma_i \models_{I_{M_r}} \psi$
$\sigma_i \models_{I_{M_r}} \neg\phi$ $\quad$ if $\neg(\sigma_i \models_{I_{M_r}} \phi)$	$\sigma_i \models_{I_{M_r}} \psi\mathsf{U}\phi$ $\quad$ if $\exists j.(j \geq i \wedge \sigma_j \models_{I_{M_r}} \phi \wedge$
$\sigma_i \models_{I_{M_r}} \mathsf{X}\phi$ $\quad$ if $\sigma_{i+1} \models_{I_{M_r}} \phi$	$\qquad\qquad \forall k.(i \leq k < j \Rightarrow \sigma_k \models_{I_{M_r}} \psi))$

A refined event system satisfies a LTL property ϕ, denoted $M_r \models_{I_{M_r}} \phi$, if $\forall \sigma \in \Sigma_{M_r}.\ (\sigma \models_{I_{M_r}} \phi)$.

Then, a LTL property, holding on a *abstract* system M_a, is *preserved* on the refined one M_r if all executions of M_r are satisfied modulo a refinement.

Definition 17 (Preservation of a LTL Property by Refinement). *Let M_a and M_r be two event systems such that $M_a \sqsubseteq M_r$. A LTL property ϕ is preserved by refinement if* $M_a \models \phi \ \Rightarrow \ M_r \models_{I_{M_r}} \phi.$

Let us now to characterize which type of LTL properties is preserved by the B refinement.

5   LTL Fragment Preserved by B Refinement

As explained above, the B event refinement introduces so-called new events during refinement. Therefore, a property such as Property ϕ_S is not preserved during the B refinement. This is due to the introduction of new events, well-known as *stuttering*. Therefore, we recall the notion of *stuttering insensitive* properties. Intuitively, a property is *stuttering insensitive* if for each accepting path, the property also accept any path where any states of the path are repeated an arbitrary number of time.

Definition 18 (Stuttering Insensitive Property [5]). *Let ϕ be a LTL formulae, ϕ is stable under stuttering if for all execution $\sigma = s_0, s_1, \ldots,$*

$$\sigma \models \phi \ \Rightarrow \ \forall i, j, \ldots \in \mathbb{N}.((\sigma' = s_0, \ldots, s_i, \ldots, s_i, \ldots, s_j, \ldots, s_j, \ldots) \Rightarrow \sigma' \models \phi)$$

Sistla [18] has shown that all LTL properties without *next* operator (X) are stuttering insensitive. We denote **L**(U) this subset of LTL. Notice that there exists some LTL properties containing a *next* operator that are stuttering insensitive (for example X $TRUE$). However, these properties have an equivalent expression without next operator [16].

In terms of B event system trace, stuttering insensitivity can be expressed as follows.

Proposition 2 (Trace Characterization of Stuttering Insensitive Property). *Let M be an event system, Let $t \in Traces(M)$ such that $t = e_0, e_1, \ldots$. Let $t' = e_0, skip, \ldots, skip, e_1, \ldots, e_i, skip, \ldots, skip, e_{i+1}, \ldots$. Let ϕ be a LTL property. $\phi \in \mathbf{L}(U)$ iff.*   path$(t) \models \phi \ \Rightarrow \ $path$(t') \models \phi$

The following lemma established an important result: if an abstract trace and a refined trace are equal modulo a refinement, then, if a **L**(U) property is satisfied on the paths of the an abstract trace, it is also satisfied on the paths of the refined trace.

Lemma 1 (Traces Inclusion modulo Refinement Preserves L(U)). *Let M_a and M_r be two event systems such that $M_a \sqsubseteq M_r$. Let $t_a \in$ Traces(M_a) and $t_r \in$ Traces(M_r). Let $\phi \in \mathbf{L}(U)$.*

$$(\forall \sigma_a \in \text{path}(t_a).(\sigma_a \models \phi)) \ \Rightarrow \ (\forall \sigma_r \in \text{path}(t_r).(\sigma_r \models_{I_{M_r}} \phi))$$

```
REFINEMENT                              Unload = SELECT Dt2 = TRUE
  Robot2                                           & De2 = FALSE
REFINES                                          THEN Dt2 := FALSE
  Robot                                               || De2 := TRUE
VARIABLES                                        END;
  De2,Dt2,On
INVARIANT                                Discard = SELECT De2 = TRUE
  Dt2 : BOOL & De2 : BOOL & On = BOOL &           THEN De2 := FALSE
  Dt2 = Dt & De2 = De                             END;
INITIALISATION
  Dt2 := FALSE || De2 := FALSE || On = FALSE  StopStart = SELECT De2 = false
OPERATIONS                                         & Dt2 = false
  Load = SELECT Dt2 = FALSE & On = TRUE           THEN
         THEN Dt2 := TRUE                             On := bool(On = FALSE)
         END;                                     END
                                         END
```

Fig. 5. An event system with a livelock on a new event

The proof is done on induction on the structure of ϕ.

This result leads to the following theorem, establishing that a LTL property without *next* operator $(\mathbf{L}(\mathsf{U}))$ is preserved by the B refinement.

Theorem 4. *Let ϕ be a LTL formula without next (X) operator ($\phi \in \mathbf{L}(\mathsf{U})$), let M_a and M_r be two event systems such that $M_a \sqsubseteq M_r$ if $M_a \models \phi$ then $M_r \models_{I_{M_r}} \phi$*

Theorem 4 is a direct consequence of Lemma 1 and Proposition 1.

Notice that this result is not surprising since a similar theorem has been established by Darlot and al. [10] in another context. Comparison with work in [10] is given in the *related work* section (see Sect.7).

6   A Particular Refinement for a Particular Formulae

6.1   Illustrating Example

Take a look at the B event system displayed in Fig. 5. This B event system satisfies the LTL Properties ϕ_S and ϕ_{L1} but it does not satisfy the refinement condition C_{live}: it introduces a new event StopStart that can take the control forever, i.e., be infinitely executed.

A naive solution is to introduce the new event e (in our example StopStart) at the abstract level. But, consider that e is a very concrete event, involving concrete variables, then these variables must also be introduced at the most abstract level. This breaks down the B methodology, which prohibits the introduction concrete variables on the abstract levels. This problem as already been addressed in [3] where a solution has been proposed. The B refinement has been introduced to preserve a certain kind of property, particularly the *total correctness* for the step by step development of algorithm. However, the *total correctness* is not always the property we aim at preserving. Therefore, we propose a new notion of refinement, *depending of the property we want to preserve*.

6.2   A Refinement Oriented by the Property

In this paper, we propose a refinement, denoted $\sqsubseteq_\phi$, depending on the LTL property ϕ we would like to preserve, i.e.,

Definition 19 (ϕ-refinement). *Given two event systems, M_a and M_r, M_r, given a $L(U)$ property ϕ, M_r is a ϕ-refinement of M_a, denoted $M_a \sqsubseteq_\phi M_r$ iff.*

- *Conditions $C_{init}, C_{old}, C_{new}$ and C_{dead} are satisfied, denoted $M_a \sqsubseteq_\tau M_r$ (See Def. 13).*
- *The Condition $\forall e_r \in \mathsf{Enew}(M_r) I_{M_a} \wedge J_{M_R} \Rightarrow (V := n)[e_r](0 \leq V < n)$ (C_{live_ϕ}) is satisfied in each state not synchronized with an accepting state.*

The ϕ-refinement differs from the classical B refinement only from the condition on the non-live-lock introduction. The condition C_{live_ϕ} is a *weaker* condition than C_{live}. It allows the new events to take the control forever under certain conditions, i.e., that the current state of the execution is synchronized with at least one accepting state of the Büchi automata.

Theorem 5 established the correctness and completeness of the approach.

Theorem 5 (ϕ-refinement Theorem). *Let $\phi \in L(U)$, let M_a and M_r such that $M_a \sqsubseteq_\tau M_b$. If $M_a \models \phi$ then $M_a \sqsubseteq_\phi M_r$ iff. $M_r \models \phi$.*

The example of Fig.5 is a ϕ_{L1}-refinement and a ϕ_{L2}-refinement of the example of Fig.1. The reader can observe that the states where the new event can be executed are synchronized with an accepting state, so no variant is needed for the proof of this weaker refinement.

7   Conclusion and Future Works

Conclusion. In this paper, we propose an approach for verifying temporal properties expressed in LTL into the B framework. The method has been proved to be sound, does not need any extension of B and has been experimented on several examples. We also have studied the problem of preservation of LTL properties during the B refinement process and we have characterized the subclass of LTL formulae and Büchi automata that are preserved by the B refinement. Finally, we have defined another condition of refinement, which depends on the property we want to preserve.

Related Work. Verification of dynamic properties and their preservation has already been addressed in several works. Abrial and Mussat have proposed to extend B with two dynamic modalities [4]. In the paper, we extend this work to the verification of all the LTL properties.

Based on the labelled transition system framework, the work in [10], adresses the verification of LTL properties by model-checking and their preservation by a refinement defined as a relation between two transition systems. In this paper, the verification of LTL is based on proof obligations and on the refinement of B event systems. To our knowledge, the first attempt for verifying properties expressed by Büchi automata on a program using proof obligation is due to Alpern and Schneider [7]. Our method adapts this approach for the B framework.

In [8], Bert and Barradas propose an approach of verification temporal properties based on the use of the deductive system of the Unity Logic.

An approach combining automata and proof has been proposed within the Genesyst [9] tool. But this approach is quite different from ours, since Genesyst generates transition systems from B event systems. Then the user can observe that the generated transition systems matches its requirement.

Current and Future Works. The approach proposed in Sect.6, defining the refinement w.r.t. the property we would like to preserve opens interesting perspective for the incremental development, since it does not consider a general refinement but a refinement depending from the properties we want to preserve. In this way, a work is to extend our refinement conditions to the whole LTL. For that, we must introduce a refinement condition ensuring that new events can only be introduced when no stability under stuttering is required.

Acknowledgement. The author thanks A. Giorgetti and F. Bellegarde for interesting comments about the paper. The author also thank N. Stouls and M-L. Potet for the Demoney specification and S. Chouali and J. Julliand for the T=1 protocol specification.

References

1. J.-R. Abrial. *The B Book.* Cambridge University Press, 1996.
2. J.-R. Abrial. Extending B without changing it (for developing distributed systems). In *1st Conference on the B method,* pages 169–190, Nantes, France, November 1996.
3. J-R. Abrial, D. Cansell, and D. Méry. Refinement and Reachability in Event B. In *ZB,* volume 3455 of *LNCS,* pages 222–241. Springer, 2005.
4. J.-R. Abrial and L. Mussat. Introducing dynamic constraints in B. In *B'98,* number 1393 in LNCS, pages 83–128. Springer, 1998.
5. B. Alpern, A. J. Demers, and F.B. Schneider. Safety without stuttering. *Information Processing Letters,* 23, 4:177–180, 1986.
6. B. Alpern and F.B.Schneider. Recognizing safety and liveness. *Distributed Computing,* 2, 3:117–126, 1987.
7. B. Alpern and F.B.Schneider. Verifying temporal properties without temporal logic. *TOPLAS,* 11, 1:147–167, 1989.
8. H.R. Barradas and D. Bert. Specification and proof of liveness properties under fairness assumption in B event systems. In *IFM'02,* LNCS 1993. Springer, 2002.
9. M-L. Potet D. Bert and N. Stouls. Genesyst: a tool to reason about behavioral aspects of b event specifications. application to security properties. In *ZB'2005,* volume 3455 of *LNCS,* pages 299–318. Springer-Verlag, 2005.
10. C. Darlot, J. Julliand, and O. Kouchnarenko. Refinement preserves PLTL properties. In *ZB'2003,* number 2651 in LNCS. Springer, 2003.
11. P. Gastin and D. Oddoux. Fast LTL to Büchi automata translation. In *CAV'01,* number 2102 in LNCS, pages 53–65. Springer, 2001.
12. A. Giorgetti and J. Groslambert. JAG: JML Annotation Generation for Verifying Temporal Properties. In *FASE,* LNCS, pages 373–376. Springer, 2006.

13. J. Groslambert. Verification of LTL on B Event System. Research Report RR2006-05, LIFC Université de Franche Comté, September 2006.
14. J. Groslambert. A JAG extension for verifying LTL properties on B Event Systems. In *B'2007, 7th International B Conference - Tool Session*, LNCS, Besancon, France. Springer, 2007.
15. L. Lamport. Proving the correctness of multiprocess programs. In *IEEE Transactions on Software Engineering*, volume 3(2), pages 125–143, 1977.
16. Doron Peled and Thomas Wilke. Stutter-invariant temporal properties are expressible without the next-time operator. *Inf. Process. Lett.*, 63(5):243–246, 1997.
17. A. Pnueli. The Temporal Logic of Program. In *18th Ann. IEEE Symp. on foundations of computer science*, pages 46–57, 1977.
18. A. Prasad Sistla. Safety, liveness and fairness in temporal logic. *Formal Asp. Comput.*, 6(5):495–512, 1994.

Patterns for B: Bridging Formal and Informal Development

Edward Chan, Ken Robinson, and Brett Welch

School of Computer Science & Engineering,
The University of New South Wales,
NSW 2052 Australia
ekfchan@gmail.com, kenr@cse.unsw.edu.au, brett.welch@gmail.com

Abstract. Patterns capture the shape of particular specifications, providing starting points for developers. The most well known design patterns in software are those of the *Gang of Four* (*GoF*), Gamma, Helm, Johnson & Vlissides[4], who have provided a set of patterns for Object-Oriented development. Starting with these patterns as a motivation, this paper discusses various issues concerning the concept of patterns for the *B Method* (*B*) and explores a number of patterns that could be used with B. The paper presents a number of case studies to illustrate use of the patterns, and discusses future exploration of design patterns for B.

A motivation for the development of patterns for B is to enable reuse and also to make B more accessible to developers from the more informal side of software development.

Keywords: B Method, design patterns, formal development, classes, objects.

1 Introduction

Among the definitions the *Concise Oxford English Dictionary* (*COED*) gives for *pattern* are: *a regular form or sequence discernible in the way in which something happens or is done*, and *an example for others to follow*.

This paper is derived from a fourth year undergraduate software engineering thesis of Chan & Welch [3]. The patterns presented here are motivated by each of those definitions. The patterns can be regarded as presenting models of particular classes of systems, or as providing examples for others to follow. One of the earliest cited examples of design patterns is Christopher Alexander's *Pattern Language* [1] for architectural and town design. In computing there are the *Design Patterns* by Gamma, Helm, Johnson & Vlissides[4], commonly referred to as the *Gang of Four* (*GoF*). The GoF patterns are intended for *Object-Oriented* (*OO*) design, and while the ambience of the these design patterns initiated thinking about patterns for the *B Method* (*B*), we are not primarily concerned with duplicating those patterns here. There are many reasons, some of which are discussed in section 2, why it is not feasible, or desirable to duplicate those patterns for B. It is also important to develop B design patterns in their own right.

J. Julliand and O. Kouchnarenko (Eds.): B 2007, LNCS 4355, pp. 125–139, 2006.
© Springer-Verlag Berlin Heidelberg 2006

Many of the patterns discussed here will be familiar to those who have used B, but that is largely the point of a pattern: it is a taxonomy of established techniques collected for the benefit of others and re-use. Sandrine Blazy, et al [2] presented a review of the use of patterns in B and a report on their research into re-use of patterns in B.

In section 2 we discuss the role of patterns in B. Then in section 3 we give some fundamental B patterns, which we call *foundational* and in section 4 we use some case studies to present patterns that extend the foundational patterns. We try to identify recurring patterns in B developments, and patterns are presented in terms of machine composition. The contents of the machines are abbreviated to show only the characteristics that are important for the pattern. Throughout this paper the examples are chosen to demonstrate structure. In the case studies, the problem being addressed is not, in itself, the central concern: it is used as a carrier for the demonstration of a class of patterns. The reason for choosing actual problems —even though highly abstracted— is to provide a "bridge" for readers who are not experienced in the use of B.

All proof obligations for the full B specifications, from which the examples given in this paper are extracted, have been discharged.

2   The Role of Patterns in B

Although this work received significant motivation from the GoF patterns, and some of the patterns discussed are clearly based on patterns from that source, we want to emphasise that we are not primarily attempting to simulate the OO world of design. There are a number of reasons for that: 1) there are significant parts of inheritance that B, at least in it's current form, cannot simulate 2) OO patterns deal mainly with concrete classes, where we intend to deal –at least in this initial attempt— with (abstract) specifications. It is interesting that some patterns, for example the GoF Template pattern, present strategies that are intrinsic to B, namely the process from abstract specification through refinement (design) to concrete implementation. An important distinction between OO design and B design is that OO design assumes an isomorphism between design classes and implementation; B development assumes no such isomorphism between the specification, the refinement constructs and the final implementation. Indeed there is no reason to expect that the structure of an implementation mirrors the structure of the specification.

Snook and Butler [6] have devised UML-B to provide a bridge between OO and B, via the *Unified Modelling Language* (*UML*).

3   B Foundational Patterns

The patterns presented in this section may be regarded as *foundational* in the sense that they are fundamental patterns that are used in many specifications.

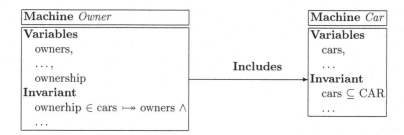

Fig. 1. Simple Association Pattern

The foundational patterns will be used in the more advanced patterns that follow.

3.1 Association Pattern

INCLUDES is used in B to compose (or decompose, depending on your point of view) machine state. But an important use of composition is to build *associations* in the UML sense. An example is shown in Fig. 1.

The inclusion is used to enable an expression of an association, or relationship (bijective function in this case), between variables in the including machine (*owners*) and variables in the included (subordinate) machines (*cars*).

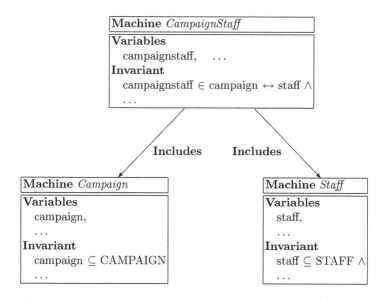

Fig. 2. Many-to-Many Association Pattern

Machine *Identity_ctx*
Sets *IDENTITY*
End

Machine *Identity* (*maxIdentity*)
Constraints *maxIdentity* $\in \mathbb{N}_1$
Sees *Identity_ctx*
Variables *Identities*
Invariant
    Identities $\subseteq$ *IDENTITY* $\wedge$
    card (*Identities*) $\leq$ *maxIdentity*
Initialisation *Identities* := {}

Operations
    newIdentity (*ids*) $\widehat{=}$
        pre *ids* $\in$ *IDENTITY* $\wedge$ card (*Identities*) $\neq$ *maxIdentity* $\wedge$
            ids $\in$ *IDENTITY* $-$ *Identities* **then**
        Identities := *Identities* $\cup$ { *ids* }
        end ;
    killIdentity (*ids*) $\widehat{=}$
        pre *ids* $\in$ *IDENTITY* $\wedge$ *ids* $\in$ *Identities* **then**
        Identities := *Identities* $-$ { *ids* }
        end
End

Fig. 3a. The Identity Pattern: variant 1

One-to-many relationships can be established with an association pattern in which many machines are included. In the example shown in Fig. 2 a third machine is introduced to build a relation between variables of two machines. An important property of the association pattern is the maintenance of the independence of the subordinate components of the pattern.

3.2   The Identity Pattern

There are many situations, known to all who have developed specifications in B, where multiple instances of some object need to be managed: a unique identity is needed for each instance. For this purpose we will use an *Identity* machine to allocate unique tokens for each instance. We will call this the *Identity* pattern, see Fig. 3a,3b. Two operations are shown: newIdentity for allocating a new token, and killIdentity for reclaiming a token. In many applications tokens are never reclaimed. There are two variants on the newIdentity operation:

$\cdots$

$newid \longleftarrow$ **newIdentity** $\widehat{=}$
  pre card ($Identities$) $\neq maxIdentity$ **then**
   any ids **where** $ids \in IDENTITY - Identities$ **then**
    $Identities := Identities \cup \{ ids \}$ $\|$
    $newid := ids$
   end
  end ;

$\cdots$

Fig. 3b. The Identity Pattern: variant 2

1. that shown in Fig. 3a, in which the new token is chosen by the invoker of the operation, and
2. an alternative, shown in Fig. 3b, in which the new token is chosen by the newIdentity operation. In this case the new token is returned to the invoker as a result.

Variant 2 is preferred, but cannot be used if the returned value is to be used subsequently in the invoking operation. This would require sequential composition, which is not available at the machine level. (Note: this is one of the few instances that justifies allowing sequential composition in machines.)

In some cases, each instance will need its own attributes and we will use an *Object* machine for that purpose. It seems sensible —and consistent with B terminology to call such aggregates *objects*.

3.3   The Object Pattern

The Object pattern includes or extends the Identity pattern. The purpose of the pattern is to add attributes for an identity and to provide operations that depend on the identity and attributes owned by the identity. A schematic version of Object is shown Fig. 4. The machine shows a *Make* operation to create a new instance of an object, initialising all attributes shown generically by *Attri*. Also shown is an operation, *Operationi*, which is a representative of all operations on attributes of the object.

3.4   The Subtype Pattern

A simple subtype pattern can be achieved by using EXTENDS, rather than INCLUDES. This pattern supports, not only subsetting of variables but also subsetting of operations as shown in Fig. 5a and Fig. 5b. Notice the subsetting of variables: *squares* $\subseteq$ *rectangles*; and also the subsetting of operations: the operation *SquareArea* finally delegates to operation *RectangleArea*.

Machine $Object$ ($maxobjects$)
Constraints $maxobjects \in \mathbb{N}_1$
Sees $Identity\_ctx$
Includes $Identity$ ($maxobjects$)
Sets $ATTR$; ARG ; $RESULT$
Variables $objects$, $attri$
Invariant $objects \subseteq Identities \wedge attri \in objects \nrightarrow ATTR$
Initialisation $objects$, $attri := \{\}$, $\{\}$

Operations
   $object \longleftarrow$ **MakeObject** ($INITattr$) $\,\widehat{=}$
     pre card ($objects$) $\neq maxobjects \wedge INITattr \in ATTR$ **then**
       any obj **where** $obj \in IDENTITY - Identities$ **then**
         $newIdentity$ (obj) $\parallel$ $objects := objects \cup \{\ obj\ \}$ $\parallel$ $object := obj$ $\parallel$
         $attri$ (obj) $:= INITattr$
       end
     end ;
   $result \longleftarrow$ **Operationi** ($ident$, $args$) $\,\widehat{=}$
     pre $ident \in Identities \wedge args \in ARG$ **then**
       $result :\in RESULT$ $\parallel$ $attri :\in Identities \nrightarrow ATTR$
     end
End

Fig. 4. Object Pattern

3.5   The Interface Pattern

The *interface* pattern provides for the organisation of a number of machines into a supermachine that plays the role of a superclass. As an example we will use the interface pattern to organise the Square and Rectangle machines (seen in the subtype pattern) together with a Triangle machine into a Shape machine, represented in the following as the Shape_Interface machine.

The essential aspects of the interface pattern are:

1. A set of machines that can form a subtype, in this case machines that compute common properties for Squares, Rectangles, Triangles, etc.
2. A machine that acts as an interface to route requests to the appropriate machines.
3. The interface machine needs to set up types and variables to enable recognition of the classification of each of member of the subtype.
4. The interface machine uses a switch to direct requests to the appropriate subtype operation.

Notice that the interface pattern is easily extensible to add new subtype members and operations.

> **Machine** *Shape_Square*
>
> **Variables** Squares, Sidelength
> **Invariant**
>   Squares $\subseteq$ SHAPE $\wedge$ Squares $\subseteq$ Rectangles $\wedge$
>   SideLength $\in$ Squares $\rightarrow \mathbb{N}_1$
> **Operations**
> newSquare(ids, side) $\widehat{=}$
> **pre** ids $\in$ SHAPE $\wedge$ ids $\notin$ Squares $\wedge$ side $\in \mathbb{N}_1$
> **then**
>   *Squares := Squares* $\cup$ *{ids}* $\parallel$ SideLength(ids) := side $\parallel$
>   newRectangle(ids, side, side)
> **end**;
> ans $\longleftarrow$ SquareArea(ids) $\widehat{=}$
> **pre** ids $\in$ Squares **then**
>   ans $\longleftarrow$ RectangleArea(ids)
> **end**;
> . . .

Extends *Shape_Rectangle*

Fig. 5a. Subtype Pattern: Subtype

> **Machine** *Shape_Rectangle*
>
> **Variables** Rectangles, Height, Width
> **Invariant**
>   Rectangles $\subseteq$ SHAPE $\wedge$ Height $\in$ Rectangles $\rightarrow \mathbb{N}_1 \wedge$ Width $\in$ Rectangles $\rightarrow \mathbb{N}_1$
> **Operations**
> newRectangle(ids, ht, wd) $\widehat{=}$
> **pre** ids $\in$ SHAPE $\wedge$ ids $\notin$ Rectangles $\wedge$ ht $\in \mathbb{N}_1 \wedge$ wd $\in \mathbb{N}_1$
> **then**
>   Rectangles := Rectangles $\cup$ {ids} $\parallel$ Height(ids) := ht Width(ids) := wd
> **end**;
> ans $\longleftarrow$ RectangleArea(ids) $\widehat{=}$
> **pre** ids $\in$ Rectangles **then**
>   ans := Height(ids) $\times$ Width(ids)
> **end**;
> . . .

Fig. 5b. Subtype Pattern: Supertype

Machine *Shape_Interface* (*maxshape*)
Constraints *maxshape* $\in \mathbb{N}_1$
Sees *Shape_ctx* , *Identity_ctx*
Includes *Identity* (*maxshape*) , *Shape_Square* , *Shape_Triangle*
Sets *SHAPE_TYPE* = { *RECTANGLE* , *SQUARE* , *TRIANGLE* }

Variables *Shapes* , *ShapeTypes*
Invariant

   $Shapes \subseteq Identities \wedge$
   card (*Shapes*) $\leq maxshape \wedge$
   $ShapeTypes \in Shapes \rightarrowtail SHAPE\_TYPE \wedge$
   $Shapes = Rectangles \cup Squares \cup Triangles \wedge$
   $Squares \subseteq Rectangles \wedge$
   $Rectangles \cap Triangles = \{\} \wedge$
   $ShapeTypes^{-1} [\{ RECTANGLE \}] = Rectangles \wedge$
   $ShapeTypes^{-1} [\{ SQUARE \}] = Squares \wedge$
   $ShapeTypes^{-1} [\{ TRIANGLE \}] = Triangles$
Initialisation *Shapes* , *ShapeTypes* := {} , {}

Operations

   $sid \longleftarrow$ **Rectangle** (*height* , *width*) $\widehat{=}$
      pre $height \in \mathbb{N}_1 \wedge width \in \mathbb{N}_1 \wedge$ card (*Identities*) $\neq maxshape$ **then**
         any   *rid* **where** $rid \in IDENTITY - Identities$ **then**
            $newIdentity (rid) \parallel sid := rid \parallel$
            $Shapes := Shapes \cup \{ rid \} \parallel$
            $ShapeTypes (rid) := RECTANGLE \parallel$
            $newRectangle (rid , height , width)$
         end
      end ;

   $sid \longleftarrow$ **Square** (*side*) $\widehat{=}$
      pre $side \in \mathbb{N}_1 \wedge$ card (*Identities*) $\neq maxshape$ **then**
         any   *rid* **where** $rid \in IDENTITY - Identities$ **then**
            $newIdentity (rid) \parallel sid := rid \parallel$
            $Shapes := Shapes \cup \{ rid \} \parallel$
            $ShapeTypes (rid) := SQUARE \parallel$
            $newSquare (rid , side)$
         end
      end ;

   Other shapes go here

   $ans \longleftarrow$ **Area** (*sid*) $\widehat{=}$
      pre $sid \in Shapes$ **then**
         select $ShapeTypes (sid) = SQUARE \wedge sid \in Squares$ **then**
            $ans \longleftarrow SquareArea (sid)$
         when $ShapeTypes (sid) = RECTANGLE \wedge sid \in Rectangles$ **then**

$$ans \longleftarrow RectangleArea ~(~sid~)$$

    end

  end

Other *shape* operations can be added, for example *Perimeter*

End

4   Examples and Extensions

In this section we will give some larger examples that use and extend the foundational patterns presented in the previous section. It is important to remember that the chosen example is not the primary point of interest. We are interested in describing some patterns that the examples provide. In all cases the examples are treated abstractly and could be regarded as the initial step in a refinement process.

4.1   Strategy

The strategy pattern is in the spirit of the GoF strategy pattern, and allows a number of different algorithms to be used as appropriate for the solution of some generic problem. The example we use to demonstrate the pattern is a Chess playing program.

The Chess game sets out to model a system of pairs of players playing a game of chess. Each player can modify their behaviour dynamically.

The strategy pattern is particularly suited to this problem as it allows us to define a series of encapsulated, interchangeable chess strategies. The strategy pattern allows players to alter their strategy during the game without altering the game or board logic.

The Structure of the Game. The basic structure of chess and abstract strategies are modelled as uninstantiated constant functions in the context machine, *Chess_ctx*. While uninstantiated, the context machines contains minimal properties required to present provably consistent machines. This context machine, carrying an abstract theory of the application being modelled, is a significant example of a B pattern itself.

The *ChessGame* machine controls the state of the Chess game, while the *ChessBoard* machine maintains the board state.

The *ChessStrategies* machine is a stateless machine which encapsulates all of the chess strategies.

The Sequence of Events. The sequence of events described by the Chess Strategy patten is as follows.

Two players obtain a new board (*NewBoard*) and attach themselves to White and Black chess pieces using, respectively, *NewBoard*, *AttachPlayerWhite* and

Machine *Chess_ctx*

  The Structure of the Game

Sets
  CHESS_BOARDS ;
  CHESS_PIECES ; *WHITE_PIECES* ; *BLACK_PIECES* ;
  POSITION ;
  CHESS_PLAYER ;
  CHESS_STRATEGIES = { *AGGRESSIVE* , *DEFENSIVE* , *RANDOM* } ;
  COLOUR = { *BLACK* , *WHITE* }
Constants
  legalMoves , *legalBlackMoves* , *legalWhiteMoves* ,
  legalDefensiveWhiteMoves , *legalDefensiveBlackMoves* ,
  legalAggressiveWhiteMoves , *legalAggressiveBlackMoves* ,
  changeBoard
Properties
  $WHITE\_PIECES \cup BLACK\_PIECES = CHESS\_PIECES \land$
  $WHITE\_PIECES \cap BLACK\_PIECES = \{\} \land$
  $\mathsf{card} (WHITE\_PIECES) = \mathsf{card} (BLACK\_PIECES) \land$
  $legalMoves \in BOARD \rightarrow MOVES (CHESS\_PIECES) \land$
  $legalWhiteMoves \in BOARD \rightarrow MOVES (WHITE\_PIECES) \land$
  $legalBlackMoves \in BOARD \rightarrow MOVES (BLACK\_PIECES) \land$
  $legalMoves = legalWhiteMoves \cup legalBlackMoves \land$
  $legalDefensiveBlackMoves \subseteq legalBlackMoves \land$
  $legalAggressiveBlackMoves \subseteq legalBlackMoves \land$
  $legalDefensiveWhiteMoves \subseteq legalWhiteMoves \land$
  $legalAggressiveWhiteMoves \subseteq legalWhiteMoves \land$
  $\forall bd . (bd \in BOARD \Rightarrow \mathsf{dom} (legalMoves (bd)) \subseteq \mathsf{ran} (bd)) \land$
  $changeBoard \in BOARD \rightarrow (CHESS\_PIECES \nrightarrow (POSITION \nrightarrow BOARD)) \land$
  $\forall (bd , pc) . (bd \in BOARD \land pc \in CHESS\_PIECES \land$
  $pc \in \mathsf{dom} (legalMoves (bd)) \Rightarrow$
    $pc \in \mathsf{dom} (changeBoard (bd))) \land$
  $\forall (bd , pc , pos) . (bd \in BOARD \land pc \in CHESS\_PIECES \land pos \in POSITION \land$
  $pos \in legalMoves (bd) (pc) \Rightarrow$
    $pos \in \mathsf{dom} (changeBoard (bd) (pc)))$
Definitions
  $BOARD \,\,\widehat{=}\,\, POSITION \nrightarrow CHESS\_PIECES$;
  $MOVES (X) \,\,\widehat{=}\,\, X \nrightarrow \mathbb{P} (POSITION)$
End

Fig. 6a. Chess_ctx: the Chess context machine

Machine *ChessGame*

Promotes
   NewBoard

Variables
   strategies, players, opponents, playerGames, playerColour

Invariant
   $players \subseteq CHESS\_PLAYER \wedge$
   $opponents \in players \rightarrow players \wedge$
   $strategies \in players \twoheadrightarrow CHESS\_STRATEGIES \wedge$
   $playerGames \in players \twoheadrightarrow chessBoards \wedge$
   $playerColour \in players \twoheadrightarrow COLOUR \wedge$
   $playing \subseteq \mathsf{dom}(strategies) \wedge$
   $playing \subseteq \mathsf{dom}(playerGames) \wedge$
   $playing \subseteq \mathsf{dom}(playerColour)$

Definitions
   $playing \mathrel{\widehat{=}} \mathsf{dom}(opponents) \cup \mathsf{ran}(opponents)$

Operations
   $player \longleftarrow NewPlayer \mathrel{\widehat{=}}$
   $SetChessStrategy(player, strat) \mathrel{\widehat{=}}$
   $AttachPlayerWhite(player, board) \mathrel{\widehat{=}}$
   $AttachPlayerBlack(player, board) \mathrel{\widehat{=}}$
   $PlayGame(player1, player12) \mathrel{\widehat{=}}$
   $MakeMove(player) \mathrel{\widehat{=}}$

Includes *ChessStrategies*

Fig. 6b. ChessGame

AttachPlayerBlack. The players then set their playing strategies and initiate playing a game as opponents, using *SetStrategy* and *PlayGame*. The first move —and all subsequent moves— is made by calling the *MakeMove* operation. For each call to *MakeMove* an operation in *ChessStrategies* is called, based on the chosen strategy for the player.

The strategy operations in *ChessStrategies* are given a board state and the colour of the player. The strategy then calculates a course of action according to the strategy that particular operation represents, choosing the piece to be moved and its new position. The move is then made on the board itself by calling the *MovePiece* operation.

It is worth noting that the flow of control always starts and ends at the same points, with only the strategy itself being variable. This is one of the key characteristics of the Strategy patterns in both the GoF and B strategy pattern.

4.2 Command

The Command pattern presented here is again in the spirit of the GoF Command pattern. The case-study presents a model of users and their calculators in a client-server view where the users can send encapsulated requests to their

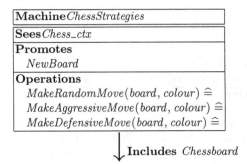

Fig. 6c. ChessStrategies

Machine *ChessBoard*
Sees *Chess_ctx*
Definitions $BOARDSTATE \cong POSITION \nrightarrow CHESS\_PIECES$
Constants $startingPositions, newPositions$
Variables $chessBoards, positions$
Invariant $chessBoards \subseteq CHESS\_BOARDS \land$ $positions \in chessBoards \rightarrow (BOARDSTATE) \land$ $\forall cb.(cb \in chessBoards \Rightarrow$ $\quad \mathsf{dom}(legalBlackMoves(positions(cb))) \subseteq ran(positions(cb))) \land$ $\forall cb.(cb \in chessBoards \Rightarrow$ $\quad \mathsf{dom}(legalWhiteMoves(positions(cb))) \subseteq ran(positions(cb)))$
Operations $board \longleftarrow NewBoard \cong$ $MovePiece(board, piece, newPos) \cong$

Fig. 6d. ChessBoard

"calculator" for calculating and storing an arithmetic result. The purpose of this case-study is to show how foundational patterns are employed in B specifications and also how they are intertwined to build more complex patterns which then become a template for new subsystems required to solve a similar problem. In this example of the calculator, the goal is to build a B specification that provides parameterised requests, request queueing and support of undo/redo functionality consequently giving rise to a pattern that forms the basis for the Calculator system example.

B Command Pattern Structure. To keep this pattern understandable, three machines are used, each of them using the Object pattern to model the Client (*User* machine), Command (*Command* machine) and Receiver (*Calculator* machine) objects respectively. These three machines are then connected using the

```
Calculator_ctx
```
```
Sets
    CALCULATOR; USER; COMMAND;
    OPERATOR = ADD, SUB, MUL, DIV, MOD, SQUARE
```

Fig. 7a. Command Pattern: Context

```
Machine Command(maxcommand, maxcalc, maxuser)
```
```
Sees
    Calculator_ctx
```
```
Promotes
    MakeUser, MakeCalculator
```
```
Variables
    userCommand, userRedo, userUndo, commands,
    comCalculators, comOperators,
    comOperands, comPrevCalcState
```
```
Invariant
```
$commands \subseteq COMMAND \land$

$card(commands) \leq maxcommand \land$

$comCalculators \in commands \rightarrow calculators \land$

$comOperators \in commands \rightarrow OPERATOR \land$

$comOperands \in commands \rightarrow \mathbb{N} \land$

$comPrevCalcState \in commands \rightarrow \mathbb{N} \land$

$\forall com.(com \in commands \land comOperators(com) = DIV \Rightarrow$
$\quad comOperands(com) \neq 0) \land$

$userCommand \in users \twoheadrightarrow commands \land$

$userUndo \in users \twoheadrightarrow \mathbf{seq}(commands) \land$

$userRedo \in users \twoheadrightarrow \mathbf{seq}(commands)$

```
Operations
```
$cmd \longleftarrow MakeCommand(calc, operator, operand) \;\widehat{=}$

$AttachCommand(user, cmd) \;\widehat{=}$

$val \longleftarrow Compute(user) \;\widehat{=}$

$val \longleftarrow Undo(user) \;\widehat{=}$

$val \longleftarrow Redo(user) \;\widehat{=}$

↓ **Includes** *User*   ↓ **Includes** *Calculator*

Fig. 7b. Command Pattern: Command

Association pattern. In this instance, the Command Machine is used to include both the Client and Receiver machines. This gives command objects access to the receiver objects so that they know which Receiver to call for a particular action. The command objects also need to be associated with a user so the commands can be placed in the undo/redo stacks for that user.

In this pattern, the Client machine itself does not contain much functionality. It follows an Identity pattern to manage the Client objects. If desired, the Object

Machine $User(maxuser)$	**Machine** $Calculator(maxcalc)$
Sees $Calculator\_ctx$	**Sees** $Calculator\_ctx$
Variables $users$	**Variables** $calculators, values$
Invariant $users \subseteq USER \wedge card(users) \leq maxuser$	**Operations** $calc \longleftarrow MakeCalculator \,\widehat{=}$
Operations $newUser \longleftarrow MakeUser \,\widehat{=}$ $DeleteUser(user) \,\widehat{=}$	$DeleteCalculator \,\widehat{=}$ $Evaluate(calc, operator, operand) \,\widehat{=}$ $SetCalculator(calc, newValue) \,\widehat{=}$ $result \longleftarrow GetCalculator(calc) \,\widehat{=}$

Fig. 7c. Command Pattern: User & Calculator

pattern could be used to add extra self-contained functionality to the Client machine.

The Receiver machine in the pattern is used to perform operations as requested by the Clients. This is facilitated through the specification of an "Evaluate" operation that can be called by the Command machine. Following the Object pattern, there is a set of Receiver objects. The Evaluate operation performs some state change on the receiver in question.

Finally, the Command machine models the encapsulation of method calls and stores the operations to be called as well as the parameters for those operations. By including both the receiver and the client machines, each command has a reference to a receiver so it knows which receiver methods it must execute. Each user can also be associated with a sequence of command objects to specify an undo stack. The same principle is used to specify a redo stack. As command objects are created and invoked, they are added to these sequences. When the user needs to undo a command, they simply take the head of the undo sequence and restore the state of the receiver to the state that is stored within the command object.

The *Calculator* machine models a simple arithmetic calculator class that is capable of storing state. Only ADD, SUB, MUL, DIV, MOD and SQUARE operations are available, however the user is free to specify more operations for the calculator by appending to the *Operation* operation and also by specifying how to undo this operation by adding the inverse operation to *UndoOperation*.

The *Undo* and *Redo* operations shown in this specification run commands to change state. In some applications it may be preferable to save and restore state. Clearly this pattern can be easily adapted to either of those alternatives. This type of choice is not central to the pattern itself, and neither is being advocated.

5   Conclusion

We have presented a small subset of the specification patterns that could be constructed in B. While the basic pattern incentive was taken from the set of GoF patterns, the objective has been to illustrate patterns that are concerned with how to use the compositional mechanisms of B and to produce patterns that can accurately be described as B patterns. We have attempted to choose examples that might make it easier for novice B users to understand and use B. As befits the notion of a pattern the examples have been kept as abstract as possible. Space limitations have meant significant condensation of the examples.

Many more patterns can be described, but it must be emphasised that, so far, these patterns are concerned only with the structuring of specifications. A very rich line to pursue, and one we intend to pursue, is the identification and development of refinement patterns, where they might address not simply the structure of a refinement construct, but also the relationship between a specification and its refinement, and between a refinement and its refinement.

Acknowledgement

We wish to thank the anonymous reviewers for valuable suggestions and corrections.

References

1. Christopher Alexander. *A Pattern Language : Towns, Buildings, Construction (Center for Environmental Structure Series)*. Oxford University Press, 1977.
2. Sandrine Blazy, Frédéric Gervais, and Régine Laleau. Reuse of Specification Patterns with the B Method. In *ZB2003: Formal Specification and Development in Z and B*, pages 40–57, 2003.
3. Edward Chan and Brett Welch. Patterns and the B Method: Bridging Formal and Informal Development. Technical report, Department of Computer Science, University of NSW, 2006. ftp://ftp.cse.unsw.edu.au/pub/doc/papers/UNSW/0620.pdf.
4. Erich Gamma, Richard Helm, Ralph Johnson, and John Vlissides. *Design Patterns: Elements of Reusable Object-Oriented Software*. Addison-Wesley, 1995.
5. Ken Robinson. Embedding Formal Methods in Software Engineering. In C Neville Dean and Raymond T Boute, editors, *Teaching Formal Methods*, volume 3294 of *LNCS*, pages 203–213. CoLogNET/FME, Springer, November 2004.
6. Colin Snook and Michael Butler. UML-B: Formal Modeling and Design Aided by UML. *ACM Trans. Softw. Eng. Methodol.*, 15(1):92–122, 2006.

Time Constraint Patterns for Event B Development

Dominique Cansell[1,5], Dominique Méry[2,3,5], and Joris Rehm[2,4,5]

[1] Université de Metz
`cansell@loria.fr`
[2] Université Henri Poincaré Nancy 1
[3] `mery@loria.fr`
[4] `rehm@loria.fr`
[5] LORIA
BP 239
54506 Vandœvre-lès-Nancy
France

Abstract. Distributed applications are based on algorithms which should be able to deal with time constraints. It is mandatory to express time constraints in (mathematical) models and the current work intends to integrate time constraints in the modelling process based on event B models and refinement. The starting point of our work is the event B development of the IEEE 1394 leader election protocol; from standard documents, we derive temporal requirements to solve the contention problem and we propose a method for introducing time constraints using a pattern. The pattern captures time constraints in a generic event B development and it is applied to the IEEE 1394 case study.

Keywords: event B, pattern, distributed systems, refinement.

1 Introduction

1.1 Overview

In this article, we present work in progress on the modelling of time in event B using *patterns*. The concept of time is not predefined in B but using set theory we can effectively model it. Generally most formal models "implement" time in the first abstraction and they explicitly express time constraints in models of computations or automata; several notations propose solutions for expressing time and time constraints (timed automata of Alur and Dill [8]). We think that it is not a good idea to introduce time too early in the development process, because invariants on time (using natural numbers and arithmetic) introduce too much noise for proof assistants and consequently most proof obligations need interaction. Using abstraction without time we can solve and prove more easily important properties of the system and obtain a first scheduling of events. For us, time can be introduced later in a specific refinement where time is a global variable.

J. Julliand and O. Kouchnarenko (Eds.): B 2007, LNCS 4355, pp. 140–154, 2006.
© Springer-Verlag Berlin Heidelberg 2006

1.2 Motivations for Integrating Time Constraints in Event B Development

Needs for integrating time constraints in event B development are motivated by observations on a case study developed by Jean-Raymond Abrial, D. Cansell and D. Méry [6] and the goal was to redevelop the leader election protocol and to provide a proof simpler and easier to understand than Devillers et al [16]. The IEEE 1394 leader election protocol works properly provided the network is acyclic; but it is sensitive to time constraints [20], since it may loop forever if no time constraint is taken into account. In fact, the problem appears when the algorithm is executed and leads to a situation where two nodes of a finite network a and b are in contention. Let us recall the problem using events. Node a sends a message to b and asks him to be its child, while node b is asking to a to be its child. The two nodes a and b have sent messages to each other and the messages were sent independently. No one wants to be the leader but no other one can be the leader, since they are the last nodes in the election process: the others nodes have already asked to be children or grand-children of a or b. This problem is called the *contention* problem. This problem can occur with only two nodes of the network (this can be proved using our models). In the "real" protocol the problem is "solved" by means of timers. As soon as a node a discovers a contention with node b, it waits for a very short delay in order to be sure that the other node b has also discovered the problem. The very short delay in question is at least equal to the message transfer time between nodes (such a time is supposed to be *bounded*). After this, each node randomly chooses (with probability $1/2$) to wait for either a "short" or a "large" delay (the difference between the two is at least twice the message transfer time). After the chosen delay has passed each node sends a new request to the other *if it is in the situation to do so*. Clearly, if both nodes choose the same delay, the contention situation will reappear. However if they do not choose the same delay, then the one with the largest delay becomes the father of the other: when it wakes up, it discovers the request from the other while it has not itself already sent its own request, it can therefore send an acknowledgement and thus become the father. According to the *law of large numbers*, the probability for both nodes indefinitely choosing the same delay is zero. Thus, at some point, they will (in probability) choose different delays and one of them will thus becomes the father of the other.

Abrial et al. [6] present a partial formalisation of the contention problem and the idea is to introduce a *virtual channel* which is used to resolve the contention. Recently, J-R. Abrial et al propose a simpler (without acknowledgement and confirmation) algorithm [7]. In both models, the contention is solved abstractly and no time reference is used. The real algorithm uses time constraints to solve this contention. Our starting questions were:

- can we add time constraints in previous abstract models to facilitate more realistic refinement?
- can we do this in a systematic way using something similar to design patterns in object-oriented software development [18]?

The questions will be partly addressed in the next sections. However, the introduction of time is not the main issue and the next sub-section motivates the introduction of patterns in the B methodology.

1.3   B Patterns

Designing models of a complex system using refinement and proofs are very hard and often not very well used. This proof-based modelling technique is not automatically done, since we need to extract some knowledge from the system in an incremental and clever way. The event B method allows one such development and many case studies have been developed, including sequential algorithms [5], distributed algorithms [6,14], parallel algorithms [4] or embedded systems for controlling train like METEOR [10] or Roissy Val [9]. The last example was developed faster because previous models were reused and a specific automatic refining tool - Edit B developed by Matra (now Siemens)- was utilised. EditB provides automatic refinement from an abstract B model, which can be proved more quickly and automatically using or adding specific rules in the B prover; EditB is a "private" tool and only Siemens uses it to develop systems. The interesting thing is that the engineer activity *(typing model)* is very much simplified. This tool seems to apply a similar technique to those used in design patterns. It is the application of well-engineered patterns for a specific domain.

Three years ago Jean-Raymond Abrial, D. Cansell and D. Méry worked on using genericity in event B [13,3]. When a designer develops a generic development (a list of models related by refinement) both modelling and proof are easily done. Models are more abstract and consequently the set of proof obligations can be discharged more automatically or in an interactive way (it is less noisy for the prover). The generic development can be reused by instantiation of the carrier sets and constants of the development (list of models). We obtain a new development (list of models) which is correct, if all instantiated sets and constants satisfy properties of the generic development. An interesting point is that we do not prove the proof obligation of the instantiated development. This technique is well known by mathematicians who prove abstract theorems and reuse these on specific cases reproving the instantiated axioms of the theorem to obtain (for free or without proof) the instantiated goal of the theorem.

Recently, Jean-Raymond Abrial has presented [2] patterns for the action/reaction paradigm to systematically develop the mechanical press controller.

These contributions follows the same direction leading to reuse previous proof-based developments, to give guidelines for mechanical refinement in daily software development. In our opinion, a B pattern is an event B development which is proved, sufficiently generic and can be partially reused in another specific B development to produce automatically new refinement models: proofs are (partly) inherited from the B pattern.

1.4 Summary

Our paper proposes initial and partial answers to these questions. We do not give an exact definition of B patterns. It is too early to propose a standard definition as many works are converging to this B pattern concept. We describe a pattern with regard to time and how we can use it to produce other patterns or to solve a specific problem. The next section introduces the time constraint pattern and its construction. Section 3 presents an application of our pattern for a message passing system. Section 4 concludes the paper by the IEEE 1394 case study and future works.

2 Time Constraint Pattern

In order to express time and time constraints we introduce a new pattern. This pattern demonstrates our modelling choice and gives a general background to reason about things like time progression, clock or timer. The main idea is to guard events with a time constraint, therefore those events can be observed only when the system reaches a specific time. The time progress is also an event, so there is no modification of the underlying language of B. It is only a modelling technique instead of a specialised formal system. The variable $time$ is in $\mathbb{N}$ but time constraints can be written in terms involving unknown constants or expressions between different times. Finally, the timed event observations can be constrained by other events which determine future activations.

2.1 Defining the Pattern

We can explain our method through an example event-B model. Later this model can be used like a pattern to refine another model adding time considerations. As you can see below, the pattern has two variables:

```
MODEL
    m0
VARIABLES
    time, /* current time */
    at/ * Active Times */
INVARIANT
    time ∈ ℕ   ∧
    at ⊆ ℕ   ∧
    (at ≠ ∅ ⟹ time ≤ min(at))
INITIALISATION
    time := 0 || at := ∅
EVENTS
    ...
```

- *time* in $\mathbb{N}$ models the current time value. The incrementation of this value denotes the time progression.
- *at* $\subseteq \mathbb{N}$ is the known future active times of the system. Each active time stands for a future event activation. For example, a simple clock will have a set of active times like $\{time + 1, time + 2, ...\}$.

Since this pattern is very general, the invariant is simple and we have only to satisfy $at \neq \emptyset \Rightarrow time \leq min(at)$. This means that active times are in the future. As a consequence of this fact the time can not be moved beyond the first active time, this is intuitively correct because if time goes beyond one event activation, then we miss the right moment for observing it.

The three events represent three different temporal aspects. The first event is the creation of a new active time. In real system this can be the initialisation of a timer or the setting of a new time constraint. We denote this by "posting" new active times in the event "post_time". This event is needed when the activation of the system is dynamic. For our example of a regular clock the active times are known for every system so we have only to initialise the set *at* with $\mathbb{N}$. In this case, the event *post_time* is not required. For more complex cases like message passing in a network, the active times are determined by the message arrival so we need an event like *post_time* observed when a message is sent to constrain the system to receiving them some time later.

> post_time $\hat{=}$
>   **any** *tm* **where**
> $tm \in \mathbb{N}$ $\wedge$
> $tm > time$
>   **then**
> $at := at \cup \{tm\}$
>   **end**

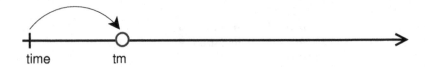

The event takes a new active time *tm* which is indeterminate in the most general case but it can be more specific like $time + delay$ with a constant *delay* in $\mathbb{N}$ and greater than 0.

The second aspect is time progression. In this modelling approach, in a system state the time is frozen and it can go with an observation of the tick_tock event.

```
tick_tock  ≘
    any  tm  where
        tm ∈ ℕ  ∧
        tm > time  ∧
        (at ≠ ∅  ⟹  tm ≤ min(at))
    then
        time := tm
    end
```

This event simply takes a new value of time in the future and assigns it at the current time.

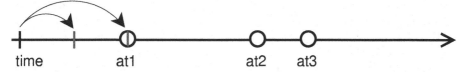

time   at1   at2   at3

As we have already said, time progress is nondeterministic, the new value tm should only satisfy the invariant with $tm \leq min(at)$, if $at \neq \emptyset$. Otherwise time can take place everywhere and let the system trigger any event potentially. But as time is a natural and $tm > time$ we are sure that the system will reach the next active time if $tick\_tock$ is activated enough. Thanks to the set at, which is very general, this event can be copied without modification when we use the time constraint pattern.

Now we can look at the last aspect which is the goal of our work. With this event "process_time" we can consider events with time constraints.

```
process_time  ≘
    when
        time ∈ at
    then
        at := at − {time}
    end
```

The guard $time \in at$ and the invariant implies that $time$ has reached the first active time. The time can have made one or more step with one or more activation on $tick\_tock$ and other temporised events may have occurred.

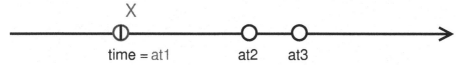

time = at1   at2   at3

The current active time is deleted from at therefore an active time can be used once and only once. After this removal the time and the system can continue to change.

2.2 Applying the Time Constraint Pattern

This model can be used as a pattern, but it is very general and the invariant is limited. The pattern can be fit to time-sensitive systems in order to introduce time behaviour and prove invariants. Consequently such B patterns can be used as a systematic help to refine systems.

As this pattern represents a way to write time arguments it can not be used directly but needs to be adapted to a specific system (except for *tick_tock* which can be used directly).

At first, events of the system involving time must be present and written in a proved model. The idea is to use refinement and make an abstract model where time is implicitly controlled by events as usual. One can already reason about a model without time and prove general or abstract properties on the system. Next, the pattern should be adapted except *tick_tock*. The two aspects involved in *post_time* and *process_time* need to be identified from the modelled system. For instance, the beginning of a timer, sending of message or other initiation of non-instantaneous actions match the posting time event. Connected to that timer ending, message reception or finalisation of non-instantaneous actions match the processing time event. The result will be a set of adapted and renamed instances of *post_time* and *process_time* events.

When this aspect of events has been identified we can use it to refine the abstract model with a superposition of modified events; we refine the abstract model; for instance, we can substitute an abstract guard model by concrete time expression; in this way, we can prove that the time constraints implements required behaviour.

Some specific adaptation or improvement may be used:

- The two ideas of posting and processing active times have been presented separately for getting the essence of the concept. However they are often mixed in the same event. One can make a chain of reactions with time constraints between events.
- There is no contradiction to consider more than one time posting in an event which refines *post_time*. We can add a number of active times in one shot. Using the same idea, an infinite number of times can be posted using generalised substitution: for example, on the initialisation of the system.
- In addition to the set *at* we can add variables to express in a more specialised and meaningful way active times. These variables have common elements with *at*. For example, we can store sending time of messages. All these added variables allow one to write more specialised time constraints and give different categories of active times inside *at*.
- With the last remark, we can have different categories but we can not simply trigger more than one event at the same time because *at* is a set and it can not contain several identical values like in a multiset. To resolve this we can take several sets like *at* or take a function to index different sets. This index will represent different processes which can run at the same time. Of course

this modification needs to be done in the same way for the rest of the model: invariant and other events. With this adaptation we can represent different local clocks or several processes.

2.3 Comparisons with Other Methods

Our solution does not require a language with explicit time expression. Consequently it is difficult to compare this work with other solutions. A big part of other work uses timed automata [8] with model checkers such as Uppaal [11] or Kronos [15]. These automata allows one to write transition systems with time. Transitions between states are instantaneous and time can progress inside a state. One can use several clocks (variables in $\mathbb{R}$). Time constraints are comparisons of clocks with numeric constants and can be set both on state and transition. Automata can only stay in a state, if clock does not exceed time constraints. In the same way system can transit, if constraints are valid. One can reset clock to zero on transition, so the time may be cyclic.

We can point out fundamental differences with our time model using connections between event B models and automata. In our model it is a transition (event) which makes time progress under some condition instead of a state such that time can grow under a limit. For this reason we can have several event activations which are instantaneous. Usually we do not reset time to zero because we can infinitely add active times in the future.

The main difference comes with the use of the active times set which are not explicit in timed automata theory. The word "clock" does not fit very well with our approach because the variable *time* denotes the general time passing. For us a clock is a relation between time progression and known future active times. This set is also the main difference with the explicit-time description in [1] and [19] by L. Lamport et al. As a result our tick_tock event is more general because it only refers to elements of this set.

Properties certification for timed automata is done by a model-checker. The infinite number of states (because of time) is reduced to a finite set of partitions over vector space make by clocks. In our case, proof are made as usual with first order classical logic and set theory inside B tools.

Some other works related to real-time systems can be found in [17] by C.J. Fidge and A.J. Wellings, their approach is different than ours because they do not use instantaneous actions.

3   Message Passing Using the Time Constraint Pattern

This section presents an application of our pattern. We design a system of two devices a and b. Device a can send a message to b. We prove that a timer triggered after sending ensure to a the effective reception of message by b (we do not take into account loss of message). The system is described by two models. The first model has basic elements and events sequencing. The second model refines the previous sequencing of events by time constraints.

3.1   Abstract Model

As a first step we introduce the problem with an abstract model. The model consists of two constants a and b for the devices, four variables A, S, B and AB, and three events :

- sendA : a sends its message to b using connection AB
- recB : b receives it from the connection AB
- quA : when a knows that the message is received by b, it modifies one of its local variable S.

The invariant of the model is:

$$
\begin{array}{l}
A \subseteq \{a\} \;\;\wedge \\
B \subseteq \{b\} \;\;\wedge \\
AB \subseteq \{a\} \;\;\wedge \\
S \subseteq \{a\} \;\;\wedge \\
(A \neq \emptyset \implies AB \neq \emptyset)
\end{array}
$$

According to a distributed system, we consider that A and S are local variables for device a, B is a local variable for device b and AB is a global variable for the channel between the two devices. Similarly events sendA and quA are local to device a and event recB is local to device b. A denotes sending of the message if and only if A is not empty, similarly B denotes its reception and S denotes the state after execution of quA. All variables are booleans (empty or not). Next we define the three events:

$$
\begin{array}{l}
\text{sendA} \;\;\widehat{=} \\
\quad \textbf{when} \\
\qquad A = \emptyset \\
\quad \textbf{then} \\
\qquad A := \{a\} \;\|\; AB := \{a\} \\
\quad \textbf{end}
\end{array}
\qquad
\begin{array}{l}
\text{recB} \;\;\widehat{=} \\
\quad \textbf{when} \\
\qquad AB = \{a\} \\
\quad \textbf{then} \\
\qquad B := \{b\} \;\|\; AB := \emptyset \\
\quad \textbf{end}
\end{array}
$$

Using A to express the sending of the message and B its reception, these events implicitly denote a delay between the execution of sendA and recB. After this delay, we make an action (the reception of the message) as a requirement. To specify this we explicitly ask the message to be received, in the guard of quA.

$$
\begin{array}{l}
\text{quA} \;\;\widehat{=} \\
\quad \textbf{when} \\
\qquad B = \{b\} \\
\quad \textbf{then} \\
\qquad S := \{a\} \\
\quad \textbf{end}
\end{array}
$$

In the abstract model we are "cheating" because event $quaA$ is intended to be local to device a but it can see the variable B which is intended to be local to device b. It is as if device a can see local information of device b. In order to enforce the localisation property as we are moving towards implementation we refine this specification with the time constraint pattern.

3.2   Introducing Time by the Time Constraint Pattern

With the method already described we need to adapt the pattern and anchor events in time. For this we need two constants : $prop$ is the propagation time needed for the message to transit from a to b and st is the sleeping time used in the timer. As an adaptation we need two new variables: stm is the "send time message" and slp the time when a will stop sleeping at the end of the timer. The tick_tock event can be copied as before and we have the two aspects of the pattern:

- Only event sendA posts two active times : $time + prop$ and $time + st$ (with the hypothesis $prop < st$).

- Events recB and quA are processing an active time.

Next we can write temporal aspects with a refinement of the abstract model.

For these two events the refinement is just a superposition, i.e. some lines have been added without changing existing expressions. On sendA we can see the two new active times $time + prop$ and $time + st$ which are the future arrival time of messages and the awake time ending the timer. On the same event the informative variables stm and slp are set up. The second event is triggered by $stm + prop$ which is equal to the posted value $time + prop$, this active time is deleted from at, as in the pattern. Now the most interesting event:

$$\begin{array}{l}
\text{quA } \widehat{=} \\
\textbf{when} \\
\quad A \neq \emptyset \ \wedge \ / * changed\ to\ a\ local\ guard * / \\
\quad time = slp \ / * added * / \\
\textbf{then} \\
\quad S := \{a\} \ \| \\
\quad at := at - \{time\} \ / * added * / \\
\textbf{end}
\end{array}$$

Here the refinement is not just a superposition: the abstract guard was $B = \{b\}$ and is changed to a more concrete $A \neq \emptyset \wedge time = slp$. The use of the non local variable B has disappeared with the use of the local variable A and of the variable $time$. Variable $time$ is universal and global so we can use it to get more information from the local state of distributed devices. In order to prove the refinement we need the following invariant:

$$\begin{array}{l}
time \in \mathbb{N} \ \wedge \\
stm \in \mathbb{N} \ \wedge \\
slp \in \mathbb{N} \ \wedge \\
at \subseteq \mathbb{N} \ \wedge \\
(A \neq \emptyset \implies stm + prop < slp) \ \wedge \\
(A \neq \emptyset \wedge time \geq stm + prop \wedge stm + prop \notin at \implies B = \{b\}) \ \wedge \\
(at \neq \emptyset \implies time \leq min(at)) \ \wedge \\
at \subseteq \{stm + prop, slp\} \ \wedge \\
(A = \emptyset \implies at = \emptyset) \ \wedge \\
(A \neq \emptyset \wedge at = \emptyset \implies time \geq slp) \ \wedge \\
(A \neq \emptyset \wedge at \neq \emptyset \implies slp \in at) \ \wedge \\
(A \neq \emptyset \wedge at = \{slp\} \implies time \geq stm + prop)
\end{array}$$

We give explanations on the most interesting part of this invariant and a derived theorem:

- $(A \neq \emptyset \wedge stm + prop \notin at \wedge time \geq stm + prop \Rightarrow B = \{b\}$:
  This part of the invariant is important to prove the refinement of quA. In this expression if time is beyond $stm + prop$ and if the time constraint $stm + prop$ has already been processed then we are sure of the reception ($B = \{b\}$).
- $(A \neq \emptyset \wedge at = \{slp\} \Rightarrow time \geq stm + prop$:
  If active times set is only $\{slp\}$ and message is gone then current time is after the message reception.
- $(A \neq \emptyset \wedge at = \emptyset \Rightarrow time \geq slp$:
  This predicate is interesting if the message has already been sent ($A \neq \emptyset$) and if there is no more time constraints on process ($at = \emptyset$), in other words once all the events were observed. In this case, one can affirm that the current time exceeded the moment when a was awaken.

– $(A \neq \emptyset \implies stm + prop < slp)$:
  This invariant uses the fact that $prop < st$ because event $sendA$ provides the following proof obligation: $\{a\} \neq \emptyset \implies time + prop < time + st$. This fact is a property on constants st and $prop$ which expresses that the propagation time is less than the sleep time.

The abstract event quA is cheating, since it looks the variable B in its guard ($B = \{b\}$); the refined version is no more cheating, since the guard is local ($A \neq \emptyset$ it has sent the message) and the temporal guard $time = slp$. Only $time$ is a global variable shared by each participant of the global system: it is local for each participant and everyone has the same time. We assume that the time is the same of everyone.

4 Concluding Remarks and Perspectives

4.1 On the Contention Problem

This work began with the time constraint problems inside the firewire protocol. The protocol, namely *IEEE 1394*, can be found in computers and devices like cameras or external hard-disks and is used to connect them together in a local network. When one or several devices are connected or disconnected, they are able to reconfigure themselves. The reconfiguration consists of the election of a network leader. The network is a symmetric acyclic graph, the algorithm of election orients edges to obtain a spanning tree rooted by a leader.

At each step of this distributed algorithm a device is submitted to another. The submitted device is a leaf node among non-submitted devices. The submission of the device is done by sending a message to the device next to it.

But, at the end of the process, a contention problem may occur with the last two devices (and only in this case). Since both devices are leaves, they can send submission almost at the same time. In this case, the two messages cross in the bi-directional channel between the last devices. The election can not be done because both devices are in a submission state.

We can see in the figure 1 an example of contention. X and Y devices are sending messages together with the arrow "1". After the first sending there is a period "a", in this period the other node can send a second message because the first is not received. The protocol has a special case for this problem, the chosen solution deletes the two submission messages and tries to choose a leader with a new message. Messages are not structured packets but constant signals, so a message can be put on or removed from the channel. To give a chance for resolving contention each device chooses a delay between a long and a short time. Then they sleep for the chosen delay. We can see a example below in figure 2 with the two delays "b" and "c" and the deletion of message with the arrow "2".

When the device awakes, there are two possibilities:

– No message has arrived during the sleeping time, so the device can send a submission message.

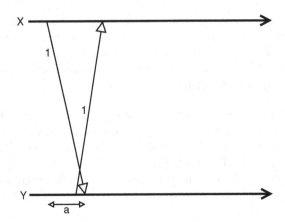

Fig. 1. Example for the contention problem

- One message has arrived during the sleep, so the device has to receive it and
  becomes the leader.

This contention solving succeeds only if the chosen times are different, in this
case only one message is re-sent and the receiver becomes the leader. We can
see this discriminatory message labelled "3" in the figure 2. On the other hand if
sleeping times are the same the contention problem occurs again and the same
process begin.

As we have seen there are a lot of time issues in this part of the protocol.
Time is needed to quantify the two different sleeping times and to represent the
progression of the message signals over the channel.

4.2   Conclusion

The starting point of our work is the proof-based development of the IEEE 1394
leader election protocol and the observation of the partiality of the resulting
proved solution [6]: the development does not take into account time constraints.
Moreover, we paid attention to capture our modelling experience in a pattern
called *time constraint pattern*. We give a light definition of patterns which are
planned to give a systematic help for specialised refinement. Our work illustrates
the use of a general and global time which interacts with a number of actives
times. The time progression is abstract and nondeterministic; the concept of
active times can be fit to various situations like simple clocks, timers or delays
for messages. We have used our pattern on a realistic problem involving messages
on channels and we have studied time constraints in contention problem of the
IEEE 1394 protocol.

The contention problem is not yet completely solved. But we have enough
elements and tools to solve the contention problem in the event B framework.
With the help of refinement we can introduce time constraints that satisfies
a sequence of events. If a concrete system refines another system with time

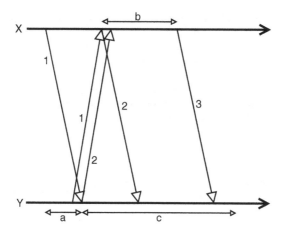

Fig. 2. Example for the contention problem

constraints we can prove the timing validity of the concrete system. For future work, we can enrich the library of patterns and we can study the applicability of such a process on others case studies.

References

1. Martín Abadi and Leslie Lamport. An old-fashioned recipe for real time. *ACM Transactions on Programming Languages and Systems*, 16(5):1543–1571, September 1994.
2. J.-R. Abrial. Using Design Patterns in Formal Devlopments - Example: A Mechanical Press Controler. Journée scientifique du PPF IAEM Transversal - Développement incrémental et prouvé de systèmes, April 2006.
3. Jean-Raymond Abrial. $B^{\#}$: Toward a synthesis between z and b. In Bert et al. [12], pages 168–177.
4. Jean-Raymond Abrial and Dominique Cansell. Formal Construction of a Nonblocking Concurrent Queue Algorithm (a Case Study in Atomicity). *Journal of Universal Computer Science*, 11(5):744–770, May 2005.
5. Jean-Raymond Abrial, Dominique Cansell, and Dominique Méry. Formal derivation of spanning trees algorithms. In Bert et al. [12], pages 457–476.
6. Jean-Raymond Abrial, Dominique Cansell, and Dominique Méry. A mechanically proved and incremental development of IEEE 1394 tree identify protocol. *Formal Asp. Comput.*, 14(3):215–227, 2003.
7. Jean-Raymond Abrial, Dominique Cansell, and Dominique Méry. A new IEEE 1394 leader election protocol. In *Rigorous Methods for Software Construction and Analysis Seminar N 06191,07.05.-12.05.06*. Schloss Dagstuhl, U. Glaser and J. Abrial, 2006.
8. Rajeev Alur and David L. Dill. A theory of timed automata. *Theoretical Computer Science*, 126(2):183–235, 1994.

9. Frédéric Badeau and Arnaud Amelot. Using B as a high level programming language in an industrial project: Roissy val. In Helen Treharne, Steve King, Martin C. Henson, and Steve A. Schneider, editors, *ZB*, volume 3455 of *Lecture Notes in Computer Science*, pages 334–354. Springer, 2005.

10. P. Behm, P. Benoit, A. Faivre, and J.-M.Meynadier. METEOR : A successful application of B in a large project. In *Proceedings of FM'99: World Congress on Formal Methods*, Lecture Notes in Computer Science, pages 369–387, 1999.

11. Johan Bengtsson, Kim Guldstrand Larsen, Fredrik Larsson, Paul Pettersson, and Wang Yi. UPPAAL - a tool suite for automatic verification of real-time systems. In *Hybrid Systems*, pages 232–243, 1995.

12. Didier Bert, Jonathan P. Bowen, Steve King, and Marina A. Waldén, editors. *ZB 2003: Formal Specification and Development in Z and B, Third International Conference of B and Z Users, Turku, Finland, June 4-6, 2003, Proceedings*, volume 2651 of *Lecture Notes in Computer Science*. Springer, 2003.

13. D. Cansell. *Assistance au développement incrémental et à sa preuve*. Habilitation à diriger des recherches, Université Henri Poincaré (Nancy 1), 2003.

14. D. Cansell and D. Méry. Formal and Incremental Construction of Distributed Algorithms:
On the Distributed Reference Counting Algorithm. *Theoretical Computer Science*, 2006. to appear.

15. C. Daws, A. Olivero, S. Tripakis, and S. Yovine. The tool KRONOS. In *Hybrid Systems III: Verification and Control*, volume 1066, pages 208–219, Rutgers University, New Brunswick, NJ, USA, 22–25 October 1995. Springer.

16. Marco Devillers, W. O. David Griffioen, Judi Romijn, and Frits W. Vaandrager. Verification of a leader election protocol: Formal methods applied to ieee 1394. *Formal Methods in System Design*, 16(3):307–320, 2000.

17. Colin J. Fidge and Andy J. Wellings. An action-based formal model for concurrent real-time systems. *Formal Aspects of Computing*, 9(2):175–207, 1997.

18. Erich Gamma, Richard Helm, Ralph E. Johnson, and John M. Vlissides. Design patterns: Abstraction and reuse of object-oriented design. In Oscar Nierstrasz, editor, *ECOOP*, volume 707 of *Lecture Notes in Computer Science*, pages 406–431. Springer, 1993.

19. L. Lamport. Real time is really simple. Technical Report MSR-TR-2006-30, March 2005.

20. Judi Romijn. A timed verification of the ieee 1394 leader election protocol. *Formal Methods in System Design*, 19(2):165–194, 2001.

Modelling and Proof Analysis of Interrupt Driven Scheduling

Bill Stoddart[1], Dominique Cansell[2], and Frank Zeyda[1]

[1] University of Teesside
[2] INRIA/LORIA, University of Metz

Abstract. Following a brief discussion of uniprocessor scheduling in which we argue the case for formal analysis, we describe a distributed Event B model of interrupt driven scheduling. We first consider a model with two executing tasks, presented with the aid of state machine diagrams. We then present a faulty variant of this model which, under particular event timings, may "drop" an interrupt. We show how the failure to discharge a particular proof obligation leads us to the conceptual error in this model. Finally we generalise the correct model to n tasks, leading to a *reduction* in proof effort.

Keywords: Formal Methods, Interrupt Driven Scheduler, Event Calculus.

1   Introduction

We present, in a simple Event Calculus of communicating state machines, the design of an interrupt driven scheduler which is a simplification of one we have deployed in a number of embedded applications. The simplifications are that we do not model the creation of tasks, and that all tasks are "interrupt driven". The resulting model still contains a particularly critical aspect of the design, which relates to a possible race hazard in interrupt timings.

The essence of our modelling technique, which is a variant of Event B, is to describe a state space along with some guarded events which can "instantaneously" modify this state. The state space description includes a formulation of invariant properties, and we incur proof obligations to show that these properties are established at initialisation and maintained across all events. Also essential to the method in general, but not required for our model, are the use of refinement to gradually introduce richer structure and techniques for reachability analysis. Current developments are described in [1].

We define separate B "Abstract Systems" which interact by means of shared events. This is not the predominant modelling technique in Event B, but it is one which can be expressed in B without difficulty. See for example [2,4]. A tutorial introduction to our style of modelling is given in [3].

Our paper has the following structure. In section two we discuss uniprocessor scheduling and justify our choice of a simple but formally modelled scheduler. In section three we present a model of our scheduler running two tasks, using state

J. Julliand and O. Kouchnarenko (Eds.): B 2007, LNCS 4355, pp. 155–170, 2006.
© Springer-Verlag Berlin Heidelberg 2006

machine diagrams to aid comprehension. In section four we present a faulty variant to emphasise the value of formal analysis. Although the scheduler is simple, the fault is difficult to spot or detect though testing. We show how proof analysis directs us precisely to the conceptual error in the design. In section five we generalise the design to n tasks, which, in sharp contrast to the model checking approach, reduces proof effort. In section six we conclude.

2   Uniprocessor Scheduling in Real Time Environments

Formal analysis of real time scheduling has a long history, but has mainly assumed the correctness of a scheduler design and analysed the ability of a certain policy to schedule a given set of tasks with assumed priorities, periodicities and execution times. In 1973 the seminal paper of Liu and Layland [5] showed that for a set of periodic non-intercommunicating tasks the optimal fixed priority scheduler could be obtained by giving higher priorities to tasks that ran at the most frequent rates. They called this scheme "Rate Monotonic Scheduling" (RMS). Assuming zero task switching overheads they obtained a least upper bound to achievable processor utilisation of about 69%. Since that time RMS scheduling and its variants have dominated scheduling policy and generated an enormous body of academic literature, some of which is summarised in [6]. One of the problems considered in this research is "priority inversion". This occurs when a higher priority task is waiting for the lower priority task to release a shared resource. There are a number of methods of dealing with priority inversion, such as 'Priority Inheritance" and the "Priority Ceiling Protocol", but these are not always used as they introduce added complexity which incurs performance penalties. RMS scheduling analysis also has difficulty in dealing with asynchronous events. A flurry of asynchronous events together with priority inversion caused the well known software crash in the NASA Mars Pathfinder mission.[7].

For our own embedded applications we use an "interrupt driven round robin" scheduler. Each i/o device has its own associated task and interrupt service routine. Events in the environment provoke interrupts. The associated interrupt service routine performs any urgent action required by the event, e.g. the dispatch of a data frame at a precise time, then sets the status flag of its associated task. The task then runs when its turn arrives and deals with the less urgent aspects of the event, e.g. the preparation and queueing of subsequent frames. Round robin (RR) scheduling is sometimes considered too simplistic for use in the most demanding applications, due to the following apparent disadvantage: a task with a hard deadline may become ready to run just after it has been considered by the scheduler. In this case it will need to wait for all other tasks before it gets its turn and is therefore likely to miss its deadline. With our scheduler however, we are able to meet hard deadlines via an interrupt response, though we consider this only appropriate if the required action is fairly simple. Very often it can be. Take another example. A tank is proceeding on a road with its gun aimed at a target, when it hits a bump which disturbs the aim. The immediate action is to set a flag which momentarily postpones any firing of the gun. The subsequent action is to re-establish its gun's orientation.

More generally we can argue a case as follows. By assigning less time to each task, the round robin will rotate more quickly and reduce variation in task service times. Indeed, if we ignore scheduling overheads, processor utilisation under RR tends to 100% as the maximum task service time tends to zero. Letting service time tend to zero whilst ignoring scheduling overheads has its limitations, but the formal result indicates why RR is particularly applicable where there is an efficient scheduling mechanism. Assuming a suitable processor architecture (one that does not impose significant task switching overheads) such a mechanism is described in this paper.

There are a number of other well known "work arounds" such as allowing the most urgent tasks to have multiple entries in the round robin. Formal analysis assists us here by ensuring that such variations do not introduce faults into the scheduler design.

Our experience has been that it is worth persisting with the round robin in order to profit from its simplicity, low overheads and fairness properties. Despite its simplicity however, we will show that even a round robin scheduler requires formal analysis, as it can exhibit subtle faults which may escape detection by testing.

3   Our First Model: The Scheduler with Two Tasks

We present the model in terms of interacting state machines which synchronise on shared events. For our previous work using such state machines and describing their translation into B see [3,4].

The model (though not its invariant properties) is simple enough for its components to be expressed as state machine diagrams. We have found this a useful way to present the design to students and real time practitioners. Although the practitioners we have collaborated with are trained engineers, they require gentle treatment when Formal Methods are mentioned, and appear to appreciate this form of description. We also hope this model will help the reader to understand the scheduler's operation. This understanding is essential of course: if we are to gain the readers confidence with respect to the results of our proof analysis, he or she needs to agree that what we have analysed is indeed an adequate model for a scheduler.

The machines in this model do not represent separate physical entities. Rather they formalise some views (i.e. abstractions) of the design, namely: scheduling policy, task status history, device interrupt and task execution protocols.

Figure 1 shows the operation of RR scheduling for two tasks. From its initial state S_0, the scheduler may either run task A or skip task A. If it skips A, it becomes ready to run or skip B. When a task runs, it must subsequently relinquish the processor to allow other tasks to run. If it has completed the action required in response to the current interrupt it will *stop*. Alternatively, if it still has more work to do but is relinquishing the processor to allow other tasks a turn, it will *pause*.

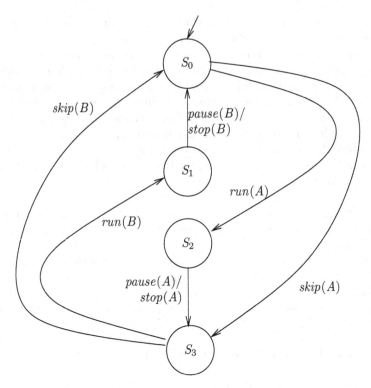

Fig. 1. Task scheduler running tasks A and B

We translate this state machine into a B abstract system. SELECT constructs express the firing condition of each event: e.g. $skipp(A)$ can occur when $t = A$ and $state = S0$. Pre-conditions are used to provide type information.[1]

SYSTEM *scheduler*

SEES *globals*/* this defines the set $TASK = \{A, B\}$ */

SETS $SSTATE = \{S0, S1, S2, S3\}$

VARIABLES *state*

INVARIANT *state* : *SSTATE*

INITIALISATION *state* := *S0*

EVENTS

   $skipp(t) \mathrel{\widehat{=}}$ PRE t : *TASK* THEN
      SELECT $state = S0 \wedge t = A$ THEN $state := S3$
      WHEN $state = S3 \wedge t = B$ THEN $state := S0$ END
   END ;

---

[1] Readers may recall the B convention of reserving single character names for meta-variables. This does not apply to the Click'n'Prove tool available on the B4free web site, www.b4free.com, and is not used here.

$run(t) \;\widehat{=}\;$ PRE $t : TASK$ THEN
    SELECT $state = S0 \wedge t = A$ THEN $state := S2$
    WHEN $state = S3 \wedge t = B$ THEN $state := S1$ END
END ;

$pause(t) =$ PRE $t : TASK$ THEN
    SELECT $state = S1 \wedge t = B$ THEN $state := S0$
    WHEN $state = S2 \wedge t = A$ THEN $state := S3$ END
END ;

$stop(t) =$ PRE $t : TASK$ THEN
    SELECT $state = S1 \wedge t = B$ THEN $state := S0$
    WHEN $state = S2 \wedge t = A$ THEN $state := S3$ END
END
END

The state machine for the scheduling policy does not indicate how a choice is made between running or skipping a task, or between *stop* or *pause*. This will be determined by event synchronisation with other state machines.

Each task is modelled in terms of a status flag, an i/o device interrupt protocol and an execution protocol. We detail those for task A.

The decision as to whether a task will be run or skipped by the scheduler is made according to the setting of the task's status flag. The status flag behaviour for A is shown as the left most state machine of figure 2.

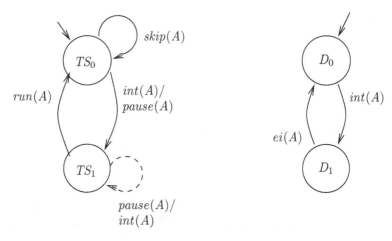

Fig. 2. Task A status flag (left) and i/o device interrupt protocol

In its initial state TS_0 this status flag permits the event $skip(A)$ but blocks $run(A)$. In state TS_1 the status flag has the opposite effect, blocking $skip(A)$ and allowing $run(A)$. It will change from TS_0 to TS_1 on the occurrence of either an interrupt for task A (event $int(A)$) or by a pause in the execution of task A (event $pause(A)$). When task A is run, (event $run(A)$) its status flag is reset to state TS_0.

From state TS_1 the status flag for task A will permit either $pause(A)$ or $int(A)$ but will remain in the same state. This pair of transitions is represented with a dotted line, a convention we use to represent the expectation that these transitions are not expected to occur within the context of the overall system, but must be included here because *it is not the job of the status flag to block them*, and that would be the effect of their omission under our interpretation of shared (synchronised) events.

We use a single B Abstract System to model the status flags of both tasks. Within this abstract system, $status(A)$ represents the status of task A and $status(B)$ the status of task B. The firing condition for $run(A)$ is $status(A) = TS_1$ and so on.

SYSTEM *status*

SEES *globals*

SETS $TASKSTATUS = \{ TS0, TS1 \}$

VARIABLES *status*

INVARIANT $status : TASK \rightarrow TASKSTATUS$

INITIALISATION $status := TASK * \{ TS0 \}$

EVENTS

   $skipp(t) \;\widehat{=}\;$ PRE $t : TASK$ THEN
      SELECT $status(t) = TS0$ THEN *skip* END
   END ;

   $run(t) \;\widehat{=}\;$ PRE $t : TASK$ THEN
      SELECT $status(t) = TS1$ THEN $status(t) := TS0$ END
   END ;

   $int(t) \;\widehat{=}\;$ PRE $t : TASK$ THEN
      BEGIN $status(t) := TS1$ END
   END;

   $pause(t) \;\widehat{=}\;$ PRE $t : TASK$ THEN
      BEGIN $status(t) := TS1$ END
   END
END

We now consider the interrupt protocol to be followed by a task's i/o device. It is the same for all tasks, so we will again just consider the case of task A. After the event $int(A)$ a further $int(A)$ is impossible until interrupts are enabled for the device (event $ei(A)$). This is shown in the rightmost state machine of figure 2. Our model does not detail what happens when an outside world event which would cause an interrupt occurs when interrupts are disabled. In this situation the hardware devices keeps the interrupt pending and will raise it when the device interrupt is next enabled.

Figure 3 defines the execution protocol of task A. From its initial non-executing state T_0 the task may be run (event $run(A)$). It returns to the non-executing state either via a pause (when it has more work still to do but other tasks are to have access to the processor) or by re-enabling the interrupts for its associated i/o device and stopping (when it has completed its work). The

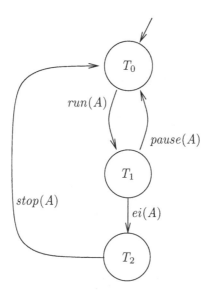

Fig. 3. Execution protocol for task A

translation of these last two state machines to B follows exactly the pattern of the status flags, and will therefore be omitted. The complete model is shown in figure 4.

The design becomes critical under conditions of heavy load, i.e. when interrupts occur more or less as soon as they are enabled. In this case an interrupt may arrive to activate a task which is still running in response to a previous interrupt. A key design decision here is that when a task is dispatched its status flag is reset to its initial state, allowing its interrupt routine to register an effect whilst the task is actually running. Event $int(B)$ in the following trace illustrates this. To indicate which machines participate in each event we use these names: S for the scheduler; AS, BS for the status flags; AD, BD for the i/o devices and A, B for the execution protocols of the two tasks.

Event	Participating Machines	Task A	Scheduler	Task B
		T_0, TS_0, D_0	S_0	T_0, TS_0, D_0
$skip(A)$	S, AS	T_0, TS_0, D_0	S_3	T_0, TS_0, D_0
$int(A)$	AS, AD	T_0, TS_1, D_1	S_3	T_0, TS_0, D_0
$int(B)$	BS, BD	T_0, TS_1, D_1	S_3	T_0, TS_1, D_1
$run(B)$	S, B, BS	T_0, TS_1, D_1	S_1	T_1, TS_0, D_1
$ei(B)$	B, BD	T_0, TS_1, D_1	S_1	T_2, TS_0, D_0
$int(B)$	BS, BD	T_0, TS_1, D_1	S_1	T_2, TS_1, D_1

Following these events, task B is running and task activation in response to an interrupt is pending for both tasks. Under the assumption that no further

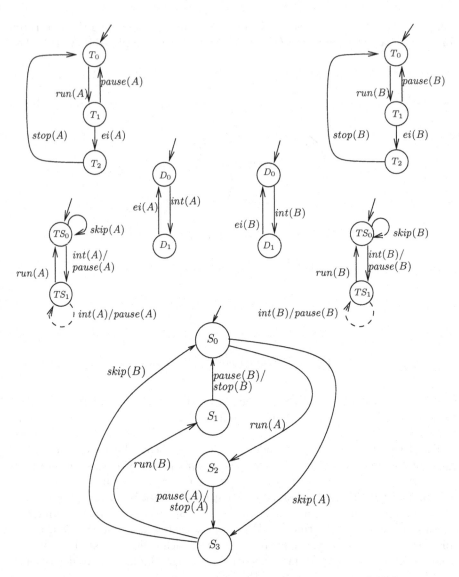

Fig. 4. Tasks A and B with status flags, i/o devices and scheduler

interrupts occur and that tasks relinquish the processor via *stop*, the following event trace will subsequently occur:

$$\langle stop(B), run(A), ei(A), stop(A), run(B), ei(B), stop(B)...\rangle$$

Now let us return to the unwanted event transitions of the status flags, which are marked by dotted lines in our diagrams, and consider exactly why we do not want them to occur but must nevertheless include them in the behaviour of our machines. For example consider the transition:

$$TS_1 \xrightarrow{\quad int(A) \quad} TS_1$$

this is unwanted since it fails to register that an interrupt has occurred. It must be included because it cannot be the business of a status flag, which will be implemented as a program variable, to control whether an interrupt can occur. On the other hand the status flag can very well be used, in an *if* statement, to control a choice, made by the scheduler, between running or skipping a task, and this is its function in our model.

A B model of the entire system is constructed by including all component machines and composing events in parallel. At this level we can also introduce system invariant properties.

SYSTEM *system*
INCLUDES *globals, Dev.device, Sched.scheduler, Task.task, Status.status*
INVARIANT
/*A task's device is not interrupt enabled when the task is dispatched*/
$\forall\, t.(t : TASK \Rightarrow (Task.state(t) = T1 \Rightarrow Dev.state(t) = D1)) \wedge$
/*If a task's device is interrupt enabled, the task does not require service*/
$\forall\, t.(t : TASK \Rightarrow (Dev.state(t) = D0 \Rightarrow Status.status(t) = TS0)) \wedge$
/* Global impossibility properties (infeasibility of dotted transitions): */
/* interrupt behaviour */
$\forall\, t.(t : TASK \Rightarrow (Status.status(t) = TS1 \Rightarrow Dev.state(t) = D1)) \wedge$
/* pausing behaviour */
$(Status.status(A) = TS1 \Rightarrow not(Sched.state = S2 \wedge Task.state(A) = T1))$
$\wedge$
$(Status.status(B) = TS1 \Rightarrow not(Sched.state = S1 \wedge Task.state(B) = T1))$
$\wedge$
/*scheduler properties*/
$(Sched.state = S0 \Rightarrow \forall\, t.(t : TASK \Rightarrow Task.state(t) = T0)) \wedge$
$(Sched.state = S1 \Rightarrow Task.state(A) = T0 \wedge Task.state(B) \neq T0) \wedge$
$(Sched.state = S2 \Rightarrow Task.state(A) \neq T0 \wedge Task.state(B) = T0) \wedge$
$(Sched.state = S3 \Rightarrow \forall\, t.(t : TASK \Rightarrow Task.state(t) = T0))$

ASSERTIONS
/*only one task runs at a time. Note that the status of an idle task is T0.*/
$\forall(t1, t2).$
$\quad (t1 : TASK \wedge t2 : TASK \wedge Task.state(t1) \neq T0 \wedge Task.state(t2) \neq T0$
$\qquad \Rightarrow$
$t1 = t2)$
EVENTS
$\quad run(t) \,\widehat{=}\, PRE\ t : TASK\ THEN$
$\qquad Sched.run(t) \parallel Task.run(t) \parallel Status.run(t)$
$\quad END ;$

$\quad skipp(t) \,\widehat{=}\, PRE\ t : TASK\ THEN\ Sched.skipp(t) \parallel Status.skipp(t)\ END ;$

$pause(t) \mathrel{\widehat{=}}$ PRE $t : TASK$ THEN
   $Sched.pause(t) \parallel Status.pause(t) \parallel Task.pause(t)$
END ;

$stop(t) \mathrel{\widehat{=}}$ PRE $t : TASK$ THEN $Sched.stop(t) \parallel Task.stop(t)$ END ;

$ei(t) \mathrel{\widehat{=}}$ PRE $t : TASK$ THEN $Dev.ei(t) \parallel Task.ei(t)$ END ;

$int(t) \mathrel{\widehat{=}}$ PRE $t : TASK$ THEN $Dev.int(t) \parallel Status.int(t)$ END

END

Let us now consider some events and invariant clauses of this system model. As an example event consider $run(t)$. This involves the scheduler, the task t, and the task's status flag. We form the system event $run(t)$ by composing the $run(t)$ events of these three components in parallel. The result is an event which can only fire if each of its components can fire: a three way event synchronisation. Checking the definitions of run in the included machines, we see that the effective firing condition is the conjunction of the following:

- The scheduler is considering whether to run t
- t is in the idle state
- The status flag for t is set.

Now let us turn to the invariant and assertions clauses. The formal checks of consistency imposed by the B method are to ensure the invariant is established by the initialisation of the system, and is preserved by any events that occur. Our system machine has no initialisation clause, and indeed no variables of its own. Its initialisation is performed within the included machines. The invariant clause, on the other hand, is quite extensive and we will pick out for discussion the part that relates to guaranteeing that interrupts cannot be "dropped".

Since the effect of an interrupt is to set the status flag for the associated task we will drop an interrupt (i.e. miss its effect) if it occurs when the relevant status flag is already set. So we want to ensure the event $int(t)$ cannot fire (is not feasible) when the status flag of t is set: i.e.

$$\forall t.(t : TASK \Rightarrow (Status.status(t) = TS1 \Rightarrow not(fis(int(t))))$$

This form is not immediately suitable for use in our invariant as our tool support does not allow us to directly refer to the feasibility of an event. However, after some obvious manipulations using the definition for fis given in the B Book [8] the property can be expressed in the following form:

$$\forall t.(t : TASK \Rightarrow (Status.state(t) = TS1 \Rightarrow not(Dev.state(t) = D0)))$$

This property ensures that whenever interrupts can occur, their effect will be registered by the system. A further obvious simplification step gives the invariant clause used above in the model.

3.1   On the Use of Input Parameters, Event Synchronisation and Feasibility

Our style differs from most Event B models in its use of parametrized events. We use what are notionally "input" parameters for this purpose, but here they serve as a general form of event parameterization.. The resulting proof obligations for invariant preservation are universally quantified over all possible parameter values.

The use of event parameters allows us to model n way synchronisations via parallel composition of events. This is similar to the primitive synchronisation of actions in CSP. However, CSP also has a more elaborate model of communication, built on top of primitive synchronisations, which describes the one way communication of a value from a sender to a receiver via a "channel". Channels are used in Michael Butler's csp2B[2] and in Steve Schneider and Helen Treharne's Communicating B Machines[9], two formalisms which provide an integration of CSP and B. Channels provide an ideal description for the communicating of information from a transmitter to a receiver along a wire (and for analogous situations) but their use would be artificial and clumsy for the more intimate style of modelling we adopt here, where shared events may arise from the intersecting life cycle histories of purely conceptual components obtained from taking different "views" of the system.

Feasibility plays an essential role in our modelling. Events are typically guarded, and may only fire if their guard is true. An event which cannot fire cannot fail to preserve the system invariant. In terms of formal proof, such an event is "miraculously" able to guarantee any post condition, and thus can guarantee the system invariant remains true. Intuitively we can interpret this miraculous behaviour as "all possible after states will satisfy the post condition". As there are no after states, any postcondition can (in this vacuous way) be satisfied.

4   A Faulty Variant and Its Proof Analysis

In our model a task status of TS_1 indicates that a request for future action by the task is pending, whereas TS_0 indicates that there is no such request. We now look at an alternative characterisation which might initially seem more appealing. A task will be "asleep" (task status TS_0) if it is not running and not requiring service, or "awake" (task status TS_1) if it is running or requiring service. The only difference from the previous model is that a task's status is reset at the *stop* event rather than the *run* event. This gives a different life cycle history for a task's status flag, as shown in figure 5 for task A.

We invite the reader to try to spot the fault in this model before we show how it is revealed by proof analysis!

For this model our tool support lists 111 non-trivial proof obligations for the establishment and preservation of static invariant properties. The large number of proof obligations means that when we encounter an obligation that we see will not be true, we can gain very precise information about the fault in our model.

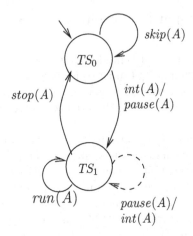

Fig. 5. Task A status flag, faulty variant

The first obligation that we find impossible to discharge is one arising from the *ei* (enable interrupt) event. It is presented to us as: $Statusstate(t\$0) = TS0$.

The invariant clause to preserved by the event is also displayed at the top of the proof tree window. Apart from slight variations due to internal normalisation, it is the clause discussed at the end of the previous section: a tasks status flag is in state $TS0$ whenever its interrupts are enabled. The tool has generated the proof obligation from this by eliminating the universal quantification (introducing, in the process, the "fresh" variable $t\$0$) and converting the left hand side of the remaining implication to a hypothesis.

The failure to discharge this obligation leads us to the following analysis. In this model, when a task is set running its status remains "awake". It cannot at this point register the effect of an interrupt, but that is not a problem (yet) because the corresponding device interrupt is currently disabled. The task enables its interrupt before it stops. This is the event at which our proof analysis fails, and it marks an interval of vulnerability when interrupts are enabled and the task is still running. At this point a device interrupt can occur without registering any effect on the status flag, i.e. the interrupt can be "dropped". This fault can escape detection by testing, as it will only manifest itself if the interrupt occurs in a certain time interval. Indeed, one can realistically envisage a situation in which the scheduler passes some tests and the fault later occurs on prototype hardware, a scenario that would completely confuse development engineers. Formal analysis, however, has precisely directed our attention to the fault.

5   Generalising the Model

To generalise our scheduler model from two to n tasks we change our *globals* machine so *TASK* is a set of unknown size but with at least one element. This is enough to generalise all the component Abstract Systems in our model with the exception of the scheduler. For that, we introduce a new B Abstract System which represents the round robin as a circular list of tasks. We have a variable *head* which indicates the currently selected tasks, and events which select the current task and move *head* to the next task in the robin.

SYSTEM *sched_data*

SEES *globals*

VARIABLES *robin*, *head*

INVARIANT
/* robin is an isomorphic function with a single cycle, representing a circular list of all tasks */
$$robin : TASK \rightarrowtail TASK \wedge$$
$$head : TASK \wedge$$
$$\forall ss.(ss \subseteq TASK \wedge robin[ss] = ss \Rightarrow ss = TASK)$$

INITIALISATION
$$robin, head : (robin : TASK \rightarrowtail TASK \wedge head : TASK \wedge$$
$$\forall ss.(ss \subseteq TASK \wedge head : ss \wedge robin[ss] \subseteq ss \Rightarrow ss = TASK))$$

EVENTS
$$this(t) \widehat{=} \text{ PRE } t : TASK \text{ THEN}$$
      SELECT $t = head$ THEN *skip* END
   END ;

$$next(t) \widehat{=} \text{ PRE } t : TASK \text{ THEN}$$
      SELECT $t = head$ THEN $head := robin(head)$ END
   END
END

A state machine representation of the scheduler which refers to these events is shown in fig. 6. In state S_0 the scheduler is running, and in state S_1 a task is running. We see once again the familiar events *run, skip pause* and *stop* but this time each of these appears in parallel with an event from the *sched_data* machine, which may be considered as representing the "internal state" of the scheduler (by which we mean a state not shown explicitly on the state diagram). The event $run(t)$ occurs in parallel with $this(t)$, which uses a feasibility filter to ensure that $run(t)$ can only fire when $t = head$. Without the inhibiting action of $this(t)$, the event $run(t)$ could fire for any t. The effect of the parallel composition is to ensure that $run(t)$ is only enabled for the task at the head of the round robin. The events *skip, pause* and *stop* occur in parallel with *next*, which, as well as using a feasibility filter to select $t = head$, updates the internal state of the scheduler to point the *head* variable at the following task.

In the translation process which converts the state machine representation to B we identify the parameter t as a variable by a convention that constants are named in upper case (e.g. the tasks A, B in the first model were constants) and variables in lower case.

SYSTEM *scheduler*

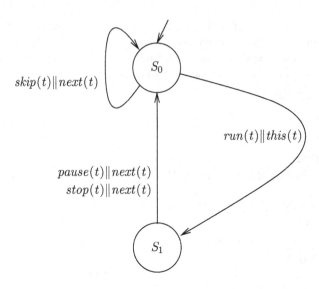

Fig. 6. Generalised Scheduler

SEES *globals*

INCLUDES *sched_data*

SETS $SSTATE = \{S0, S1\}$

VARIABLES *state*

INVARIANT *state* : *SSTATE*

INITIALISATION *state* := *S0*

EVENTS

  skipp(t) $\widehat{=}$ PRE t : *TASK* THEN
    SELECT *state* = *S0* THEN *next*(t) END
  END ;

  run(t) $\widehat{=}$ PRE t : *TASK* THEN
    SELECT *state* = *S0* THEN *state* := *S1* || *this*(t) END
  END ;

  pause(t) $\widehat{=}$ PRE t : *TASK* THEN
    SELECT *state* = *S1* THEN *state* := *S0* || *next*(t) END
  END ;

  stop(t) $\widehat{=}$ PRE t : *TASK* THEN
    SELECT *state* = *S1* THEN *state* := *S0* || *next*(t) END
  END
END

    As with the two task model, we produce a system machine which includes all distributed components with events composed in parallel to define the system level events. The definition of this new system machine is identical to that for the two task model apart from a re-expression of the invariant in the following more general terms.

INVARIANT
/*a task's device is not interrupt enabled when the task is dispatched*/
   $\forall t.(t : TASK \Rightarrow (Task.state(t) = T1 \Rightarrow Dev.state(t) = D1)) \wedge$
/*if a task's device is interrupt enabled, the task does not require service*/
   $\forall t.(t : TASK => (Dev.state(t) = D0 \Rightarrow Status.state(t) = TS0)) \wedge$
/* Global impossibility properties (infeasibility of dotted transitions): */
/* interrupt behaviour */
   $\forall t.(t : TASK => (Status.state(t) = TS1 \Rightarrow Dev.state(t) = D1))$
   $\wedge$
/* pausing behaviour */
   $\forall t.(t : TASK \Rightarrow (Status.state(t) = TS1 \Rightarrow$
      $not(Sched.state = S1 \wedge Sched.head = t \wedge Task.state(t) = T1))) \wedge$
/*scheduler properties*/
   $(Sched.state = S0 \Rightarrow \forall t.(t : TASK \Rightarrow Task.state(t) = T0)) \wedge$
   $(Sched.state = S1 \Rightarrow$
      $(Task.state(Sched.head) \neq T0 \wedge \forall t.(t : TASK \wedge t \neq Sched.head \Rightarrow$
         $Task.state(t) = T0)))$

   Our first model, specific to two tasks, generated 111 non-trivial proof obligations of which 77 were discharged automatically and 34 were proved interactively. For the generalised model, although the scheduler component now has a significant invariant of its own, the number of non-trivial proof obligations fell to 41, of which 21 were discharged automatically and 20 were proved interactively. The higher proportion of automatic proofs for the first model is due to the proof obligation generator producing separate proof obligations for task A and task B in some of the simpler cases. Overall, the generalisation has led to a reduction in the proof effort required. The models were analysed with the "Click'n'Prove" tool [10].

6   Conclusions

This paper has presented a formal model which captures the essential aspects of an interrupt driven scheduler. We have demonstrated how proof analysis of a faulty variant leads us directly to a subtle fault which could be missed in testing. We have shown how the model is generalised from two to n tasks, and that, in contrast to the model checking approach, such a generalisation reduces proof effort.

   We also conjecture that interrupt driven RR scheduling, with some variations, is a viable choice for demanding real time applications. We propose to elaborate the extent of this claim in future work, along with a formal analysis of variations in our scheduler design, such as including multiple entries for urgent tasks.

References

1. J-R Abrial and D Cansell. Refinement and Reachability in Event B. In D Bert et al, editor, *ZB2005*, To appear in Lecture Notes in Computer Science, 2005.
2. M Butler. csp2B: A practical approach to combining CSP and B. In J M Wing, Woodcock J, and Davies J, editors, *FM99 vol 1*, number 1708 in Lecture Notes in Computer Science. Springer Verlag, 1999.
3. W J Stoddart, S E Dunne, Galloway A J, and Shore R. Abstract State Machines: Designing Distributed Systems with State Machines and B. In D Bert, editor, *B'98: Recent Developments in the Use of the B Method.*, number 1393 in Lecture Notes in Computer Science, 1998.
4. A Papatsaras and W J Stoddart. Global and Communicating State Machine Models in Event Driven B: A Simple Railway Case Study. In Bert D, Bowen J, Henson M, and Robinson K, editors, *ZB2002*, number 2272 in Lecture Notes in Computer Science, 2002.
5. C L Liu and J W Layland. Scheduling algorithms for multiprogramming in a hard real-time environment. *Journal of the ACM*, 20(1), 1973.
6. M Klein et al. *A Practitioners Handbook for Real time Analysis*. Kluwer Academic Pub., 1993.
7. Glenn Reeves. What really happened on Mars? *Risks Forum Digest*, 19: Issue 58, 1998.
8. J-R Abrial. *The B Book*. Cambridge University Press, 1996.
9. S Schneider and H Treharne. Communicating B Machines. In D Bert, J Bowen, M Henson, and K Robinson, editors, *ZB2002*, number 2272 in Lecture Notes in Computer Science, 2002.
10. J-R Abrial and D Cansell. Click'n'Prove: Interactive Proofs in Set Theory. In D Basin and B Wolff, editors, *TPHOLs 2003*, number 2758 in Lecture Notes in Computer Science, 2003. Invited Paper.

Refinement of Statemachines Using Event B Semantics[*]

Colin Snook[1] and Marina Waldén[2]

[1] University of Southampton, Southampton, SO17 1BJ, UK
[2] Åbo Akademi University, Joukahaisenkatu 3-5A, 20520 Turku, Finland

Abstract. While refinement gives a formal underpinning to the development of dependable control systems, such models are difficult to communicate and reason about in a non-formal sense, particularly for validation by non-specialist industrial partners. Here we present a visualisation of, and guidance for, event B refinement using a specialisation of UML statemachines. Furthermore, we introduce design patterns and process rules that are aimed at assisting in the software development process leading to correct refinements. The specialisation will be incorporated into the UML-B notation to be integrated with the Event B platform developed by the RODIN project.

1 Introduction

Formal software construction techniques are beneficial when developing complex distributed control systems. Such systems often demand high integrity to achieve safety requirements. The use of formal analysis tools can increase confidence in the correctness of the system. These tools are, however, not always easy to use, or well accepted, in an industrial environment. This barrier can be overcome by a graphical presentation of the formal models. In many cases, rules of the formal development can be built into the graphical notation and supported directly within the drawing tool.

We use the Event B [1] formalism as our formal framework for developing distributed control systems. Event B is a method with tool support for applying distributed systems in the B Method [2] that is based on Action Systems [5,6] and related to B Action Systems [26]. Hence, we can benefit from the useful formalism for reasoning about distributed systems given by Action Systems and from the tool support in B. Development within Event B is performed in a stepwise manner from abstract specification to concrete implementation using superposition refinement. The correctness of each step is proved in order to achieve a reliable system. The tool assists the development process by generating the proof obligations needed. These proof obligations can then be proved with the automatic or the interactive prover of the tool.

An approach of integrating B with the UML [9] has been developed at Southampton. The UML-B [22] is a specialisation of UML that defines a formal modelling notation combining UML and B. It is supported by the U2B tool [21], which translates UML-B models into B. The translation of UML-B statemachines is similar to that proposed by Sekerinski [18]. A closer integration of UML-B and Event B tools is being developed in the RODIN project [17]. In this paper we describe part of this ongoing work

---

[*] Work done within the EU research project RODIN: IST 511599.

J. Julliand and O. Kouchnarenko (Eds.): B 2007, LNCS 4355, pp. 171–185, 2006.

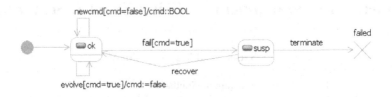

Fig. 1. Abstract model of a controller failing and recovering

to extend support for the refinement of event models expressed as UML-B statemachines. This work is based on previous work to develop control systems using UML and B [23,24]. We use hierarchical states to model the addition of detail to the state space and corresponding events. We use *junction* pseudostates to visualise the required event refinement relationships and choice pseudostates to visualise how events are decomposed.

The rest of the paper is structured as follows. In Section 2 we show how to model a control system in UML-B. Section 3 describes the refinement concept. In Section 4 we give a practical view of the refinement process via a graphical interface and illustrate the process with examples. We conclude in Section 5.

2 Modelling Event B Systems in UML

We depict the functional requirements of the system in class diagrams. For each class we give the attributes and their types, as well as the methods. Hence, the classes model the state independent properties of the components. The behaviour of each component of the system is specified with a statemachine diagram. The specification of the eventual system is then gradually captured and made more and more precise throughout a series of these diagrams. In the most abstract class diagram we only consider the state value for the state machine and the command that the component is required to obey. The methods cover the functionality of the system and an abstract representation of the types of errors, as well as the possibility to fix these errors. Here, we focus on refinement of statemachines.

The first abstract statemachine diagram of a control system is shown in Figure 1. When the system is given proper commands (cmd = true), and is functioning successfully (evolve), it remains in state ok. The transition evolve is an abstraction of the behaviour of the system. New commands may be given to the system (new_command) when it is in state ok and the previous command has been processed (cmd = false). If the system fails, it will go to state susp via transition fail. The controller recovers (recover) to state ok, if the fault is recoverable. If a non-recoverable fault occurs, the controller terminates (terminate) in state failed where it is deadlocked. Note that we do not use the state machine to illustrate the sequencing of the events new_command and evolve. This is because we wish to refine the data representation of the command separately from the state of the system.

2.1   Event B Models

In Event B the variables of a system are given in the **VARIABLES**-clause. The types and the invariant properties of the variables are given in the **INVARIANT**-clause and their initial value in the **INITIALISATION**-clause. The events that alter the variables are given in the **EVENTS**-clause.

With Event B we model systems, where events are selected for execution in a non-deterministic manner. This enables modelling of parallel and distributed systems. The events are given in the form e = **WHEN** P **THEN** S **END**, where P is a predicate on the variables (also called a guard) and S is a substitution (i.e. the values of zero or more variables are substituted with new values which may be selected non-deterministically). When P holds the event e is said to be enabled. Only enabled events are considered for execution. When there are no enabled events the system terminates. We note that control systems are designed only to terminate when an unrecoverable failure occurs. The events are considered to be atomic, and hence, only their pre and post states are of interest.

In order to be able to ensure the correctness of the system, the abstract model should be consistent and feasible [3,14]. This can be ensured by proving the following proof obligations:

1. The initialisation should be feasible and establish the invariant.
2. Each event should be feasible and preserve the invariant.

These proof obligations can be generated automatically and then verified using the tool Atelier B [11] that supports the B Method and Event B (previously via Evt2B transla-tion). The proof obligations are generated via before-after predicates denoting the rela-tion between the variable values before and after the execution of a substitution [3,14]. For example, the before-after predicate, BA, of the simple substitution $v := E(v)$ is $BA(v, v') \mathrel{\hat=} v' = E(v)$, where v is the variable value before and v' after the execution of the substitution. The proof obligation stating that event e above preserves the invari-ant I is then $I(v) \;\wedge\; P(v) \;\wedge\; BA(v, v') \;\Rightarrow\; I(v')$. In this paper we give informal and intuitive descriptions of the proof obligations. Their formal descriptions are given in [3,14].

2.2   Creating a B-Model from UML

The first step in our formal development is to create an abstract Event B system from the abstract class diagrams and statemachines. The tool U2B [20] supports this translation. Attributes in class diagrams correspond to variables in B. Such variables are 'lifted' and modelled as functions so that the separate values for each instance can be represented. However, for simplicity, we do not show this lifting in the examples that follow.

UML-B is given a semantics by translation to Event B as provided by the U2B trans-lator. Hence, a statemachine represents a variable, s, whose value is one of the states and a transition path from state A to state B represents an event that is guarded by s=A and takes action s:=B. UML provides a mechanism for constructing a transition path via intermediate pseudostates (representing junction and choice). We require exactly one segment of a transition path to be named and this name is used as the name of the corresponding event. Unnamed transition segments (between pseudostates) are not separate events, but may contribute to the guard and action of the named transitions. Hence, an event is constructed for each complete transition path. Its guard includes the conjunction of the guards of all the segments in its path and its substitution includes the parallel composition of the actions of these segments. As there is no branch construct in Event B, each branch is represented as a separate event. Therefore, if a named transition segment contributes to multiple paths it translates into multiple events, one for each path (a naming scheme is used to provide a unique name for each event). Hierarchical statemachines are represented with further variables, one for each statemachine.

The statemachine of the controller in Figure 1 can be translated to the Event B system below.

```
SYSTEM Controller
VARIABLES      cmd, state
INVARIANT      cmd ∈ BOOL ∧ state ∈ {ok, susp, failed}
INITIALISATION cmd := false ‖ state := ok
EVENTS
  new_command == WHEN cmd = false THEN cmd :∈ BOOL END
  evolve ==      WHEN state = ok ∧ cmd = true THEN cmd := false END
  fail ==        WHEN state = ok ∧ cmd = true THEN state := susp END
  recover ==     WHEN state = susp THEN state := ok END
  terminate ==   WHEN state = susp THEN state := failed END
END
```

Here, the variable cmd models the command of the controller and is initially set to false. The state is initialised to value ok. New commands are provided by the environment via event new_command, which can occur when the previous command has been processed (cmd = false). Note that at this stage we model the input of a new command as internal choice. Later the representation of commands will be refined and determined via external choice. The guards and substitutions of the other events evolve, fail, recover and terminate are formed in a similar manner from the guards and actions of the corresponding transitions in the statemachine in Figure 1.

3   Refining Models

An important feature provided by the Event B formalism is the ability to stepwise refine specifications. Refinement is a process that transforms an abstract, non-deterministic, specification into a concrete, deterministic, system that preserves the functionality of the original specification. We use a particular refinement method, *superposition refinement* [5,13], where we extend the state space while preserving the old variables. Superposition refinement is a special case of Event B refinement [3,14], which is based on refinement calculus [7]. When dealing with complex control systems it is especially convenient to stepwise introduce details about the system to the specification and not to have to handle all the concrete implementation issues at once [16]. As the system development proceeds we also add more elaborated information about faults and conditions of failure occurrence [16,25].

During the refinement process new features that are suggested by the requirements are represented by new variables added to the system. Simultaneously, events are refined to take the new features into account. This is performed by strengthening their guards and adding substitutions on the new variables. Furthermore, events may be split so that several events refine one old event. New events that only assign the new variables may also be introduced.

In order to gain confidence in the refinement process we need to prove the correctness of each refinement step. With the tool Atelier B we can formally verify that the refinement is sound by discharging a number of proof obligations. For proving that a system C is a correct refinement of a system A ($A \sqsubseteq C$) the following proof obligations have to be satisfied [6,26,14]:

1. The initialisation in C should be a refinement of the initialisation in A, and it should establish the invariant of C.
2. Each old event in C should refine an event in A, and preserve the invariant of C. (If the event is renamed in C, the event it refines must be explicitly stated).
3. Each new event in C (that does not refine an event in A) should only concern the new variables, and preserve the invariant.
4. The new events in C should eventually all be disabled, if they are executed in isolation, so that one of the old events is executed. (Non-divergence).
5. Whenever an event in A is enabled, either the corresponding event in C or one of the new events in C should be enabled. (Strong relative deadlock freeness.)
6. Whenever an error occurs in C (an error detection event in C is enabled), an error should also be possible in A (an error detection event in A should be enabled).

With the error detection events in (6) we mean the events leading to state susp. Hence, an abstract representation of an error type is partitioned into distinct concrete errors during the refinement process [25].

The Proof Obligations (1)-(3) above are automatically generated by Atelier B, while Proof Obligations (4)-(6) can be generated after introducing some additional constructs discussed in [10,26]. Moreover, Proof Obligation (4) requires a variant that is decreased by all of the new events. A new Event B tool [4] is being developed that will be able to generate Proof Obligations (1)-(5). Proof Obligation (6) can be generated in a similar manner as (5) merely considering the guards of the error detection events. These events could be discovered via their assignment of the value susp to the variable representing the state. By discharging all these proof obligations for each refinement step in the control system development we have proved the correctness of the system with respect to its specification.

4   Graphical Interface for Refinements

In order to get a graphical interface to the formal development process, the development is performed via UML artefacts. New features are introduced in a stepwise manner into the class diagrams and statemachines. As a starting point we 'clone' the current model to obtain a copy to be refined. The refinement process is further facilitated by only allowing events, which guarantee that the refinement rules for Event B (and B Action Systems) are applied [1,26]. The new features are modelled with new variables. The transitions (events) in the corresponding statemachines are modified to take into account these new variables. The more concrete behaviour of the system can be modelled with

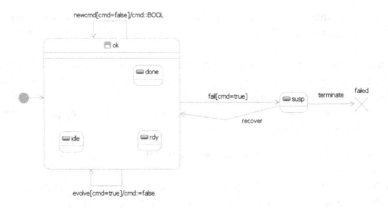

Fig. 2. The controller refined by adding hierarchical substates

hierarchical states by adding sub-states and more complex transitions in the statemachines. Furthermore, new events may be added between the sub-states. When refining the class and state-machines in UML we consider two kinds of refinement: data refinement and event refinement. Using these refinement patterns within the UML diagrams with subsequent translation to Event B assists in discharging the proof obligations given in Section 3.

4.1   Data Refinement

When refining a system we model the behaviour of the system in a more detailed manner. Before adding more detailed behaviour we need to reveal more detailed state space. This can be done using hierarchical states to introduce sub-states within a state. For example, in Figure 1 we model abstractly with state ok that the controller is working, while in Figure 2 state ok is split into sub-states to model that when the controller is working it can be pending (idle), ready (rdy) or running (done).

A new state variable, ok_state, of type {idle, rdy, done} will be generated in B to model the substates. Note that ok_state retains its value when state is not equal to ok, even though it then has no meaning in terms of the current state of the system. This corresponds to the UML notion of states having a memory (*history*) that can be returned to. Here we have shown this step separately for illustration. Normally we would combine it with the next step, where new events make use of the new states.

The hierarchy of states is usually given in a refined statemachine diagram by elaborating a state with substates. However, after several consequent splittings into substates, it could be preferable to flatten the hierarchy (i.e. remove old superstates) in order to reduce the complexity of the diagram.

4.2   Event Refinement - Adding New Transitions to Use Refined States

The more detailed behaviour that is revealed by the hierarchical states is reflected by refining the old events and adding new transitions (new events) between the substates. The old transitions (events) may be renamed during the refinement to better describe the

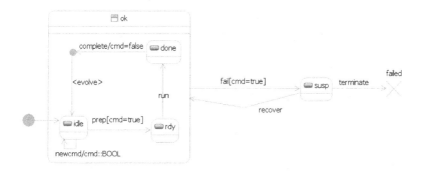

Fig. 3. The controller refined by adding new transitions

scenario. The guards of the old events may be strengthened and assignments concerning the new feature added in line with the Proof Obligations (1) and (2) in Section 3. The new events are only allowed to assign the new variables, but may refer to the old variables as stated in Proof Obligation (3).

In our controller example the abstract transition, evolve, is replaced by a sequence of the transitions prep, run, and complete. It is the last transition in this sequence that leaves the system in an equivalent state to the post-state of evolve (i.e., ready to start the sequence again). Hence, it is the new transition, complete, that refines evolve. This is specified using a junction pseudostate as shown in Figure 3 indicating the old, refined, transition in angled brackets (<evolve>). In UML, junctions are 'semantic-free' vertices that are used where two transitions share a common part of their path [15]. Junctions are appropriate where we wish to indicate secondary information such as the refinement relation of new transitions with previous abstract ones. The two new transitions, prep and run, are introduced to establishi the enabling guard for the refining transition complete. Note that we do not want the sequence of transitions to start unless it can complete (i.e. is feasible) so we put the guard of evolve on the first transition, prep. This is fulfilling Proof Obligation (5). The guard of complete must not be weaker than that of evolve according to Proof Obligation (2). This is the case in our refinement because the only possible path of transitions to the state done starts with prep. To reinforce this (and assist the proof) we attach the invariant cmd=true to the states rdy and run. Note that the U2B translator automatically adds the premises ok_state=rdy and ok_state=done.

According to the refinement rules (Proof Obligation (4)) the new events should not take over the execution. This can be guaranteed by disallowing the new transitions (corresponding to new events) from forming a loop in the statemachine diagram. The loop could be checked for automatically via graph theory. For proof in B, a variant must be generated. This is done by numbering the states in the diagram with the minimum path length to a refining transition. If loops are unavoidable, it must be the case that ancillary variables are modified during the loop in such a way as to cause its eventual termination. These ancillary variables must be used in the variant otherwise the proof

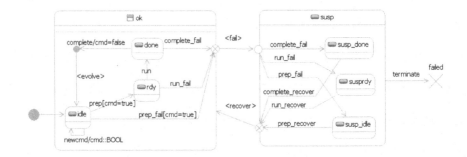

Fig. 4. The refinement of failure management

obligation will not be satisfiable. Each new transition between the substates should decrease the variant, i.e., lead to a new state with a lower designated number or decrease the variant by altering the ancillary state variables. If there is no route whereby a sequence of new transitions can reach one that refines an old transition, then the new events terminate without enabling an old event and a new deadlock has been introduced. Hence, for relative deadlock freeness, it is a necessary (but not sufficient) condition for there to be a route from every new transition to one that refines an old transition.

As features are added to the system the failure management should also be refined. If a fault occurs at a substate it should be possible to return to that substate after recovery. Note that we are not introducing new failure situations, but only splitting up the current non-deterministic failures (according to Proof Obligation (6)).

In Figure 4, the failure management of the controller is refined by splitting the suspended state (**susp**) into substates corresponding to the substates of state **ok**. From each substate of **ok** a failure transition (**prep_fail**, **run_fail** and **complete_fail**) takes the controller to the corresponding faulty state. Also the recovery transition **recover** should be refined so that the controller returns after recovery to the state where the failure was detected. Notice that the recovery transition utilises the history that is retained by the substates. That is, the substate that was current when **ok** was left, is reinstated. Since the recovery transitions may contain different actions depending on the **susp** substates, we refine **recover** to separate recovery transitions from each of these substates.

Hence, when states are refined into substates to give a more precise description of the system there is often a corresponding refinement of the superstate's incoming and outgoing transitions so that they utilise the new substates. When adding these new transitions to the statemachine diagram, it is convenient to utilise UML's *entry* and *exit* pseudostates. These have similar semantic-free interpretation as *junction*, but are used to indicate that a transition enters/exits a superstate. An example of using *entry* and *exit* pseudostates is shown in Figure 4 where transition **fail** is refined by the transitions **prep_fail**, **run_fail** and **complete_fail**. The refined controller in Figure 4 is translated to the refined B machine **Controller_Ref** below.

REFINEMENT Controller_Ref
REFINES Controller
VARIABLES   cmd, state, ok_state, susp_state
INVARIANT   cmd $\in$ BOOL $\land$ state $\in$ {ok, susp, failed} $\land$ ok_state $\in$ {idle, rdy, done} $\land$
                susp_state $\in$ {susp_idle, susp_rdy, susp_done} $\land$
                (ok_state = rdy $\Rightarrow$ cmd = true) $\land$ (ok_state = done $\Rightarrow$ cmd = true)
INITIALISATION cmd := false $\|$ state := ok $\|$ ok_state := idle $\|$
                susp_state :$\in$ {susp_idle, susp_rdy, susp_done}
EVENTS
  new_command == ...
  complete (refines evolve) ==
      WHEN state = ok $\land$ ok_state = done **THEN** cmd := false $\|$ ok_state := idle **END**
  prep (refines skip) == ...
      WHEN state = ok $\land$ ok_state = idle $\land$ cmd = true **THEN** ok_state := rdy **END**
  run (refines skip == ...
  prep_fail (refines fail) ==
      WHEN state = ok $\land$ ok_state = idle $\land$ cmd = true
      THEN state := failed $\|$ susp_state := susp_idle **END**
  run_fail (refines fail) == ...
  complete_fail (refines fail) == ...
  prep_recover (refines recover) ==
      WHEN state = susp $\land$ susp_state = susp_idle **THEN** state := ok **END**
  run_recover (refines recover) == ...
  complete_recover (refines recover) == ...
END

During the refinement steps described above, it is usual to also add more details about the operation of the system by adding guards that describe when each transition/event occurs. In this way we can reduce the non-determinism between alternative transitions/events, such as operation or failure. At the same time, assignment substitutions are added to the transitions/events to modify the variables controlling these guards. For clarity we have omitted such detail.

4.3   Data and Event Refinement - Superposition of New Regions

When we refine a simple state by replacing it with a composite one, we elaborate the behaviour of that particular state separately from any other abstract state. For example, the behaviour of ok was refined differently to that of susp. Sometimes we wish to specify a new behaviour that is common to all the current states. This can be done by adding an orthogonal region to the superstate. In Figure 5, the susp state is refined by adding a common behaviour pattern that is applicable to all three kinds of failure.

The events/transitions introduced in the orthogonal region are new events in the refinement and should only concern new features (Proof Obligation (3)). Hence, they must also be proved to terminate (Proof Obligation (4)) in order to show that the new transitions relinquish control. In Figure 5 it is readily observed that there are no loops, so all that is needed is to generate a variant based on the distance to an *exit* transition. The enabling of failure events is not affected by the orthogonal region (Proof Obligation (6)). After entering the orthogonal region at least one of the new transitions (unfixable, or diagnose followed by fix) must be enabled in order to satisfy Proof Obligation (5). This is because the recovering transitions (exit transitions) are not enabled until the orthogonal region is ready to synchronise with them.

The entry and exit transitions to the orthogonal region are unnamed indicating that they are not events in their own right. They connect to the named events via fork and

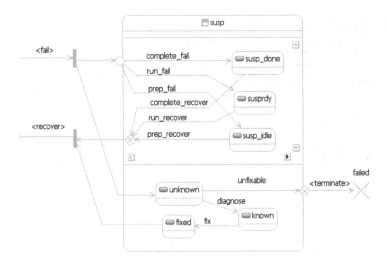

Fig. 5. Superposition of an orthogonal region

join pseudostates, respectively, meaning that they must be synchronised with the other events from the same pseudostate. That is, if the lower region is called status, status:=unknown is a substitution to be performed in parallel by complete_fail, prep_fail and run_fail. Similarly, status=fixed is a guard of complete_recover, prep_recover and run_recover. The composed events are then refinements of the old events complete_fail etc. in accordance with Proof Obligation (2). The states of the orthogonal regions are treated as two independent variables in the translated Event B. They are used to perform synchronisation of entry and exit transitions, but elsewhere each can be altered only by the transitions of the region it represents.

4.4   Event Refinement - Separating Existing Transitions

When refining an event we may wish to split it into several separate events. Each event uses newly introduced variables in its guards and actions to reduce non-determinism (Proof Obligation (2)). While adding conditions concerning new features to the guards we also refine the failure management. We divide an abstract failure into more specific failures on the new features according to Proof Obligation (6). Here many events refine one event.

In UML statemachine diagrams, a transition can choose from multiple paths indicated by splitting the transition with a *choice* symbol (a diamond shape). The guards of the outgoing paths depend on the value of variables when the choice point is reached (i.e. dynamically calculated guards). In our case we wish to show alternative paths resulting from an initial one, but the choice is static, since there is no sequential composition in Event B. Each choice represents a separate event whose guard includes the conjunction of all the segments leading up to that path. Since the conceptual representation is similar, but the semantics are more constrained, we represent these alternatives

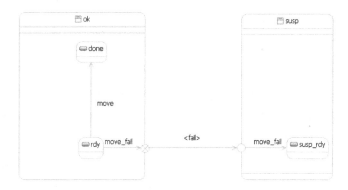

Fig. 6. The abstract move event and its corresponding failure

with a black diamond shape symbol (which we call *salmiakki* after a Finnish liquorice of that shape). We use salmiakki to visualise common parts of transitions and their relationship to the old refined events.

We illustrate the use of salmiakki with an abstract example of a height positioning system that drives a motor up or down to achieve a commanded position. The example was part of a drugs testing machine, Fillwell, and is dealt with in more detail elsewhere [8]. Here we focus on the event/transition to move shown in the statemachine diagram in Figure 6. (Event move corresponds to event run in the previous examples). The system is prepared to move when it is in state rdy. This either results in a success transition move that takes the system to state done or in a failure transition move_fail that suspends the system. At this stage no details are given as to how this choice is made. The transitions in the statemachine diagram in Figure 6 translate to the following events in B.

move ==   **WHEN** state = rdy **THEN** state := done **END**
move_fail == **WHEN** state = rdy **THEN** state := susp_rdy **END**

In the first refinement step we introduce salmiakki to visualise refinement of the move and move_fail transitions as shown in Figure 7. The failure transition move_fail is split into three different failures (Proof Obligation (6)); sensor_fail modelling failure of the position sensor, motor_fail modelling failure when the motor does not respond and move_fail1 representing remaining undetermined failures. The guards sf and mf represent the two specific failure conditions. At this level of abstraction the variables used in these guards could be boolean values representing the prescence of a failure. We have chosen to prioritise failures via a sequence of salmiakki. If both sf and mf are true, the sensor_fail failure will occur since move_fail is guarded by ¬sf. Note that we do not yet know whether the undetermined failures take priority over the ones we have specified. Hence, we do not add the negated failure guards to move_fail1. A join is used to show that the new failure transitions refine the abstract transition move_fail. The guard for transition move is strengthened (Proof Obligation (2)) by the conjunction of the negation of all the specific failures (Proof Obligation (5)).

The refined statemachine diagram in Figure 7 translates to the following B events.

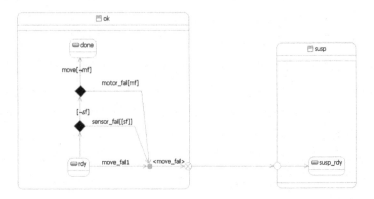

Fig. 7. The first refinement of the move event

```
move ==
    WHEN state = rdy ∧ ¬sf ∧ ¬mf THEN state := done END
move_fail1 (refines move_fail) ==
    WHEN state = rdy THEN state := susp_rdy END
sensor_fail (refines move_fail) ==
    WHEN state = rdy ∧ sf THEN state := susp_rdy END
motor_fail (refines move_fail) ==
    WHEN state = rdy ∧ ¬sf ∧ mf THEN state := susp_rdy END
```

The second refinement step in Figure 8 shows further decomposition of the remaining undetermined failures in move_fail1. For the motor failure we introduce transition motor_underspeed that suspends the system due to the motor not running at the expected speed (Proof Obligation (6)). This corresponds to the superposition of an integer variable measuring the speed of the motor. In this refinement we have chosen not to prioritise between motor_fail and motor_underspeed, either may be chosen if both failures are present. This non-determinism may be used when there is functional equivalence between the kinds of failures. The undetermined failure is again still represented in move_fail2. We also refine the move transition to show that a decision is made over the direction to move. Hence, move is split into two transitions, up and down, strengthening the guards by ¬mu , as well as lp and hp, respectively (Proof Obligations (2) and (5)). This corresponds to the introduction of variables representing the desired position and the current position. Unlike the refinement of failures, the desired action is refined without retaining an undetermined representation of the action.

The transitions in the statemachine diagram in Figure 8 of the second refinement step translate to the following B events.

```
up (refines move) ==
    WHEN state = rdy ∧ ¬sf ∧ ¬(mf ∨ mu) ∧ lp THEN state := done END
down (refines move) ==
    WHEN state = rdy ∧ ¬sf ∧ ¬(mf ∨ mu) ∧ hp THEN state := done END
move_fail2 (refines move_fail1) ==
    WHEN state = rdy THEN state := susp_rdy END
sensor_fail ==
    WHEN state = rdy ∧ sf THEN state := susp_rdy END
motor_fail ==
    WHEN state = rdy ∧ ¬sf ∧ mf THEN state := susp_rdy END
motor_underspeed (refines move_fail1) ==
    WHEN state = rdy ∧ ¬sf ∧ mu THEN state := susp_rdy END
```

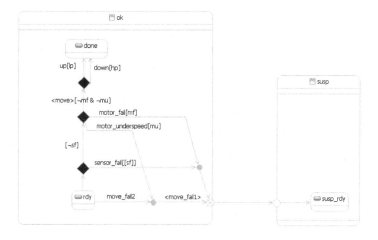

Fig. 8. The second refinement of the move event

In subsequent refinements we only show the latest event/transition refinement step in the statemachine diagram, e.g. move_fail2 refines move_fail1 in Figure 8. This agrees with the corresponding B specification where only the last event refined needs to be indicated. When adding a new feature we usually also add assignment substitutions to the events and give more detailed recovery functions. Here we have focused on the guards of the events for clarity.

Refinements should be made until all the possible failures have been identified and made specific. At this stage the original undetermined failure has been completely refined away. However, since the undetermined failure abstracts away from any detail the process does not indicate when this is the case. We envisage further work to explore how this can be assured. For example, hazard analysis could be used to identify all the specific failure categories and provide an abstract failure analysis model.

5 Conclusions

We have illustrated a specialisation of the UML statemachine notation that enables it to be used to visualise event models and their refinements including specification of the refinement relationship between events of the abstract and concrete models. The techniques we have proposed form development patterns that are intended to assist in the design process of a system where correctness and safety are important issues. The UML statemachines are translated to Event B, where tool support is available for proving the correctness of the refinement steps. In the refinement process we use hierarchical substates to provide the additional state space needed for defining new event transitions. Hence, we provide pragmatic transformation rules relying on Event B semantics for making the state space and the transitions increasingly fine-grained. In addition to hierarchical state spaces orthogonal regions can be introduced to refine several simple states with a common compositional one. Moreover, pseudostates for adding secondary information to the model such as the prioritisation of newly determined events is also a useful visualisation technique.

Simons [19] includes a "theory of compatible object refinement" giving a theoretical treatment to the refinement of states. However, our notion of event refinement, with refinement relations between events, is richer than Simons. Sekerinski [18] also translates statemachines into B specifications. However, he does not cover refinement. He uses parallel regions in his specifications, but for modelling synchronised computation between objects, instead of modelling common computation of states. UML has also previously been used as a graphical view of a B development by Idani et al [12]. They apply abstraction techniques to deal with the development of large systems. However, they do not provide guidance for the refinement process as we do.

Further investigations are required to explore how orthogonal regions can be better utilized for visualising the superposition of new features to a system. This is particularly interesting in relation to the theoretical underpinning suggested by Simons [19], which utilises intersecting (non-orthogonal) regions to unify the treatment of refined states. We have found the techniques introduced in this paper to be very useful in communicating models with colleagues and especially with industrial partners who have less experience with formal notations. We envisage improving the existing tool support for refinement in UML-B as part of the RODIN project, in order to make the techniques more attractive for industrial use.

References

1. J. R. Abrial and L. Mussat. Event B Reference Manual, 2001.
   http://www.atelierb.societe.com/ressources/evt2b/eventb_reference_manual.pdf
2. J.-R. Abrial. *The B-Book: Assigning Programs to Meanings.* Cambridge University Press, 1996.
3. J.R. Abrial, D. Cansell and D. Méry. Refinement and Reachability in Event B. In *Proceedings of the 4th International Conference of B and Z users - ZB2005: Formal Specification and Development in Z and B*, Guildford, UK, LNCS 3455, Springer, pp. 222-241, 2005.
4. J.R. Abrial, S. Hallerstede, F. Mehta, C. Métayer and L. Voisin. Specification of Basic Tools and Platform, RODIN Deliverable D10 [17], 2005.
5. R.J.R. Back and R. Kurki-Suonio. Decentralization of process nets with centralized control. In *Proceedings of the 2nd ACM SIGACT-SIGOPS Symposium on Principles of Distributed Computing*, pp. 131-142, 1983.
6. R.J.R. Back and K. Sere. From modular systems to action systems. *Software - Concepts and Tools* 17, pp. 26-39, 1996.
7. R.J.R Back and J. von Wright. *Refinement calculus: A systematic introduction.* Springer-Verlag New York, 1998.
8. P. Boström, M. Jansson, and M. Waldén. A healthcare case study: Fillwell. TUCS Technical Reports No 569, Turku Centre for Computer Science, Finland.
9. G. Booch, I. Jacobson, and J. Rumbaugh. *The Unified Modeling Language - a Reference Manual.* Addison-Wesley, 1998.
10. M. Butler, and Waldén. Distributed system development in B. In *Proceedings of the 1st Conference on the B Method.* Nantes, France, November 1996, pp. 155-168.
11. ClearSy. Atelier B. *http://www.atelierb.societe.com/*
12. A. Idani and Y. Ledru. Dynamic Graphical UML Views from Formal B Specifications. *Information and Software Technology*, 48(3), pp. 154-169, March 2006. Elsevier Science.

13. S.M. Katz. A superimposition control construct for distributed systems. *ACM Transactions on Programming Languages and Systems*, 15(2):337-356, April 1993.
14. C. Métayer, J.R. Abrial and L. Voisin. Event-B Language, RODIN Deliverable D7 [17], 2005.
15. *UML 2.0 Superstructure Specification*, (Document-formal/05-07-04 (UML Superstructure Specification, v2.0)), August 2005, *http://www.omg.org/cgi-bin/doc?formal/05-07-04* (accessed 16.07.2006)
16. L. Petre, E. Troubitsyna, M. Waldén, P. Boström, N. Engblom, and M. Jansson. Methodology of integration of formal methods within the healthcare case study. TUCS Technical Reports No 436, Turku Centre for Computer Science, Finland. October 2001.
17. Rigorous Open Development Environment for Complex Systems (RODIN) - IST 511599. *http://rodin.cs.ncl.ac.uk/*
18. E. Sekerinski. Graphical Design of Reactive Systems. In *Proceedings of the 2nd International B Conference*, Montpellier, France, April 1998, pp. 182 - 197. Springer-Verlag, 1998.
19. A. Simons. A theory of regression testing for behaviourally compatible object types. *Software Testing, Verification and Reliability*, 16 (3), pp. 133-156, *UKTest 2005 Special Edition*, September 2006, John Wiley.
20. C. Snook and M. Butler. U2B Downloads. *http://www.ecs.soton.ac.uk/~cfs/U2Bdownloads.htm*
21. C. Snook and M. Butler. U2B -a tool for translating UML-B models into B. In J. Mermet (ed.), *UML-B Specification for Proven Embedded Systems Design*. Springer, 2004.
22. C. Snook, I. Oliver, and M. Butler. The UML-B profile for formal systems modelling in UML. In J. Mermet (ed.), *UML-B Specification for Proven Embedded Systems Design*. Springer, 2004.
23. C. Snook, L. Tsiopoulos and M. Waldén. A case study in requirement analysis of control systems using UML and B. In *Proceedings of RCS'03 - International workshop on Refinement of Critical Systems: Methods, Tools and Experience*, Turku, Finland, June 2003. *http://www.esil.univ-mrs.fr/~spc/rcs03/rcs03.html*
24. C. Snook and M. Waldén. Refinement of Statemachines using Hierarchical States, Choice Points and Joins. In *Proceedings of the EPSRC RefineNet Workshop*, UK, 2005.
25. E. Troubitsyna. *Stepwise Development of Dependable Systems*. Turku Centre for Computer Science, TUCS, Ph.D. thesis No.29. June 2000.
26. M. Waldén and K. Sere. Reasoning About Action Systems Using the B-Method. *Formal Methods in Systems Design* 13(5-35), 1998. Kluwer Academic Publishers.

Formal Transformation of Platform Independent Models into Platform Specific Models*

Pontus Boström[1], Mats Neovius[1], Ian Oliver[2], and Marina Waldén[1]

[1] Åbo Akademi University, Department of Information Technologies
Turku Centre for Computer Science (TUCS)
Joukahaisenkatu 3-5, 20520 Turku, Finland
{Pontus.Bostrom,Mats.Neovius,Marina.Walden}@abo.fi
[2] Nokia Research Center
Itämerenkatu 11-13, 00180 Helsinki, Finland
Ian.Oliver@nokia.com

Abstract. This paper introduces a method for formal transformation of platform independent models (PIM) to platform specific models (PSM) in a model driven architecture (MDA) context. The models are constructed using state-machines in the Unified Modeling Language (UML). As a formal framework for reasoning about the models we use Event B. In this paper we illustrate our method by introducing fault tolerance to the PSM. Fault tolerance is not considered in the PIM in order to make the models reusable for different platforms. On the other hand, the PSM often has to consider platform specific faults. However, fault tolerance mechanisms cannot usually be introduced as a refinement in the PSM. We present a model transformation of the PIM in order to preserve refinement properties in the construction of the PSM. Design patterns are used for guiding the development. Our method can be beneficial for developing reliable applications in many different areas, since both UML and B are used for practical applications.

1 Introduction

A platform independent model (PIM) in a Model Driven Architecture (MDA[1]) context considers only features in the problem domain. In order to implement the platform independent model, the model is transformed into a platform specific model (PSM) that takes into account implementation issues for the platform where the system will run. For example, fault tolerance and other platform specific features should not be included in the PIM, since every possible platform where the system could run would have to be considered. All potential platforms might not even be known at the time the PIM is created [4,11]. In order to anticipate all the different restrictions that will be encountered on a specific platform, the fault handling mechanisms and other platform specific features in the PIM would have to be very general. Hence, they would not provide any

---

* Work done within the RODIN-project, IST-511599.
[1] Model Driven Architecture, http://www.omg.org/mda/

J. Julliand and O. Kouchnarenko (Eds.): B 2007, LNCS 4355, pp. 186–200, 2006.

useful information and could restrict future transformations to other platforms. However, the PSM is not necessarily a refinement of the PIM, since the PSM can introduce behaviour that is not considered in the PIM at all [13]. We introduce a method that involves an automatic transformation of the PIM to allow a very abstract definition of platform specific features. These features can then be refined to concrete features in the platform specific model. In this paper we introduce fault tolerance as an example of platform specific features. We then use patterns to facilitate its introduction.

We have chosen to use UML[2] for describing the platform independent and platform specific models, since it is a specification language that is widely used in industry. Here we concentrate on state-machines [7]; we do not consider the object oriented features of UML. To have a formal semantics and good tool support for analysis, the state-machines are translated to Event B. Event B [3,12] is a formalism based on Action Systems [5] and the B Method [2] for reasoning about distributed and reactive systems. It supports stepwise refinement of specifications and it is also compatible with UML state-machines [14,17]. For the state-machine transformation from PIM to PSM we give extra rules for ensuring deadlock freeness and preserving the behaviour of the PIM. Although we use UML for specification, some of the rules are not UML specific and they can be used in ordinary Event B as well.

Section 2 gives a short presentation of UML and Section 3 describes Event B. The translation of UML state-machines to Event B is then given in Section 4. The PIM to PSM transformation is introduced in Sections 5 and 6, together with an example. In Section 7 we conclude.

2   UML

UML is a popular language for modelling object oriented software. An application developed using object oriented methodology [1,15] consists of a set of objects that communicate by sending messages. Each object consists of a set of variables and a set of operations describing the functionality of the object. Messages are assumed to be operation calls. Furthermore, objects run concurrently and the communication between them is instantaneous. The behaviour of the objects is described by state-machines [7]. Here we assume that at most one state-machine is used for each object.

The state-machine specification in UML is large and complex. For simplicity we will only use a subset of it. We consider only state-machines containing normal, initial and final states and no composite states. We assume that all state-machines containing composite states have been flattened.

The transitions in a state-machine describe the behaviour of the enclosing object. Each transition can be labelled by an event and each event corresponds to an operation in the object. Hence, state-machines in different objects can communicate by sending events (operation calls). In UML, events that cannot fire a transition are normally implicitly consumed. However, we assume that

---

[2] Unified Modeling Language, http://www.uml.org

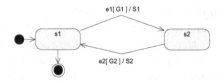

Fig. 1. A simple state-machine

events are always deferred until they can fire a transition. The events in UML will later be referred to as *UML events*. Transitions can have *guards* and *actions* that take into account other variables than the state in the enclosing object. A guard is a predicate that has to evaluate to *true* before the transition can be fired. An action is a substitution that is executed when the corresponding transition is fired.

A simple state-machine is shown in Figure 1. The state-machine contains two states s_1 and s_2. There are two transitions E_1 and E_2 between the states. Transition E_1 is triggered by UML event e_1 and it has the guard G_1 and the action S_1.

The specification of state-machines in UML contains also other features than those described here, such as e.g., composite states, history states, activities, entry- or exit-actions inside states. However, the aim of this paper is not to give a complete formal semantics to UML state-machines, but to consider mapping a PIM into a fault tolerant PSM.

3   Event B

Event B [12] is a formalism based on Action Systems [5] and the B Method [2], and it is related to B Action Systems [19]. It has been developed for reasoning about distributed and reactive systems. Both the B Method and Event B have received interest from industry and they have been applied to practical problems. An Event B specification consists of an abstract model that can be refined to a concrete model in a stepwise manner.

3.1   Abstract Model

An Event B model consists of variables giving the statespace and events for describing the behaviour of the system [12].

Consider model $\mathcal{M}$ in Figure 2. The context $\mathcal{C}$ of the model provides definitions of sets s and constants c, where $P(s,c)$ describes their properties. The set of variables in the model is given by v. Their types and properties are given in the invariant $I(s,c,v)$. The behaviour of the model is described by the events E_1 and E_2. Each event consists of a guard G_i and a substitution S_i. When the guard G_i evaluates to *true* the event E_i is said to be enabled and the substitution S_i can be executed. Enabled events are chosen non-deterministically for execution.

```
MODEL  M                          CONTEXT  C
SEES                              SETS
  C                                 s
VARIABLES                         CONSTANTS
  v                                 c
INVARIANT                         PROPERTIES
  I(s, c, v)                        P(s, c)
INITIALISATION                    END
  S_0(s, c, v)
EVENTS
E_1 ≘
   WHEN G_1(s, c, v) THEN S_1(s, c, v) END ;
E_2 ≘
   WHEN G_2(s, c, v) THEN S_2(s, c, v) END ;
END
```

Fig. 2. An abstract Event B model

A number of proof obligations need to be discharged in order to show that an Event B model is consistent [12]. To generate the proof obligations every substitution $S_i(s, c, v)$ is translated to a before-after predicate $BA(S_i)(s, c, v, v')$. For example, if the substitution is $S(s, c, v) \mathrel{\hat{=}} (v := F(s, c, v))$ then the before-after predicate is $BA(S)(s, c, v, v') \mathrel{\hat{=}} (v' = F(s, c, v))$. The first two proof obligations concern the correctness of the initialisation.

Mod1: $P(s, c) \Rightarrow \exists v'.BA(S_0)(s, c, v')$
Mod2: $P(s, c) \wedge BA(S_0)(s, c, v') \Rightarrow I(s, c, v')$

The proof obligations state that the initialisation should be possible (Mod1) and it should establish the invariant (Mod2). Note that the before-after predicate for the initialisation only refer to the new value of the variables v. The correctness of each event E_i is ensured by the following proof obligations.

Mod3: $P(s, c) \wedge I(s, c, v) \wedge G_i(s, c, v) \Rightarrow \exists v'.BA(S_i)(s, c, v, v')$
Mod4: $P(s, c) \wedge I(s, c, v) \wedge G_i(s, c, v) \wedge BA(S_i)(s, c, v, v') \Rightarrow I(s, c, v')$

The first proof obligation states that the substitution in each event E_i should be possible (Mod3) and the second one that the event has to maintain the invariant (Mod4).

3.2   Refinement

An Event B model can be refined [12]. As an example consider a model $\mathcal{M}_1$ that is a refinement of the model $\mathcal{M}$ in Figure 2. Assume $\mathcal{M}_1$ has concrete variables w and the relation between the variables in the abstract model and the refined model is given by the refinement invariant $J(s, c, v, w)$. The event E_i is refined to $E_i \mathrel{\hat{=}} \textbf{WHEN } H_i(s, c, w) \textbf{ THEN } R_i(s, c, w) \textbf{ END }$. New events F_i may also be introduced. In order to show that model $\mathcal{M}$ is refined by $\mathcal{M}_1$, $\mathcal{M} \sqsubseteq \mathcal{M}_1$, a number of proof obligations need to be discharged. Event E_i is correctly refined if the following conditions hold:

Ref1: $P(s,c) \wedge I(s,c,v) \wedge J(s,c,v,w) \wedge H_i(s,c,w) \Rightarrow \exists w'.BA(R_i)(s,c,w,w')$

Ref2: $P(s,c) \wedge I(s,c,v) \wedge J(s,c,v,w) \wedge H_i(s,c,w) \Rightarrow G_i(s,c,v)$

Ref3: $P(s,c) \wedge I(s,c,v) \wedge J(s,c,v,w) \wedge H_i(s,c,w) \wedge BA(R_i)(s,c,w,w') \Rightarrow$
      $\exists v'.(BA(S_i)(s,c,v,v') \wedge J(s,c,v',w'))$

The proof obligations states that the refined substitution R_i is possible (Ref1), the guard of the event is strengthened (Ref2) and that there is an assignment to the variables in the abstract model corresponding to the assignment in the refined substitution under relation J (Ref3). The proof obligations for new events $F_i \mathrel{\hat=} \textbf{WHEN } N_i(s,c,w) \textbf{ THEN } T_i(s,c,w) \textbf{ END}$ are similar to the ones above. However, they refine $skip$ and, hence, the before-after predicate in the abstract specification is $BA(S_n)(s,c,v,v') \mathrel{\hat=} (v' = v)$.

In order to ensure the correctness of the entire model, two additional proof obligations need to be discharged. The refined system cannot deadlock or terminate more often than the abstract one (Ref4).

Ref4: $P(s,c) \wedge I(s,c,v) \wedge J(s,c,v,w) \wedge G_i(s,c,v) \Rightarrow$
       $H_i(s,c,w) \vee N_1(s,c,w) \vee \ldots \vee N_n(s,c,w)$

If an event is enabled in the abstract model it is also enabled in the refined model or some new events are enabled. This is the strong version of the proof obligation for deadlock freeness. Finally, we need to show that the new events terminate when executed in isolation, since they are not allowed to take control forever. We assume that we have a variant $V(s,c,w)$ that maps the state space to a well founded structure $(\mathbb{N}, \leq)$. Each new event then has to decrease the variant (Ref5).

Ref5: $P(s,c) \wedge I(s,c,v) \wedge J(s,c,v,w) \wedge N_i(s,c,w) \wedge BA(T_i)(s,c,w,w') \Rightarrow$
       $V(s,c,w') \in \mathbb{N} \wedge V(s,c,w') < V(s,c,w)$

These proof obligations are necessary and sufficient to show that an Event B model is consistent and that the refinement is correct.

A recently introduced feature in Event B is the, so called, anticipating events [3]. Sometimes a new event is needed in a refinement that also modifies old variables. The event is then added as an anticipating event in previous refinement steps. An anticipating event can perform any substitution that maintains the invariant and does not increase the variant of the current refinement level (if any). We still have to prove that the new events refining the anticipating events terminate when executed in isolation. Anticipating events is only syntactic sugar for actually introducing the events in earlier refinement steps and introducing extra variables for their variant.

4   Translation of State-Machines to Event B

In order to be able to formally reason about the UML state-machines, we translate them to Event B. There are several translations from UML state-machines

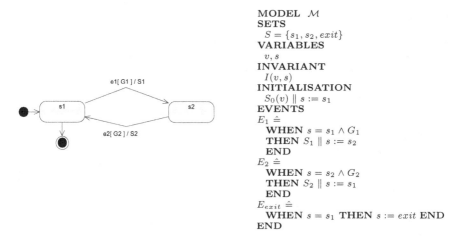

MODEL $\mathcal{M}$
SETS
$\quad S = \{s_1, s_2, exit\}$
VARIABLES
$\quad v, s$
INVARIANT
$\quad I(v, s)$
INITIALISATION
$\quad S_0(v) \parallel s := s_1$
EVENTS
$E_1 \mathrel{\hat{=}}$
$\quad$ **WHEN** $s = s_1 \wedge G_1$
$\quad$ **THEN** $S_1 \parallel s := s_2$
$\quad$ **END**
$E_2 \mathrel{\hat{=}}$
$\quad$ **WHEN** $s = s_2 \wedge G_2$
$\quad$ **THEN** $S_2 \parallel s := s_1$
$\quad$ **END**
$E_{exit} \mathrel{\hat{=}}$
$\quad$ **WHEN** $s = s_1$ **THEN** $s := exit$ **END**
END

Fig. 3. Translation of a UML state-machine $\mathcal{M}$ to Event B

to B [14,17]. The translation of a subset of UML presented here is similar to those approaches. However, we use a different semantics concerning UML events that is suitable for our purpose.

The state-machine in Figure 1 is translated to Event B as shown in Figure 3. The states of the state-machine are given as an enumerated set $S = \{s_1, s_2, exit\}$ in Event B. The current state of the state-machine is modelled as a variable $s \in S$. The initial state in a UML state-machine gives the initial value of the state variable s. The exit states are modelled as a single state, $exit \in S$. The variables v in $\mathcal{M}$ are the variables of the UML state-machine. The transitions correspond to events in Event B. The events E_1 and E_2 in Event B (later called *B events* to distinguish them from UML events) corresponds to the transitions triggered by the UML events e_1 and e_2, respectively. The guards G_i and substitutions S_i refer to the variables v.

The proof obligations for transitions are the standard proof obligations for events in Event B. However, it is a desirable property that a state-machine should not deadlock. The only state where no transition should be enabled is in state $exit$. To ensure that this holds we introduce an extra proof obligation (Exit1).

Exit1: $I(v, s) \wedge \neg((s = s_1 \wedge G_1) \vee \ldots \vee (s = s_n \wedge G_m)) \Rightarrow s = exit$

The abstract model in Figure 3 can be refined to take into account more features and to make the model implementable. In figure 4 we refine the abstract variables v with concrete variables w. The guards and actions in the transitions of the abtract model are refined to H_i and R_i, respectively, to take the concrete variables w into consideration. The state variable s is refined by r. The relation between s and r is given as $J_S(s, r) \mathrel{\hat{=}} (s = s_1 \Leftrightarrow r = r_1) \wedge (s = s_2 \Leftrightarrow r \in \{r_2, r_3\})$. Two new transitions with UML event f_1 have also been introduced in the model

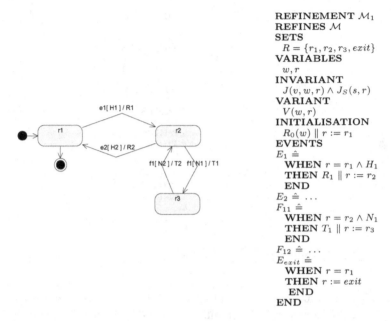

REFINEMENT $\mathcal{M}_1$
REFINES $\mathcal{M}$
SETS
$\quad R = \{r_1, r_2, r_3, exit\}$
VARIABLES
$\quad w, r$
INVARIANT
$\quad J(v, w, r) \wedge J_S(s, r)$
VARIANT
$\quad V(w, r)$
INITIALISATION
$\quad R_0(w) \parallel r := r_1$
EVENTS
$E_1 \triangleq$
$\quad$ WHEN $r = r_1 \wedge H_1$
$\quad$ THEN $R_1 \parallel r := r_2$
$\quad$ END
$E_2 \triangleq \ldots$
$F_{11} \triangleq$
$\quad$ WHEN $r = r_2 \wedge N_1$
$\quad$ THEN $T_1 \parallel r := r_3$
$\quad$ END
$F_{12} \triangleq \ldots$
$E_{exit} \triangleq$
$\quad$ WHEN $r = r_1$
$\quad$ THEN $r := exit$
$\quad$ END
END

Fig. 4. Translation of a refined UML state-machine $\mathcal{M}_1$

(transitions F_{11} and F_{12} in Event B). Translation of the refined state-machine $\mathcal{M}_1$ is performed in the same manner as for the abstract model.

An object-oriented application consists of a set of objects. Here we only model individual objects and their environment is considered to be a black-box that calls the operations of the object, i.e. sends UML events to the object as described in Section 2. We can consider the behaviour of each UML event to be the non-deterministic choice of all transitions labelled with that event. Assume UML event e labels transitions $E_1, \ldots, E_n$. Then the behaviour in Event B for e is given as $E_1 \parallel \ldots \parallel E_n$, where E_i is a B event. The behaviour of e should also be refined when the state-machine is refined. This interpretation of UML events gives rules for labeling transitions with UML events: A transition without a UML event can be refined to a transition with a private, possibly new, UML event. The UML event cannot be changed on a transition during the refinement process. Furthermore, if a UML event e can trigger a transition in the abstract state-machine, it should also be possible in the refined state-machine. This can be proved by showing the strong version of deadlock freeness in combination with termination of new transitions, since we have deferred UML events.

5   Introduction of Platform Specific Features

In order to implement a PIM we need to transform it into a PSM. The PSM is not necessarily a refinement of the PIM, since the PIM does not consider platform specific features. In this paper we exemplify the introduction of platform specific features with the introduction of fault tolerance features; we can even consider fault tolerance to be a platform in its own right (cf. [4,11]). We can make the following observations: the behaviour in the PIM should be the "normal" behaviour of the PSM and the new behaviour in the PSM relates mainly to hardware restrictions and to tolerance of faults that can occur on that specific platform.

To guarantee the behaviour in this transformation, we would like to preserve as many refinement properties as possible. The following properties of the PIM are required to be preserved in the PSM:

1. The sequence of valid calls to public operations are maintained in the PSM or the state-machine has reached state *exit*.
2. New public operations (UML events) are not introduced. Hence, an object does not require new interactions from its environment.
3. New behaviour violating the refinement relation between the PIM and the PSM cannot take control forever.
4. There should be a trace in the PIM that is also a possible trace in the PSM. Hence, it should be possible to execute the PSM using only the transitions in the PIM.

To better illustrate the rules above, they can also be expressed as restrictions on the state-machine in the PSM. In the view of the environment, a UML state-machine accepts a language over an alphabet consisting of the events. Assume that the state-machine in the platform independent model accepts the language L. The alphabet of the language is the operations of the object. Consider two, possibly empty, strings L_1 and L_2 in L such that $L = L_1 L_2$. Assume that the platform specific behaviour is represented by the finite string of events α. The state-machine of the PSM with one platform specific behaviour can then accept the following language $L_1 L_2 + L_1 \alpha L_2 + L_1 \alpha$. This means that the state-machine operates either normally, performs some platform specific computation and continues with its normal operation or it prematurely terminates after the platform specific behaviour.

Fault tolerance is used as an example of platform specific features in this paper. In general, a fault is a defect in the system that possibly can manifest itself as an error, which might result in a system failure [18]. Because of the unpredictability of the environment, faulty behaviour is evident. Fault tolerance refers to a method for designing a system so that it is capable of operating, possibly at a reduced level, rather than failing completely when some error occurs. Consequently, a fault tolerant system is capable of handling unexpected erroneous events in a sensible manner.

A fault tolerance procedure always starts with error detection, followed by a diagnosis and the outcome of the error handling method. The error diagnosis is completely dependent on the uniqueness of the current state. The outcome of the fault tolerance is achieved through applying a handling method designed for errors occurring in that specific state. Consequently, an error in a certain state is always tackled according to the same pattern.

The faults that can be handled by the application can be divided into three groups: the first group consists of faults where the only remedy is to terminate the application. The second group consists of faults that cannot be recovered from when the mechanisms for fault tolerance are introduced as a refinement of the PIM. An example of such a fault could be inserting an item into a buffer. The PIM considered the buffer to have infinite length, while in the PSM it has a finite length. When the buffer gets full, messages are dropped, but the application can otherwise continue its operation. The last group of faults consists of faults that the fault tolerance mechanisms always can recover from and where the fault tolerance mechanism can be introduced as a refinement. This group of faults are not a problem, since the PSM can still be a refinement of the PIM in this case. If the fault is not considered in the application the behaviour of the system is undefined, and the system may suffer an uncontrolled "total" failure, i.e., a crash.

In our transformation from PIM to PSM we do not allow usage of history states and of traces. Hence, if there is more than one possible path leading to the present state, the system cannot know its prior events. Consequently, any pattern preserving the system conditions is deduced from a unique situation of the system, making checkpoint dependent recovery [8] unattainable. These constraints demand more of the development of fault tolerance.

6   Transforming a PIM into a PSM

The PIM is transformed to a PSM in such a manner that the properties in Section 5 are preserved. In order to transform the PIM into a PSM we use design patterns. Design patterns are template solutions for solving commonly occurring problems. Patterns will be discussed in more detail in Subsection 6.3.

6.1   Introducing Anticipating Events

To enable transformation of the PIM to a PSM we use anticipating events in Event B. We transform the PIM to a model having all the possible *anticipating transitions* (B events) modelling very abstract platform specific behaviour. Figure 5 illustrates how a platform independent model M is transformed into a platform specific model M''. First M is automatically translated to a model $T(M)$ including all the possible anticipating transitions. The model $T(M)$ is hidden from the developer of the PIM. He/She will only have to consider the models M, M' and M''. To obtain a model M' with platform specific features, a pattern p_1 is applied to the PIM M by the developer. This procedure can be repeated until all platform specific features have been introduced. However, the order in which the patterns are applied is significant and has to be considered. The result obtained is a model that have similar functionality as M, but can have several platform specific features, e.g. fault tolerance for memory limitations and network problems. The obtained model M' is a refinement of $T(M)$, but not necessarily of the platform independent model M.

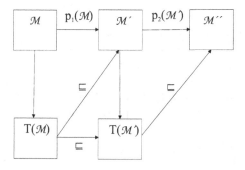

Fig. 5. Transforming a platform independent model $\mathcal{M}$ into a platform specific model $\mathcal{M}''$

The fault tolerance example can be divided into two separate parts, the modelling of the detection of an error and the error handling as described in Section 5. To model the detection of errors in this example, we introduce one new anticipating transition in $T(\mathcal{M})$ for each transition in the PIM $\mathcal{M}$. These transitions $e_i[G_i]/keep$ (see Figure 6) have the same source, destination and guard as their corresponding transitions. They contain the action $keep \mathrel{\hat{=}} v :\in I(v)$, modelling that the execution of the action failed. To model error handling we introduce two extra anticipating transitions $/keep$ for each state in the platform independent model. These anticipating transitions have no event and they are later labelled by new private UML events or removed if they are unused. One transition models errors that the system can recover from, the other models termination of the system in the state *exit*. All the anticipating transitions can be refined to any behaviour restricted by the invariant, as for example fault tolerance. The choice of anticipating events is a trade-off between being able to introduce new features in the PSM and ensuring that the behaviour of the PIM is preserved. This also implies that we cannot introduce arbitrary new behaviour.

An abstract platform independent model is presented in Figure 1 in Section 2. The model contains two states, s_1 and s_2 and two transitions between them. The corresponding transformed PIM $T(\mathcal{M})$ is shown in Figure 6, where anticipating transitions are introduced for both the states s_1 and s_2, as well as between these two states.

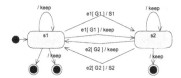

Fig. 6. The transformation of the platform independent model $T(\mathcal{M})$ in Figure 1

6.2   Validation of the Platform Specific Model

We transform the PIM $\mathcal{M}$ to a PSM $\mathcal{M}'$ using a pattern p that takes into account the transformation rules in this paper. An example of such a transformation from a PIM to a PSM with fault tolerance is shown in Figure 8. Validation of the PSM is performed within the Event B framework, where we can show that the PSM $\mathcal{M}'$ is a refinement of the transformed platform independent model $T(\mathcal{M})$. In Section 5 we gave four additional properties that the PSM $\mathcal{M}'$ should satisfy with respect to the original PIM $\mathcal{M}$. They are related to proof obligations in Event B as follows. The sequence of valid events (1) is preserved, since we have deferred events and we prove deadlock freeness. All UML events are deferred until a possible transition is encountered. The proof of strong deadlock freeness (Ref4) and that the state-machine only deadlocks in state $exit$ (Exit1) guarantees that transitions in the PIM will either eventually be enabled or the state-machine will be in state exit. We can check syntactically on the UML model that no new public events are introduced (2). New behaviour is not allowed to take control forever (3), which is guaranteed with the proof obligations for anticipating transitions and new transitions in Event B. Condition (4) stating that there is behaviour common to the PIM and PSM requires extra proof obligations in Event B.

The fourth requirement in Section 5 is needed, since we introduce several extra transitions in $T(\mathcal{M})$ compared to $\mathcal{M}$. It is necessary to show that the behaviour of the PIM is still feasible in the PSM after anticipating transitions have been labelled with UML events or removed. First, we check that the initialisation $R_0(w, r)$ of the PSM $\mathcal{M}'$ can enable an already existing transition in the PIM or that it moves to state $exit$ (PSM1).

PSM1: $\exists w', r'.(BA(R_0)(w', r') \wedge (H_1(w', r') \vee \ldots \vee H_n(w', r') \vee r' = exit))$

Here every H_i denotes the Event B guard of a transition in the PSM that refines a transition in the PIM. Furthermore, let **WHEN** $H_j(w, r)$ **THEN** $R_j(w, r)$ **END** be a transition in the PSM that is a refinement of a transition in the PIM. For every such transition there should be assignment w', r' to the variables that enables a transition in the PIM or leads to the state $exit$ (PSM2).

$$\text{PSM2: } \begin{array}{l} I(v, s) \wedge J(v, w, s, r) \wedge H_j(w, r) \Rightarrow \\ \exists w', r'.(BA(R_j)(w, w', r, r') \wedge (H_1(w', r') \vee \ldots \vee H_n(w', r') \vee r' = exit)) \end{array}$$

When these proof obligations hold the state-machine is not allowed to use solely platform specific transitions. This rule can also be beneficial in Event B when using anticipating events in order to ensure that the behaviour from the abstract model is preserved. Note that these proof obligations are the same as the feasibility proof obligation (see Section 3) with the extra condition $(H_1(w', r') \vee \ldots \vee H_n(w', r') \vee r' = exit)$. The generation of this proof obligation can be implemented in Event B by introducing extra events with the non-deterministic assignment $: |$ [12] containing the conditions in (PSM1) and (PSM2):

```
WHEN H_j(w,r)
THEN w,r : |(BA(R_j(w_0, w, r_0, r)) ∧ (H_1(w,r) ∨ ... ∨ H_n(w,r) ∨ r = exit))
END
```

These extra rules ensure that the desired properties given in Section 5 hold.

6.3   Patterns

A pattern introducing new functionality is dependent upon the original model and must satisfy the system constraints. This means that the pattern must allow the original functionality of the system. Thus, for all traces in the original $\mathcal{M}$, there must be corresponding valid traces in the successively developed systems, including the transition containing *keep*. Consequently, after e.g. fault tolerance has been introduced, it can be seen as a "slave" system evolving in parallel with the original model.

When developing a fault tolerant system according to the method in this paper, it is deadlock free and preserves the invariant. The patterns are bounded within the strict constraints proposed here. This means that the system $T(M)$ will have the following structure, where L_i stands for a subset of the language (UML events) accepted by a state-machine in the PIM, f for an erroneous event and $*$ denotes the Kleene closure: $L_1 f^* L_2 f^* \dots L_n f^*$. Hence, any number of faults can occur between the events of the PIM. If fault tolerance would evolve in parallel with the model, every added feature could potentially change the desired recovery method.

In the PSM we can refine the platform specific behaviour α (anticipating transition) in $T(\mathcal{M})$ to a combination of handled crash h and error recovery r in $\mathcal{M}'$. The expression $L_1 L_2 + L_1 r L_2 + L_1 h$ in $\mathcal{M}'$, gives the refined fault tolerance. Every error state would have to contain at least the worst case scenario of unexpected total breakdown, leading to hard reboot. However, the unexpected total breakdown is out of the scope of this paper and is not modelled here. Our expression models normal behaviour ($L_1 L_2$), successful recovery ($L_1 r L_2$) and handled crash after possible recovery attempts ($L_1 h$). By following this method we can introduce fault tolerance in the PSM while preserving the main functionality of the PIM.

The benefit of using patterns are twofold. Patterns give a template solution for common problems and, hence they give the developer a good solution to the problem at hand. In order to prove that a PSM is correctly derived from the PIM a number of proof obligations need to be discharged. If the PSM is obtained by using a pattern, certain proof obligations can be automatically ensured by the pattern.

To illustrate how a pattern is defined for a state-machine consider the patterns $p(s_1, s_2, s_3, e_1, ack, send)$ in Figure 7. The original model fragment to the left models sending a message ($e_1/send$) and waiting for a reply (ack). The pattern p then introduces fault tolerance timeout to handle lost acknowledgements. If the acknowledgement does not arrive on time, the message is re-transmitted. The message can be re-transmitted at most *max* number of times. When a part of the model where the pattern should be applied matches the model fragment to the left, it can be substituted for the model fragment to the right. The original state-machine fragment accepts the language $e_1\,ack$, while the resulting fragment accepts

$$e_1((\langle timeout\rangle\,\langle retry\rangle)^k\,\langle ack\rangle + (\langle timeout\rangle\,\langle retry\rangle)^{max})$$

where $k < max$.

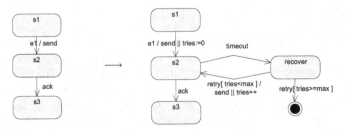

Fig. 7. An example of a pattern $p(s_1, s_2, s_3, e_1, send, ack)$

Even if patterns are used to obtain the PSM we still need to prove it is a correct derivation of the PIM. Consider a PIM $\mathcal{M}$ where we make the pattern application $p(r_1, r_2, r_3, e, rcv, snd)$ to obtain the PSM $\mathcal{M}'$. We get the refinement relation

$$(r' \in \{r_2, recover\} \Rightarrow r = r_2) \wedge (r' \notin \{r_2, recover\} \Rightarrow r' = r)$$

between the states r in $\mathcal{M}$ and r' in $\mathcal{M}'$. To prove that $\mathcal{M}'$ is a valid PSM for the PIM $\mathcal{M}$ we only need to prove that the transition $retry[tries < max]/snd$ is a refinement of an anticipating transition, since the proof obligation of all other transitions are guaranteed by the pattern. The proof obligations for deadlock freeness and termination of new transitions, as well as the extra constraints given in this paper are also ensured automatically by the pattern.

6.4 Example Application

To apply a pattern on the PIM $\mathcal{M}$, we have to make sure that the pattern is applicable for the scenario. Consequently, $\mathcal{M}$ and the pattern prerequisites must match, as discussed in Subsection 6.3. The proposed pattern matching and model substitution is clarified with an example of a communication timeout. Consider the simple communication system implementing hand-shaking in Figure 8. The system reads, sends and waits for an acknowledgment before sending the next segment. The pattern introducing timeout fault tolerance is illustrated in Figure 7. The application $p(send, sending, sent, b, ack, send)$ of the pattern p matches with a fraction of model $\mathcal{M}$, $a(\mathbf{b}\,\langle ack\rangle c)^* d$. Applying the pattern results in

$$a(\mathbf{b}(\langle\mathbf{timeout}\rangle\,\langle\mathbf{retry}\rangle)^{\mathbf{k}}\,\langle\mathbf{ack}\rangle\,c)^* d + a(\mathbf{b}(\langle\mathbf{timeout}\rangle\,\langle\mathbf{retry}\rangle))^{\mathbf{max}}$$

7   Conclusions

In this paper we presented a method for transforming a PIM into a PSM in a MDA context. Our transformation rules are mainly aimed at introducing fault tolerance features into the models. We consider behavioural models constructed using UML state-machines and we use Event B as the underlying formal framework. A PIM does not consider platform specific fault tolerance, while it has to

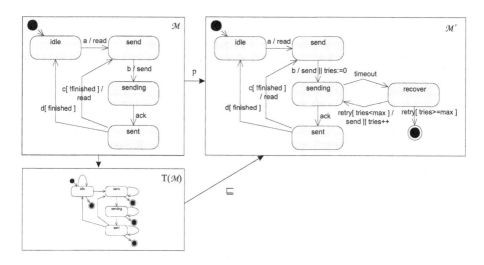

Fig. 8. Transformation of the PIM $\mathcal{M}$ into a PSM $\mathcal{M}'$

be considered in the PSM. However, fault tolerance cannot always be introduced in the PSM as a refinement of the PIM. The transformation rules in this paper will ensure that certain desirable properties are preserved in the PSM. Here models were created using UML and Event B, but the idea of using patterns for platform specific features and the extra proof obligations can also be beneficial when using only Event B to create the PIM and the PSM.

Adding features to a model that do not obey refinement rules has been investigated before. Retrenchment [6] is an approach to make exceptions to refinement rules in a structured manner. Retrenchment is more flexible than the method presented in this paper because it has fewer restrictions on the new features that can be added in the PSM. However, our method better ensures that behaviour of the PIM is preserved in the PSM. The rules in this paper has been developed to give a reasonable compromise between preserving behviour of the PIM and flexibility in introducing platform specific features.

Fault tolerance is often considered directly in the abstract specification (PIM). Adding fault tolerance in B has been investigated before by Laibinis and Troubitsyna in e.g. [9,10]. However, we like to construct the PIM without considering platform specific fault tolerance, in order to focus on the desired functionality and to make the models more reusable for different platforms.

As future work, we aim at applying the method on a case study to investigate its practicality and to develop reusable patterns. The method is not limited to only the subset of UML given in the paper, but it can be extended to consider more features from the UML standard. Since UML and B are used in industry this type of transformation rules can be beneficial in many application areas.

References

1. M. Abadi and L. Cardelli. *A Theory of Objects.* Springer, 1998
2. J. R. Abrial. *The B Book: Assigning Programs to Meanings.* Cambridge University Press. 1996
3. J. R. Abrial, D. Cansell and D. Méry. Refinement and Reachability in Event B. In *Proceedings of the 4th International Conference of B and Z users - ZB2005: Formal specification and Development in Z and B*, Guildford, UK, LNCS 3455, Springer, pp. 222-241, 2005
4. C. Atkinson and T. Kuhne. A Generalised Notion of Platforms for Model-Driven Development. In: Sami Beydeda, Mattias Book and Volker Gruhn (eds.) *Model-Driven Software Development.* Springer, pp. 119-136, 2005
5. R. J. R. Back and R. Kurki-Suonio. Decentralization of process nets with centralized control. In *Proceedings of the 2nd ACM SIGACT-SIGOPS Symposium of Principles of Distributed Computing*, pp. 131-142, 1983
6. R. Banach and M. Poppleton. Retrenchment: an Engineering Variation on Refinement. In *Proceedings of FM-99*, LNCS 1709, Springer, 1999
7. D. Harel. Statecharts: A Visual Formalism for Complex Systems. *Science of Computer Programming*, 8, Elsevier Science Publishers, pp. 231-274, 1987
8. R. Koo and S. Toueg. Checkpointing and rollback-recovery for distributed systems. IEEE Computer Society Press, pp. 1150 - 1158, 1986, ISBN: 0-8186-4743-4
9. L. Laibinis and E. Troubitsyna. Fault Tolerance in a Layered Architecture: A General Specification Pattern in B. In *Proceedings of SEFM 2004*, IEEE Computer Society, 2004
10. L. Laibinis and E. Troubitsyna. Refinement of Fault Tolerant Control Systems in B. In *Computer Safety, Reliability and Security - Proceedings of SAFECOMP 2004*, LNCS, 3219, Springer, pp. 254-268, 2004
11. T. Margaria and B. Steffen. Aggressive Model-Driven Development: Synthesising Systems from Models viewed as Constraints. *The Monterey Workshop Series 2003 Theme: Workshop on Software Engineering for Embedded Systems: From Requirements to Implementation*, Chicago, Illinois, September, 2003
12. C. Métayer, J. -R. Abrial and L. Voisin. Event-B Language, *Rodin Deliverable D7.* RODIN project, IST-511599, 2005 (accessed 29.09.2006) http://rodin.cs.ncl.ac.uk/deliverables.htm
13. I. Oliver. Model Based Testing and Refinement in MDA Based Development. In: *Pierre Boulet (ed.) Advances in Design and Specification Languages for SoCs.* The ChDL Series, Springer, 0-387-26149-4, 2005
14. E. Sekerinski and R. Zurob. Translating Statecharts to B. In *Proceedings of the third international Conference on Integrated Formal Methods, IFM 2002*, Turku, Finland, May 2002, LNCS 2335, Springer, 2002
15. B. Selic, G. Gullekson and P. T. Ward. *Real-Time Object-Oriented Modelling.* John Wiley & Sons. 1994
16. K. Sere and M. Waldén. Data Refinement of Remote Procedures. *Formal Aspects of Computing*, 12, pp. 278-297, 2000
17. C. Snook and M. Waldén. Refinement of Statemachines using Hierarchical States, Choice Points and Joins. In P*roceedings of the EPSRC RefineNet Workshop*, UK, 2005 (accessed 29.09.2006) http://www.tucs.fi/publications/attachment.php?fname=inpSnWa05a.pdf
18. N. Storey. *Safety-Critical Computer Systems.* Addison-Wesley, 1996
19. M. Waldén and K. Sere. Reasoning About Action Systems Using the B-Method. *Formal Methods in Systems Design*, 13:5-35, 1998

Refinement of EB³ Process Patterns into B Specifications

Frédéric Gervais[1,2], Marc Frappier[2], and Régine Laleau[3]

[1] CEDRIC, ENSIIE
18 Allée Jean Rostand, 91025 Évry Cedex, France
gervais_frederic@yahoo.fr
[2] GRIL, Département d'informatique, Université de Sherbrooke
Sherbrooke (Québec), J1K 2R1, Canada
marc.frappier@usherbrooke.ca
[3] LACL, Université Paris 12
IUT Fontainebleau, 77300 Fontainebleau, France
laleau@univ-paris12.fr

Abstract. On one hand, EB³ is a trace-based formal language created for the specification of information systems (IS). In particular, EB³ points out the dynamic behaviour of the system. On the other hand, B is a state-based formal language well adapted for the specification of the IS static properties. We are defining a new approach called EB⁴ that integrates both EB³ and B to specify IS. EB³ process expressions are used to represent and validate the behaviour of the system. Then, the specification is translated into B in order to specify and verify the main static properties of the IS. In this paper, we deal with the refinement of EB³ process expressions into B specifications. Since this process cannot be automated, we define refinement patterns that can be reused to obtain B specifications that refine the event ordering properties specified in EB³.

Keywords: Information systems, data integrity constraints, EB³, process expressions, refinement.

1 Introduction

Our aim is the formal specification of information systems (IS). An IS is a system that helps an organization to collect and manipulate all its relevant data. In the context of our work, we mainly consider the specification of database (DB) applications. The use of formal methods to design IS [8,13,16] is justified by the relevant value of data from corporations like banks, insurance companies, high-tech industries or government organizations. There exist several paradigms to specify IS, but we are interested in two specific formal languages. On one hand, EB³ [8] is a trace-based formal language created for the specification of IS. EB³ provides process expressions that represent the valid traces of the system and recursive functions that compute attribute values from the valid traces. On the other hand, B [1] is a state-based formal language that is well adapted to specify IS data models [13]. In B, state variables represent the state space of the system and invariant properties must be preserved by each operation.

J. Julliand and O. Kouchnarenko (Eds.): B 2007, LNCS 4355, pp. 201–215, 2006.

We are defining EB^4, an integrated approach that combines both EB^3 and B. Indeed, EB^3 and B are complementary when taking the main properties of IS into account [6]. There exist many integrated methods that combine state-based specifications with event-based specifications, like csp2B [3], CSP || B [4] or Circus [17], but none of them is well adapted for the specification of IS, althought a first attempt with CSP || B has been proposed in [4]. In IS, each action of the system requires an answer, possibly an error message. We use B rather than Event B [2], because guarded operations cannot be executed if their guards are not satisfied, whereas operations with preconditions as in B can be implemented with the relevant error messages. EB^4 is closer to the csp2B approach, where the CSP specification is translated into B. However, the main characteristics of IS lead us to choose EB^3 rather than CSP for specifying them. A discussion on the different couplings of state-based specifications with event-based specifications can be found in [9].

Considering the complementarity between B and EB^3 for IS specification, we are working on a new method that consists of using EB^3 to specify the behaviour of IS, and then using B to specify and prove safety properties on the model. In that aim, the EB^3 specification must be translated into an equivalent B specification. In [11], we have proposed an algorithm to partly automate the translation from EB^3 to B. This algorithm generates: i) the state space of the B specification; ii) the substitution of each operation body that updates the state variables; iii) the weakest precondition of each operation such that the invariant of the B specification is satisfied. However, one part of the operation preconditions was missing in this translation to represent the exact behaviour of the EB^3 specification. In [7], Frappier and Laleau have shown how to prove EB^3 event ordering properties on a B specification by using the B refinement relation. However, this refinement step is difficult to automate and often requires sound mathematical skills to prove its correctness. In this paper, we reuse the main principles of [7] to define refinement patterns for typical EB^3 process expressions.

The paper is organized as follows. Section 2 is an introduction to the EB^4 method. Then, we present in Sect. 3 the main components of an EB^3 specification. Section 4 deals with the synthesis of B specifications that correspond to the data model of EB^3. In Sect. 5, we show how to refine EB^3 event ordering properties into B specifications by using refinement patterns. Finally, Sect. 6 concludes the paper.

2   The EB^4 Method

In this section, a general overview of EB^4 is provided. The different steps of the method will be detailed in the next sections. Generally, the main issue for integrating two different paradigms is the way each representation is related to the other one. In EB^4 [11], we have chosen to adopt an "embedding" of EB^3 in B. In other words, an EB^3 specification of the IS is refined by a B specification. However, such a refinement is not straightforward and several steps are required

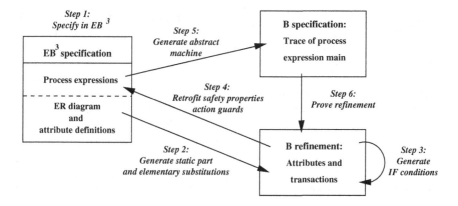

Fig. 1. Main steps of the EB⁴ method

to simplify the process. Fig. 1 shows the main steps of the EB⁴ method. Their description is the following:

- **Step 1:** The IS is first specified in EB³. EB³ [8] provides a formal notation to describe a specification of the input-output behaviour of an IS. An EB³ specification consists of the following elements:

  1. a diagram which includes the entity types and associations of the IS, and their respective actions and attributes. In EB³, the terms *entity type* and *entity* are used instead of class and object, respectively. The diagram is based on entity-relationship (ER) model concepts and uses a subset of the UML graphical notation for class diagrams. This graphic is called ER diagram in the remainder of the paper.
  2. a process expression, denoted by *main*, which describes the sequences of events accepted by the IS, called the *valid input traces* of the system. An *event* is simply an action call by IS end-users.
  3. input-output rules, which assign an output to each valid input trace.
  4. recursive functions, defined on the valid input traces of *main*, that assign values to entity type and association attributes. These particular functions are called *attribute definitions*.

- **Step 2:** The ER diagram and attribute definitions are translated into a B refinement. The rules of this translation are detailed in [10,11]. The B description obtained at this step is mainly used as a skeleton for the next steps. Indeed, EB³ attribute definitions represent the state space and the effects of transactions of the IS. Consequently, the resulting B refinement is not complete, since it does not take the dynamic properties described by EB³ process expressions into account. Moreover, the B operations do not preserve the invariant properties automatically generated from the ER diagram, because some preconditions are missing. However, this preliminary step makes the refinement of EB³ specification into B easier, since it provides the relevant state variables and invariant properties for the B refinement.

- **Step 3:** One of the benefits of the complementarity between EB^3 and B is exploited in this step. Static data integrity constraints are safety properties that IS entity types and associations must always satisfy. In this step, additional static integrity constraints can be described by means of invariant properties if they are missing in the B model obtained at Step 2. Then, new preconditions are generated for each operation of the B refinement such that all the invariant properties are preserved. In [14], we have defined systematic rules in order to generate such preconditions. This process can be automated because the general form of B invariant properties is restricted to a subset of invariant expressions that are characteristic of the domain of IS. At this step, we can also detect inconsistencies between static properties. In particular, if some constraints are too strong, then some B operations may be abortive (*i.e.,* their precondition is always equivalent to *false*). In that case, we come back to Step 1.
- **Step 4:** EB^3 actions can be guarded by first-order predicates involving attribute definitions. To reflect the new preconditions of B operations from Step 3, equivalent guards are generated in this step for the actions in EB^3 process expressions.
- **Steps 5 and 6:** The crux of these steps is to obtain a B refinement that refines the EB^3 specification. For that aim, EB^3 process expressions are first translated into B in Step 5; the translation is detailed in [7]. Then, Step 6 consists of refining this B model of the EB^3 specification. The B description obtained at the end of Step 3 provides the skeleton of the refinement. In particular, we have already generated: i) the state space of the refinement (Step 2); ii) the substitution of each operation body that updates the state variables (Step 2); iii) the precondition of each operation such that the static integrity constraints are satisfied (Step 3). The only parts that are now missing in the refinement are the operation preconditions that represent the behaviour entailed from the ordering constraints expressed in EB^3 process expressions and the gluing invariant.

Most of the aforementioned steps can be automated. In particular, systematic rules have been defined for steps 2, 4 and 5. Nevertheless, steps 3 and 6 still require a human intervention. The final B refinement obtained at the end of the process satisfies both the dynamic properties described in the initial EB^3 specification and the safety properties described in B. Step 1 is discussed in Sect. 3. Then, the translation into B and the verification of safety properties (steps 2 and 3) are presented in Sect. 4. Section 5 deals with steps 5 and 6.

3   EB^3 Specification

Step 1 is an important step of the EB^4 method since it provides the initial specification of the IS. We begin to specify the IS with EB^3, because this event-based language points out the dynamic behaviour of the system, while many existing IS specification methods tend to focus on the data model. We rather aim at describing the IS behaviour as soon as possible, because behaviour specification is more abstract than the description of the static part.

In EB³, an IS is considered as a black box. Each action has an implicit output which determines whether an event of this action is valid ("ok") or not ("error"). An event is considered as valid if it is accepted by the main process called *main*. The denotational semantics of an EB³ specification is given by a relation R defined on $T(main) \times O$, where $T(main)$ denotes the finite traces accepted by *main* and O is the set of output events. Let *trace* denote the system trace, which is the list of valid input events accepted so far by the system. Let $t :: \sigma$ denote the right append of an input event σ to trace t, and let $[\,]$ denote the empty trace. The operational behaviour of an EB³ specification is defined as follows:

> $trace := [\,]$;
> **forever do**
> > receive input event σ;
> > **if** *main* can accept $trace :: \sigma$ **then**
> > > $trace := trace :: \sigma$;
> > > send output event o such that $(trace, o) \in R$;
> > **else**
> > > send error message;

To be concise, we describe only the relevant parts of an EB³ specification that are of interest for the remainder of the paper. We consider a simplified library management system to illustrate the main aspects of the paper. The system has to manage book loans to members. A book is acquired (action Acquire) by the library. It can be discarded (Discard), but only if it is not borrowed. A member must join (Register) the library in order to borrow a book (Lend). A member can transfer a loan to another member (Transfer). A member can relinquish library membership (Unregister) only when all his loans are returned (Return) or transferred. The title of a book can be modified by action Modify and displayed with action DisplayTitle. Figure 2 shows the ER diagram for the library management system.

3.1   Process Expressions

The process expressions of an EB³ specification describe the valid input traces of the system. The special symbol "_" may be used as an actual parameter of an action, to denote an arbitrary value of the corresponding type. The EB³ notation for process expressions is similar to Hoare's CSP [12]. Complex EB³ process expressions can be constructed from elementary process expressions using the following operators: sequence (denoted by .), choice (|), Kleene closure (*), interleaving (|||), parallel composition (||, *i.e.,* CSP's synchronization on shared actions), guard ($\Longrightarrow$), process call, and quantification of choice ($|x : T : ...$) and of interleaving ($|||x : T : ...$). The complete syntax and semantics of EB³ can be found in [8].

For instance, the EB³ process expression for entity type *book* is of the following form:

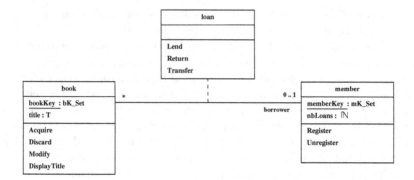

Fig. 2. ER diagram of the library

$book(bId : bK\_Set) \triangleq$
Acquire$(bId, \_)$.
(
　　　(| $mId : mK\_Set : loan(mId, bId)$)*
　|||
　　　Modify$(bId, \_)$*
　|||
　　　DisplayTitle(bId)*
).
Discard(bId)

The process *book* describes the life-cycle of each book entity of the system. First, book entity *bId* is produced by action Acquire. Then, it can be borrowed by only one member entity *mId* at once (quantified choice "| $mId : mK\_Set : ...$"). Indeed, the process *book* calls the subprocess *loan* that involves actions Lend, Return and Transfer. The Kleene closure on *loan* means that an arbitrary finite number of loans can be made on book entity *bId*. At any moment, actions Modify and DisplayTitle can be interleaved with the actions of *loan*. Finally, book entity *bId* is consumed by action Discard. The complete process expressions for the example are given in [10].

3.2　Attribute Definitions

In IS, attributes of associations and entity types are the main elements, because they represent the knowledge contained in the IS that can be read to answer requests from users or updated to reflect evolutions of the IS. The definition of an attribute in EB³ is a recursive function on the valid input traces of the system. The function is total and is given in a functional style, as in CAML. It outputs the attribute values that are valid for the state in which the system is, after having executed the input events in the trace.

We distinguish key attributes from non-key attributes. A key definition outputs the set of existing key values, while a non-key attribute definition outputs

$bookKey(s : \mathcal{T}(\mathsf{main})) : \mathbb{F}(bK\_Set) \quad \triangleq$	$title(s : \mathcal{T}(\mathsf{main}), bId : bK\_Set) : T \quad \triangleq$	
match $last(s)$ **with**	**match** $last(s)$ **with**	
$\perp : \emptyset,$	$\perp : \perp,$	(I1)
$\mathsf{Acquire}(bId, \_) : bookKey(front(s)) \cup \{bId\},$	$\mathsf{Acquire}(bId, ttl) : ttl,$	(I2)
$\mathsf{Discard}(bId) : bookKey(front(s)) - \{bId\},$	$\mathsf{Discard}(bId) : \perp,$	(I3)
$\_ : bookKey(front(s));$	$\mathsf{Modify}(bId, ttl) : ttl,$	(I4)
	$\_ : title(front(s), bId);$	(I5)

Fig. 3. Examples of EB³ attribute definitions

the attribute value for a key value given as an input parameter. For instance, the key of entity type *book* is defined by function *bookKey* in Fig. 3. *bookKey* has a unique input parameter $s \in \mathcal{T}(\mathsf{main})$, *i.e.*, a valid trace of the system, and it returns the set of key values of entity type *book*. Note that type $\mathbb{F}(bK\_Set)$ denotes the set of finite subsets of bK_Set. Function *title* in Fig. 3 is an example of non-key attribute definition. Expressions of the form *input : expr*, like $\mathsf{Acquire}(bId, ttl) : ttl$, are called *input clauses*. Expression *expr* is a term composed of constants, variables and attribute calls. Expressions of the form **if then else end** can also be used. The symbol "$\perp$" denotes undefinedness.

For instance, we have: $title([], b_1) = \perp$, because $last([]) = \perp$. To evaluate $title([\mathsf{Register}(m_1)], b_1)$, we first apply (I5) and we have: $title([], b_1)$. Then, we obtain the result by applying (I1): $title([\mathsf{Register}(m_1)], b_1) = \perp$. A more detailed description of EB³ attribute definitions can be found in [10].

4   Generating B Specifications from EB³ Attribute Definitions

We now focus on steps 2 and 3 of the EB⁴ method. Figure 4 shows the B refinement generated from the EB³ specification of the library management system by using the algorithms discussed in this section. For the sake of brevity, some operations have been omitted.

4.1   State Space and Substitutions

Step 2 of the EB⁴ method allows us to generate a B model of the state space and the effects of the system transactions. The static part of B specifications is automatically generated from the ER diagram. The translation is inspired from the formalization in B of OMT and UML class diagrams [13,15,16]. In particular, each recursive function k defining a key in the EB³ specification is translated into a state variable k_B whose invariant is an inclusion of the form $k_B \subseteq T_B$, where T_B represents the set of all the possible values of k. Each non-key attribute definition b is translated into a state variable b_B such that $b_B \in k_B \rightarrow T_B$ or $b_B \in k_B \nrightarrow T_B$ (depending on whether b admits null values), where k_B is the state variable that corresponds to the key of the entity type or the association in which b is defined and T_B represents the set of all the possible values of b.

REFINEMENT $B\_Library$
REFINES $EB3\_Library$ /* abstract sets mK_Set, bK_Set and T
                      will be defined in the abstract machine */
VARIABLES $memberKey, nbLoans, bookKey, title, loan$
INVARIANT $memberKey \subseteq mK\_Set \ \wedge \ nbLoans \in memberKey \rightarrow NAT$
    $\wedge \ bookKey \subseteq bK\_Set \ \wedge \ title \in bookKey \rightarrow T$
    $\wedge \ loan \in bookKey \rightarrowtail memberKey \ \wedge \ J$
DEFINITIONS $borrower(x) \triangleq loan(x)$
INITIALISATION
    $memberKey, nbLoans, bookKey, title, loan := \emptyset, \emptyset, \emptyset, \emptyset, \emptyset$
OPERATIONS
$res \longleftarrow$ **Acquire**$(bId, ttl) \triangleq$
    PRE $bId \in bK\_Set \ \wedge \ ttl \in T$
    THEN
        IF $SC1 \ \wedge \ DC1$ THEN
            $bookKey := bookKey \cup \{bId\}$ ||
            $title := title \mathbin{\lhd\!\!\!-} \{bId \mapsto ttl\}$ ||
            $res :=$ "ok"
        ELSE
            $res :=$ "error"
        END
    END;
$res \longleftarrow$ **Discard**$(bId) \triangleq$
    PRE $bId \in bK\_Set$
    THEN
        IF $SC2 \ \wedge \ DC2$ THEN
            $bookKey := bookKey - \{bId\}$ ||
            $title := \{bId\} \mathbin{\lhd\!\!\!-} title$ ||
            $res :=$ "ok"
        ELSE
            $res :=$ "error"
        END
    END;
$res \longleftarrow$ **Lend**$(bId, mId) \triangleq$
    PRE $bId \in bK\_Set \ \wedge \ mId \in mK\_Set$
    THEN
        IF $SC3 \ \wedge \ DC3$ THEN
            $loan := loan \mathbin{\lhd\!\!\!-} \{(bId, mId)\}$ ||
            $nbLoans := nbLoans \mathbin{\lhd\!\!\!-} \{mId \mapsto nbLoans(mId) + 1\}$ ||
            $res :=$ "ok"
        ELSE
            $res :=$ "error"
        END
    END;

Fig. 4. B refinement generated from EB[3] attribute definitions

The translation rules for the static part are detailed in [5,16]. For the sake of brevity, we generate a single B machine that contains all the operations. This has no influence on the algorithms described in the paper.

EB^3 attribute definitions describe the dynamic behaviour of IS data. Thus, each attribute definition specifies what the effects of each action on the attribute values are. In B, attributes are defined as state variables of the system and each B operation specifies what the substitutions on the state variables are. During Step 2, a B operation is generated for each action defined in EB^3. The translation rules are detailed in [11]. For instance, let us consider operation **Discard** in Fig. 4. Parameter *res* corresponds to the implicit output of EB^3 actions that determines whether an input event is valid or not. The generated precondition is only a typing constraint on the input parameter. The body of each operation is of the form IF THEN ELSE END, in order to reflect the semantics of EB^3 specification; the ELSE part corresponds to the case where the new event is invalid.

In addition to the substitutions associated with *res*, a substitution is generated for each attribute definition affected by the action. For example, action Discard occurs only in functions *bookKey* and *title* (see Sect. 3.2). The generation of substitutions is quite straightforward. For a key definition like *bookKey*, the substitution is simply the expression associated with input clause Discard, where each occurrence of *bookKey(front(s))* is replaced by *bookKey*. For the non-key attribute definition, we have to determine the key value affected by the execution of Discard. In that case, *bId* is directly determined from the pattern matching and the substitution is generated according to the type of state variable *title*. However, if the input clause contains **if then else end** expressions, then we must analyse the different conditions in the **if** predicates to determine the values of the key attributes that are not bound by the pattern matching [10].

At this step, we are not able to generate the predicates for the IF part of B operations; they are determined by steps 3 and 6 of the EB^4 method. The IF predicates can be divided in two parts: i) the weakest precondition required to preserve the invariant of the machine (denoted by SC in the remainder of the paper) and ii) the condition required to impose ordering constraints on operations (denoted by DC).

4.2 Static Properties

Contrary to other translation methods from semi-formal notations into B [15,13], where the operation preconditions and invariant properties are automatically generated from the class diagram, the translation presented in Sect. 4.1 does not synthesize the preconditions that correspond to the static integrity constraints of the ER diagram. Consequently, we have developed in [14] a set of systematic rules that compute preconditions to preserve the invariant of the B specification. These rules have been defined for a relevant subset of invariant properties that are characteristic to IS static data integrity constraints. For instance, condition $SC1$ of operation **Acquire** is *true*, since the precondition is sufficient to discharge the proof obligation, but condition $SC2$ for operation **Discard** is: $bId \notin dom(loan)$.

The latter predicate has been generated to preserve the invariant property $loan \in bookKey \twoheadrightarrow memberKey$. Note that such a condition is not sufficient to represent the exact behaviour of the EB^3 specification; operation **Discard** still requires condition $DC2$, which is the ordering constraint that a book must have been created before it can be deleted (*i.e.*, $bId \in bookKey$).

The main interest of Step 3 is the use of B to specify and verify additional static data integrity constraints that are not explicit in the EB^3 specification. By using the aforementioned technique, we are able to generate preconditions for the safety properties directly expressed in B. For instance, we can state that the number of loans of each member must be less or equal than five books. This constraint is specified in B by the following invariant: $\forall mId \in memberKey \bullet nbLoans(mId) \leq 5$. In that case, the generated condition SC for operation **Lend** is: $nbLoans(mId) \leq 4$. The IF predicates generated at Step 3 are called *safety constraints*. They should appear as action guards in the EB^3 process expressions, in order to keep the equivalence between the two representations. This change is addressed by Step 4 of the EB^4 method. For instance, the following guard is then synthesized for action Lend: $nbLoans(trace, mId) \leq 4$.

5 Refinement of EB^3 Process Expressions

Steps 5 and 6 of the EB^4 method consist of proving that the B model obtained after several iterations of steps 1, 2 and 3 is a refinement of the B model of EB^3 process expressions. Thus, the B refinement will satisfy the dynamic properties described in the EB^3 specification.

5.1 Refinement Proof

Step 5 reuses the B representation of EB^3 process expressions introduced by Frappier and Laleau in [7]. The form of the B abstract machine is shown in part (a) of Fig. 5. State variable t is the current trace of the system, $T(main)$ represents the set of all the valid input traces of the IS and, in each operation, Typ denotes the typing constraints on the input parameters. Informally, the **IF** predicate means that an event of Operation(*parameters*) is executed only if the current trace augmented with the new event is a valid trace.

The form of the B refinement obtained at the end of Step 3 is recalled in part (b) of Fig. 5. In each operation, Typ' denotes the typing constraints, SC the safety constraints generated during Step 3, and $Subst$ the B substitutions synthesized by Step 2. Our aim is to define the dynamic constraints DC of each operation such that the event ordering properties specified in EB^3 are preserved by the operations.

Let I be the invariant of the abstract machine and J the gluing invariant of the refinement. Since the concrete variables are automatically generated from the ER diagram in Step 2, the gluing invariant J is straightforward. By convention, expression V_e denotes the B state variable which represents key definition or non-key attribute definition e. Then, for each attribute definition e, J includes

MACHINE *EB3_Library*	REFINEMENT *B_Library*
SETS *mK_Set*; *bK_Set*; *T*;	REFINES *EB3_Library*
SEES ... /* definition of $T(main)$ */	
VARIABLES *t*	VARIABLES ... /* see Fig. 4 */
INVARIANT $t \in T(main)$	INVARIANT ... /* see Fig. 4 */
...	...
OPERATIONS	OPERATIONS
res ⟵ **Operation**(*parameters*) $\triangleq$	*res* ⟵ **Operation**(*parameters*) $\triangleq$
PRE *Typ*	PRE *Typ'*
THEN	THEN
IF *t* :: Operation(*parameters*) $\in T(main)$	IF $SC \wedge DC$
THEN	THEN
$t := t$ :: Operation(*parameters*) ‖	*Subst* ‖
res := "ok"	*res* := "ok"
ELSE *res* := "error"	ELSE *res* := "error"
END	END
END	END
(a) Abstract Machine	(b) Refinement

Fig. 5. Abstract machine and refinement

a predicate of the form $e(t) = V_e$. By analysing the refinement proof obligation for the operations of Fig. 5 and by performing a case analysis on the possible values of output parameter *res*, we deduce that the proof obligation is satisfied if and only if the three following lemmas are satisfied, under the hypotheses *I* and *J*:

(PO1) $Typ \Rightarrow Typ'$

(PO2) $SC \wedge DC \Rightarrow [Subst][t := t$ :: Operation(*parameters*)]*J*

(PO3) $SC \wedge DC \Leftrightarrow t$ :: Operation(*parameters*) $\in T(main)$

Proof obligation (PO1) is straightforward, since *Typ* and *Typ'* are exactly the same. Proof obligation (PO2) means that the effects *Subst* are consistent with respect to the effects of EB³ actions. By definition of our translation rules, the B substitutions generated by Step 2 are equivalent to EB³ attribute definitions. The proof of (PO3) is quite difficult. Such a proof requires some creativity, since the specifier needs to propose the dynamic constraint *DC* for the operation. Predicate *t* :: Operation(*parameters*) $\in T$(main) can be decomposed, by case analysis during the proof, in two parts: $G \wedge OC$. Predicate *G* corresponds to the guard that is specified in the EB³ process expressions for the equivalent action. Predicate *OC* is the ordering constraint that must be satisfied when the guard *G* is supposed to be satisfied. In the EB⁴ method, EB³ action guards are generated from the safety constraints specified in the B model; hence, *SC* is equivalent to *G*. Consequently, the specifier has to define, for each operation, a condition *DC* such that: $DC \Leftrightarrow OC$. To assist in specifying such conditions, we have defined some refinement patterns.

5.2 Refinement Patterns

During Step 1, the IS valid input traces are specified by means of EB^3 process expressions. Obviously, this step cannot be automated, but a set of characteristic process patterns have been defined in [8] to help the specifier. Since these patterns are representative of most common IS behaviours, we have proposed refinement patterns based on these typical process expressions. Thus, the patterns provide, for each kind of action in the processes, an ordering constraint DC such that proof obligation (PO3) is satisfied. In the next sections, we present two patterns.

5.2.1 Elementary Pattern for Entity Types and Associations

Actions involved in the life-cycle of an IS entity often follow the pattern "producer, modifier, consumer". This pattern [8] describes the typical behaviour of an entity type e, whose actions are either producers $(P_1, ..., P_l)$, modifiers $(M_1, ..., M_n)$, or consumers $(C_1, ..., C_m)$:

$$
\begin{aligned}
&e(k : K\_Set) = \\
&\quad P_1(k, \_) \mid ... \mid P_l(k, \_). \\
&\quad (\\
&\qquad (M_1(k, \_) \mid ... \mid M_n(k, \_))^* \\
&\quad \| \\
&\qquad AP_1 \, \| \, ... \, \| \, AP_r \\
&\quad \|\| \\
&\qquad Rq_1^* \, \|\| \, ... \, \|\| \, Rq_p^* \\
&\quad). \\
&\quad C_1(k, \_) \mid ... \mid C_m(k, \_)
\end{aligned}
$$

where k is the key of e and K_Set the type of k. Expressions $Rq_1, ..., Rq_p$ denote the EB^3 actions that output one or more attribute values. Expressions $AP_1, ..., AP_r$ represent the possible process calls corresponding to IS associations; r depends on the number of associations in which entity type e participates. Each AP_i, $1 \leq i \leq r$, must be replaced by one of the process patterns described in Sect. 5.2.2 to reflect the cardinalities of each association. Analogously, the process that describes the life-cycle of an association follows the same pattern, except for expressions $AP_1, ..., AP_r$ that are removed from it. For instance, the process of entity type *book* described in Sect. 3.1 follows the aforementioned pattern. Actions Acquire, Modify and Discard are respectively producer, modifier and consumer of *book*, while action DisplayTitle is a query on attribute *title*.

The ordering constraint for a producer P_j of an entity of e whose key value is k must check that this entity does not exist before the execution of P_j. Hence, DC is of the form: $k \notin V_k$. For instance, condition $DC1$ in the IF part of operation **Acquire** is: $bId \notin bookKey$. Modifiers and consumers must check that the entity identified by k exists before their execution. Consequently, condition DC is of the following form: $k \in V_k$. For instance, condition $DC2$ of operation **Discard** is: $bId \in bookKey$.

5.2.2 Patterns for Entities Participating in Binary Associations

We consider binary associations with cardinalities $1 : N$, $1 : 1$ and $M : N$. In EB^3, the process corresponding to an association is a subprocess of one or more entity types. Such process calls are represented by expressions AP_j in the pattern described in Sect. 5.2.1. Let e_1 and e_2 be the entity types participating in binary association a. Let $k1$ and $k2$ be their respective key. Let AP_{i1} and AP_{i2} be the process calls to a in the process expressions of e_1 and e_2. The form of AP_{i1} and AP_{i2} depends on the cardinalities in association a. If a is a $1 : N$ association, then expressions AP_{i1} and AP_{i2} are respectively of the form (AP-Multi) and (AP-One):

$$\||| \; k2 : K\_Set2 : a(k1, k2)^* \qquad \text{(AP-Multi)}$$
$$(\; | \; k1 : K\_Set1 : a(k1, k2) \;)^* \quad \text{(AP-One)}$$

Thus, subprocess a is called in process e_1 as a quantified interleaving; hence, an entity identified by $k1$ can be associated with several entities $k2$. In the process of e_2, subprocess a is called as a quantified choice; an entity $k2$ is therefore associated with at most one entity $k1$ at once. Let us consider process *book* to illustrate this particular pattern: the process call to *loan* in *book* is of the form (AP-One), since a book can be borrowed by only one member at once. For $1 : 1$ associations, the process calls in the entity types participating in the association are both of the form (AP-One), while for $M : N$ associations, they are both of the form (AP-Multi).

Let us now consider $1 : N$ associations; such an association is represented by a partial function in B. For instance, V_a may be defined by: $V_a \in V_{k1} \nrightarrow V_{k2}$. The ordering constraint for an association producer must check that: i) the entities identified by $k1$ and $k2$ already exist; ii) the entity identified by $k1$ is not already associated with an entity $k2$, because of the cardinality. The constraint DC is then of the following form: $k1 \in V_{k1} \wedge k2 \in V_{k2} \wedge (k1, k2) \notin V_a \wedge k1 \notin dom(V_a)$. Note that the first three conditions are common to all kinds of associations. The last predicate depends on the cardinality of a. For instance, condition $DC3$ of operation **Lend** is: $bId \in bookKey \wedge mId \in memberKey \wedge (bId, mId) \notin loan \wedge bId \notin dom(loan)$. The ordering constraint for modifiers or consumers must check that: i) the entities identified by $k1$ and $k2$ already exist; ii) the entity identified by $(k1, k2)$ is an existing association. Hence, DC is of the following form: $k1 \in V_{k1} \wedge k2 \in V_{k2} \wedge (k1, k2) \in V_a$.

5.2.3 Key Idea of the Proof

We now present an overview of the analysis that we have performed to prove lemma (PO3) for each refinement pattern. For the sake of illustration, we deal with actions from type producer in $1 : N$ associations. Let P_j be such a producer in an association a. We suppose that expressions AP_{i1} and AP_{i2} are of the form (AP-Multi) and (AP-One), as described in Sect. 5.2.2. To prove that the condition DC provided by the refinement pattern is equivalent to condition OC, we have to compare the state transitions associated with action P_j in the valid input traces with the state transitions of the corresponding B operation.

By analysing the pattern described in Sect. 5.2.1, we deduce that the following kind of actions must be executed before the producer P_j of an association entity identified by $(k1, k2)$: 1) a producer of the entity identified by $k1$ (in the process of entity type $e1$), 2) a producer of the entity identified by $k2$ (in the process of $e2$). To determine OC, we first describe the form of trace t. Let T_{k1} be the set of valid input traces of the form $t1 :: P_{k1} :: t2$, where P_{k1} is a producer of the entity identified by $k1$, $t1$ is an arbitrary trace, and $t2$ is a trace that does not include any consumer of $k1$. Similarly, T_{k2} is the set of valid input traces of the form $t1 :: P_{k2} :: t3$, where P_{k2} is a producer of the entity identified by $k2$ and $t3$ is a trace that does not include any consumer of $k2$. In that case, the trace t we are analysing satisfies the predicate $t \in T_{k1} \cap T_{k2}$. By definition of P_{k1} and P_{k2}, this predicate is equivalent to $k1 \in e1(t) \wedge k2 \in e2(t)$, where $e1$ and $e2$ are the key definitions of entity types $e1$ and $e2$. We denote this predicate by (OC1).

We deduce from the life-cycle of an association that: i) either a producer of the association entity identified by $(k1, k2)$ has never been executed since the initialization of the system, or ii) a finite number of producers of $(k1, k2)$ have already been executed (Kleene closure on association a), but each of them has been followed by a consumer. Thus, we can determine the form of t and deduce that $(k1, k2) \notin a(t)$, where a denotes the key definition of association a. This predicate is denoted by (OC2). By following the same pattern of analysis, we can deduce for the cardinalities that trace t satisfies the following predicate, that we denote by (OC3): $k1 \notin \{k \in K\_Set1 \mid \exists k2 \in K\_Set2 \bullet (k, k2) \in a(t)\}$.

Gluing invariant J allows state variable t to be linked to the state variables representing the different attributes of the IS in the B specification from Step 3. In particular, we have: $e1(t) = V_{k1}$, $e2(t) = V_{k2}$, and $a(t) = V_a$. Predicate (OC1) is then equivalent to $k1 \in V_{k1} \wedge k2 \in V_{k2}$, (OC2) to $(k1, k2) \notin V_a$, and (OC3) to $k1 \notin dom(V_a)$. Consequently, (OC1) $\wedge$ (OC2) $\wedge$ (OC3) is equivalent to the condition DC that we have proposed in Sect. 5.2.2.

6   Conclusions

The key idea of the EB^4 method is the refinement of an EB^3 specification into a B specification. Thus, the B refinement specification satisfies both the dynamic properties described in EB^3 and the safety properties described in B. In order to facilitate the refinement, we generate a skeleton of B specification from the data model of the EB^3 specification. Hence, the state space and the relevant concrete variables are automatically generated. The proof of correctness of this translation is a work in progress. The main issue addressed in this paper is the preservation of the dynamic properties specified in EB^3. The approach consists of defining refinement patterns for the most typical EB^3 process expressions. The refinement proof then ensures that the behaviour of the B specification is consistent with respect to the behaviour of the EB^3 specification. As future work, we aim at providing techniques to verify dynamic properties in EB^3. For instance, the verification of dynamic integrity constraints is an open issue that we now aim at tackling.

References

1. J.R. Abrial. *The B-Book: Assigning programs to meanings*. Cambridge University Press, 1996.
2. J.R. Abrial and L. Mussat. Introducing dynamic constraints in B. In *B'98*, volume 1393 of *LNCS*, pages 83–128, Montpellier, France, April 1998. Springer-Verlag.
3. M. Butler. csp2B : A practical approach to combining CSP and B. In *FM'99*, volume 1708 of *LNCS*, pages 490–508, Toulouse, France, September 1999. Springer-Verlag.
4. N. Evans, H. Treharne, R. Laleau, and M. Frappier. How to verify dynamic properties of information systems. In *SEFM 2004*, pages 416–425, Beijing, China, September 2004. IEEE Computer Society Press.
5. P. Facon, R. Laleau, and H.P. Nguyen. Mapping object diagrams into B specifications. In *Methods Integration Workshop*, eWiC, Leeds, UK, March 1996. Springer-Verlag.
6. B. Fraikin, M. Frappier, and R. Laleau. State-based versus event-based specifications for information systems: a comparison of B and EB^3. *Software and Systems Modeling*, 4(3):236–257, July 2005.
7. M. Frappier and R. Laleau. Proving event ordering properties for information systems. In *ZB 2003*, volume 2651 of *LNCS*, pages 421–436, Turku, Finland, June 2003. Springer-Verlag.
8. M. Frappier and R. St-Denis. EB^3: an entity-based black-box specification method for information systems. *Software and Systems Modeling*, 2(2):134–149, July 2003.
9. F. Gervais. *EB^4 : Vers une méthode combinée de spécification formelle des systèmes d'information*. Dissertation for the general examination, GRIL, Université de Sherbrooke, Québec, June 2004.
10. F. Gervais, M. Frappier, and R. Laleau. *Synthesizing B substitutions for EB^3 attribute definitions*. Technical Report 683, CEDRIC, France, November 2004.
11. F. Gervais, M. Frappier, and R. Laleau. Synthesizing B specifications from EB^3 attribute definitions. In *IFM 2005*, volume 3771 of *LNCS*, pages 207–226, Eindhoven, The Netherlands, November-December 2005. Springer-Verlag.
12. C.A.R. Hoare. *Communicating Sequential Processes*. Prentice-Hall, 1985.
13. A. Mammar. *Un environnement formel pour le développement d'applications base de données*. PhD thesis, CNAM, Paris, France, 2002.
14. A. Mammar, F. Gervais, and R. Laleau. Systematic identification of preconditions from set-based integrity constraints. In *INFORSID 2006*, volume 2, pages 595–610, Hammamet, Tunisia, June 2006. INFORSID.
15. E. Meyer and J. Souquières. A systematic approach to transform OMT diagrams to a B specification. In *FM'99*, volume 1708 of *LNCS*, pages 875–895, Toulouse, France, September 1999. Springer-Verlag.
16. H.P. Nguyen. *Dérivation de spécifications formelles B à partir de spécifications semi-formelles*. PhD thesis, CNAM, Paris, France, 1998.
17. J.C.P. Woodcock and A.L.C. Cavalcanti. The Semantics of Circus. In *ZB 2002*, volume 2272 of *LNCS*, pages 184–203, Grenoble, France, January 2002. Springer-Verlag.

Security Policy Enforcement Through Refinement Process

Nicolas Stouls[*] and Marie-Laure Potet

Laboratoire Logiciels Systèmes Réseaux - LSR-IMAG - Grenoble, France
{Nicolas.Stouls, Marie-Laure.Potet}@imag.fr

Abstract. In the area of networks, a common method to enforce a security policy expressed in a high-level language is based on an ad-hoc and
manual rewriting process [24]. We argue that it is possible to build a formal link between concrete and abstract terms, which can be dynamically
computed from the environment data. In order to progressively introduce
configuration data and then simplify the proof obligations, we use the B
refinement process. We present a case study modeling a network monitor. This program, described by refinement following the layers of the
TCP/IP suite protocol, has to warn for all observed events which do
not respect the security policy. To design this model, we use the event-B
method because it is suitable for modeling network concepts.

This work has been done within the framework of the POTESTAT[1]
project [9], based on the research of network testing methods from a
high-level security policy.

Keywords: Security policy enforcement, refinement, TCP/IP layers.

1 Introduction

The separation between *policies* and *mechanisms* is considered as a main specification principle in security. The policy describes the authorized actions while
the mechanism is the method to implement the policy [24,17]. Those two concepts do not have the same abstraction level. The classical process to enforce a
policy consists of manually rewriting the policy in the same terms as the mechanism, with ad-hoc methods. We argue that a policy can be formally enforced
in a mechanism by gradually building, through a refinement process, a link between abstract and concrete terms. We propose to design a specification with
the same abstraction level as the policy and to refine it to obtain the concrete
mechanism. In the case of critical software, using an abstract specification is, for
example, required for test and audit processes or for certification according to
the Common Criteria [7].

To illustrate our approach, we describe a network security software which has
to enforce an abstract security policy in a TCP/IP network. Modern TCP/IP

---

[*] Work supported by CNRS and ST-Microelectronics by the way of a doctoral grant.
[1] Security policies: test directed analysis of open networks systems.
http://www-lsr.imag.fr/POTESTAT/

J. Julliand and O. Kouchnarenko (Eds.): B 2007, LNCS 4355, pp. 216–231, 2006.

networks are heterogeneous and distributed, and their management becomes more and more complex. Thus, the use of an abstract security policy can give a global and comprehensive view of a network security [22]. We choose to focus more specifically on an access control policy because it is the main concept in network security [10,20].

We aim at designing a monitor, which warns if an action, forbidden by the policy, is observed on the network. In order to achieve that, we use the event-B method [1] for modeling network concepts.

The next section is an overview of the event-B method. Section 3 introduces networks and their security policy concepts. Then, Section 4 presents our approach, Section 5 describes our method based on the refinement process. Section 6 is a presentation of the case study. Finally, we conclude by comparing this work to related ones and by giving some prospects.

2 Event-B

The B method [2] is a formal development method as well as a specification language. B components can be refined and implemented. The correctness of models and refinements can be validated by proof obligations.

Event-B [1] is an extension of the B language where models are described by events instead of operations. The most abstract component is called *system*. Each event is composed by a guard G and an action T such that if G is enabled, then T can be executed. If several guards are enabled at the same time then the triggered event is chosen in a nondeterministic way.

Through the refinement process, data representation can be changed. The gluing invariant describes the relationship between abstract and concrete variables. If an event e_A is refined by an event e_R, then the refinement guard has to imply the abstract one. Moreover, some events can be introduced during the refinement process (refining the skip event), according to the same principles as the *stuttering* in TLA [15]. Due to the guard strengthening through refinement process, we have to prove that there is always at least one enabled event (no dead-lock) and that new events do not introduce live-locks.

Table 1. Used sets operators

Operator		Meaning
$A \leftrightarrow B$	$\hat{=}$	$\{R \mid R \subseteq A \times B\}$
$\mathsf{dom}(R)$	$\hat{=}$	$\{a \mid \exists b \cdot ((a,b) \in R)\}$
$\mathsf{ran}(R)$	$\hat{=}$	$\{b \mid \exists a \cdot ((a,b) \in R)\}$
$R[A]$	$\hat{=}$	$\{b \mid \exists a \cdot (a \in A \ \wedge \ (a,b) \in R)\}$
R^{-1}	$\hat{=}$	$\{(b,a) \mid (a,b) \in R\}$
$R_1 \; ; \; R_2$	$\hat{=}$	$\{(a,c) \mid \exists b \cdot ((a,b) \in R_1 \ \wedge \ (b,c) \in R_2)\}$
$R_1 \parallel R_2$	$\hat{=}$	$\{((a,b),(c,d)) \mid (a,c) \in R_1 \ \wedge \ (b,d) \in R_2\}$
$R \rhd B$	$\hat{=}$	$\{(a,b) \mid (a,b) \in R \ \wedge \ b \in B\}$
$A \nrightarrow B$	$\hat{=}$	$\{F \mid F \in A \leftrightarrow B \ \wedge \ \forall(b_1, b_2) \cdot ((a,b_1) \in F \ \wedge \ (a,b_2) \in F \Rightarrow b_1 = b_2)\}$

Table 2. Used primitives substitutions

Substitution	Syntactical notation	Mathematical notation
Do nothing	skip	skip
Assignment	$x := E$	$x := E$
Unbounded choice	ANY z WHERE P THEN T END	$@z \cdot (P \Rightarrow T)$
Condition	IF P THEN T_1 ELSE T_2 END	$P \Longrightarrow T_1 \parallel \neg P \Longrightarrow T_2$

To conclude, Table 1 defines the set notations which are used thereafter and Table 2 summarizes generalised substitutions.

3   Introduction to Networks and Their Security Policies

3.1   The TCP/IP Protocol Suite

Computer networks use a standard connection model, called OSI (Open Systems Interconnection) [13], composed of seven layers. The TCP/IP protocol suite implements this model but is described with only four layers: application, transport, network and link. Each of these layers plays a particular role:

- The *Application* layer is the interface between the applications and the network (client-side protocol).
- The *Transport* layer manages the host-to-host communications, but not the route between them (peer-to-peer networks).
- The *Network* layer manages the route between networks by selecting the network interface to use and the first router.
- The *Link* layer performs the signal translation (analogic/numeric) and synchronizes the data transmission. This layer is most often provided by the hardware. Therefore, it is not considered in the following sections.

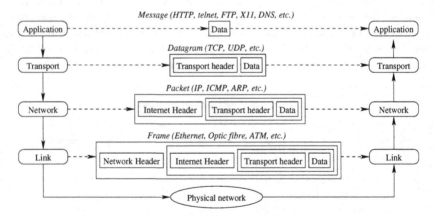

Fig. 1. Layers of the TCP/IP suite with some examples of protocols

Communications using TCP/IP protocol are composed of protocols for each layer in the suite. For example, a TCP datagram (Transport layer) is contained in the data field of an IP packet (Network layer). Figure 1 shows an example of communication using TCP/IP.

3.2   Network Security Policies

In the area of networks, security is mainly expressed in terms of access rights. An access control policy is defined on a set of actions by a set of rules. These rules determine, for each action, whether the action is authorized or not. Among the various types of access control policies [11,16], *open policies* and *closed policies* can be distinguished. An open policy (Fig. 2.A) expresses all *forbidden actions* (called *negative authorizations*): a not explicitly denied access is allowed. In a closed policy (Fig. 2.B), all *authorized actions* have to be fully specified (called *positive authorizations*). Finally, some policies are expressed with both positive and negative rules (Fig. 2.C). In this case, some actions can be *conflicting* or *undefined*.

A. Open policy   B. Closed policy   C. Both policies

Fig. 2. Example of open, closed and both policies

In the following, readers should distinguish *network events*, which are the elementary communication steps of the network, and B *events*, which are the description of actions in the B method.

In the proposed approach, a closed policy defined by a single set (SP) of authorized actions is used. However, each of these abstract actions can be associated to one or more concrete network events and conversely.

Definition 1 (Types of Events). *An event is **correct** with regard to a security policy if it corresponds only to authorized actions of the policy (Fig. 3.A). If the event is associated only to forbidden actions then this event **violates** the policy (Fig. 3.B). If an event is linked to some authorized actions and to some forbidden ones, then this event is in **conflict** with the policy (Fig. 3.C).*

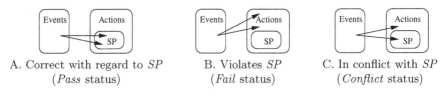

A. Correct with regard to SP B. Violates SP C. In conflict with SP
    (*Pass* status)   (*Fail* status)   (*Conflict* status)

Fig. 3. Events correct with regard to SP, in violation of SP or in conflict with SP

Several conformity relations [11,19] can be used when conflicting events can occur. The approach proposed in this article is the following:

Definition 2 (Network Conformity). *A network conforms to a security policy if each event of this network is correct with respect to the policy.*

Finally, if a security policy is relevant only to a part of the network, then all events that are not associated to any action of the policy are *unspecified*.

4   Policy Security Through TCP/IP Levels

4.1   Traceability from Policy to Implementation

The proposed approach aims to express a security policy at an abstract level (on actions) and to preserve it through the refinement process until its implementation (on network events). However, each refinement level can only access information from the protocol header of the corresponding TCP/IP layer (Fig. 1) and has to implement the same security policy as the specification.

The model used to illustrate this approach is a monitor. A monitor has to detect at least each network event which violates *SP* or which is in conflict with *SP*. In the ideal case, no event correct w.r.t. *SP* is detected. The monitor has then to guarantee, at each refinement level, the next two properties:

Property 1 (Monitor Correctness)
Each event that is not detected is correct with respect to the security policy.

Property 2 (Monitor Completeness)
Each event that is detected violates or is in conflict with the security policy.

In the model, the network events representation gradually changes at each refinement (from actions to concrete events). To implement these properties, the link between the different representations has then to be modeled, in a systematic way, at each refinement level. So, the end user (the administrator of a network) can choose the abstraction level of his policy (by using or not the more abstract levels of the model) and each event is traced through the refinement, as needed for some certification process such as the one of the Common Criteria [7].

Table 3. Networks concepts by refinement level

Level of specification	Network concepts	TCP/IP layer
0 (Policy level, actions)	Users, services	
1	Daemons, Terminal servers	Application
2	Hosts, ports	Transport
3 (implementation)	Interfaces, ports	Network

Daemon: software server providing some services.
Terminal server: particular daemon providing some logging services.
Host: machine of the network.
Ports: channels associated, on each host, to zero or one daemon.
Interface: network interface (e.g. a network card).

Each refinement level represents how the communication is seen between two elements of the network. At level 0, events correspond to the access by a user to a service. They are considered as actions of the security policy. At level 1, events are messages between daemons (*Application layer*). At level 2, events are requests between hosts and are attached to particular ports (*Transport layer*). At level 3, each event is a connection between interfaces and is attached to particular ports (*Network layer*). Table 3 summarizes these different representations.

These network concepts can be extracted from information contained in configuration files. For example the list of registered Linux users can be found in the /etc/passwd file and the list of daemons hosted on each machine can be found in /etc/init.d/. This information can then be used to associate each network event to an action of the policy.

Finally, an observer is introduced in the model to give the internal status (*Pass*, *Fail* or *Conflict* - Fig. 3) associated to each observed network event. As the event representation changes through the refinement process, the parameters of the observer are described in global variables.

4.2 Example

To illustrate the notions of conflict and failure, here is a short example (Fig. 4) of a monitor that receives a copy of each message from the network and that is parametrized by a security policy and the network configuration.

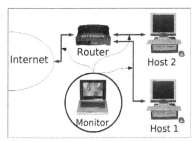

Network installation

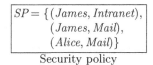

Security policy

$Host_1$ is used by *James* or *Alice*
Intranet is hosted on the port 80 from $Host_2$
Mail is hosted on the port 993 from $Host_2$.

Network configuration information

Fig. 4. Example of the monitor installation

A message coming from $Host_1$ and going to $Host_2$ at port 80, is necessarily sent by *James* or *Alice*, because they are the only referenced $Host_1$ users. Moreover, due to the accessed port of $Host_2$, and according to the configuration information, the service can only be the *Intranet*. However, the security policy SP only allows *James* to access to the *Intranet*. Thus, the observed message is in *Conflict*.

Now, if the message comes from $Host_1$ and goes to port 993 of $Host_2$, then the accessed service is *Mail* and all the users of $Host_1$ are authorized to access it. Therefore, this message is correct w.r.t. the security policy (*Pass* case).

Finally, if a message is exchanged with a host ($Host_3$) which is not in the described part of the network, then no user or action is associated to it by the network configuration: the event is ignored.

5 Description of Refinement Levels

As previously said, each refinement level represents a different layer of the TCP/IP protocol suite (Table 3). In the first subsection, we define the data domain attached to each refinement level. Next, we present a systematic approach to model the links between refinements, based on configuration files. Then, we introduce journals in order to establish the monitor correctness and completeness properties (Properties 1 and 2). Finally, we describe the observer allowing to trace the status of each event through the refinement process.

5.1 Events Representation

Table 4 gives the representation of the events for each refinement level, according to the network concepts presented in Table 3. Moreover, the incoming ports are modeled while the outgoing ports are not so (Levels 2 and 3, Table 4). Outgoing ports are useless as long as the history of connections is not taken into account. Indeed, outgoing ports are dynamically and randomly chosen and cannot be used to identify a daemon or a user, contrary to the incoming ports, that are statically reserved for each service (managed by the IANA[2]).

Table 4. Network events representation for each refinement level

Level of specification	Network events representation
0 *(Policy level)*	$Net_0 = USERS \times SERVICES$
1	$Net_1 = DAEMONS \times DAEMONS$
2	$Net_2 = HOSTS \times (HOSTS \times PORTS)$
3 *(Implementation)*	$Net_3 = INTERFACES \times (INTERFACES \times PORTS)$

The policy is enforced only on the known part of the network. The constant $KnownNet_i$ represents the known network subset at each level i. Each set is divided into a known and an unknown part, as follows:

Known Network Definition

$Users \subset USERS \wedge Services \subset SERVICES \wedge Daemons \subset DAEMONS \wedge Hosts \subset HOSTS$
$\wedge\ TerminalServers \subseteq Daemons \wedge Ports \subset PORTS \wedge Interfaces \subset INTERFACES$

$\wedge\ KnownNet_0\ =\ Users \times Services$
$\wedge\ KnownNet_1\ =\ TerminalServers \times Daemons$
$\wedge\ KnownNet_2\ =\ Hosts \times (Hosts \times Ports)$
$\wedge\ KnownNet_3\ =\ Interfaces \times (Interfaces \times Ports)$

These abstract sets correspond to concrete data extracted from configuration files. Finally, the security policy is described by the constant set SP of all authorized actions of the known network.

Security Policy Definition

$$SP \subseteq KnownNet_0$$

---

[2] IANA = Internet Assigned Numbers Authority.

5.2   Representation Relation

The event representation changes through the refinement process. The relation $Represents_i$ defines the representation link between the ith and $(i-1)^{th}$ refinement levels. For example, $Represents_1$ associates each terminal server to a set of users and each daemon to a set of services. Note that $Represents_i$ is a relation and not a function because a concrete event is not always associated to a single abstract event (as seen in the example from Section 4.2). It is neither a function from $KnownNet_{i-1}$ to $KnownNet_i$ because an action can be associated to several concrete events. These relations can be composed to define $Represents_{i \leadsto 0}$ between the ith level and the policy level.

Representation Relation axioms	
$Represents_i \in KnownNet_i \leftrightarrow KnownNet_{i-1}$	*(with $i \in 1..3$)*
$\wedge\ Represents_{i \leadsto 0} \in KnownNet_i \leftrightarrow KnownNet_0$	*(with $i \in 1..3$)*
$\wedge\ Represents_{i \leadsto 0} = (Represents_i; Represents_{i-1}; \ldots; Represents_1)$	*(with $i \in 1..3$)*

In order to simplify some further invariants, we define $Represents_0$ as the identity ($\mathrm{id}(Net_0)$). Finally, each element mentioned in the configuration has to be associated with at least one action and one network event:

The Described Sub-Network is Known as a Whole
$$\mathrm{dom}(Represents_i) = KnownNet_i \quad \wedge \quad \mathrm{ran}(Represents_i) = KnownNet_{i-1}$$

5.3   Journalizing Observed Events

Three journals are maintained: the one of observed events ($Monitored_i$) and two other ones of warned events ($FAIL_i$ and $CONFLICT_i$ respectively for the events which violate and are in conflict with the policy). All these journals are defined as non-ordered sets, because the considered policy does not take into account the history. Moreover, all warned events are observed and all events observed in a concrete level are also observed in the abstract level. At the policy level, no conflict can occur, then $CONFLICT_0$ is empty.

Invariant (General Journals Definition)	
$Monitored_0 \subseteq KnownNet_0$	
$\wedge\ Monitored_i \subseteq Represents_i^{-1}[Monitored_{i-1}]$	*(with $i \in 1..3$)*
$\wedge\ CONFLICT_0 = \emptyset$	
$\wedge\ FAIL_i \cup CONFLICT_i \subseteq Monitored_i$	*(with $i \in 0..3$)*
$\wedge\ FAIL_i \cap CONFLICT_i = \emptyset$	*(with $i \in 0..3$)*

Properties 1 and 2 can be expressed on these journals, by the next two invariants:
(1) All observed events associated with *Pass* status are correct w.r.t. *SP*:

Invariant (Monitor Correctness - Property 1)	
$Represents_{i \leadsto 0}[Monitored_i - FAIL_i - CONFLICT_i] \subseteq SP$	*(with $i \in 0..3$)*

(2) No event associated with *Conflict* or *Fail* status is correct w.r.t. *SP*:

Invariant (Monitor Completeness - Property 2)	
$Represents_{i \leadsto 0}[FAIL_i] \cap SP = \emptyset$	*(with $i \in 0..3$)*
$\wedge\ \forall e_i \cdot (e_i \in CONFLICT_i \Rightarrow Represents_{i \leadsto 0}[\{e_i\}] \not\subseteq SP)$	*(with $i \in 0..3$)*

5.4   Observer Introduction

The B event *Get_status* is an observer of the network events. It returns the status of an event chosen in a nondeterministic way. Because of the change of event representation, the observer is modeled with two new global variables: Obs_{Event} and Obs_{Status}. Obs_{Event} is the chosen observed event ($Obs_{Event\,i} \in KnownNet_i$) and Obs_{Status} is its status ($Obs_{Status\,i} \in \{Pass, Fail, Conflict\}$). Fig. 5 gives the general implementation of the observer *Get_status*.

The variables Obs_{Event} and Obs_{Status} are defined at each refinement level with the following invariant:

$$
\begin{aligned}
&Get\_status \mathrel{\widehat{=}} \text{ANY } e_i \text{ WHERE } e_i \in Monitored_i \text{ THEN} \\
&\quad \text{IF } e_i \in FAIL_i \text{ THEN} \qquad\qquad Obs_{Event\,i} := e_i \parallel Obs_{Status\,i} := Fail \\
&\quad \text{ELSIF } e_i \in CONFLICT_i \text{ THEN } Obs_{Event\,i} := e_i \parallel Obs_{Status\,i} := Conflict \\
&\quad \text{ELSE} \qquad\qquad\qquad\qquad\quad Obs_{Event\,i} := e_i \parallel Obs_{Status\,i} := Pass \\
&\quad \text{END} \\
&\text{END}
\end{aligned}
$$

Fig. 5. General definition of the *Get_status* event

Invariant (Observed Variables)

$Monitored_i \neq \emptyset \Rightarrow$
$\quad ((Obs_{Status\,i} = Fail) \Leftrightarrow (Obs_{Event\,i} \in FAIL_i))$
$\quad \wedge\ ((Obs_{Status\,i} = Conflict) \Leftrightarrow (Obs_{Event\,i} \in CONFLICT_i))$
$\quad \wedge\ ((Obs_{Status\,i} = Pass) \Leftrightarrow (Obs_{Event\,i} \in Monitored_i - FAIL_i - CONFLICT_i))$

The observed event is traced through the refinement process:

Invariant (Relation through Refinement)

$$(Obs_{Event\,i}, Obs_{Event\,i-1}) \in Represents_i$$

Finally, correctness and completeness of the monitor (Properties 1 and 2) are implemented on the journals with the invariants defined in Section 5.3. However, these properties can also be checked on the observed variables. So, if the following assertions hold, then Properties 1 and 2 are verified:

Assertion 1 (Monitor Correctness on Observed Variables)

$Monitored_i \neq \emptyset\ \wedge\ Obs_{Status\,i} = Pass \Rightarrow Obs_{Status\,i-1} = Pass$ *(with $i \in 0..3$)*

Assertion 2 (Monitor Completeness on Observed Variables)

$Monitored_i \neq \emptyset \Rightarrow$ *(with $i \in 0..3$)*
$\quad (Obs_{Status\,i} = Fail \Rightarrow Obs_{Status\,i-1} = Fail)$
$\quad \wedge\ (Obs_{Status\,i} = Conflict \Rightarrow Represents_{i \leadsto 0}[\{Obs_{Event\,i}\}] \not\subseteq SP)$
$\quad \wedge\ (Obs_{Status\,i} = Conflict \Rightarrow Represents_{i \leadsto 0}[\{Obs_{Event\,i}\}] \cap SP \neq \emptyset)$

Therefore we only discuss the verification of those assertions that are sufficient to show Properties 1 and 2.

6   Model Description

In the previous section, we have presented, in a systematic way, all data required for the model development. In this section, we describe successively each level by introducing: the configuration data, the B events and the construction of the $Represents_i$ relation. All invariants and properties described in the previous section are included at each description level.

In this description, we also focus on the verification of the correctness and the completeness properties of the monitor by checking Assertions 1 and 2.

6.1   Level 0: User-Service View

The SP constant set is given by the user while constants $Users$ and $Services$ are retrieved from configuration files. Journals are represented as abstract variables and are empty in the initial state ($Monitored_0 := \emptyset$ and $FAIL_0 := \emptyset$). Consequently, the observed variables are initially undefined ($Obs_{Event0} :\in Net_0 \wedge Obs_{Status0} :\in \{Pass, Fail, Conflict\}$). If an event e_0 occurs on the network then:

- if e_0 is not in the observed sub-network then $Event\_filter$ (Figure 6.B) is launched and e_0 is ignored,
- else $Check\_event$ (Figure 6.A) is launched and e_0 is stored in $Monitored_0$. Moreover, if e_0 violates the policy then it is journalized in $FAIL_0$.

$Check\_event \mathrel{\widehat{=}} \text{ANY } e_0 \text{ WHERE } e_0 \in KnownNet_0 \text{ THEN}$ $\quad Monitored_0 := Monitored_0 \cup \{e_0\} \parallel$ $\quad \text{IF } e_0 \notin SP \text{ THEN } FAIL_0 := FAIL_0 \cup \{e_0\} \text{ END}$ END	$Event\_filter \mathrel{\widehat{=}} \text{ANY } e_0$ $\text{WHERE } e_0 \in Net_0$ $\quad \wedge\ e_0 \notin KnownNet_0$ THEN skip END
A. $Check\_event$	B. $Event\_filter$

Fig. 6. Code of B events $Check\_event$ and $Event\_filter$ at the policy level

Finally, this level establishes Properties 1 and 2 by verifying Assertions 1 and 2 with the observed variables only, since there is no conflict at this level.

6.2   Level 1: Servers View

According to Table 3, the daemons sets ($Daemons$ and $TerminalServers$) are now described. The relation between this level and the more abstract one, i.e. the policy level, is extracted from configuration files. Each daemon is configured with its registered users and its provided services. We model this information with two relations ($Provide$ and $Used\_By$) describing which user can be connected to a particular terminal server and which daemon provides a particular service. For example, the registered users list of a telnet server can be found in /etc/passwd.

$Represents_1$ **Definition**
$$Used\_By \in TerminalServers \leftrightarrow Users \quad \wedge \quad Provide \in Daemons \leftrightarrow Services$$
$$\wedge\ Represents_1 = (Used\_By \parallel Provide)$$

$Check\_event \triangleq$ ANY e_1 WHERE $e_1 \in KnownNet_1$ THEN
  $Monitored_1 := Monitored_1 \cup \{e_1\}$ ||
  LET E_0 BE $E_0 = (Used\_By \ || \ Provide)[e_1]$ IN
  IF $E_0 \cap SP \neq \emptyset$ THEN
    $FAIL_1 := FAIL_1 \cup \{e_1\}$
  ELSIF $E_0 \not\subseteq SP$ THEN
    $CONFLICT_1 := CONFLICT_1 \cup \{e_1\}$
  END
  END
END

$Event\_filter \triangleq$ ANY e_1
  WHERE $e_1 \in Net_1$
    $\wedge \ e_1 \notin KnownNet_1$
  THEN skip END

A. *Check_event*   B. *Event_filter*

Fig. 7. Code of the B events *Check_event* and *Event_filter* at level 1

The journals and the observed variables are defined according to the invariants given in Section 5. At this level of refinement, the relation $Represents_1$ is used dynamically by the B event *Check_event* (Figure 7.A) to compute the status of the observed network event, while the B event *Event_filter* (Figure 7.B) ignores all messages exchanged with the unknown part of the network.

The observer refinement (Fig. 5) produces 18 proof obligations, which, associated to the three ones generated for Assertions 1 and 2, establish Properties 1 and 2 on the model.

6.3   Level 2: Hosts View

As described in Table 3, this level introduces the notions of *Hosts* and *Ports*. The relation between these concepts and the daemons is extracted from hosts configuration information. They are summarized by two functions: *Hosting*, which associates the hosts to the daemons, and *Run_on*, which precises the ports used by a particular daemon on a host. Configuration data is such that:

$Represents_2$ **Definition**
  $Hosting \in Hosts \leftrightarrow Daemons \quad \wedge \quad Run\_on \in Hosts \times Ports \rightarrowtail Daemons$
  $\wedge \ Represents_2 = (Hosting \rhd TerminalServers) \ || \ Run\_on$

Just as in previous levels, the journals and the observed variables are defined according to the invariants given in Section 5. The relation $Represents_2$ is used by *Check_event* (Figure 8.A) to compute the status of the observed network event, while *Event_filter* (Figure 8.B) ignores all messages exchanged with the unknown part of the network.

The main contribution of this level is the implementation of the *Check_event* event (Figure 8.A), which progressively refines the method to compute the E_0 set of all actions associated to the observed network events e_2.

In the same way as in the previous level, Properties 1 and 2 are established by proving the three proof obligations generated for Assertions 1 and 2 and the 32 proof obligations generated for the observer event *Get_status*.

$Check\_event \ \widehat{=} \ \text{ANY } e_2 \ \text{WHERE } e_2 \in KnownNet_2 \ \text{THEN}$
$\quad Monitored_2 := Monitored_2 \cup \{e_2\} \ ||$
$\quad \text{LET } E_1 \ \text{BE } E_1 = ((Hosting \rhd TerminalServers) \ || \ Run\_on)[\{e_2\}] \ \text{IN}$
$\quad\quad \text{LET } E_0 \ \text{BE } E_0 = (Used\_By \ || \ Provide)[E_1] \ \text{IN}$
$\quad\quad\quad \text{IF } E_0 \cap SP \neq \emptyset \ \text{THEN}$
$\quad\quad\quad\quad FAIL_2 := FAIL_2 \cup \{e_2\}$
$\quad\quad\quad \text{ELSIF } E_0 \nsubseteq SP \ \text{THEN}$
$\quad\quad\quad\quad CONFLICT_2 := CONFLICT_2 \cup \{e_2\}$
$\quad\quad\quad \text{END}$
$\quad\quad \text{END}$
$\quad \text{END}$
END

A. *Check_event*

$Event\_filter \ \widehat{=} \ \text{ANY } e_2 \ \text{WHERE } e_1 \in Net_2 - KnownNet_2 \ \text{THEN skip END}$

B. *Event_filter*

Fig. 8. Code of the B events *Check_event* and *Event_filter* at level 2

6.4 Level 3: Implementation

At this level, hosts are valuated into their IP address (32 bit natural which identifies hosts for the Network layer) and ports remain unchanged. For example, the host anchieta.imag.fr can be valuated into its IP address 129.88.39.37 by using its 32 bit natural value[3]: 2170038053.

The *Represents*$_3$ relation is thus the identity and all invariants are inherited and do not need to be proven again. All other constants (security policy and configuration information) have also to be valuated. Network parameters can be retrieved in configuration files while the security policy has to be given by the administrator. Table 5 gives some concrete examples for Fedora-Core (a Linux distribution) of files containing usable data.

Table 5. Example of configuration files for Fedora-Core system

Refinement level	Constant	Data file
0 (Policy level)	*Users* and *Services*	/etc/passwd and /etc/init.d/
1	*Provide* and *Used_By*	Configuration files of each server
2	*Run_on* and *Hosting*	/etc/services and /etc/init.d/
3 (Implementation)	*Interfaces*	/etc/hosts

However, the event-B language cannot be directly implemented. The model is translated into classical B. This transformation is done by some ad-hoc methods based on the results of the MATISSE[4] project [6,3]. Since the guards of *Event_filter* and *Check_event* are disjoint, the events are replaced by the single

---

[3] $2170038053 = ((129 * 256 + 88) * 256 + 39) * 256 + 37$

[4] Methodologies and Technologies for Industrial Strength Systems Engineering (MATISSE): IST Programme RTD Research Project (2000-2003).

operation *Check_event_and_Event_filter* (Fig. 9). Moreover, the network event e_3 chosen in the guard ANY e_3 WHERE $e_3 \in Net_3$ is replaced by three input parameters IP_1, IP_2 and Po representing respectively the IP address of the two hosts and the incoming port.

Check_event_and_Event_filter$(IP_1, IP_2, Po) \; \hat{=}$ BEGIN
  /* *Typing precondition:* $(IP_1, (IP_2, Po)) \in Net_3$ */
  VAR *tmp* IN
    $tmp \longleftarrow$ *Is_In_KnownNet*(IP_1, IP_2, Po) ;
    IF *tmp* =TRUE THEN   /* *Case of Check_event* */
      $Src := IP_1$; $Dest := IP_2$; $Port := Po$;
      $tmp \longleftarrow$ *Is_e3_Out_Of_SP*(IP_1, IP_2, Po) ;
      IF *tmp* =TRUE THEN $Status := Fail$; $WriteFail(IP_1, IP_2, Po)$
      ELSE
        $tmp \longleftarrow$ *Is_e3_In_SP*(IP_1, IP_2, Po) ;
        IF *tmp* =FALSE THEN $Status := Conflict$; $WriteConflict(IP_1, IP_2, Po)$
        ELSE $Status := Pass$ END
      END
    END   /* *Else case of Event_filter:* skip */
  END
END

Fig. 9. Implementation of the B event *Check_event*

Figure 9 is the implementation of *Check_event_and_Event_filter* operation. It uses three local operations (*Is_In_KnownNet*, *Is_e3_Out_Of_SP* and *Is_e3_In_SP*) to compute the correctness of each observed event. These operations are implemented as refinements of the corresponding parts of *Check_event* at level 2. For example, the local operation *Is_e3_Out_Of_SP* is defined in Figure 10.

$rr \longleftarrow$ *Is_e3_Out_Of_SP*$(IP_1, IP_2, Po) \; \hat{=}$
  PRE $(IP_1, (IP_2, Po)) \in KnownNet_3$ THEN
    $rr =$ bool$(($*Used_By* $\parallel$ *Provide*$)[$ /* *Represents*$_1$[*/
                $((Hosting \rhd TerminalServers) \parallel Run\_on)[$ /* *Represents*$_2$[*/
                $\{(IP_1, (IP_2, Po))\}$ /* $\{(IP_1, (IP_2, Po))\}$ */
                $]$ /*] */
              $] \cap SP = \emptyset)$ /* $] \cap SP = \emptyset$ */
  END

Fig. 10. Abstract definition of the *Is_e3_Out_Of_SP* local operation

The *Monitored*$_i$ set, modeled to store the monitored events, is not implemented, while *FAIL* and *CONFLICT* sets are stored in files. That is managed by an external component providing the operations *WriteFail* and *WriteConflict*. However, Properties 1 and 2 still hold, since the observed variable $Obs_{Status2}$ and Obs_{Event2} remain unchanged.

Finally, constants (configuration data and security policy) are exported in an external component as shown in Fig. 11. Thus, the model is generic and can be completely proved independently of the configuration data. The user just needs to provide some network information, or to retrieve it from configuration files, and to fulfill the conditions on configuration stated in Sections 5.3 and 5.2. A similar approach has been used in Météor [5], the Parisian subway without driver, to develop some generic and reusable components.

If the model is valuated for a simple example of network with two hosts, two daemons, one service and one user, then 31 proof obligations are generated and only 26 of them are discharged by the automatic prover. The five remaining proof obligations have been interactively discharged, but are really obvious and only need two commands : replace (eh) and predicate prover (pp(rp.0)).

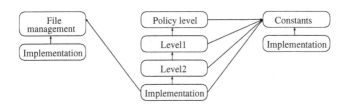

Fig. 11. General model organisation

7   Conclusion

This work has been done within the framework of the POTESTAT[5] project [9], which aims at proposing a methodology for network security testing from high-level security policies. The main problem is to establish the conformity relation in order to automatically generate test cases and oracles from an abstract specification, as it has been implemented in the TGV tool [12] from IRISA and Verimag french laboratories.

Our contribution is a method to automatically enforce an abstract security policy on a network. In order to achieve that, we build a formal relation ($Represents_{i \rightsquigarrow 0}$) between abstract and concrete levels. The dynamic part of the program ($Check\_event\_and\_Event\_filter$) computes all actions associated to each observed event. Finally, we guarantee, by using an observer (Get_status), that all violations and conflicts are detected at each refinement level (Property 1) and that no warning is issued for an event which is correct with respect to the policy (Property 2).

The work of D. Senn, D. Basin and of G. Caronni [21] and of G. Vigna [23] are also dealing with the modeling of network conformity of a security policy. The model of [23] supports all the TCP/IP layers but does not provide a formal definition of the policy and needs human interaction to produce the test cases, while the model introduced in [21] only considers the first two layers and uses a low-level policy.

---

[5]   Security policies: test directed analysis of open networks systems.

In this paper, we described the development of a network monitor, and the same approach can be used for generation, verification or test of a network configuration. The relationship is built in the same way and only the dynamic part of the model has to be modified.

In particular, many works have been developed relative to the generation of firewall configurations. For example, Firmato [4] is a tool generating the firewall configuration from a security policy and a network topology, and the POWER tool [18], of Hewlett-Packard, can rewrite a security policy into devices configuration. However, Firmato needs some topology information and uses a low-level policy, and POWER requires some human interactions during the process. The work presented here does not need human interaction (if all proof obligations are automatically discharged) or topology information. Due to the existence of the conflict status, it seems more adapted to the monitoring approach.

Finally, in our model, the conflict case can be removed if $Represents_{i \rightsquigarrow 0}$ is a function from $KnownNet_i$ to $KnownNet_0$, as done in [8] with a security policy expressed in the OrBAC framework [14]. In order to achieve that, we have to recognize the user and the service associated to each event. It can be realistic to associate only one service to each port, but it is too strict to impose that each host can be used by only one user. An investigation should be done to properly compare their approach with ours.

Acknowledgments. The authors would like to thank D. Bert, V. Darmaillacq, V. Untz, F. Dadeau and Y. Grunenberger for their advises and their reviews.

References

1. J.R. Abrial. Extending B without Changing it. In Nantes H. Habrias, editor, *First Conference on the B method*, pages 169–190, 1996. ISBN 2-906082-25-2.
2. J.R. Abrial. *The B-Book*. Cambridge University Press, 1996.
3. J.R. Abrial. Event driven sequential program construction. Technical report, ClearSy, 2001.
4. Y. Bartal, A. Mayer, K. Nissim, and A. Wool. Firmato: A novel firewall management toolkit. *ACM Transactions on Computer Systems*, 22(4), 1999.
5. P. Behm, P. Benoit, A. Faivre, and J-M. Meynadier. Météor: A Successful Application of B in a Large Project. In J. M. Wing, J. Woodcock, and J. Davies, editors, *FM'99 : World Congress on Formal Methods*, volume 1708 of *LNCS*, pages 369–387. Springer-Verlag, 1999.
6. M. Butler. A System-Based Approach to the Formal Development of Embedded Controllers for a Railway. *Design Automation for Embedded Systems*, 6(4), 2002.
7. Common Criteria. *Common Criteria for Information Technology Security Evaluation, Norme ISO 15408 - version 3.0 Rev. 2*, 2005.
8. F. Cuppens, N. Cuppens-Boulahia, T. Sans, and A. Mige. A formal approach to specify and deploy a network security policy. In T. Dimitrakos and F. Martinelli, editors, *Formal Aspects in Security and Trust (FAST)*. Springer, 2004.
9. V. Darmaillacq, J.-C. Fernandez, R. Groz, L. Mounier, and J.-L. Richier. Eléments de modélisation pour le test de politiques de sécurité. In *Colloque sur les RIsques et la Sécurité d'Internet et des Systèmes, CRiSIS, Bourges, France*, 2005.

10. D. Denning and P. Denning. Data Security. *ACM Computing Survey*, 11(3):227–249, 1979.
11. S. Jajodia, P. Samarati, and V. S. Subrahmanian. A logical language for expressing authorizations. In *IEEE Symp. on Research in Security and Privacy*, 1997.
12. C. Jard and T. Jeron. TGV: theory, principles and algorithms. *International Journal on Software Tools for Technology Transfer (STTT)*, 7(4):297–315, 2005.
13. JTC1. Information technology – Open Systems Interconnection (OSI model). Technical report, Standard ISO 7498, 1997.
14. A. Abou El Kalam, R. El Baida, P. Balbiani, S. Benferhat, F. Cuppens, Y. Deswarte, A. Mige, C. Saurel, and G. Trouessin. Organization Based Access Control. In *IEEE 4th International Workshop on Policies for Distributed Systems and Networks (POLICY'03)*, pages 120–131, 2003.
15. L. Lamport. The Temporal Logic of Actions. *ACM Transactions on Programming Languages and Systems*, 16(3):872–923, may 1994.
16. T. E Lunt. Access control policies for database systems. *Database Security II: Status and Prospects*, pages 41–52, North–Holland, Amsterdam, 1989.
17. M. Masullo. Policy Management: An Architecture and Approach. In *IEEE First International Workshop on Systems Management*, pages 13–26, 1993.
18. M. Casassa Mont, A. Baldwin, and C. Goh. POWER Prototype: Towards Integrated Policy-Based Management. Technical report, HP Laboratories, 1999.
19. P. Samarati and S. de Capitani di Vimercati. Access Control: Policies, Models, and Mechanisms. In R. Focardi and R. Gorrieri, editors, *Foundations of Security Analysis and Design*, volume 2171 of *LNCS*, pages 137–196. Springer, 2000.
20. R. S. Sandhu, E.J. Coyne, H.L. Feinstein, and C.E. Youman. Role-Based Access Control Models. *IEEE Computer*, 29(2):38–47, 1996.
21. D. Senn, D. Basin, and G. Caronni. Firewall Conformance Testing. In F. Khendek and R. Dssouli, editors, *TestCom*, volume 3502 of *LNCS*. Springer, 2005.
22. M. Sloman. Policy Driven Management for Distributed Systems. *Journal of Network and Systems Management*, 2(4):333–360, 1994.
23. G. Vigna. A Topological Characterization of TCP/IP Security. In K. Araki, S. Gnesi, and D. Mandrioli, editors, *FME*, volume 2805 of *LNCS*. Springer, 2003.
24. T. Y.C. Woo and S.S. Lam. Authorization in Distributed Systems: A Formal Approach. In *Symposium on Security and Privacy*. IEEE Computer Society, 1992.

Integration of Security Policy into System Modeling

Nazim Benaïssa[2,4,5], Dominique Cansell[1,5], and Dominique Méry[2,3,5,*]

[1] Université de Metz
cansell@loria.fr
[2] Université Henri Poincaré Nancy 1
[3] mery@loria.fr
[4] benaissa@loria.fr
[5] LORIA
BP 239
54506 Vandœuvre-lès-Nancy
France

Abstract. We address the proof-based development of (system) models satisfying a security policy. The security policy is expressed in a model called OrBAC, which allows one to state permissions and prohibitions on actions and activities and belongs to the family of role-based access control formalisms. The main question is to validate the link between the security policy expressed in OrBAC and the resulting system; a first abstract B model is derived from the OrBAC specification of the security policy and then the model is refined to introduce properties that can be expressed in OrBAC. The refinement guarantees that the resulting B (system) model satisfies the security policy. We present a generic development of a system with respect to a security policy and it can be instantiated later for a given security policy.

Keywords: refinement, integration, security policy.

1 Introduction

One of the most challenging problems in managing large networks is the complexity of security administration. Role-based access control has become the predominant model for advanced access control because it reduces the complexity and cost of security administration in large networked applications. Other models, like OrBAC [1], have been introduced by providing a structure based on the application domain and by introducing the concept of organisation. Networks or software systems can be abstracted by action systems or event B models; however, security requirements should be integrated into the proof-based design of such systems and we address the integration of security policy - expressed in a security model OrBAC - in the final systems. This leads us to deal with security properties like permissions and prohibitions. We leave obligations as

* The research is supported by the DESIRS project of the ACI Sécurité et Informatique of the Ministry of Research. The first author has obtained a partial PhD grant from the Région Lorraine.

J. Julliand and O. Kouchnarenko (Eds.): B 2007, LNCS 4355, pp. 232–247, 2006.
© Springer-Verlag Berlin Heidelberg 2006

out of the scope of the current work. J.-R. Abrial [2] contributes to the access control problem: the study consists of elaborating a system that controls access to a building for different persons. He does not refer to a security model but his work influences our current work.

1.1   Integration of Security Policies in System Development

When a system is under development, it is necessary to consider requirements documentation. The document is either written in a natural language, or in a semi-formal language, or in a formal language and it may include different aspects or views of the target system. Security policy is a possible part of this document and it may be expressed in a specific modelling language designed for expressing permissions, prohibitions, recommendations, obligations, . . . related to the target system. Now, a key question is to ensure that the resulting system conforms to the security policy and it appears to us that in existing systems the link between the system and its security policy is not clearly established and formally validated, as shown in figure 1: the satisfaction relation should be established in a formal way. We illustrate the problem to be solved by considering two modelling languages:

- the OrBAC modelling language for security policy
- the event B modelling language for systems

Another important point is that we focus on the access control problem and as shown in figure 1.2, we describe several steps to obtain an implementation of the system from the statement of the security policy:

1. Generating a B model OM from the security policy O: the translation relation is explained in the current paper and can be mechanized.
2. Generating a B model RM by refining OM and by adding progressively details of the document which are not yet integrated into the current model: the refinement of B models is the key concept ensuring the validation of the satisfaction relation.
3. Writing a system model SYS from the last B model: the implementation of a refined B model into a system language can be directed by transformations over events.

1.2   Proof-Based Incremental Modelling

Proof-based development methods [3] integrate formal proof techniques in the development of software systems. The main idea is to start with a very abstract model of the system under development. Details are gradually added to this first model by building a sequence of more concrete ones. The relationship between two successive models in this sequence is that of *refinement* [3,8,4]. The essence of the refinement relationship is that it preserves already proved *system properties* including safety properties and termination. A development gives rise to a number of, so-called, *proof obligations*, which guarantee its correctness. Such proof obligations are discharged by the proof tool using automatic and interactive proof procedures supported by a proof engine [10].

The goal of the paper is to address the proof-based development of models satisfying a security policy. The security policy can be expressed in a formal language and it is possible to analyse the security policy, especially the consistency of the policy. The refinement ensures the correctness of the satisfaction relation: the system satisfies the security policy.

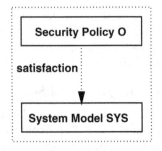

Fig. 1. The satisfaction relation

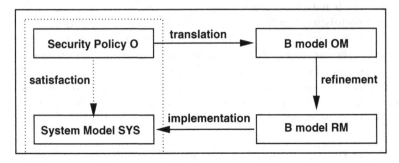

At the most abstract level it is obligatory to describe the static properties of a model's data by means of an "invariant" predicate. This gives rise to proof obligations relating to the consistency of the model. These are required to ensure that data properties which are claimed to be invariant are preserved by the events or operations of the model. Each refinement step is associated with a further invariant which relates the data of the more concrete model to that of the abstract model and states any additional invariant properties of the (possibly richer) concrete data model. These invariants, so-called *gluing invariants*, are used in the formulation of proof obligations related to the refinement.

The goal of a B development is to obtain a *proved model*. Since the development process leads to a large number of proof obligations, the mastering of proof complexity is a crucial issue. Even if a proof tool is available, its effective power is limited by classical results over logical theories and we must distribute the complexity of proofs over the components of the current development, e.g. by refinement. Refinement has the potential to decrease the complexity of the proof process whilst allowing for traceability of requirements.

B models rarely need to make assumptions about the *size* of a system being modelled, e.g. the number of nodes in a network. This is in contrast to model checking approaches [9]. The price to pay is to face possibly complex mathematical theories and difficult proofs. The re-use of developed models and the structuring mechanisms available in B help in decreasing the complexity. Where B has been exercised on known difficult problems, the result has often been a simpler proof development than has been achieved by users of other more monolithic techniques.

2   Models for Security Policy

The interaction of people with IT systems generate various security needs to guarantee that each system user benefits of its advantages without trespassing on another user's rights. These needs vary according to the activity field required. It could be regarding: Confidentiality (Non disclosure of sensitive information to non authorised persons), Integrity (Non alteration of sensitive information), Availability (Supply of information to users according to their rights of access these information), Auditability (The ability to trace and determine the actions carried out in the system).

Such requirements usually result in setting up an access control model that expresses security policies, defining for each user his permissions, prohibitions and obligations. Users (or subjects) are active entities operating on objects (passive entities) of the system.

Several access control models have been proposed: DAC [14], MAC [5,6], RBAC [12,15,13] or OrBAC [1]. In the Role-Based access control model, the RBAC model, security policy does not directly grant permissions to users but to roles [12]. A role is an abstraction for users. Each user is assigned to one or several roles, and will inherit permissions or prohibitions associated with these roles. Such a security model states security properties on the target system and on a hidden state of the current system. The hidden state clearly expresses dynamic properties related to permissions and prohibitions. The classical role-based models have no explicit state variable; the context information might be used to express the state changes but we think that a state-based approach like B provides a simpler framework for integrating security policy specification in the design of a system. Moreover, the refinement may help us in introducing security properties in a proof-based step.

2.1   Organization-Based Access Control Model: OrBAC

The OrBAC (Organization-Based Access Control model) for modelling the security policies is an extension of the RBAC model. OrBAC is based on the concept of organization. The specification of the security policy is completely parametrized by the organization such that it is possible to handle simultaneously several security policies associated with different organizations [1]. Another advantage of the OrBAC model compared to other models is that it makes it possible to express contextual permissions or prohibitions.

OrBAC takes again the concept of role such as it was defined in RBAC. Users are assigned to roles and inherit their privileges. The concept of *view* (or object's groups) is also introduced as an abstraction of the objects of the system. The construction of these groups of objects must be semantically well founded, this construction is related to the way in which the various roles carry out various actions on these objects. It should be noted that there are similarities with the concept of *view* in relational databases where it is a question of gathering objects which have similar properties. Just as for the objects, the actions are also gathered in activities, this implies that there are two levels of abstraction in OrBAC:

- Abstract level: roles (doctor, nurse), activities (management) and views (patient files, administration files) of the system on which various permissions and prohibitions are expressed.
- Concrete level: subjects (Paul, Peter, John), actions (create, delete) and objects (patient_file1, patient_file2) of the system.

Subjects, actions and objects are respectively assigned to roles, activities and views by relations defined over these entities(see figure 2). We detail relations in the next sub-section.

Empower, Use and Consider. *Assignment of subjects to roles*: subjects are assigned to one or more roles in order to define their privileges. Contrary to RBAC, subjects play their roles in organizations, which implies that subjects are assigned to roles through a ternary relation including the organization:

> $empower(org, s, r)$: means that the subject s plays the role r in the organization org.

Assignment of actions to activities: As for roles and subjects, activities are an abstraction of various actions authorized in the system. The relation binding actions to activities is also a ternary relation including the organizations:

> $consider(org, a, act)$: means that the action a is considered as an activity act in the organization org.

Assignment of objects to views: As in relational databases, a view in OrBAC corresponds to a set of objects having a common property. The relation binding the objects to the views to which they belong is also a ternary relation including the organization:

> $use(org, o, v)$: means that the organization org uses the object o in the view v.

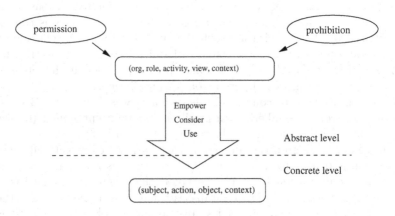

Fig. 2. Abstract and Concrete level of OrBAC

Modeling a Security Policy with OrBAC. When subjects, actions, and objects are respectively assigned to roles, activities and views, it is now possible to describe the security policy. It consists of defining different permissions and prohibitions:

- $permission(org, r, act, v, c)$: means that the organization org grants to the role r the permission to carry out the activity act on the view v in context c.
- $prohibition(org, r, act, v, c)$: means that the organization org prohibits the role r to carry out the activity act on the view v in the context c.

The concept of context, which did not exist in RBAC, is important in OrBAC, since it makes it possible to express contextual permissions (or prohibitions). Let us consider the example of a security policy in a medical environment. If one wants to restrict the access to patients records or files to their attending practitioner, the following permission should be added to the security policy:

$$permission(hospital, physician, consult, patient\_file, attending\_practitionar)$$

If there is no context: $permission(hospital, physician, consult, patient\_file)$.

A physician could therefore access the file of any patient, which needs to be avoided. To be able to use this concept of context, a new relation $define$ should be introduced:

> $Define(org, s, a, o, c)$: means that within organization org, the context c is true between subject s, the object o and action a.

Hierarchy in OrBAC. The OrBAC model makes it possible to define role hierarchies (as in RBAC) but also with respect to the organization hierarchies. The hierarchies allow the inheritance of the privileges (permissions or prohibitions), if for example $r2$ is a sub-role of $r1$, for an organization org, an activity av and a view v in the context ctx:

- When $permission(org, r1, av, v, ctx)$ holds then $permission(org, r2, av, v, ctx)$ holds.
- When $prohibition(org, r1, av, v, ctx)$ holds then $prohibition(org, r2, av, v, ctx)$ holds.

In the same way for the organizations, if $org2$ is a sub-organization of $org1$ then, for a role r an activity av and a view v in the context ctx:

- When $permission(org1, r, av, v, ctx)$ holds then $permission(org2, r, av, v, ctx)$ holds.
- When $prohibition(org1, r, av, v, ctx)$ holds then $prohibition(org2, r, av, v, ctx)$ holds.

The concept of inheritance is a key concept in OrBAC, since it allows gradual building of the security policy. Indeed, it is necessary to start by establishing a flow chart of the organizations (and roles) and defining the privileges on the basic organizations, it will then be enough to add gradually the privileges of the sub-organisations(sub-roles).

3   Event B Models from OrBAC

A complete introduction of B can be found in [7]. The question is to integrate the event B method and the OrBAC method; we have shortly introduced the event B concepts and the OrBAC concepts. In a B model, we should define the mathematical structures on which is based the development and the system under development; this information can be used to derive further properties that will be used in the validation of models. The B models have a static part and a dynamic part and in the specification of a security policy in OrBAC one has to state dynamic properties and to check the consistency of the resulting theory. The MOTOrBAC tool [11] provides a framework for defining a security policy and for checking the consistency of the set of facts and rules in a PROLOG-like style; this approach is clearly based on a fixed-point definition of permissions. The question of expressing administration model in OrBAC is also crucial and it is very simple to express the administration of security policy in B, since one can model the permissions as a variable satisfying the security policy expressed in an invariant. These points will be recalled when we present the effective translation of OrBAC models into event B models.

The current status of the work is as follows:

- We assume that we have an OrBAC description of the security policy.
- The security policy is supposed to be stable and consistent; the consistency is checked using tools like, for instance MOTOrBAC.
- The security policy states permissions and prohibitions.

The problem is to translate OrBAC statements into the event B modelling language. The translation of the security policy into event B includes several successive stages. A first B model is built and then other successive refinements are made as shown by figure 3. The first refinement validates the link between the abstract level (role, ...) and the concrete level (subject, ...).

The approach is based on refinement and each model or refinement model is enriched either by a constraint required by the OrBAC specification or by constraints like workflow constraints or separation of duties. Each constraint is attached to an invariant. The invariant becomes stronger through the refinement steps.

3.1   Abstract Model with Permissions and Prohibitions

As presented in the paragraph 2.1, the OrBAC specification has two levels of abstraction (see figure 2). The first step consists of an event B model modelling the abstract part of the security policy, i.e. initially, only concepts of organization, role, view, activity and context are considered. In the first model, permissions and prohibitions of the OrBAC model should be described.

- The clause SETS in the event B model contains basic sets such as organisations, roles, activities, views and contexts: ORGS, ROLES, ACTIVITIES, VIEWS, CONTEXTS.

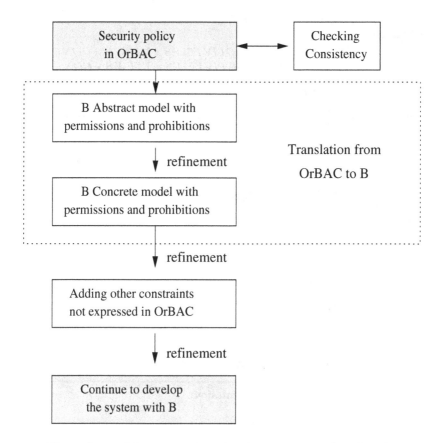

Fig. 3. Steps of the passage from OrBAC to a B event-based model

- The clauses CONSTANTS and PROPERTIES contain the constants like *permission* and *prohibition* that will contain privileges of the OrBAC description. One of the most important concepts contained in OrBAC is the concept of hierarchy: whether it is organization hierarchy or role hierarchy. Two new constants *sub_role* and *sub_org* are introduced to take into account respectively the role and organization hierarchy. It is enough to specify which roles and which organizations are concerned with inheritances, and the permissions and prohibitions corresponding to inheritances are deductively generated.

SETS	CONSTANTS
ORGS;	*permission*,
ROLES;	*prohibition*,
ACTIVITIES;	*sub_org*,
VIEWS;	*sub_role*,
CONTEXTS	*default* / * *default context value* * /

PROPERTIES

$permission \subseteq ORGS \times ROLES \times ACTIVITIES \times VIEWS \times CONTEXTS$
$prohibition \subseteq ORGS \times ROLES \times ACTIVITIES \times VIEWS \times CONTEXTS$

$sub\_org \subseteq ORGS \times ORGS$
$sub\_role \subseteq ROLES \times ROLES$

$default \in CONTEXTS$

/ * Organization hierarchies * /
$\forall(org1, org2, r, av, v, ctx).($
$\quad (org1 \in ORGS \wedge org2 \in ORGS \wedge$
$\quad r \in ROLES \wedge av \in ACTIVITIES \wedge$
$\quad v \in VIEWS \wedge ctx \in CONTEXTS \wedge$
$\quad (org1 \mapsto org2) \in sub\_org \wedge$
$\quad (org2 \mapsto r \mapsto av \mapsto v \mapsto ctx) \in permission)$
$\Rightarrow$
$\quad (org1 \mapsto r \mapsto av \mapsto v \mapsto ctx) \in permission)$

/ * Role hierarchies * /
$\forall(org, r1, r2, av, v, ctx).($
$\quad (r1 \in ROLES \wedge r2 \in ROLES \wedge$
$\quad org \in ORGS \wedge av \in ACTIVITIES \wedge$
$\quad v \in VIEWS \wedge ctx \in CONTEXTS \wedge$
$\quad (r1 \mapsto r2) \in sub\_role \wedge$
$\quad (org \mapsto r2 \mapsto av \mapsto v \mapsto ctx) \in permission)$
$\Rightarrow$
$\quad (org \mapsto r1 \mapsto av \mapsto v \mapsto ctx) \in permission)$

/ * Same properties for prohibitions * /

For a given particular case, it is enough to initialize sets in the clause SETS by entities, organizations, roles, views, activities, contexts. Properties of constants, like *permission, prohibition, sub_role* and *sub_org*, should also be set in the clause PROPERTIES. Consequently, permissions and prohibitions can not be modified, since they are defined as constants; the OrBAC definitions are expressing properties satisfied by a consistent theory of permissions and prohibitions. We will address later the administration of OrBAC.

Introducing State Variables. An event B model expresses properties over state and state variables; the main problem is effectively that OrBAC has no explicit variables. In fact, OrBAC users are using some kind of state modifications but no explicit state exists in OrBAC, even if contexts might be used to model it. Variables are used to model the status of the system with respect to permissions and prohibitions:

- The clause VARIABLES contains two variables, the state variable *hist_abst* that contains the history of system activities; the variable *context* determines the running context of the system.

Variables satisfy the following properties added to the invariant:

INVARIANT
$\quad$ $context \in CONTEXTS$
$\quad$ $hist\_abst \subseteq ORGS \times ROLES \times ACTIVITIES \times VIEWS \times CONTEXTS$
$\quad$ $hist\_abst \subseteq permission$

The initial values of the two variables are set as follows:

$$context := default \,\| hist\_abst := \emptyset$$

As the security policy is supposed to be consistent, we should be able to prove in the clause ASSERTIONS :

ASSERTIONS
$\quad$ $pemission \cap prohibition = \emptyset$
$\quad$ $hist\_abst \cap prohibition = \emptyset$

– The clause EVENTS contains the following events :
$\quad$ • The event *action* models when an authorization request for the access of a subject to an object of the system occurs.
$\quad$ • The two events *set_default* and *set_context_value* are attached to the changes of the system context.

action $\;\widehat{=}$
$\quad$ **any** $\;org, r, v, av\;$ **where**
$\quad\quad$ $org \in ORGS$
$\quad\quad$ $r \in ROLES$
$\quad\quad$ $v \in VIEWS$
$\quad\quad$ $av \in ACTIVITIES$
$\quad\quad$ $(org \mapsto r \mapsto av \mapsto v \mapsto context) \in permission$
$\quad$ **then**
$\quad\quad$ $hist\_abst := hist\_abst \cup \{(org \mapsto r \mapsto av \mapsto v \mapsto context)\}$
$\quad$ **end**

set_context_default $\;\widehat{=}$
$\quad$ **begin**
$\quad\quad$ $context := default$
$\quad$ **end**

set_context_value $\;\widehat{=}$
$\quad$ **begin**
$\quad\quad$ $context :\in CONTEXTS - \{default\}$
$\quad$ **end**

The invariant should be preserved and it means that any activity in the system is controlled by the security policy through the variable *hist_abst*.

3.2   First Refinement: Concrete Model with Permissions and Prohibitions

One of our goals is to use the refinement to validate the relation between security models; OrBAC defines two levels of abstraction and the current model is refined into a concrete model. The refinement introduces subjects, actions and objects: sets $SUBJECTS$, $ACTIONS$ and $OBJECTS$ contain respectively subjects, actions and objects of the system under development. The clause CONSTANTS includes the following constants: $empower$ (assignment of $subjects$ to $roles$), use (assignment of objects to $views$) and $consider$ (assignment of $actions$ to $activities$). Properties of constants are stated as follows:

> PROPERTIES
> $empower \subseteq ORGS \times ROLES \times SUBJECTS$
> $use \subseteq ORGS \times VIEWS \times OBJECTS$
> $consider \subseteq ORGS \times ACTIVITIES \times ACTIONS$

Concrete Variables. A new variable $hist\_conc$ models the control of the system according to the security policy; it contains the history of the actions performed by a subject on a given object. The context in which the action occurred is also stored in this variable.

The relation between $hist\_conc$ and the variable $hist\_abst$ of the abstract model is expressed in the gluing invariant; the first part of the invariant states properties satisfied by variables with respect to permissions.

> INVARIANT
> $\forall(s, a, o, ctx).($
> $\quad (s \in SUBJECTS \land a \in ACTIONS \land$
> $\quad o \in OBJECTS \land ctx \in CONTEXTS \land$
> $\quad (s \mapsto a \mapsto o \mapsto ctx) \in hist\_conc)$
> $\Rightarrow$
> $\quad (\exists(org, r, av, v).($
> $\quad org \in ORGS \land r \in ROLES \land$
> $\quad av \in ACTIVITIES \land v \in VIEWS \land$
> $\quad (r \mapsto s) \in empower \land$
> $\quad (v \mapsto o) \in use \land$
> $\quad (av \mapsto a) \in consider \land$
> $\quad (org \mapsto r \mapsto av \mapsto v \mapsto ctx) \in hist\_abst)))$

The invariant states that each action performed by the system satisfies the security policy. For the prohibitions, when a subject s wants to carry out an action a on an object o in an organization org, it is necessary to check that no prohibition exists for that action. The second part of the invariant states properties satisfied by variables with respect to prohibitions:

INVARIANT
$\forall(s,a,o,ctx).($
$\quad(s \in SUBJECTS \wedge a \in ACTIONS \wedge$
$\quad o \in OBJECTS \wedge ctx \in CONTEXTS \wedge$
$\quad(s \mapsto a \mapsto o \mapsto ctx) \in hist\_conc)$
$\Rightarrow$
$\quad(\forall(org,r,av,v).($
$\quad org \in ORGS \wedge r \in ROLES \wedge$
$\quad av \in ACTIVITIES \wedge v \in VIEWS \wedge$
$\quad(r \mapsto s) \in empower \wedge$
$\quad(v \mapsto o) \in use \wedge$
$\quad(av \mapsto a) \in consider)$
$\Rightarrow$
$\quad(org \mapsto r \mapsto av \mapsto v \mapsto ctx) \notin prohibition)))$

```
action  ≙
   any  s, a, o, org, r, v, av  where
      s ∈ SUBJECTS ∧ a ∈ ACTIONS ∧ o ∈ OBJECTS∧
      org ∈ ORGS ∧ r ∈ ROLES∧
      av ∈ ACTIVITIES ∧ v ∈ VIEWS∧
      (r ↦ s) ∈ empower∧
      (v ↦ o) ∈ use∧
      (av ↦ a) ∈ consider∧
   / * permission * /
      (org ↦ r ↦ av ↦ v ↦ ctx) ∈ permission∧
   / * prohibition * /
      (∀(orgi, ri, avi, vi).(
      (orgi ∈ ORGS ∧ ri ∈ ROLES∧
      avi ∈ ACTIVITIES ∧ vi ∈ VIEWS∧
      (ri ↦ s) ∈ empower∧
      (vi ↦ o) ∈ use∧
      (avi ↦ a) ∈ consider)
      ⇒
      ((orgi ↦ ri ↦ avi ↦ vi ↦ ctx) ∉ prohibition))
   then
      hist_conc := hist_conc ∪ {(s ↦ a ↦ o ↦ context)}
   end
```

The Events. The abstract model should consider the permissions and the prohibitions for a subject s that asks to perform an action a on an object o.

Discussion on Contextual Security Policies. In the different cases we studied, it appeared that the context notion has two different aspects. The first aspect concerns the contexts that are global to the system. An example of a global context is a system managing accesses to a building in a company. We may have a permission (or a prohibition):

$$permission(company, agent, access, building, opening\_hours)$$

In this permission, the context *opening_hours* is global to the system, i.e. the whole system is, at a given moment, in the context *default* or *opening_hour*. A state variable *context* indicating the running context of the system is used in this case. On the other hand, in the case, for example, of a system managing the access to the patient files in a hospital, we may have permissions of the form:

$$permission(hospital, physician, consult, patient\_file, attending\_practitioner)$$

In this permission, the context *attending_practitioner* (that means that the permission is valid only if the physician is the attending practitioner of the patient) is not global to the system but links subjects to the objects. In this case a new constant *define* (as in OrBAC) is used. This constant defines links between objects and subjects with respect to some actions, and has the following form :

$$define \subseteq ORGS \times SUBJECTS \times ACTIONS \times OBJECTS \times CONTEXTS$$

In order to give the system designer the possibility of expressing contextual permissions of each type, modifications must be made to the B model. If *context_value* is a value of a global context, the invariant should be modified as follows:

```
INVARIANT
∀(s, a, o, ctx).(
    (s ∈ SUBJECTS ∧ a ∈ ACTIONS∧
    o ∈ OBJECTS ∧ ctx ∈ CONTEXTS∧
    (s ↦ a ↦ o ↦ ctx) ∈ hist_conc)
⇒
    (∃(org, r, av, v).(
    org ∈ ORGS ∧ r ∈ ROLES∧
    av ∈ ACTIVITIES ∧ v ∈ VIEWS∧
    (r ↦ s) ∈ empower∧
    (v ↦ o) ∈ use∧
    (av ↦ a) ∈ consider∧
    (((org ↦ s ↦ a ↦ o ↦ ctx) ∈ define) ∨ (ctx = context_value))∧
    (org ↦ r ↦ av ↦ v ↦ ctx) ∈ hist_abst)))
```

3.3   Second Refinement: Adding Other Constraints Not Expressed in OrBAC

The state variables of the event B model give additional information on the system which was not available with OrBAC. It was impossible to know at a given moment the state of the system and, for example, which member of a company staff consulted or modified which file. This point is important since in practice the security policies are increasingly complex and new types of constraints appear. The passage towards B allows us to implement the security policy such as it was established in OrBAC, and enrich it with the possibility of introducing new constraints such as workflow constraints or the duty separation.

Workflow Constraints. Workflow constraints express properties on the task scheduling in a system. For instance, a rule for a given workflow states that an action act should be executed, only if a set of actions $act1$, $act2...$, $actn$ have already executed. Those constraints can not be expressed in OrBAC, because, when a subject is assigned to a given role, it obtains its complete privileges. A permission is systematically delivered to execute the action act, if one of the roles to which a subject is assigned has the appropriate privilege, even if one of the actions $act1$, $act2,...$, $actn$ has not yet been executed. The implementation of these constraints in a B model leads to the following invariant:

$$
\begin{aligned}
&\text{INVARIANT} \\
&\forall (s, o, ctx).(\\
&\quad (s \in SUBJECTS \wedge \\
&\quad o \in OBJECTS \wedge \\
&\quad ctx \in CONTEXTS \wedge \\
&\quad (s \mapsto act \mapsto o \mapsto ctx) \in hist\_conc) \\
&\Rightarrow \\
&\quad (\exists (sw, cw).(sw \in SUBJECTS \wedge cw \in CONTEXTS \wedge \\
&\quad\quad (sw \mapsto act1 \mapsto o \mapsto cw) \in hist\_conc) \wedge \\
&\quad \exists (sw, cw).(sw \in SUBJECTS \wedge cw \in CONTEXTS \wedge \\
&\quad\quad (sw \mapsto act2 \mapsto o \mapsto cw) \in hist\_conc) \wedge \ldots \\
&\quad \exists (sw, cw).(sw \in SUBJECTS \wedge cw \in CONTEXTS \wedge \\
&\quad\quad (sw \mapsto actn \mapsto o \mapsto cw) \in hist\_conc)))
\end{aligned}
$$

The refinement provides a way to add such a constraint to the model and proof obligations ensure the correctness of the transformation. Another refinement can be done to introduce specific rules for aspects such as duty separation.

3.4 Separation of Duties

Separation of duties aims to prevent fraud and errors by disseminating an action's execution privileges among different subjects. To implement a system satisfying this type of constraints, it is necessary that when a subject asks for the authorization to execute an action on an object, to be able to check if it did not already act throughout the process, which is impossible to do with OrBAC in a simple way. However, there is a form of separation of duties known as static separation of duties (implemented with RBAC [12]). This one consists of preventing a subject from accumulating several important functions, and it can be achieved when subjects are assigned to roles. In the B model, the following assertion should be proved to guarantee that no subject accumulates two critical given roles $r1$, $r2$. In the clause ASSERTIONS:

$$\forall s.((s \in SUBJECTS \wedge (org \mapsto r1 \mapsto s) \in empower)$$
$$\Rightarrow (org \mapsto r2 \mapsto s) \notin empower)$$

Proceeding this way may be too rigid in some cases. A subject s can cumulate several functions if it does not intervene many times in the management of the same object o. To prevent a subject s executing two critical actions $act1$, $act2$ on an object o with $act1 \neq act2$, the following invariant has to be proved:

INVARIANT
$\forall(s1, s2, o, ctx1, ctx2).($
$\quad(s1 \in SUBJECTS \wedge s2 \in SUBJECTS\wedge$
$\quad o \in OBJECTS\wedge$
$\quad ctx1 \in CONTEXTS \wedge ctx2 \in CONTEXTS\wedge$
$\quad(s1 \mapsto act1 \mapsto o \mapsto ctx1) \in hist\_conc)\wedge$
$\quad(s2 \mapsto act2 \mapsto o \mapsto ctx2) \in hist\_conc)$
$\Rightarrow$
$\quad(s1 \neq s2))$

The separation of duties and workflow constraints are only particular cases of constraints where instant system state must be known in order for them to be expressible.

4   Conclusion and Open Issues

The development of software systems satisfying a given security policy should be based on techniques for validating the link between the security policy and the resulting system. The link between the security policy and the system is called *satisfaction* and we have used the event B method, especially refinement, for relating the security policy expressed in OrBAC and the final system. The link between the two levels of abstractions in OrBAC is proved to be a B refinement. Our work is greatly influenced by the case study developed by J.-R. Abrial [2]; he shows how a system for controling access to buildings can be derived by refinement, and he starts by expressing the essence of the access control. In our case, we use an elaborate formalism OrBAC for expressing the security policy and for checking its consistency; we derive a mathematical theory from OrBAC specification and we define an explicit state of a system which is not explicit in OrBAC. The refinement provides us with a way to develop a list of models which progressively integrate details that do not seem to be possible to express in OrBAC: workflow constraints, for instance. Our models are generic with respect to the security policy and can be reused to develop a real system. A crucial question would be to use our models for developing an infrastructure for controlling an existing system with respect to a security policy. Moreover, security policy expresses permissions and prohibitions but it remains to consider obligations which are very difficult to refine because they are close to liveness properties and should be expressed on traces. Moreover, the administration of security policy (ADOrBAC) leads to modifiable permissions and prohibitions:

our constants should be transformed into state variables and decisions should be taken to handle situations, which are not satisfying the invariant (some person might become undesirable whilst in a building, when security policy is modified by the administration). Finally, case studies should be developed using these models.

References

1. A. Abou El Kalam, R. El Baida, P. Balbiani, S. Benferhat, F. Cuppens, Y. Deswarte, A. Miège, C. Saurel, and G. Trouessin. Organization Based Access Control. In *4th IEEE International Workshop on Policies for Distributed Systems and Networks (Policy'03)*, June 2003.
2. J.-R. Abrial. Etude système: méthode et exemple. http://www.atelierb.societe.com/documents.html.
3. J.R. Abrial. *The B Book - Assigning Programs to Meanings*. Cambridge University Press, 1996. ISBN 0-521-49619-5.
4. R.-J. Back and J. von Wright. *Refinement Calculus*. Springer-Verlag, 1998.
5. D. E. Bell and L. J. LaPadula. Secure computer systems: Unified exposition and multics interpretation. MTR-2997, (ESD-TR-75-306), available as NTIS AD-A023 588, MITRE Corporation, 1976.
6. K. Biba. Integrity consideration for secure computer systems. Technical Report MTR-3153, MITRE Corporation, 1975.
7. Dominique Cansell and Dominique Méry. Logical foundations of the B method. *Computers and Informatics*, 22, 2003.
8. K. M. Chandy and J. Misra. *Parallel Program Design A Foundation*. Addison-Wesley Publishing Company, 1988. ISBN 0-201-05866-9.
9. E. M. Clarke, O. Grumberg, and D. A. Peled. *Model Checking*. The MIT Press, 2000.
10. ClearSy. *Web site B4free set of tools for development of B models*, 2004.
11. F. Cuppens. Orbac web page. http://www.orbac.org.
12. D.F. Ferraiolo, R.Sandhu, S.Gavrila, D.R. Kuhn, and R.Chandramouli. Proposed nist standard for role-based access control. *ACM Transactions on Information and System Security*, 4(3):222–274, 2001.
13. Serban I. Gavrila and John F. Barkley. Formal specification for role based access control user/role and role/role relationship management. In *ACM Workshop on Role-Based Access Control*, pages 81–90, 1998.
14. Butler Lampson. Protection. In *Proceedings of the 5th Annual Princeton Conference on Information Sciences and Systems*, pages 437–443, Princeton University, 1971.
15. R.Sandhu, E.J. Coyne, H.L. Feinstein, and C.E. Youman. Role-based access control models. *IEEE Computer*, 29(2):38–47, 1996.

Experiences in Using B and UML in Industrial Development

Ian Oliver

Nokia Research Center, Itämerenkatu 11-13, 00180 Helsinki, Finland

1   Introduction

We describe in this paper the results[1] of our experiences on the use of formal methods with UML and B in the specification and development of part of Nokia's NoTA (Network on Terminal Architecture) platform for providing Service Oriented abilities to the embedded, mobile platform.

Nokia's Network on Terminal Architecture (NoTA) is designed to allow the notions of service orientation [4] in an embedded environment within a mobile device. It is based around the combination of two ideas: the first is that the hardware platform becomes modular by simplifying the connection interface to just power lines and just two data communication lines. Secondly that the system provides resource and session management to components which provide 'services' in much the same way as contemporary webservices.

2   The Specifications

In order to evaluate the integration of B and UML [8,1] we made three major attempts made to model the the upper layers of the NoTA interconnection protocol (session and transport). The first attempt was by 'traditional methods' based around the SDL language [3], the second by making a straight mapping from a UML class diagram based domain model to B and the third by first *architecting* the previous domain model into layers and then mapping one of those layers into B.

The SDL development was based around a use case driven approach in which the system is a black box and the use cases describe interactions from outside the system [6]. During the course of development, the black box is refined to a state machine and then further decomposed using SDL's block structures to more detailed communicating state-machines. The block structure forms a tree-like hierarchy with the behaviour encoded in the state-machines being found in the leaf nodes of the block hierarchy.

Rather than taking the use case and functional decomposition approach, when using object oriented methods it is more beneficial to take advantage of the class structuring mechanisms - OO is more about the unification of functionality and structure and this must be taken into consideration. This basically means the

---

[1] Work made in conjunction with the EU funded Rodin project (IST 511599 RODIN).

J. Julliand and O. Kouchnarenko (Eds.): B 2007, LNCS 4355, pp. 248–251, 2006.

production of a domain model describing the system in terms of the problem. The use cases utilised earlier were used as tests to this domain model rather than the primary development artifact. The domain model in UML complete with a number of constraints expressed in OCL was mapped to B using the U2B tool [10] - the OCL constraints being mapped by hand.

When working with a layered approach, we started with the domain model from the previous attempt and then undertook a process of architecting (or partitioning) the model according to the suggested four layer model of NoTA. In particular we concentrated on the high level interconnect protocol layer which provides service registration, discovery and session management protocols to services. The lower level protocol are concerned with the transport of data.

3   Experiences

All three attempts produced models by which some form of reasoning could be made about the system. However what was noticed was the effect that the method employed had upon the particular design.

In the first case with SDL, the functional decomposition to state machines resulted in very early implementation decisions - it was impossible not to include implementation details in order to make the models 'simulatable' (or 'executable'). This compromised the intended code generation engine - we have a customised engine specifically for the mobile device environment - and in particular this meant that hardware generation was not possible. As the system was constructed through use cases, which were also the tests for the system, these tests always ran correctly - if not then this meant that the actual design did not conform. But this also means that the structure of the system closely follows the tests rather than what is actually needed. Furthermore the amount of testing of the system is compromised by the amount of test cases that can be examined - exhaustive testing can not be made and certain aspects of the system will always remain untested [5].

Using UML and domain modelling principles forced the developer to think more about the structure of the system and more importantly the relationships between those structures. Systems should (must) be constructed to support the required use cases and not be implementations of use cases.

Mapping the domain model directly to B via U2B produced a much larger block of B than was anticipated with a large amount of OO superstructure explicitly encoded inside the B. Specifically here the relationships between the objects, constructor/destructor functions and general management of the relationships. We estimate that approximately 70% of the proof obligations (with AtelierB 3.6) from a total of approximately 1200 were concerned with this superstructure. The writing of the OO navigation expressions across the classes to encode the invariants, pre and post-conditions was complicated by having to know how the U2B translation works. This had an effect on the provability of the proof obligations and also our ability to work the manual proof. The final attempt is basically a simplification of the previous but rather than try to utilise the U2B and the OO superstructure within the chosen architectural layer we simply used B in a much purer sense as per the B-Method. We expected this to be simpler and regarding the proof, much simpler - this is precisely what happened with approximately 200 proof obligations and 80-90% discharge automatically.

4 Conclusions

The mobile phone is not considered a saftey critical device and the usage of formal methods and in particular verification and proof in this environment in not common.

The results[2] of each of the experiments in terms of time taken showed that the development time spent designing increases the more formal the approach. In the three attempts here the 3rd (B) approach spent approximately 150% more time in design then the 1st (SDL). However much of this time is spent more precisely figuring out what the customer requires and working with the verification and validation.

When it came to producing the final working code, the SDL based method was much faster but the code contained more bugs than either of the UML or B approaches. Many of these bugs were logical errors from the design resulting in much more time reworking the original models. Verification of the system which was not possible with SDL removes many logical errors (buffer overflows probably being the most visible) while validation through animation and theorem proving in conjunction with the verification ensure that the system is meeting the customer's requirements. We estimate that the code generated from the B specification contained approximately only 5% of the errors that were seen in the SDL version.

Overall development time was approximately 50% shorter for the UML versus the SDL and 30% shorter for B versus the SDL modelling. Much of this can be explained in terms of the amount of remodelling work required to counteract errors due to misspecification.

The major problem in industrial development is that of requirements change. We made no attempt to manage this in order to evaluate somewhat the effects of this upon the process. Many changes of course affect the use of refinement but we did not investigate this in detail here. The major result however was that when working with SDL each requirements change was integrated into the model as if it were necessary, while in the more formal models we could more accurately investigate the likely effects upon the system. Overall we saw that almost 90% of changes could be dismissed due to misunderstanding of the workings of the system - something that was not possible to ascertain with certainty when working with a non-formal method.

Regarding tools, whatever the situation, a theorem prover is not user friendly and is not suitable for demonstration of the system. However animations such as ProB [7] are much more accessible and we found can be used by the customer.

---

[2] Precise figures can not be given due to confidentiality reasons, although we present here percentages which are indicative of the results instead.

Interestingly the use of ProB versus traditional prototypes (complete with user-interface) resulted in the customer being more focussed on what the system does rather than how the user-interface was constructed. The interface to the tools is not as critical as we expected, although engineers do expect tools to interact easily - specifically transfer of models between tools. Sadly for the tool vendors, the cost of many of these tools is prohibitive in non-safety critical environments thus hampering the uptake of said tools and formal methods in general. Environments such as the forthcoming open-source, Eclipse-based Rodin toolset [2] and newer ProB versions greatly help in this respect.

Overall we consider that the use of formal methods and tools is at a stage where they can be accepted in *normal* software engineering practises. Despite claims that engineers do not accept 'mathematical methods' we have found almost the opposite when relevant and reasonable analysis of their work can be made. We also find that coaching of the engineers is required until familiarity with the analysis techniques has development sufficiently. Finally we make note that strict adherence to formal techniques is often counter productive in this environment and a much more pragmatic approach [9] must be taken when introducing and using these techniques.

References

1. J. R. Abrial. *The B Book: Assigning Programs to Meanings*. Cambridge University Press. 1996
2. Joey Coleman, Cliff Jones, Ian Oliver, and Elena Troubitsyna Alexander Romanovsky. RODIN (Rigorous Open Development Environment for Complex Systems). In *Fifth European Dependable Computing Conference EDCC-5, Budapest, Hungary*, 2005.
3. Jan Ellsberger, Dieter Hogrefe, and Amardeo Sarma. *SDL, Formal Object-oriented Language for Communicating Systems*. Prentice Hall, 1997. 0-13-632886-5.
4. Thomas Erl. *Service-Oriented Architecture*. Prentice Hall, 2005. 0-13-185858-0.
5. Antti Huima. A Note on an Anomaly in Black-Box Testing. In *Formal Approaches to Software Testing*, volume 3997 of *LNCS*, pages 47–61. Springer, 2005.
6. Klaus Kronlof, Samu Kontinen, Ian Oliver, and Timo Eriksson. A Method for Mobile Terminal Platform Architecture Development. In *Proceedings of Forum on Design Languages 2006. Darmstadt, Germany*, 2006.
7. Michael Leuschel and Michael Butler. ProB: A Model Checker for B. In Keijiro Araki, Stefania Gnesi, and Dino Mandrioli, editors, *FME 2003: Formal Methods*, volume 2805 of *LNCS*, pages 855–874. Springer, 2003.
8. Object Management Group. UML Superstructure Specification v2.0, omg document number ad/02-09-02 edition. OMG Document Number formal/05-07-04, 2004.
9. Michael Poppleton and Richard Banach. Requirements Validation by Lifting Retrenchments in B. In *Proceedings of ICECCS2004: IEEE International Conference on Engineering of Complex Computer Systems, Florence, Italy*, pages 87–96, 2004.
10. Colin Snook and Michael Butler. UML-B: Formal modeling and design aided by UML. *ACM Trans. Softw. Eng. Methodol.*, 15(1):92–122, 2006.

B in Large-Scale Projects: The Canarsie Line CBTC Experience

Didier Essamé and Daniel Dollé

Siemens Transportation Systems
150, avenue de la République, BP 101, 92323 Châtillon Cedex, France
{didier.essame,daniel.dolle}@siemens.com

Abstract. Eight years ago, Siemens Transportation Systems accomplished the first successful application of the B Method on an industrial project. The vital software of the METEOR automatic train control system, with very strong dependability and safety needs, was specified and coded in B. Beyond the technological challenge of using such a complex formal method in an industrial context, it is now clear for us that building software using B is not more expensive than using conventional methods. Better, due to our experience in using this method, we can assert that using B is cheaper when considering the whole development process (from specification to validation and sometimes certification). Since METEOR, Siemens Transportation Systems has generalized the use of B for building all vital software of its systems in particular its Communication Based Train Control Systems (CBTC) recently enacted on the New York City Canarsie Line. This short paper shares the Canarsie line experience in the B landscape.

1 Introduction

METEOR was the first project where Siemens Transportation Systems used the B method to build vital software. The feedback on this project was extremely positive with respect to the quality of the validation and to the cost effectiveness of the method. With B, we were able to have a concise and unambiguous high level software specification that was clearly separated from the low level algorithms of the code. This allowed our validation team to concentrate on the specification rather than lose time and energy on the nitty-gritty details of the code. This approach was made possible for two reasons. On the theoretical side, B ensures that the code preserves the properties of the formal specification. On the practical side, the tool we used - the Atelier B - matured in the course of METEOR from a R&D status to a robust tool capable of dealing with tens of thousands of proof obligations. Even though METEOR was the company's first large scale project using formal methods it induced no significant budget overhead. The introduction of a new method is indeed costly but we observed that it was offset by our suppression of unit testing and by an earlier detection of errors. Rather than having the system go wrong during site tests, all the errors in the B software were found during reviews and development tests.

J. Julliand and O. Kouchnarenko (Eds.): B 2007, LNCS 4355, pp. 252–254, 2006.
© Springer-Verlag Berlin Heidelberg 2006

The B method is now completely embedded in our safety critical software development process. Since METEOR, the major shortcomings of our process have been corrected and we have gained in effectiveness and in profitability. The single most important step is automatic refinement. The introduction of this technique into our development process made it possible to make transparent the most technical and complex aspect of using the B method and thus making it accessible to anyone with a very reduced effort of training.

2 The Canarsie Line Experience

After METEOR, the B method has been used to build some parts of the SACEM systems for new projects in San Juan and in Hong Kong. But the second biggest experience of SIEMENS Transportation Systems building a large scale system with B is the Canarsie Line CBTC. The CBTC system with radio communication and online track database data processing adds new challenges to our vital software. The software of the Canarsie CBTC is much more complex than that of METEOR. To give an idea, the onboard vital software of the Canarsie CBTC is bigger than all vital software of METEOR. Moreover, unusual elements of the B language such as sequences or generalized concatenation have been deeply used. Here are some keys indicators for the onboard vital software development:

Activities	Persons	Average Load in months	Person with METEOR experience
Software Requirement formalisation	4	7	1
Refinement to ADA code	3	3	0
Proof	3	3	1
Functional test	3	3	0

In fact, the onboard vital software was carried out with a team of 4 persons with little knowledge of METEOR and within not much more than one year. In addition only 25% of development time was devoted to the coding, the remainder was devoted to the formalization of the software specification and to the proof. In addition, two team members had never practised a B development even if one among them knew the language theoretically.

For us the main feedback is that using B to build vital software is effective and does not require a pool of experts in formal methods.

3 Is Your Company Ready to Join the "B Landscape"?

B, like any formal method, uses mathematics. But this aspect does not make it a method reserved to mathematicians. Our daily practice shows it to us. Do you need a pool of mathematicians experts to start? From our point of view the answer is no. The real question is what is necessary to launch a B development? For us, a pilot project and a team with a person having a first B experience and tools.

In addition, the whole activities of a B development process is partitioned and each company can concentrate on the activities which adds value to its product. It is the case for example for software specification formalization activity, which brings value to the customer because it enables him to apprehend what the software does by properties and not by means of algorithms (we shall illustrate that in the presentation). Once this choice made, the company can request assistance for the others activities.

4   Conclusion

Our conviction is that this method is compatible with the industrial constraints. Moreover its use adds real value to the system owner. This method is now tested and our experience proves it. The use of automatic refinement makes it available to all with very reduced effort of training. One can introduce this method in its software development process safely with possibly an external support for a pilot or a test project.

About the Authors

Didier Essamé is a B expert. He is Equipment Manager at Siemens Transportation Systems and leading the development of the Carborne Controller of Barcelone L9 CBTC.

Daniel Dollé is a B expert who took part in the great adventure of METEOR. He is now leading the development of the Wayside Controller vital software of TRAINGUARD CBTC the Siemens Transportation Systems product for rail automation.

A Tool for Firewall Administration

Mathieu Clabaut

Systerel
Porte de l'Arbois, bât. A,
1090 rue René Descartes,
Parc d'activités de la Duranne,
13857 Aix-en-Provence cedex 3, France
mathieu.clabaut@systerel.fr

Abstract. Firewall administration is not a task free from pitfalls. Some interfaces exist to alleviate the administrator burden, but none is formally proven, and none is generic enough to manage appliances from different vendors. A study[1] was lead to develop such a formal interface.

1 Firewall Administration, a Tough Job

A security officer and a network administrator in charge of designing and implementing security policies face two difficulties:

1. configure each network device to implement the security policies for one,
2. get the intimate conviction that the configuration correctly implements the policies for the other.

Indeed, configuring a firewall may be a daunting task on an heterogeneous network, when one knows that each network appliance provider designed a specific configuration language and use different filtering concepts. Getting the conviction for the security officer that the policies are correctly implemented is not easier when he does not master all the tip and tricks of each network appliance.

Some existing configuration interfaces may alleviate the administrator burden, but they appear to suffer from several problems:

– they often are proprietary and work for one type of network appliance only,
– they often do not provide the abstraction level needed to let the security officer verify the policies enforcement,
– they may introduce some unadvertised (and unwanted) side effects.

Considering these difficulties, a study aimed at designing a firewall configuration tool was launched with the prerequisite to use formal methods.

Its scope was restricted to the configuration of *one* generic firewall and the *netfilter*[2] firewall was chosen as an implementation target.

---

[1] This study was funded by the SGDN (*Secrétariat Général de la Défense Nationale*) under contract number 2005000110021507501.

[2] Firewall implemented in the linux OS.

J. Julliand and O. Kouchnarenko (Eds.): B 2007, LNCS 4355, pp. 255–256, 2006.

2   Interfaces Design

A two levels decomposition based on languages tailored to fit the firewall administration task was envisioned.

A *high level language* (HLL) was designed to define security policies at the firewall level and to allow abstraction, modularity and reuse of policy chunks.

A *low level language* (LLL) was in turn designed to define firewall configurations with two constraints in mind: be vendor independent and translate easily into a specific firewall configuration idiom (i.e. no formal method for this task).

3   Tools

Two tools were then designed to accomplish the transformation from HLL to firewall configuration:

- a so called *compiler*, in charge for translating the security policies expressed in HLL to firewall configuration expressed in LLL,
- a *translator*, in charge for producing the final *netfilter* configuration file from the LLL configuration.

4   Use of Formal Method

The language design task in itself constitutes a response to two of the three difficulties listed in Sect. 1, but in order to improve the confidence and get rid of unwanted side effects, the *compiler* and the *translator* behavior had to be proven (given the simplicity of the later, the proof was only done for the *compiler*).

The *B method* was elected to prove that the LLL configuration produced by the tools correctly implements the HLL policies. We have chosen to prove the tool, that is, to prove that the *HLL compiler* preserves the semantic of the security policies. Note that only the core HLL translation, which works on abstract syntax trees, has been modelled and proved. The other components (language parsing, language production, LLL translation) were classically developed in C/C++.

5   Results and Future Works

The three main tasks in term of effort were the design of a *formal, but nonetheless natural* semantic, B modelling and model proving. The proof was quite difficult even when the model mainly describes a "simple" task, roughly equivalent to the transformation of a binary formula into its Disjunctive Normal Form.

Even if the modelling task would probably have deserved more work, the study leads successfully to two functional prototypes, the *compiler* one being proved.

Several themes were only briefly addressed during this study and may deserve some future work: *policy testing, configuration of statefull firewalls, policies equivalence, modelling of firewall behaviour,* ...

The B-Method for the Construction of Microkernel-Based Systems

Sarah Hoffmann[1], Germain Haugou[1], Sophie Gabriele[1], and Lilian Burdy[2]

[1] STMicroelectronics
[2] ClearSy

1 Introduction

Microkernels have been developed to minimize the size of software that needs to run in privileged CPU-Mode. They provide only a set of general hardware abstractions, which then can be used to implement an operating system with a high level of reliability and security on top. L4 is a second generation microkernel based on the principles of minimalism, flexibility and efficiency. Its small size (about 15,000 lines of C++) and its relevance for security make it a good candidate for formal analysis. This paper describes our approach to develop a formal model of the API of the L4 microkernel. The goal was to evaluate the possibility to model such software with formal techniques, moreover, the objectives were:

- to describe precisely the mechanisms of L4,
- to obtain a more extensive documentation of the microkernel,
- to highlight the points where the specification was incomplete,
- to prove some static properties on the kernel.

The formalism used to model the system is the Event B formalism. Event B allows to describe a system through a set of data with properties and the events modifying that data: an event either describes an internal behavior of the system or how the system reacts to external actions. Finally, B provides automatic and interactive tools to help proving formally that each event always respects the properties.

2 Basic Concepts of L4

As a microkernel L4 aims to avoid the implementation of any system policies. It focuses on the basic mechanisms that allow constructing a complete operating system in non-privileged mode. The three fundamental abstractions are: tasks, threads and inter-process communication (IPC).

Tasks provide virtual address spaces. The address space translation towards physical memory is established decentralized by the tasks themselves. Initially, sigma0, the task created first, finds the available physical memory in its address space. It can share this memory with other tasks by sending one or more pages of virtual memory. The receiving task specifies the place where to put the pages and

J. Julliand and O. Kouchnarenko (Eds.): B 2007, LNCS 4355, pp. 257–259, 2006.
© Springer-Verlag Berlin Heidelberg 2006

the kernel establishes the new mapping. The task can then access the memory or map it recursively on to other tasks. Page faults are forwarded to a specific thread, the pager, which has to resolve the fault by providing a mapping.

Mappings may be revoked (unmapped) at any time, which results in a recursive unmapping of all further mappings that have been established from that page. For this, the kernel needs to track all mappings in what is conventionally called the mapping database.

Threads are execution contexts. As such they are attached to a task and are scheduled by the kernel according to the parameters that can be changed through system calls.

IPC allows to send messages synchronously and unbuffered between two threads. The content of these messages may consists of simple registers contents and of memory regions that are copied directly into the receiving address space. Memory pages are sent to other tasks via IPC as well.

3   Model of the L4 API

We have constructed a representation of the L4 microkernel API using this event B formalism. We have developed an abstract model of the data inside the microkernel and described the different ways to interact with it. Those interactions are, in fact, the different system calls. In L4, a system call is an entry point that allows carrying out many different actions. We have split those different actions into different events. This allows defining more clearly what is necessary to perform a single action and what this action will modify in the kernel. We have obtained a model describing all the system calls and a manual outlining:

- the structure and the properties of the system abstractions
- and for each possible action its prerequisites as well as the modifications carried out by this action.

The data structures mainly represent the memory and the threads. These structures are not described in the API, but they appear through the specification of the system calls. In the model, they correspond to the definition of constants and variables. On the other hand, each action is guarded by a predicate on those variables defining the conditions on which the corresponding system call can be called. This guard depends also on the system call parameters.

4   Animation and Test

To validate the model against the running code (and vice versa), we have used the Brama animator framework in order to test the code using the model as an oracle. A test case consists of a kernel pre- state and a system call with specific parameters. The corresponding test application first makes some system calls to position the kernel in the pre-state, then it executes the system call, and finally the kernel post-state is dumped into a file. Using the animator, one can also set the model in a given state, execute some events and dump the model state into a file.

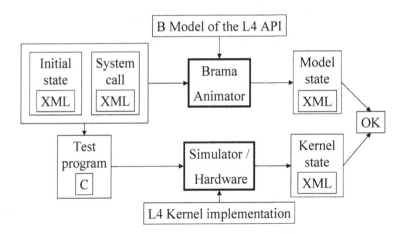

We have developed an interface that allows to convert a kernel state into a model state, associating the model variables with the implementation data. We have also converted a system call into a sequence of event executions. This allows to put the kernel and the model in an equivalent state starting from a unique description, to execute the system call and to compare the two resulting states in order to validate the conformance of the code to the model.

5 Conclusion

To conclude, we consider that the development of this model allows us to obtain more confidence in the correctness of the API, to describe its behavior from a different point of view and to establish a deeper understanding on how it works. The test framework allows to validate the model against an implementation; the relation between the model and the implementation is not proven (as it could be in a complete formal development with code generation) but the test allows to ensure more confidence. For software where efficiency is such a crucial requirement that it rules out code generation, this kind of test framework can be a realistic solution to construct a validation at two levels: at specification level, when constructing the model, and at implementation level when testing it.

Hardware Verification and Beyond: Using B at AWE

Neil Evans and Wilson Ifill

Atomic Weapons Establishment, Aldermaston, Reading, UK

The Atomic Weapons Establishment (AWE) has been responsible for the United Kingdom's nuclear deterrent for more than 50 years. Its work covers the entire development lifecycle - from the initial research and design, through manufacture, in- service support and, finally, decommissioning and disposal. In order to maintain its reputation as a world-class company, AWE upholds strict working procedures and demands high standards.

The nature of the work at AWE demands precision. In many aspects of the work, well established engineering principles exist to enforce the necessary rigour. Historically, the same level of rigour has not been forthcoming in the development of computer systems (in both software and hardware). The simple answer to this problem is, of course, formal methods (the choice of which formal method to use is a bit more difficult). The B Method is AWEs formal method of choice, and this talk will present its early role in the development and verification of hardware at AWE, how B is being used today, and its role in the future.

The history of formal methods at AWE began about 15 years ago. The development of computerised control systems introduced a need for verified hardware. Since no commercial processors were available to meet this requirement, an in-house chip was developed: the Arming System Processor (ASP) -a RISC processor with separate data and program buses, only three registers, and built-in test utilities. A collaboration with Ib Sorensen at B-Core (U.K.) resulted in the addition of hardware component libraries and a VHDL code generator to the B Toolkit (this is documented in [3]). This approach to the formal development of hardware was named B-VHDL. Using this approach, the ASP was formally verified [4]. All hardware specifications written in B-VHDL mimic the structure of a traditional VHDL program[1]. This was necessary to gain acceptance from AWE engineers, many of whom were familiar with VHDL but had no experience with formal methods. In addition to the ASP, B-VHDL has been used in the development of other pieces of hardware. For example, in [1], B-VHDL was used to prove the absence of hazards in a example pipelined processor.

One of the problems with mimicking VHDL is the relatively low-level of abstraction attainable in the B. In particular, the clocked nature of VHDL means that constructing B-VHDL models and animating them is very difficult. At the early stages of a development, it is desirable to abstract away the clock in order to focus on the more conceptual features of a system. Then the clock can be introduced at a later stage in the development.

---

[1] www.vhdl.org

J. Julliand and O. Kouchnarenko (Eds.): B 2007, LNCS 4355, pp. 260–261, 2006.

An alternative hardware description language is Handel-C[2], which can be used without the need to refer to the clock. Currently, research is being undertaken to generate Handel-C code from abstract B specifications. However, certain features of Handel-C are difficult to express in B. In particular, modelling the concurrent aspects of Handel-C is not straightforward in B. It is possible to use an integrated approach such as CSP||B [5] but, once again, the sensitivities of AWE engineers must be taken into consideration: it would be unreasonable to expect them to learn yet another formal notation. Instead, an augmentation to the B language itself is proposed in [2]. Each operation is annotated with control information to model the possible execution sequences of the operations.

Looking ahead, AWE is funding a number of academic research projects to investigate how B and its associated tool support can be exploited in other areas. Within this environment it is possible to pursue more ambitious lines of research without fear of alienating the AWE workforce. An ongoing project with the University of Surrey, called SystemB at AWE, is looking at ways to formalise software/hardware co-design using both CSP and B, and a research contract is being set up to provide formal analysis techniques in the development of executable UML (xUML) models. The work with UML will offer a route to formalize high-level system specifications, whereas the co-design work will afford an implementation route from CSP||B to platform solutions. All of the work described in this proposal will contribute to a long term AWE project to built high integrity systems from formal specifications.

References

1. W. Ifill. The Formal Development of an Example Processor in AMN, C and VHDL. Technical report, MSc thesis, Royal Holloway, University of London, 1999.
2. W. Ifill, S. Schneider, and H. Treharne. Annotating B for Control. Technical report, 2007.
3. Wilson Ifill, Ib Sorensen, and Steve Schneider. The use of B to specify, design and verify hardware. In *High integrity software*, pages 43–62, Norwell, MA, USA, 2001. Kluwer Academic Publishers.
4. I. Sorensen. A Mathematical AMN State Based Description of the ASP. Technical report, AWE, 1998.
5. Helen Treharne and Steve Schneider. Using a Process Algebra to Control B Operations. In *IFM '99: Proceedings of the 1st International Conference on Integrated Formal Methods*, pages 437–456, London, UK, 1999. Springer-Verlag.

---

[2] www.celoxica.com

A JAG Extension for Verifying LTL Properties on B Event Systems*

Julien Groslambert

Université de Franche-Comté - LIFC - CNRS
16 route de Gray - 25030 Besançon cedex France
groslambert@lifc.univ-fcomte.fr

Abstract. This paper presents an extension of the tool JAG for verifying temporal properties expressed in LTL (Linear Temporal Logic) on B Event Systems. The tool generates a machine containing a B representation of the Büchi automaton associated with the LTL property to verify and includes it within the original B event system. Then, the user have to prove the consistency of the generated event system. This proof of consistency implies the satisfaction of the LTL property on the executions of the original event system.

Keywords: LTL, Büchi Automaton, Verification.

1 Introduction

This article presents an extension of the JAG tool [3], initially written for Java/ JML. The extension permits to verify temporal properties expressed in LTL on B event systems[1]. This is an implementation of the work presented in [4]. The tool generates, from a B event system S and a property ϕ, a new system S_ϕ, whose correctness ensures the satisfaction of ϕ on the executions of the original event system S. The tool has been experimented on different examples.

2 B Event System Example

First introduced by J.-R Abrial [1], event B is both a formal development method and a specification language. Figure 1 displays an example of B event system, describing a system composed of two platforms: an *input* and an *output* platform (respectively modeled by two booleans De and Dt). An empty platform (resp. busy, i.e., a piece is on the platform) is modeled by a value set to FALSE (resp. TRUE. An event load describes the loadong of a piece on the input platform. An event unload puts the piece on the output platform and an event discard leaves out the piece from the output platform. In this paper, we are interested in verifying that this B event system satisfies some temporal requirements.

---

* Research partially founded by the french ACI *Geccoo*.

[1] This extension will be fully integrated in the next release of the JAG tool, however, a demo version is available http://lifc.univ-fcomte.fr/~groslambert/JAGB/

J. Julliand and O. Kouchnarenko (Eds.): B 2007, LNCS 4355, pp. 262–265, 2006.
© Springer-Verlag Berlin Heidelberg 2006

```
MACHINE
   Robot                                   Unload = SELECT Dt = TRUE
VARIABLES                                             ∧ De = FALSE
   De,Dt                                        THEN Dt := FALSE
INVARIANT                                         || De := TRUE
   Dt ∈ BOOL ∧ De ∈ BOOL                         END;
INITIALISATION
   Dt := FALSE || De := FALSE             Discard = SELECT De = TRUE
OPERATIONS                                         THEN De := FALSE
   Load = SELECT Dt = FALSE                      END
          THEN Dt := TRUE            END
          END;
```

Fig. 1. Example of a B event system

3   Temporal Requirements

The extension of JAG uses temporal properties expressed in LTL [5]. The LTL operators are F P ("eventually P"), meaning that there is eventually a state in the future where P holds; G P ("always P"), meaning that all the states in the future satisfy P; X P ("next P") meaning the next state of the execution satisfies P; and finally P U Q, meaning that all the future states satisfy P until a state where Q holds is reached.

Examples of LTL formulae. On the example, one would like to express a temporal requirement such as *"an unload can be done only if the evacuation is free"*. This can be expressed in the LTL logic by the following formula:

$$G((Dt = true ∧ X (Dt = false)) ⇒ De = false) \qquad (1)$$

It must be understood as follows: in all the states of the execution (G), if the input platform is not free (Dt = true) and if it is free in the next state (X (Dt = false)), i.e., an unload has occured, then the output platform must be free (De = false).

Our tool automatically translates such properties into the B framework. The architecture of the tool is explained in the next section.

4   Tool Structure and Experiments

The general dataflow of the tool is displayed in Fig. 2. It works as follows.

1. On the one hand, the LTL property ϕ is firstly translated into a equivalent Büchi automaton (an automaton representation of the property) using the LTL2BA tool [2]. The automata generated from the LTL property (1) is displayed in Fig. 3.
2. Then, the automata's states and transitions are translated into a B machine M_ϕ by the JAG *converter* module. The machine automata (see Fig. 4 - left side) is the result of the conversion of the automaton in Fig. 3. It is built as follows:
   - Each state of the automaton is described by a boolean variable. The variable associated to the initial state is set to TRUE, and the others to FALSE.

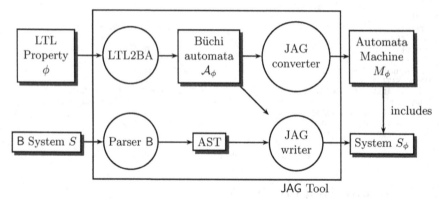

Fig. 2. Tool Architecture

- An operation `automata_1` represents the transitions of the automaton. For example, the variable `ASS0`, representing the initial state of the automata, is set to `TRUE` if (i) the automaton was synchronized with the initial state (`ASS0 = TRUE`) and the guard of the transition (`Dt = FALSE or De = FALSE`) is satisfied. ; or if (ii) the automata was synchronized with the second state (`ASS1 = TRUE`) and the guard of the transition was satisfied (`Dt = TRUE & De = FALSE`).

3. On the other hand, the system S is parsed and the JAG *writer* module extends it by including in it the B machine M_ϕ. Figure 4 displays, on the right side, the event system obtained for the `Robot` example. States of the machine are synchronized with the automaton by invocations of the `automata_1` operation. An invariant ensures that the event system is synchronized with at least one state of the automata.

Details and soundness of the translation can be found in [4]. The generated event system S_ϕ can be proved using the Atelier B. Table 1 displays the results of the proof obligation generation of LTL properties on two B models, the (T=1) communication protocol and a Javacard application (Demoney). Generated proof obligations have often been done in an interactive way.

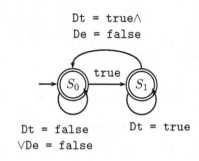

Fig. 3. Automaton of Property (1)

5   Conclusion and Future Works

The extension of JAG [3] presented is this paper is an implementation the work presented in [4]. An interesting future work is to generate the proof obligation implying the preservation of the LTL properties during a refinement. In our experimentations,we have observed that the success of automatic proof can be

```
                                          SYSTEM
                                            Robot_1
MACHINE                                   INCLUDES
BA                                          BA_S
VARIABLES                                 VARIABLES
   ASS0,ASS1                                De,Dt
INVARIANT                                 INVARIANT
ASS0 ∈ BOOL ∧ ASS1 ∈ BOOL                   Dt ∈ BOOL ∧ De ∈ BOOL
INITIALIZATION                              ∧ (ASS0 = TRUE ∨ ASS1 = TRUE)
   ASS0 := TRUE ‖                         INITIALISATION
   ASS1 := FALSE                            Dt := FALSE ‖ De := FALSE
OPERATION                                 EVENTS
automata_1(De,Dt) =                         Load = SELECT Dt = FALSE
  PRE De ∈ BOOL ∧ Dt ∈ BOOL                   THEN Dt := TRUE
  THEN                                        ‖ automata_1(De,Dt)
     ASS0 := bool((Dt = TRUE                  END;
       ∧ De = FALSE ∧ ASS1 = TRUE)          Unload = SELECT Dt = TRUE
       ∨ (Dt = FALSE ∨ De = FALSE)             ∧ De = FALSE
       ∧ ASS0 = TRUE))                         THEN Dt := FALSE
     ‖                                         ‖ De := TRUE
     ASS1 := bool(ASS0 = TRUE                  ‖ automata_1(De,Dt)
       ∧ (Dt = TRUE                            END;
       ∨ ASS1 = TRUE))                       Discard = SELECT De = TRUE
     END                                       THEN De := FALSE
END                                            ‖ automata_1(De,Dt)
                                               END
                                          END
```

Fig. 4. JAG outputs

increased by adding extra invariants gluing states of the automaton with states of the event system. Therefore, a future work is to characterize the relation between these invariants and the structure of the automaton in the goal of generating them automatically.

Table 1. Results of the proof obligation generation

Example	Property	# of PO
Protocol T = 1	$(P \wedge \mathsf{X}Q) \Rightarrow (\mathsf{X}\neg R)$	4
Protocol T = 1	$\mathsf{FG}P \Rightarrow \mathsf{FG}Q$	12
Demoney	$\mathsf{G}(P \Rightarrow \mathsf{G}P)$	7
Demoney	$\mathsf{G}(P \Rightarrow \mathsf{X}(Q \vee R))$	7

References

1. J.-R. Abrial. *The B Book*. Cambridge University Press, 1996.
2. P. Gastin and D. Oddoux. Fast LTL to Büchi automata translation. In *CAV'01*, number 2102 in LNCS, pages 53–65. Springer, 2001.
3. A. Giorgetti and J. Groslambert. JAG: JML Annotation Generation for Verifying Temporal Properties. In *FASE*, LNCS, pages 373–376. Springer, 2006.
4. J. Groslambert. Verification of LTL on B event systems. In *B'2007, 7th International B Conference*, LNCS, Besancon, France. Springer, 2007.
5. A. Pnueli. The Temporal Logic of Program. In *18th Ann. IEEE Symp. on foundations of computer science*, pages 46–57, 1977.

A Generic Flash-Based
Animation Engine for ProB*

Jens Bendisposto and Michael Leuschel

Heinrich-Heine Universität Düsseldorf
{bendisposto,leuschel}@cs.uni-duesseldorf.de

Abstract. Writing a formal specification for real-life, industrial problems is a difficult and error prone task, even for experts in formal methods. In the process of specifying a formal model for later refinement and implementation it is crucial to get approval and feedback from domain experts to avoid the costs of changing a specification at a late point of the development. But understanding formal models written in a specification language like B requires mathematical knowledge a domain expert might not have. In this paper we present a new tool to visualize B Machines using the PROB animator and Macromedia Flash. Our tool offers an easy way for specifiers to build a domain specific visualization that can be used by domain experts to check whether a B specification corresponds to their expectations.

Keywords: B-Method, Tool Support, Animation.

1 Motivation

In [1] A. Hunt and D. Thomas describe a shortcoming on formal methods:

> *Most formal methods capture requirements using a combination of diagrams and some supporting words. These pictures represent the designers' understanding of the requirements. However in many cases these diagrams are meaningless to the end users, so the designers have to interpret them. Therefore there is no real formal checking of the requirements by the actual user of the system - everything is based on the designers' explanations, just as in old-fashioned written requirements. We see some benefit in capturing requirements this way, but we prefer, where possible, to show the user a prototype and let him play with it.*

In previous work [2] we presented the Prolog based PROB animator and model checker for the B Method,

which addresses the problems mentioned by Hunt and Thomas. PROB can help a specifier gain confidence that the model that is being specified, refined and implemented, does meet the domain requirements. This is achieved by the

---

* This research is being carried out as part of the EU funded research projects: IST 511599 RODIN (Rigorous Open Development Environment for Complex Systems).

J. Julliand and O. Kouchnarenko (Eds.): B 2007, LNCS 4355, pp. 266–269, 2006.

animation component of PROB, that allows to check the presence of desired functionality and to inspect the behaviour of a specification.

For a domain expert with little knowledge about the mathematical notation of B, however, it might still be too difficult to understand the meaning of a specific B state; in other words, understanding a model still relies on the designers' explanations. We believe that a broad industrial acceptance of formal methods needs tools that can mediate between domain experts and formal method experts.

In this work we present a generic Flash-based animation engine as a plug-in for PROB which allows to easily develop visualizations for a given specification. Our tool supports state-based animations, using simple pictures to represent a specific state of a B specification, and transition-based animations consisting of picture sequences. To avoid the creation of many different animations the tool supports composing visualizations from individual subcomponents.

2   Flash Animation Server

The Flash animation server is a plug-in for the Eclipse version of PROB that offers support for rapid creation of domain specific visualizations. Such an animation can be seen as a prototype for the software as mentioned by Hunt and Thomas. A domain expert can get a feeling what a B operation does and he can check whether his expectations are met, without having to know the mathematical notation or relying on the specifiers' explanations.

Each state of a B machine can be represented by a set of graphical objects such as text labels or pictures. In addition it is possible to attach a movie to a state changing operation. We use Macromedia Flash which is the de facto industry standard for web animations. It is available on many platforms and, in contrast to dynamic HTML, a Flash movie looks the same in different browsers. Also it comes with many features and tools that help create professional animations.

Obviously one has to define the mapping between a state and its graphical representation. This *gluing code* could be written using the Flash built-in programming language ActionScript. Unfortunately, ActionScript is very limited and error prone, therefore we developed an animation framework which frees the user from having to use ActionScript. Our animation framework comprises a generic Flash movie on the client side, i.e., it is not necessary to create different Flash movies for different machines. The only thing one has to provide for each client is the generic movie together with the required pictures. However, it is also possible to use ActionScript, if desired, but for most applications the generic movie is sufficient.

For the server side a piece of gluing code is needed, that defines the mapping between a state (or two states plus an operation) and a graphical representation. This gluing code can be written in Java. In addition to the generic movie, we have developed a set of Java objects that can be used inside the gluing code as an abstraction for the Flash objects. These objects live inside a container named *canvas*. For example, if we want to create a new image named "image1" in the upper left corner and load the file "old.jpg", we call *canvas.createNewFlashMovie("image1","old.jpg",0,0)* if we want to replace that image with a new one called "new.jpg", we could use *canvas.get("image1").setUrl ("new.jpg")*. The gluing code has also access to the machine's current state, the last operation executed and the machine's state before executing this operation using a Java object named *machine*. This gives the opportunity to write more sophisticated gluing code.

When any operation is being executed the Flash animation server will be notified by PROB. The animation server then calls the statechange method of the gluing code for the particular machine. The gluing code will typically read information from the machine object, do some updates on the canvas and finally call the method *canvas.commitChanges()*. Our animation server then calculates a XML message from the changed canvas and broadcasts it to all connected clients whose generic movie will display the new representation.

3   Example of an Application

We applied our generic solution to several nontrivial B specifications. The waterlock example (a detail view of an animation is shown in figure 1) is inspired by a case study from [3]; the model describes a system of waterlocks that can be operated separately. The artwork for the example has been rendered using Bryce[1]. Setting up the scene in Bryce took about two days; excluding the time to render the scene and the animations. Writing the gluing code took less than one hour. This shows that the effort to create an animation is mainly determined by the artwork. There is another example, downloadable on the tool's website, that has been developed during a workshop within three hours including writing the gluing code and creating the artwork. This example shows that our plug-in can be used for rapid visualization development.

4   Related and Future Work

The company ClearSy is currently developing a commercial visualization tool for B specifications, also based on Macromedia Flash technology called Brama. Brama will be available as a plug-in to the RODIN platform[2] and it also uses a B animator. In contrast to our generic solution, Brama does require programming in Flash since it provides a library for Action Script instead of an abstraction layer.

Several items can be pointed out for the most pressing future work:

1. Writing the gluing code is still a relatively cumbersome task, we are developing a graphical interface to setup the animation and an automatic code generator to generate the code.

---

[1] http://bryce.daz3d.com
[2] http://rodin-b-sharp.sourceforge.net/

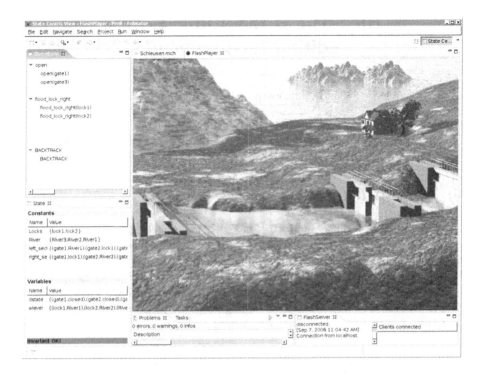

Fig. 1. Visualization of a waterlock system - animation stills

2. We will extend the abstraction layer for Flash components to enable two-way-communication. Therefore we will support Flash Buttons, this will help to generate prototype user interface from B machines.

In summary, we have presented a generic animation framework to visualize B specifications using Flash technology and PROB. We hope that this new tool will help make formal methods more appealing in an industrial setting, notably by allowing domain experts to understand formal specifications. Our tool is available on http://www.stups.uni-duesseldorf.de/ProB/eclipse.

References

1. Andrew Hunt and David Thomas. *The Pragmatic Programmer - From Journeyman to Master.* Addison-Wesley, 2005.
2. Michael Leuschel and Michael Butler. ProB: A model checker for B. In Keijiro Araki, Stefania Gnesi, and Dino Mandrioli, editors, *FME 2003: Formal Methods*, LNCS 2805, pages 855–874. Springer-Verlag, 2003.
3. Bram De Wachter. *dSL, a Language and Environment for the Design of Distributed Industrial Controllers.* Dissertation, Université Libre de Bruxelles, December 2005.

BE⁴: The B Extensible Eclipse Editing Environment*

Jens Bendisposto and Michael Leuschel

Heinrich-Heine Universität Düsseldorf
{bendisposto,leuschel}@cs.uni-duesseldorf.de

1 Introduction

The open-source Eclipse platform[1] has become hugely popular as an integrated development environment for Java, and a considerable number of plug-ins have been developed for other programming languages (e.g., C++,PHP, Eiffel, Python, Fortran, etc.). In this paper we present a new plug-in for Eclipse, supporting the B-method and B's abstract machine notation (AMN) [1]. In addition to providing editing and syntax highlighting, the plug-in displays syntax and structural errors in the B source code, as well as suggesting fixes for those errors.

2 Building a Document Object Model from B

The centerpiece of a semantic-aware editor for programming languages is a parser that generates a model from source-code. In Eclipse, a parser can be integrated by creating a plug-in that extends *org.eclipse.core.resources.builders*. Because we want to allow later contributions to the parser from other plug-ins, we decided to build a multi-phase parsing framework for B projects (Fig. 1).

Table 1. Parser phases

Phase	Objective
I	Create and modify the syntax tree
II	Run file based build tools
III	Analyze all resources
IV	Run tools to decorate the models

For each phase it is guaranteed, that all tools from a previous phase have finished their work. Since Phases I and II work on a file basis, it is possible that the builder[2] for file1 is in Phase II and for file2 in Phase I.

---

* This research is partially being carried out within the EU research project: IST 511599 RODIN (Rigorous Open Development Environment for Complex Systems).

[1] http://www.eclipse.org/

[2] A builder is a tool that runs every time a project is being rebuilt.

J. Julliand and O. Kouchnarenko (Eds.): B 2007, LNCS 4355, pp. 270–273, 2006.

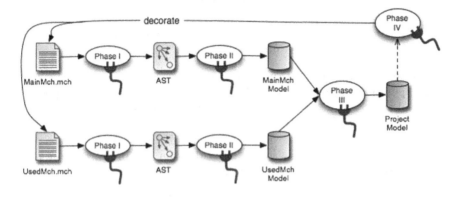

Fig. 1. Phases of the building framework

Phase I generates an abstract syntax tree (AST) from a B file. This is done by applying a modified version of Tatibouet's jbtools [6] Parser. If the AST-Generator completes its work without error, then other plug-ins can be called. For example, one of our extensions to Phase I checks if the name of the component matches the filename and if the type of the component matches the file extension. Any plug-in that modifies the syntax tree should be run in this phase, that means that in the second phase the syntax tree is stable.

Phase II contains file based builders that must not modify the syntax tree, but can create abstractions of the syntax tree or other artifacts. For instance, our standard builder creates a simplified syntax tree that is easier to handle for some of the editor views (like the outline view). Tools in Phase II run if and only if the AST-Generator completed its work without an error.

Phase III runs on all resources even when some AST generation failed. This phase can be used to perform a "global analysis". Currently, our standard builder uses this phase to check if all dependencies (SEES, INCLUDES, etc.) are being satisfied. In future, we also plan to check the structuring guidelines from [5].

Phase IV must not modify the model in any way, it contains plug-ins that only read from the model and update other parts of the plug-ins. For example, our builder uses the final phase to update some properties of the so called markers³.

In Phase I - III it is also possible to give dependencies for a tool. For example, if a tool C relies on the output of tool A and B it is possible to specify this dependency in the extension configuration. If the dependencies do not contain cycles, the building framework will automatically generate an order via topological sorting.

Our architecture was designed for extensibility by new, as of yet unknown, plug-ins (without this requirement, a simple dependency graph of the various tools would have been sufficient).

---

³ http://www.eclipse.org/articles/Article-Mark My Words/mark-my-words.html

3   Using the Model for Editing B

The model created by the parser can be used for several tasks; so far we have implemented the following features:

- **Context based completion:** Since the editor knows if the user types within an operation or the machine's head, it can choose different proposals to complete the word the user types[4]. In addition, we support templates that contain parts to be filled by the user.
- **Hover information:** The Editor is aware of the token the mouse points to and can display information about that token. For instance, if the mouse points to the token $\backslash/$, the editor displays the information "$S \backslash/ T$: *union of sets S and T*" as a hover text.
- **Error Displaying and Correction:** (Syntax) Errors are caught and displayed directly in the source code window (line 1 and 18 in Fig. 2) and additionally in a special "Problems view". As shown in the screenshot, the editor supports auto-correction.[5] Based on the error it determines a set of actions called quick-fixes that might be applied to correct the error.
- **Outline view:** The editor produces an outline view of the machine, e.g., the variables used, the operations defined, etc. If the user clicks on any item in the outline, the editor jumps to the line, where the item is being defined.

4   Related and Future Work

The BZ testing tool (BZTT) [3] as well as PROB [4] provide simple editing and highlighting, but lack the features of a dedicated editing/development tool. The EmacsPri[6] and the more recent Click'N'Prove [2] by Dominique Cansell and J.-R. Abrial provide syntax highlighting and an interface to AtelierB within Emacs. Bruno Tatibouet's jbtools package [6] also contains a B plug-in for the Java-based Editor jEdit, with syntax-highlighting, type checking and a shortcut pane for the mathematical symbols.

Finally, the Rodin EventB (BSharp) Toolkit[7] is also developed within Eclipse, but has moved away from an ASCII AMN encoding to an internal storage in an XML database of the components of B machines, which can be manipulated directly by various graphical editors. It is actually our goal to combine these two Eclipse plug-ins, so as to also allow editing of EventB components in AMN as well as linking PROB directly to the Rodin EventB core and the associated provers. We are also working on integration of refactorings into the editor, as well as more semantic checks and quick-fixes. Our tool is available from http://www.stups.uni-duesseldorf.de/ProB/be4.

---

[4] As in Java mode, the autocompletion can be invoked typing **CTRL+SPACE**.
[5] **CTRL+1** invokes the auto-correction.
[6] http://www.atelierb.societe.com/emacspri/emacspri_uk.html
[7] http://sourceforge.net/projects/rodin-b-sharp/

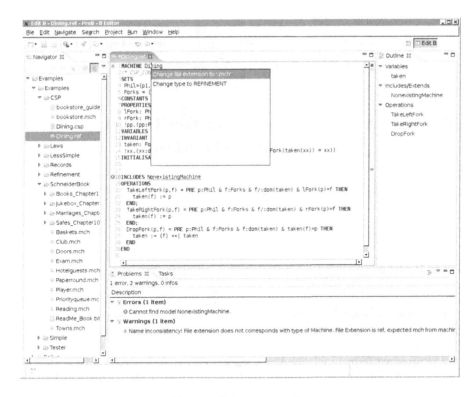

Fig. 2. B-Editor screenshot

References

1. J.-R. Abrial. *The B-Book*. Cambridge University Press, 1996.
2. J.-R. Abrial and D. Cansell. Click'n prove: Interactive proofs within set theory. In D. A. Basin and B. Wolff, editors, *TPHOLs*, volume 2758 of *Lecture Notes in Computer Science*, pages 1–24. Springer, 2003.
3. B. Legeard, F. Peureux, and M. Utting. Automated boundary testing from Z and B. In *Proceedings FME'02*, LNCS 2391, pages 21–40. Springer-Verlag, 2002.
4. M. Leuschel and M. Butler. ProB: A model checker for B. In K. Araki, S. Gnesi, and D. Mandrioli, editors, *FME 2003: Formal Methods*, LNCS 2805, pages 855–874. Springer-Verlag, 2003.
5. M.-L. Potet and Y. Rouzaud. Composition and refinement in the b-method. In D. Bert, editor, *B*, volume 1393 of *Lecture Notes in Computer Science*, pages 46–65. Springer, 1998.
6. B. Tatibouet. The jbtools package. Available at http://lifc.univ-fcomte.fr/PEOPLE/tatibouet/JBTOOLS/BParser_en.html, 2001.

BRAMA: A New Graphic Animation Tool for B Models
Clearsy - 2007 B Conference

Thierry Servat

Clearsy System Engineering

Introduction

Clearsy is an engineering company specialized in system dependability.

It verifies the concepts and tools required to create secure systems and uses formal techniques to define, design and validate systems, then create critical software for their integration.

The principal formal tools used by Clearsy to create, refine and prove models are the *Atelier B and B4free,* and *CompoSys* to create formal system models and related documentation.

Based on our various experiments using formal tools in an industrial setting and our desire to disseminate formal methods, we have imagined a new approach to present models to our customers. The Brama tool supports this approach.

The objective of this document is to explain the approach and related Brama tool.

Context: The Need to Validate Models

Method B is often used in industrial settings to create proven secure software in the context of SIL 4 level certification pursuant to the 61508 standard.

It has now been used for a few years to model systems.

This new practice has revealed a deficiency.

When you want to specify a system, you need to:

- Know what you want
- Ensure the feasibility of what you want.

Modeling and proof activities reveal specification issues. This is the very point of modeling. An advantage of the B method is it is based on mathematics and therefore allows for specifications to be written with unparalleled precision.

However, we discovered that, when faced with a model, our customers, and in general those who did not write the model, have difficulty in understanding it, on the one hand, and, on the other, have difficulty in affirming that the model represents the system.

The completeness and quality of the model are therefore problematic.

J. Julliand and O. Kouchnarenko (Eds.): B 2007, LNCS 4355, pp. 274–276, 2006.

Translation of Models into Natural Language

A first response to the issue of B model comprehension was provided by Clearsy with its offer of the ComposSys tool, allowing the modeler to prepare model documentation at the same time as the model. This allows the user to automatically produce a model translation, with various graphic views of dependencies between the different system components. The documentation in natural language is an accurate reflection of the model and may be read "easily" by all to ensure the model matches the system.

Animation to "Test" Models

The Brama model animation tool provides a further response as it may be used by the modeler throughout the modeling process. The animation functions allow him to "create" various model events, filters and properties; he can "test" the model.

Graphic Visualization of the System

A third means consists in using the model to graphically view the system in specific operational contexts.

This approach consists in offering the model's author tools that allow for:

- The representation by graphic drawings and animations of the system and its different types of states
- "Linking" these drawings and animations to different events and B model B variables
- Representation by buttons of the various interactions of the elements external to the system and re-actualization of the system's graphic representation in accordance with these interactions.

The model is therefore not shown to the client. The system's graphic representation is presented, as it is based on the B model itself.

More Details on the Brama Tool

The modeler creates B models with Atelier B, B4free or the Rodin platform, then uses the Brama animation tool that in turn uses these models.

Brama was designed to communicate with Flash tools configured with a communication extension that is delivered with Brama.

The modeler's task consists in representing his system with the Flash tools and configuring scripts that allow for communication with the Brama animation engine.

When the user is satisfied, Brama lets him export the finished animation in the form of files which, once saved on a CD, will launch the graphic animation without prior installation and on any PC using Windows or Linux.

Brama is presented as an Eclipse plug-in suite and Flash extension that can be used with Windows and Linux.

Brama contains the following principal modules: BtoRodin: an animation engine (predicate solver), event and B variable visualization tools, an automatic event linkage management module, a variable management module, observed predicates and expressions, and a Flash communication module.

Examples and Feedback

The first examples were developed on the basis of experimental models: mechanical press, island/continent road traffic, locks, switches, verification of Ariane's nozzles.

The work on these samples demonstrated the deficiencies present in the analyzed models and confirmed the value of visualizing the system to better ensure model reliability.

This graphic representation work is not burdensome: approximately one week to perfect the animation of a model created over two months. The largest model represents 450 events and 17 refinement levels.

Distribution: In Beta Test on the Rodin Platform

Brama tools will be made available in Beta test. They can be used from the Open Source Rodin modeling platform.

A converter allows for the transformation of existing B models to this platform's format.

The Future

The model animation interface requires improvement. For the time being, the Brama tool is used most often to create graphic animations for existing models.

LEIRIOS Test Generator: Automated Test Generation from B Models

Eddie Jaffuel[1] and Bruno Legeard[1,2]

[1] LEIRIOS Technologies
TEMIS Innovation - 18 Rue Alain Savary - 25000 Besançon, France
{eddie.jaffuel,bruno.legeard}@leirios.com
http://www.leirios.com
[2] University of Franche-Comté
LIFC - 16 route de Gray - 25000 Besançon, France
legeard@lifc.univ-fcomte.fr
http://lifc.univ-fcomte.fr

1 Introduction

Since 2003, automated test generation from B abstract machines has been trying out in the smart card industry, using LEIRIOS Test Generator (LTG) for Smart-Card tool. Now the major card manufacturers, such as Gemalto and Giesecke & Devrient, are regularly deploying model-based testing in their validation processes. The purpose is black-box functional testing: from the specifications (a standard or specific requirements), a B formal model is developed which is the basis for test generation. Generated test cases are then translated into executable test scripts and then run on the application.

This summary gives the main lessons of experience from these large experiments of automated test generation using B abstract machines [1, 2] for smart card applications [3]. We analyze the effectiveness of B modeling for testing, the way for controlling test case explosion from the formal model [4], the translation of generated test cases in executable test scripts [5]and the integration of this new approach in the validation process. In the sequel of this abstract, we first introduce the test generation process and then we discuss these various issues.

2 Test Generation Process

The test generation process (see figure 1) is structured in five main stages:

1. **Formal model development:** The application under test is specified with a B abstract machine [6], which has a state space (consisting of several state variables) and several operations that are specified via preconditions and post-conditions. Usually, for smart card software, each operation corresponds to an APDU or API of the application. The model abstraction level depends directly on the overall test objectives.
2. **Formal model validation:** The B abstract machine is validated using the LTG symbolic animator. It makes it possible to animate use cases and, step by step, to verify the invariant properties.

J. Julliand and O. Kouchnarenko (Eds.): B 2007, LNCS 4355, pp. 277–280, 2006.

3. **Test case generation:** From the model, the test cases are generated by covering all the symbolic execution paths for all operations with input parameter boundary values. Therefore, a test case is a sequence of operation (APDU) invocations structured in a preamble, a body and a postamble to automatically link several test cases. Each operation call provides the expected results for test verdict assignment. Various model coverage criteria help the test engineer to control the test generation.

4. **Test script generation:** Previously generated abstract test cases are then translated in executable test scripts using the format of the targeted test execution environment. This process is fully automated, using a data dictionary to give the mapping between abstract names (from the model) and concrete names (used in the test execution environment).

5. **Test execution and verdict assignment:** The tests are run with the test execution environment, successively on the simulator platform and then on the card itself. Each test case includes expected results and the verdict is automatically computed.

More details on the LTG test generation strategy can be found in the book "Practical Model-Based Testing - A Tools Approach" [7].

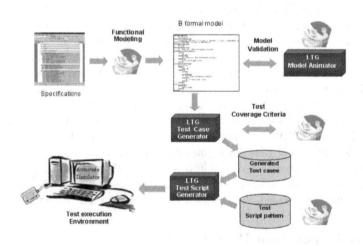

Fig. 1. Test Generation Process

3   B Modeling for Model-Based Testing

LTG for Smartcard tool uses the B abstract machine notation as modeling notation. Here, B machines are used to formalize models that provide the expected behavior of the system under test.

There are four main steps to writing a B model for model-based testing:

1. Choose a high-level test objective.
2. Design the signatures of the operations in the model.
3. Design the state variables of the model and choose their types.
4. Write the precondition and action part of each operation.

As we discuss each of these steps, we shall see that the central theme that runs through them all is how to choose a good level of abstraction for the model. The goal is to have just enough detail in the model to be able to generate test inputs and check the correctness of outputs, while avoiding unnecessary detail that would make the model larger and more complex.

The **first step** is to choose a high-level test objective that says which aspects of the SUT we want to test. For example, if we are testing the software for a GPS navigation system in a vehicle, we might decide that we want to test just its position tracking capabilities (including its interaction with the GPS satellites, the car speedometer and gyroscope). Alternatively, we might decide that we want to test just its route planning capabilities. The B models for these two alternatives would be quite different, since they would be modeling different aspects of the navigation system. The generated tests would also be quite different, since they would use different subsets of the control and observation ports of the GPS navigation system. While it would be possible to write a single B model to test both these aspects at once, this would be undesirable, because the model would be much more complex, so test generation would be more difficult and we could get a useless combinatorial explosion between the position tracking and route planning functions when computing test cases. Whenever possible, it is preferable to use separate B abstract machines to test different aspects of a system.

The **second step** is to decide which control and observation ports of the SUT we need to use to satisfy our high-level test objective, and how those ports should be mapped into operations of the B model. As well as choosing a name for each model operation, we must also decide what input and output parameters it will have. The input parameters will correspond to the inputs to the SUT control ports, while the output parameters will correspond to the output from the SUT observation ports. Typically, the operations of the model will match the control and observation ports of the SUT quite closely.

The **third step** is to design the data structures that will be used within the model. This involves choosing some state variables for the model, with an appropriate data type for each variable. The goal here is for the model to record just enough of the internal state of the SUT to make it possible to check the correctness of its outputs.

The **fourth step** is to write the preconditions and action part of each operation. We start by putting the typing conditions of the inputs into the preconditions. For example, the signature may define size:int, but we actually want to limit the inputs to size < 100, or say that size must be less than the length of some other input. These kinds of constraints go into the precondition, so that we only generate test inputs that satisfy these constraints. The action part of each operation represents the expected behavior of the system under test depending with the abstraction level and the test objectives.

4   Lessons of Experience

- **Modeling for testing with B abstract machines** is cost effective: We show on several applications (see [7]) that the automatic test generation process was 30% lower cost than a classical, manually test design process, including the cost for modeling. Moreover, we show that functional test coverage was always higher with the automated test generation process.
- **Model coverage criteria help to control test case explosion:** The test generation strategy is based on model coverage principles (cause-effect and boundary testing). The test engineer drives the test generation using various criteria like multiple-conditions coverage, boundary values coverage and effect coverage. Therefore, the tester can control the number of generated test cases with these criteria.
- **Automated test generation is not disruptive for the overall development process:** The generated test scripts have the same format than the classical one. The existing tools, like Test execution environment and version management are used to execute generated test cases and stored it.

References

[1] B. Legeard, F. Peureux, and M. Utting. Automated boundary testing from Z and B. In *Proc. of the Int. Conf. on Formal Methods Europe, FME'02*, volume 2391 of *LNCS*, pages 21–40, Copenhaguen, Denmark, July 2002. Springer.

[2] F. Ambert, F. Bouquet, S. Chemin, S. Guenaud, B. Legeard, F. Peureux, N. Vacelet, and M. Utting. BZ-TT: A tool-set for test generation from Z and B using constraint logic programming. In *Proc. of Formal Approaches to Testing of Software, FATES 2002 (workshop of CONCUR'02)*, pages 105–120, Brnö, République Tchèque, August 2002. INRIA report.

[3] E. Bernard, B. Legeard, X. Luck, and F. Peureux. Generation of test sequences from formal specifications: GSM 11-11 standard case study. *International Journal of Software Practice and Experience*, 34(10):915–948, 2004.

[4] B. Legeard, F. Peureux, and M. Utting. Controlling test case explosion in test generation from B formal models. *Software Testing, Verification and Reliability, STVR*, 14(2):81–103, 2004.

[5] F. Bouquet and B. Legeard. Reification of executable test scripts in formal specification-based test generation: The java card transaction mechanism case study. In *Proc. of FME'03, Formal Method Europe*, volume 2805 of *LNCS*, pages 778–795, Pisa, Italy, September 2003.

[6] S. Schneider. *The B-Method - An Introduction*. 2001. 370 pages, ISBN 0-333-79284-X.

[7] M. Utting and B. Legeard. *Practical Model-Based Testing - A Tools Approach*. 2006. 528 pages, ISBN 0-12-372501-1.

Meca: A Tool for Access Control Models

Amal Haddad

LSR-IMAG, Grenoble, France
Amal.Haddad@imag.fr

1 Introduction of Meca

Access Control is a technique which insures security by preserving confidentiality and integrity of information. Meca (Models for access control) is a tool which generates, in a B machine, operational conditions that should be verified by an application to insure security.

The inputs of Meca are a B machine offering a format for presenting a security model and a functional model containing the presentation of an application with its sensitive entities like variables and operations. The format of a security model provides a declarative representation of the access distribution in the system at a given moment. It is done according to various models related to three branches policies: discretionary policies model (DAC)[4], Bell and LaPadula model (BLP) [1], Biba model (Biba) [2] and role based access control model (RBAC) [3]. Meca generates access rules in a B machine called security kernel. Security kernel offers secure services under witch sensitive entities of functional model can be manipulated. The format of the security kernel varies depending of the security policy model type.

In access control scope, Objects are passive entities that represent system resources and should be protected. Subjects are active entities accessing to objects and possessing rights to manipulate them. Figure 1 presents Meca with his inputs and outputs components.

We illustrate our approach and Meca with a small part of a bank card example.

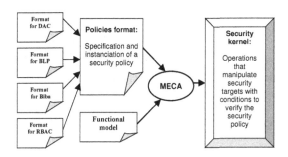

Fig. 1. MECA schema

J. Julliand and O. Kouchnarenko (Eds.): B 2007, LNCS 4355, pp. 281–284, 2006.

2   Use Case and the Functional Model

The bank card is a smart card with an electronic purse. As the other smart cards [5], the purse can be debited from a terminal in a shop to pay a purchase and credited at an ATM from a cash or by withdrawing from a bank account. There are three different hierarchical levels to operate the purse: debiting the purse, crediting the purse from cash or from a bank account and performing administrative operations. With these three access levels correspond three kind of terminals from which the purse can be manipulated: a terminal in a shop for debiting the purse, a bank terminal for crediting the purse and an administration terminal for updating configuration parameters. We note that any operation allowed on a specific level is allowed on lower levels.

During its life cycle, the card passes through different operating modes load, use or invalid. When the card is in the load mode, its issuer (the bank) records the holder pin code (hpc). We present the specification of SetHPC operation in the functional model:

MACHINE *BankCard*
SETS
   $MODE=\{load, invalid, use\}$
CONSTANTS
   HPC
PROPERTIES
   $HPC = 0000 .. 9999$ /*pin has four digits*/
ABSTRACT_VARIABLES
   mode,hpc
INVARIANT
   $mode \in MODE \wedge hpc \in HPC$ /*variable hpc is typed in the invariant*/
INITIALISATION
   $hpc := 1000 \parallel mode := load$
OPERATIONS
   setHPC$(pin) =$
      PRE
         $pin \in \textbf{INT} \wedge pin \in HPC \wedge mode = load$
      THEN
         $hpc := pin$
      END
END

Thereafter, we present the second entry component for Meca, it is the format for the security model.

3   Policies Format

As a part of our work, we deal with three models of security policies: The access matrix model (belonging to DAC policies), Bell Lapadula model (BLP), Biba model (belonging to MAC policies) and Role Based Model (RBAC). We will give a short definition about each of these policies. In the scope of discretionary policies (DAC), access control on objects is granted to their creator. Access permissions are read and write [4]. Mandatory policies (MAC) provide a classification for subjects and objects. According to this classification, read and write operations are allowed to preserve secrecy (BLP model) [1] or integrity of information (Biba model) [2]. The originality of role based access control policies (RBAC) is that they introduce role concept that intercepts permissions, subjects and objects [3]. Permissions are granted to roles. Subjects obtain permissions according to roles that they hold. Permissions are operations that could be executed on objects. Roles inherit between each others permissions and users [6]. We will give a detailed account of RBAC instanciated with bank card example. The aim is to safeguard security when the card is manipulated from various terminals.

MACHINE *rbac_format_BankCard*
SETS
  SUJET $=\{shop\_terminal, bank\_terminal, admin\_terminal\}$;
  ROLE $=\{debit, credit, admin\ \}$;
  PERMISSION $=\{OP\_\ checkHPC, OP\_setHPC, OP\_\ debitPurse,$
  $OP\_creditPurse\}$
CONSTANTS
  sujet_role, role_permission, herite_de
PROPERTIES
  sujet_role $\in$ *SUJET* $\rightarrow$ *ROLE*
  $\wedge$ *role_permission* $\in$ *ROLE* $\leftrightarrow$ *PERMISSION*
  $\wedge$ *herite_de* $\in$ *ROLE* $\leftrightarrow$ *ROLE*
  $\wedge$ *closure1 (herite_de)* $\cap$ *id (ROLE)* $= \emptyset$
  $\wedge$ *sujet_role* $= \{(shop\_terminal \mapsto debit),$
  $(bank\_terminal \mapsto credit), (admin\_terminal \mapsto admin)\}$
  $\wedge$ *role_permission* $= \{(admin \mapsto OP\_setHPC),$
  $(credit \mapsto OP\_creditPurse), (debit \mapsto OP\_debitPurse),$
  $(debit \mapsto OP\_checkHPC)\}$
  $\wedge$ *herite_de* $= \{(admin \mapsto credit), (credit \mapsto debit)\}$
END

The entities represented in bold are fixed by Meca format while those in simple depend on the application. A commentary introduced in the header component announces for Meca the security model used.

The set PERMISSION refers to operations of the application. Subjects are terminals. Roles are various levels that exist. The relation sujet_role is the association between a subject and a role. In this example we suppose that a subject can have only one role. Role_permission is the association between a role and one or several permissions. The hierarchy is presented by the relation called herite_de. We use constants to present these sets since we don´t deal with updating access distribution. The prefix OP_ is used for operations in order to avoid names clash with functional component.

4   The Generated Security Kernel

The security kernel is the component that contains conditions that should be verified to insure the respect of security. This kernel is produced according to access rules that govern each model type of security policy. Thereafter, we present security kernel for RBAC format.

Meca generates for every operation, that belongs to set PERMISSION of RBAC format, a new predicate to control access. SetHPC operation becomes:

setHPC $(pin, su) =$
   PRE
      $pin \in$ **INT** $\wedge\ pin \in HPC \wedge\ mode = invalid$
      $\wedge\ su \in SUJET$
      $\wedge\ (sujet\_role(su), OP\_setHPC):(\textbf{closure}(herite\_de);$
      $role\_permission)$
   THEN
      $hpc := pin$
   END

This mechanism reinforces the precondition of each operation that should be performed by a specific role. The generated component should be used instead of the old functional model. Hence, whenever SetHPC is called its precondition should be satisfied.

5   Contribution and Future Works

Our contribution is materialised by the approach to introduce security in the development of certified products. The security kernel could be used in the scope of a static verification (by B proofs) to reason about the security of an application. In a sooner future work, we will exploit the use of the security kernel for a validation with tests. In the scope of Meca, we formalize also model for security policies. We are now interested to develop object oriented security models and to formalize it in the B method. This is done in the scope of POSE project (http:/wwwrntl-pose.info/).

References

1. D. E. Bell and L. J. Lapadula. Secure computer systems: A mathematical model. Technical report esd-tr-278, vol. 2, The Mitre Corporation, Bedford, 1973.
2. K. J. Biba. Integrity considerations for secure computer systems. Technical report tr-3153, The Mitre Corporation, Bedford, 1997.
3. D. F. Ferraiolo and D. R. Kuhn. Role based access control. In *15th National Computer Security Conference*, 1992.
4. Butler W. Lampson. Protection. In *5th Princeton Symposium on Information Science and Systems*, pages 437–443, 1971.
5. Renaud Marlet and Cédric Mesnil. A demonstrative electronic purse -Card specification-. pages 1–53, 2002.
6. R.S. Sandhu. Role hierarchies and constraints for lattice-bases access controls. *Lecture Notes in Computer Science*, 1146:65–79, 1996.

JML2B: Checking JML Specifications with B Machines

Fabrice Bouquet, Frédéric Dadeau, and Julien Groslambert

Laboratoire d'Informatique (LIFC)
Université de Franche-Comté, CNRS - INRIA Cassis Project
16, route de Gray - 25030 Besançon cedex, France
{bouquet, dadeau, groslambert}@lifc.univ-fcomte.fr

Abstract. This paper introduces a tool, named JML2B, destined to check the consistency of JML specifications. JML2B is a solution to the lack of tool-support for the JML models verification. Our tool translates JML specifications into the B abstract machines notation. The generated B machines can then be checked to ensure their correctness. When the proof fails, it is possible to retrieve the mistakes in the original JML specification.

1 Introduction

In recent years, the Java Modeling Language –JML– [5] has been introduced to act as a behavioral interface specification language to formally describe Java programs. Since its syntax is close to Java, this specification language may even be used by non-specialists of modeling.

Nevertheless, most of the JML-related tools [1] concentrate on ensuring the conformance of the Java code w.r.t. the JML annotations. But the verification of a JML model itself, to the best of our knowledge, is not tool-supported. Since we want to use JML as a modeling language, we would like to be able to easily prove the correctness of the JML model, without taking account to the Java code.

Therefore, we introduce a tool, named JML2B[1], which provides a solution to the verification of JML specifications, by rewriting them into semantically equivalent B machines. This tool is the implementation of the formal work presented in [2].

2 Java Modeling Language

The Java Modeling Language was introduced by Leavens et al. at the Iowa State University [5]. This specification language, describing Java modules behavior, aims at being used by developers as well as by specifiers. The JML annotations are embedded within Java comments by using //@ for a single-line annotation

---

[1] The JML2B tool is freely available at:
http://lifc.univ-fcomte.fr/~{}groslambert/JML2B

J. Julliand and O. Kouchnarenko (Eds.): B 2007, LNCS 4355, pp. 285–288, 2006.

```
class Purse {                          /*@ public normal_behavior
   //@ invariant balance >= 0;          @  requires p != null && p != this
   protected short balance;             @  assignable balance;
                                        @  ensures balance == p.getBalance();
   /*@ public normal_behavior           @*/
    @   requires amount >= 0;          public void transfer(Purse p) {...}
    @   assignable balance;
    @   ensures balance == amount;      /*@ public behavior
    @*/                                  @  requires amount >= 0;
   public Purse(short amount) {...}      @  assignable balance;
                                        @  ensures
   /*@ public normal_behavior           @     balance == \old(balance) + amount;
    @   requires amount >= 0;           @  signals (NoCreditException E1)
    @   assignable balance;             @     balance == \old(balance)
    @   ensures                         @     && s > amount
    @      balance == \old(balance) + amount;    @*/
    @*/                                public void withdraw(short amount)
   public void credit(short amount) {...}        throws NoCreditException {...}}
                                      }
```

Fig. 1. JML specification of a Purse

and /*@ ... @*/ for multiple-lines annotations. Moreover, the JML syntax is based on the Java syntax for expressing predicates, enriched with several new operators and keywords.

The example presented in Fig. 1 specifies a simplified electronic purse. The Purse class describes a basic purse, managing only one attribute named balance representing the amount of money available in the considered purse. An JML invariant specifies that this attributes must be greater than zero. This property must hold for each *visible* state of the model, i.e., before and after each method execution.

The constructor specification is given with the normal_behavior keyword. The requires clause defines a precondition that must be true before when the constructor is invoked. The assignable clause expresses the frame condition, i.e., the attributes modified by the method (here balance) and the ensures clause defines a condition that must be true at the end of the execution. In the case of the constructor of Purse(short), the attribute balance must be assigned to 0. The credit(short) method is used to add money to the purse, whereas the withdraw(short) method removes money from the purse. Notice that this latter may possibly throw an exception named NoCreditException, specified by the signals clause, when there is not enough money in the purse. Finally, the transfer(Purse) method makes it possible to transfer the amount contained in the purse in parameter into the current purse.

3 Tool Presentation

JML2B is a compiler that translates the JML files into the B formalism. It produces as an output abstract machines, that can be used with the usual tools supporting the B notation (AtelierB, ProB, BZ-Testing-Tools, B4Free, Balbulette). Running provers on these machines makes it possible to check the coherence of the original JML model.

By running the tool JML2B of the file Purse.java, two B machines are generated: (i) global.mch (given in [2]) and (ii) Purse.mch displayed in Fig. 2.

```
MACHINE Purse                                   {this ↦ assigned_balance}
INCLUDES global                            END
CONSTANTS exc_NoCreditException            END;
PROPERTIES                              ...
   exc_NoCreditException ∈ EXCEPTIONS   b_Purse_withdraw_short(this, b_amount) ≘
   ∧ exc_NoCreditException ≠ no_exception   PRE
VARIABLES                                    this ∈ b_PurseInstances
   b_PurseInstances, b_Purse_balance         ∧ b_amount ∈ -32768..32767 ∧
INVARIANT                                    b_amount ≥ 0 ∧ exception = no_exception
   /* Purse class expression */           THEN
   b_PurseInstances ⊆ instances ∧         CHOICE
   b_Purse_balance ∈                        ANY assigned_balance
       b_PurseInstances ⟶  -32768..32767 ∧     WHERE
   /* Purse class invariant */                assigned_balance ∈ -32768..32767 ∧
   (∀xx_inv.(xx_inv ∈ b_PurseInstances         b_amount ≤ b_Purse_balance(this) ∧
     ⇒ b_Purse_balance(xx_inv)≥0))             assigned_balance =
INITIALISATION                                     b_Purse_balance(this) - b_amount
   b_PurseInstances := {} ||                THEN
   b_Purse_balance := {}                      b_Purse_balance(this) :=
OPERATIONS                                         assigned_balance
b_Purse_constructorPurse_short(this,b_amount) ≘   END
   PRE                                    OR
       this ∈ INSTANCES - instances ∧       ANY assigned_balance
       this ≠ null ∧                        WHERE
       b_amount ∈ -32768..32767 ∧             assigned_balance ∈ -32768..32767 ∧
       b_amount ≥ 0 ∧                         assigned_balance =
       exception = no_exception                 b_Purse_balance(this)
   THEN                                      THEN
       ANY assigned_balance                   b_Purse_balance(this) :=
       WHERE assigned_balance = b_amount          assigned_balance
       THEN                                   || throw(exc_NoCreditException)
           new({this}) ||                   END
           b_PurseInstances :=            END
               b_PurseInstances ∪ {this} ||   END;
           b_Purse_balance :=             ...
               b_Purse_balance ∪
```

Fig. 2. Extract of the machine Purse.mch

(i) The machine global.mch manages two Java mechanism, that are not related
    to classes but to the language itself.
    – *object management.* An abstract set of addresses named INSTANCES rep-
      resents of the memory heap. A variable, named instances, subset of
      INSTANCES designates the used addresses in the heap. A constant, named
      null, represents a null pointer. The operation new permits to allocate a
      new address.
    – *exception management.* Exceptions described in the specifications are
      referenced in an abstract set, named EXCEPTIONS and a variable named
      exception specifies which exception is currently thrown. Two operations
      represent the throwing or the catching of exceptions.
(ii) The machine Purse.mch represents the class Purse itself. Details and sound-
     ness proof of the translation are given in [2]. It must be intuitively understood
     as follows.
     (a) A variable b_PurseInstances, subset of INSTANCES is declared to rep-
         resent the set of the instances of Purse. A variable b_Purse_balance,
         mapping the instances of Purse to the B representation of the short
         integers, represents the attributes balance.

(b) Each JML invariant is expressed as a B invariant containing a universal quantification over the instances of the class.
(c) Each method is translated by an operation having at least one parameter representing the instance on which the method is invoked.
(d) The precondition of the operation is composed of the typing predicate of the parameters and a translation of the precondition.
(e) The assignable clause and the ensures clause are translated into an ANY...WHERE...THEN...END substitution.
(f) In case of a constructor, the new operation is called to allocate the heap memory. In case of exceptional postcondition (signals clause) the operation throw is called.

The JML2B tool as been experimented on the example illustrating this paper, but also on the 500 lines JML model of an industrial case study. The B models generated from the industrial case study produced 157 proof obligations, 100% were automatically discharged by the B4Free prover.

4 Conclusion and Future Work

In this paper, we have described JML2B, a tool implementing the work presented in [2], consisting in expressing JML specifications with B abstract machines, and therefore using all the B verification tools to prove the model. We have successfully used on an industrial case study that has further been used to automatically generate tests [3]. Most of the JML tools aim at validating or proving the implementation with respect to the model. Our tool is different but complements them, since it permits to detect model inconsistencies before trying to prove the implementation. One important point is that our translation generates human-readable B specifications, so unchecked proof obligations messages may easily be transposed back into the original JML specifications to provide an assistance for the writing of correct JML models. However, one interesting future work is to automate this task, and then, try to automatically find a counter-example by symbolic animation with JML-Testing-Tools symbolic animator (see [4]).

References

1. L. Burdy, Y. Cheon, D. Cok, M. Ernst, J. Kiniry, G.T. Leavens, K.R.M. Leino, and E. Poll. An overview of JML tools and applications. In *FMICS 03*, volume 80 of *ENTCS*, pages 73–89. Elsevier, 2003.
2. F. Bouquet, F. Dadeau, and J. Groslambert. Checking JML specifications with B machines. In *ZB'05,LNCS* 3455, pages 435–454. Springer, 2005.
3. F. Bouquet, F. Dadeau, J. Groslambert, and J. Julliand. Safety property driven test generation from JML specifications. In *FATES/RV'06*, LNCS 4262, pages 225–239. Springer-Verlag, 2006. To appear.
4. F. Bouquet, F. Dadeau, B. Legeard, and M. Utting. Symbolic animation of JML specifications. In *FM'2005*, LNCS. Springer-Verlag, 2005.
5. G.T. Leavens, A.L. Baker, and C Ruby. JML: A notation for detailed design. *Behavioral Specifications of Businesses and Systems*, pages 175–188. Kluwer, 1999.

Plug-and-Play Nondeterminacy

(Extended Abstract⋆)

Joseph M. Morris

School of Computing
Dublin City University
Ireland
and
Lero – the Irish Software Engineering Research Centre
Joseph.Morris@computing.dcu.ie

Nondeterminacy occurs commonly in computing, much more than we recognise. Indeed it deserves to be recognised as a fundamental notion, meriting a place alongside other fundamental notions such as algorithm, recursion, data type, concurrency, object, etc. Essentially the same notion of nondeterminacy manifests itself in a range of different contexts, among them imperative, functional, and concurrent programming, competing agents, data refinement, and fixpoint theory. Nondeterminacy can be recognised, extracted, and studied in isolation such that the properties we discover are applicable more-or-less without change in the various domains in which it occurs.

The status of nondeterminacy is analogous to recursion as it occurs in programming.

1. At the language level, programmers reason about recursion using two logical rules, typically called the *unfolding* rule and the *induction* rule. Analogously, nondeterminacy can be presented as a set of axioms that allows programmers to understand it intuitively or to formally verify nondeterministic code.

2. The rules of recursion are justified "under the hood" by a mathematical theory of *fixpoints on complete partial orders* that guarantees that the rules are sound. Similarly, nondeterminacy can be justified by an under-the-hood theory, in this case that of *free completely distributed lattices over a poset*.

3. The basic theory of recursion is fundamental in that it is applicable across many programming paradigms, with local "wiring in" to each host language. Similarly, the axioms of nondeterminacy account for nondeterminacy in many paradigms, with some local wiring in.

4. Formally, recursion is defined in terms of two operators, μ and ν corresponding to least and greatest fixpoints, respectively, together with a partial ordering relation. Analogously, nondeterminacy is described in terms of two choice operators $\sqcap$ and $\sqcup$, together with a partial ordering relation $\sqsubseteq$ (called the *refinement order*).

⋆ This extended abstract of an invited talk has been included in late-stage editing.

J. Julliand and O. Kouchnarenko (Eds.): B 2007, LNCS 4355, pp. 289–292, 2006.

For example, the function specified informally as "Given a name n and a phone book b return a phone number for n" can be expressed as

$$\lambda n{:}Name, b{:}PhoneBook \cdot \textstyle\bigcap\{x{:}PhoneNumber \mid (n, x) \in b\}$$

Here, $\bigcap S$, where S denotes a set of elements of some type T, is a term of type T and denotes *some* element of S nondeterministically chosen.

$\bigsqcup S$ also represents a nondeterministic choice over set S. The two choice operators and refinement are intimately related, e.g. they satisfy the classic lattice-theoretic relationship $t \sqsubseteq u \Leftrightarrow t \sqcap u = t \Leftrightarrow t \sqcup u = u$ where $\sqcap$ and $\sqcup$ are the binary infix versions of $\bigcap$ and $\bigsqcup$, respectively. Two choice operators are necessary in general to capture the fact that choices may be exercised by different agents, as when a client interacts with a server. We call this *dual nondeterminacy*. For a simple example, consider the game of *Nim* in which two players alternately remove from 1 to 4 matches from a pile until none remain. The player who removes the last match loses. The game can be formally specified as follows. The *Home* player's game is described by *playH*, and the *Away* player's by *playA*.

$$playH \triangleq \lambda n{:}\mathbb{N}\cdot \textbf{if } n = 0 \textbf{ then } Home$$
$$\textbf{else } (playA \circ moveH)\, n$$
$$\textbf{fi}$$

$$playA \triangleq \lambda n{:}\mathbb{N}\cdot \textbf{if } n = 0 \textbf{ then } Away$$
$$\textbf{else } (playH \circ moveA)\, n$$
$$\textbf{fi}$$

$$moveH \triangleq \lambda n{:}\mathbb{N} \cdot \textstyle\bigsqcup\{m{:}\mathbb{N} \mid 0 < n - m \leq 4\}$$

$$moveA \triangleq \lambda n{:}\mathbb{N} \cdot \textstyle\bigcap\{m{:}\mathbb{N} \mid 0 < n - m \leq 4\}$$

By defining the refinement order on $\{Home, Away\}$ to be $Away \sqsubseteq Home$, we can encode "there is a winning strategy for the *Home* player in *Nim* when offered n matches $(n > 0)$" as $playH\, n = Home$. The first example showed nondeterminacy in the body of a function, and this example throws up nondeterminacy in arguments. Clearly any theory of nondeterminacy that purports to be widely applicable must cater for nondeterministic functions.

Turning to data refinement, we address the following question. How does a function f in an abstract domain translate to one in a concrete domain? Let F denote the abstraction function from the concrete to the abstract domain. It turns out that the concrete version of f is $F^{\mathsf{L}} \circ f \circ F$ where F^{L} denotes the left adjoint of F. This may appear to have nothing to do with nondeterminacy, but not so: F^{L} is not in general well defined, but in the presence of dual nondeterminacy large classes of functions have both a left and a right adjoint. Occasionally, the abstract and concrete domains are related by a function G from the abstract to the concrete; in that case the concrete version of function f on the abstract space is $G \circ f \circ G^{\mathsf{R}}$ where G^{R} denotes the right adjoint of G.

We may introduce nondeterminacy into an imperative language via its term language; e.g. we can define $x := 0 \sqcap x := 1$ to be equivalent to $x := 0 \sqcap 1$. With this approach, however, predicate transformers no longer make sense in general. For example, the predicate transformer semantics of the assignment statement, $wp(x{:=}t, R) \triangleq (t \neq \perp) \wedge R[x \backslash t]$, isn't meaningful when t may be nondeterministic. We need something better, and the theory of nondeterminacy tells us what it should be: we should move from predicate transformers to the more general "term transformers" (as a first approximation, think of these as predicate transformers in which the postcondition is replaced by a term of any type). Term transformers rely on the availability of a general theory of non-determinacy. Predicate transformers can be derived as special instance of term transformers, and it turns out that the version we get via this route is totally accommodating of nondeterminacy wherever it may arise. For example, the semantics of assignment we get is $wp(x{:=}t, R) \triangleq true \sqsubseteq (\lambda x{:}T \cdot R)\, t$ where T stands for the type of x. Weakest precondition semantics is thus reduced to a theory of nondeterministic functions. We can reconstruct the refinement calculus based on nondeterministic functions, and we get a better return. Traditionally it has been troublesome to accommodate functions (even regular deterministic ones) in a nondeterministic imperative language because it is extremely difficult to prevent nondeterminacy leaking from the level of commands to the level of terms. That worry now disappears because nondeterminacy in terms is welcome.

In the basic theory of nondeterminacy, $\sqcap$ and $\sqcup$ represent choice as made by two neutral agents that are perfect duals of one another. When we wire them in to a host language, however, we may introduce asymmetry between them, for example by postulating different distribution laws with respect to the operators of the host language. Wiring in also entails fixing the refinement order on base types. It is usual for base types to be discretely ordered (i.e. refinement is identified with equality), but sometimes we depart from this. The more we depart from the discrete ordering, the more we are imparting benign behaviour to $\sqcup$ and and malicious behaviour to $\sqcap$. For example, if base types contain $\perp$ to represent the "outcome" of a non-terminating computation, and if we postulate $\perp \sqsubseteq t$ for all terms t, then the agent of $\sqcup$ tries to avoid nontermination, while the agent of $\sqcap$ seeks out nontermination. For these reasons we classically refer to $\sqcup$ as *angelic* choice, and $\sqcap$ as *demonic* choice. $\sqcup$ and $\sqcap$ do indeed represent angelic and demonic nondeterminacy, respectively, when they are plugged into imperative programming as described above.

Knowing that taking an adjoint is facilitated by nondeterminacy, it is natural to seek other operations that benefit similarly. Taking fixpoints is one such. It turns out that just about every function in a "reasonable" specification language has least and greatest fixpoints. To take an extreme example, the successor function on the naturals $\lambda x{:}\mathbb{N} \cdot x + 1$ has fixpoints $\bigsqcup\{m{:}\mathbb{N} \cdot \bigsqcap\{n{:}\mathbb{N} \mid n \geq m\}\}$ and $\bigsqcap\{m{:}\mathbb{N} \cdot \bigsqcup\{n{:}\mathbb{N} \mid n \geq m\}\}$ (if you want to check this, appeal to the lattice relationship given earlier, and the fact that function application distributes over choice). The pervasiveness of fixpoints can exploited to give a semantics for recursive functions in terms of nondeterminacy.

The theory of nondeterminacy explains how to add nondeterminacy to any type in a type hierarchy. A process algebra for reasoning about communicating sequential processes is, putting it rather crudely, a theory of event sequences with nondeterminacy added. It is therefore reasonable to ask if we can construct a process algebra as a theory of event sequences enriched with a theory of nondeterminacy. Indeed, one can do so, and it gives rise to process algebras with elegant algebraic laws.

We have constructed a plug-and-play theory of dual nondeterminacy, in which nondeterminacy is described by five axioms [4]. We have empirically confirmed that it is plug-and-play by using it as a basis for theories of nondeterministic functions [2], term transformers (and predicate transformers as a special case) [1], recursion [3], and communicating sequential processes [5]. We are currently employing it on a theory of adjoints and data refinement.

References

1. J. M. Morris and A. Bunkenburg. Term transformers: a new approach to state. 2006. submitted.
2. J. M. Morris and M. Tyrrell. Dually nondeterministic functions and functional refinement. 2005. submitted.
3. J. M. Morris and M. Tyrrell. Dual unbounded nondeterminacy, recursion, and fixpoints. *Acta Informatica*, 2006. to appear.
4. J. M. Morris and M. Tyrrell. Terms with unbounded demonic and angelic nondeterminacy. *Science of Computer Programming*, 2006. to appear.
5. Malcolm Tyrrell, Joseph M. Morris, Andrew Butterfield, and Arthur Hughes. A lattice-theoretic model for an algebra of communicating sequential processes. In *Proc. 3rd Int. Colloquium on Theoretical Aspects of Computing*, Lecture Notes in Computing Science. Springer Verlag, 2006. to appear.

Author Index

Lecture Notes in Computer Science

For information about Vols. 1–4246

please contact your bookseller or Springer

Vol. 4286: P. Spirakis, M. Mavronicolas, S. Kontogiannis (Eds.), Internet and Network Economics. XI, 401 pages. 2006.

Vol. 4285: Y. Matsumoto, R. Sproat, K.-F. Wong, M. Zhang (Eds.), Computer Processing of Oriental Languages. XVII, 544 pages. 2006. (Sublibrary LNAI).

Vol. 4284: X. Lai, K. Chen (Eds.), Advances in Cryptology – ASIACRYPT 2006. XIV, 468 pages. 2006.

Vol. 4283: Y.Q. Shi, B. Jeon (Eds.), Digital Watermarking. XII, 474 pages. 2006.

Vol. 4282: Z. Pan, A.D. Cheok, M. Haller, R.W.H. Lau, H. Saito, R. Liang (Eds.), Advances in Artificial Reality and Tele-Existence. XXIII, 1347 pages. 2006.

Vol. 4281: K. Barkaoui, A. Cavalcanti, A. Cerone (Eds.), Theoretical Aspects of Computing - ICTAC 2006. XV, 371 pages. 2006.

Vol. 4280: A.K. Datta, M. Gradinariu (Eds.), Stabilization, Safety, and Security of Distributed Systems. XVII, 590 pages. 2006.

Vol. 4279: N. Kobayashi (Ed.), Programming Languages and Systems. XI, 423 pages. 2006.

Vol. 4278: R. Meersman, Z. Tari, P. Herrero (Eds.), On the Move to Meaningful Internet Systems 2006: OTM 2006 Workshops, Part II. XLV, 1004 pages. 2006.

Vol. 4277: R. Meersman, Z. Tari, P. Herrero (Eds.), On the Move to Meaningful Internet Systems 2006: OTM 2006 Workshops, Part I. XLV, 1009 pages. 2006.

Vol. 4276: R. Meersman, Z. Tari (Eds.), On the Move to Meaningful Internet Systems 2006: CoopIS, DOA, GADA, and ODBASE, Part II. XXXII, 752 pages. 2006.

Vol. 4275: R. Meersman, Z. Tari (Eds.), On the Move to Meaningful Internet Systems 2006: CoopIS, DOA, GADA, and ODBASE, Part I. XXXI, 1115 pages. 2006.

Vol. 4274: Q. Huo, B. Ma, E.-S. Chng, H. Li (Eds.), Chinese Spoken Language Processing. XXIV, 805 pages. 2006. (Sublibrary LNAI).

Vol. 4273: I. Cruz, S. Decker, D. Allemang, C. Preist, D. Schwabe, P. Mika, M. Uschold, L. Aroyo (Eds.), The Semantic Web - ISWC 2006. XXIV, 1001 pages. 2006.

Vol. 4272: P. Havinga, M. Lijding, N. Meratnia, M. Wegdam (Eds.), Smart Sensing and Context. XI, 267 pages. 2006.

Vol. 4271: F.V. Fomin (Ed.), Graph-Theoretic Concepts in Computer Science. XIII, 358 pages. 2006.

Vol. 4270: H. Zha, Z. Pan, H. Thwaites, A.C. Addison, M. Forte (Eds.), Interactive Technologies and Sociotechnical Systems. XVI, 547 pages. 2006.

Vol. 4269: R. State, S. van der Meer, D. O'Sullivan, T. Pfeifer (Eds.), Large Scale Management of Distributed Systems. XIII, 282 pages. 2006.

Vol. 4268: G. Parr, D. Malone, M. Ó Foghlú (Eds.), Autonomic Principles of IP Operations and Management. XIII, 237 pages. 2006.

Vol. 4267: A. Helmy, B. Jennings, L. Murphy, T. Pfeifer (Eds.), Autonomic Management of Mobile Multimedia Services. XIII, 257 pages. 2006.

Vol. 4266: H. Yoshiura, K. Sakurai, K. Rannenberg, Y. Murayama, S. Kawamura (Eds.), Advances in Information and Computer Security. XIII, 438 pages. 2006.

Vol. 4265: L. Todorovski, N. Lavrač, K.P. Jantke (Eds.), Discovery Science. XIV, 384 pages. 2006. (Sublibrary LNAI).

Vol. 4264: J.L. Balcázar, P.M. Long, F. Stephan (Eds.), Algorithmic Learning Theory. XIII, 393 pages. 2006. (Sublibrary LNAI).

Vol. 4263: A. Levi, E. Savaş, H. Yenigün, S. Balcısoy, Y. Saygın (Eds.), Computer and Information Sciences – ISCIS 2006. XXIII, 1084 pages. 2006.

Vol. 4262: K. Havelund, M. Núñez, G. Roşu, B. Wolff (Eds.), Formal Approaches to Software Testing and Runtime Verification. VIII, 255 pages. 2006.

Vol. 4261: Y. Zhuang, S. Yang, Y. Rui, Q. He (Eds.), Advances in Multimedia Information Processing - PCM 2006. XXII, 1040 pages. 2006.

Vol. 4260: Z. Liu, J. He (Eds.), Formal Methods and Software Engineering. XII, 778 pages. 2006.

Vol. 4259: S. Greco, Y. Hata, S. Hirano, M. Inuiguchi, S. Miyamoto, H.S. Nguyen, R. Słowiński (Eds.), Rough Sets and Current Trends in Computing. XXII, 951 pages. 2006. (Sublibrary LNAI).

Vol. 4257: I. Richardson, P. Runeson, R. Messnarz (Eds.), Software Process Improvement. XI, 219 pages. 2006.

Vol. 4256: L. Feng, G. Wang, C. Zeng, R. Huang (Eds.), Web Information Systems – WISE 2006 Workshops. XIV, 320 pages. 2006.

Vol. 4255: K. Aberer, Z. Peng, E.A. Rundensteiner, Y. Zhang, X. Li (Eds.), Web Information Systems – WISE 2006. XIV, 563 pages. 2006.

Vol. 4254: T. Grust, H. Höpfner, A. Illarramendi, S. Jablonski, M. Mesiti, S. Müller, P.-L. Patranjan, K.-U. Sattler, M. Spiliopoulou, J. Wijsen (Eds.), Current Trends in Database Technology – EDBT 2006. XXXI, 932 pages. 2006.

Vol. 4253: B. Gabrys, R.J. Howlett, L.C. Jain (Eds.), Knowledge-Based Intelligent Information and Engineering Systems, Part III. XXXII, 1301 pages. 2006. (Sublibrary LNAI).

Vol. 4252: B. Gabrys, R.J. Howlett, L.C. Jain (Eds.), Knowledge-Based Intelligent Information and Engineering Systems, Part II. XXXIII, 1335 pages. 2006. (Sublibrary LNAI).

Vol. 4251: B. Gabrys, R.J. Howlett, L.C. Jain (Eds.), Knowledge-Based Intelligent Information and Engineering Systems, Part I. LXVI, 1297 pages. 2006. (Sublibrary LNAI).

Vol. 4250: H.J. van den Herik, S.-C. Hsu, T.-s. Hsu, H.H.L.M. Donkers (Eds.), Advances in Computer Games. XIV, 273 pages. 2006.

Vol. 4249: L. Goubin, M. Matsui (Eds.), Cryptographic Hardware and Embedded Systems - CHES 2006. XII, 462 pages. 2006.

Vol. 4248: S. Staab, V. Svátek (Eds.), Managing Knowledge in a World of Networks. XIV, 400 pages. 2006. (Sublibrary LNAI).

Vol. 4247: T.-D. Wang, X. Li, S.-H. Chen, X. Wang, H. Abbass, H. Iba, G. Chen, X. Yao (Eds.), Simulated Evolution and Learning. XXI, 940 pages. 2006.